The Night Canada Stood Still

The Night Canada Stood Still

How the 1995 Quebec Referendum Nearly
Cost Us Our Country

ROBERT WRIGHT

HARPERCOLLINS PUBLISHERS LTD

HarperCollins books may be purchased for educational, business, or sales
promotional use through our Special Markets Department.

HarperCollins Publishers Ltd
2 Bloor Street East, 20th Floor
Toronto, Ontario, Canada
M4W 1A8

www.harpercollins.ca

Library and Archives Canada Cataloguing in Publication
information is available upon request

ISBN 978-1-44340-965-0

Printed and bound in the United States
RRD 9 8 7 6 5 4 3 2 1

For Michael, Anna, Helena, and Laura

Le vrai Québécois sait qu'est-ce qu'y veut. Pis qu'est-ce qu'y veut,
c't'un Québec indépendant, dans un Canada fort.

The real Québécois knows what he's after,
and that's an independent Quebec in a strong Canada.

—YVON DESCHAMPS

Contents

XIII   PREFACE

1   PROLOGUE: Free Falling

16   CHAPTER ONE: Ottawa, 1993

35   CHAPTER TWO: Quebec City, 1994

51   CHAPTER THREE: Sovereignty for What?

62   CHAPTER FOUR: *Noui*

77   CHAPTER FIVE: Clever, Quite Clever

96   CHAPTER SIX: Sovereignist Setbacks

110   CHAPTER SEVEN: *Les Virages*

130   CHAPTER EIGHT: Declaring Sovereignty

153   CHAPTER NINE: Down to Business

173   CHAPTER TEN: *L'Effet Lucien*

194   CHAPTER ELEVEN: Federalist Setbacks

218   CHAPTER TWELVE: *Amour à Montréal*

238   CHAPTER THIRTEEN: The Night Canada Stood Still

260   CONCLUSION: Numb and Number

277   ABBREVIATIONS USED IN NOTES

279   NOTES

343   INDEX

The Night Canada Stood Still tells the story of the second Quebec referendum on sovereignty, held on October 30, 1995. (The first was held in May 1980.) The premise of this book is that the referendum debate was a national event not just for Quebecers but for all Canadians. I have therefore been mindful of three considerations: to get the story right, to treat all of its principal characters fairly, and to allow them to speak for themselves wherever possible. In case it is not immediately apparent, I write from the perspective of "earnest Upper Canadianism," a term coined by John Duffy in Catherine Annau's wonderful 1999 documentary film *Just Watch Me: Trudeau and the '70s Generation*. When I reference the Anglo-Canadian "My-Canada-includes-Quebec crowd" in the pages that follow, readers should know that this is my crowd.

A note on sources. In contrast with my last two books, where the narratives tended to be hidden in once-secret documents, I found the story of the 1995 referendum to be hidden in plain view. The challenge was not the dearth of sources but rather the extraordinary abundance. Hundreds of thousands of words were spoken during the sovereignty debates in the National Assembly and the House of Commons, while the number of what we now call "hits" in the popular media ran into the tens of thousands. This book is, therefore, a work of analysis but also of synthesis. For ease of reading, I have taken two minor liberties with the text. I have standardized the spellings of terms like *Quebecer* and *sovereignist* wherever they appear. I have also closed extended excerpts without ellipses and square brackets in instances where I judged continuity and context to be unaffected. In every other respect, the sources cited in the endnotes conform to established scholarly standards. There is no invented dialogue in this book. All translations from the original French are my own unless otherwise noted.

The Night Canada Stood Still could not have been written without the help of others. It gives me great pleasure to acknowledge them here.

Research funding was provided by the Canada Council for the Arts and the Symons Trust Fund for Canadian Studies, for which I am indebted. For putting themselves at my disposal early on in my research, I am grateful to Joe Clark, Edmond Chiasson, Heather Chiasson, Peter Donolo, Derek Lipman, Paul Daniel Muller, Eddie Goldenberg, Patrick Parisot, and John Rae. I owe a special debt of gratitude to my research assistants Rianna Genore, Kailey Miller, and Anna Harrington. Thanks as well to Ken Field and John Wales of the Trent Oshawa Library, to Karen Benacquista and Heather Gildner of the Toronto Public Library, and to R.K. Wright, Pat Wright, Lee Anne Farrow, Dennis Molinaro, Judy Cornish, Drew Taylor, Patricia Taylor, Rena Zimmerman, Amber Ashton, and Hailey Wright.

The publication of *The Night Canada Stood Still* marks a decade of collaboration with my friend and editor Jim Gifford, whose tireless efforts on my behalf have introduced my work to a far broader audience than academic historians normally enjoy. Thanks to Jim and everyone at HarperCollins Canada, and to Noelle Zitzer, Allegra Robinson, Rebecca Vogan, and Lisa Rundle in particular.

Quebec MNA and cabinet member Jean-François Lisée, Professor Louis Balthazar, Professor David Sheinin, former ambassador Ken Taylor, and my brother Daniel Wright each read a manuscript draft of this book in its entirety, providing invaluable commentary and rescuing me from pitfalls large and small. For their unstinting generosity, I am deeply indebted. I need hardly add the standard authorial caveat. I have tried to bring balance and objectivity to the referendum story, but where I have failed, I have done so single-handedly.

My wife, Laura, and our children, Helena, Anna and Michael, spent more time living with this project than they might have liked. As always, this book is for you, guys.

Free Falling

The morning of Tuesday, October 24, 1995, the phone rang in Jean Pelletier's Ottawa boardroom. Pelletier, a former mayor of Quebec City and now Prime Minister Jean Chrétien's chief of staff, was chatting amicably as he did almost every morning with a handful of Chrétien's senior political advisors. On the line, as usual, was John Rae from Montreal. This morning, Rae was the bearer of bad news. Quebec's second referendum on sovereignty in fifteen years was less than a week away, and overnight polling showed the sovereignist Yes side leading by seven points. Eddie Goldenberg, Chrétien's senior policy advisor, glanced at Pelletier. Both men were plainly anxious. "We seem to be in free fall," Goldenberg observed bluntly.[1]

No sooner had Rae hung up than Jean Chrétien rang. "Is there anything new this morning?" he asked.

"We have good news and bad news," said Goldenberg. "The bad news is that we are seven points behind. The good news is that everyone is counting on you to turn it around tonight."

"I guess that's why we are paid the big bucks," replied Chrétien.[2]

The prime minister hung up the phone and returned to the document on his desk, notes for a speech he would give that evening in the Montreal borough of Verdun. He had been up late the night before, hashing out the major points of the address with Goldenberg and his press secretary, Patrick Parisot. Chrétien knew that some of the best speeches of his career had been unscripted. But not this time. "I was going to have to stick closely to the written text," he acknowledged. "This one was too important for me to risk flying without a net."[3]

Chrétien knew that the stakes were high. After months of polls showing that the No side would coast to victory, a *Toronto Star/La Presse* survey published on October 18 had stunned Quebecers and Canadians alike with the news that the two sides were in a virtual dead heat. "It's Neck and Neck!"shouted the headlines, *"La Marée Haute du OUI"* (The High Tide of YES).[4] The next day, October 19, the No camp's internal polling numbers revealed that the situation was, in fact, far more dire. "An overnight poll showed a dramatic reversal of fortune," Chrétien himself later recalled. "The Yes forces were now in the lead, 54–46, and the No side was in freefall. No one had a clue how to stop it."[5]

To appease Quebec Liberal leader Daniel Johnson, the official *chef* of the No side, Chrétien had kept a low public profile in Quebec up to that point—even though his every instinct told him that he should be fighting tooth and nail for Canada. A majority of Quebecers would vote against separatism, Chrétien had reasoned, so there was no reason to paint a target on his own back. Now the sovereignists had the wind at their backs. With just days to go in a vote that threatened to break up the country, Chrétien was determined to pull out all the stops. He told his subordinates to clear his calendar, even cancelling meetings with foreign leaders that had been on the books for months. "At last I was going to act on my basic instincts and plunge into the campaign," Chrétien resolved. "It was time to speak to the hearts of Quebecers."[6]

～

The last time Quebecers had voted in a referendum on sovereignty, in May 1980, Prime Minister Pierre Trudeau had been at the helm of the No forces. Jean Chrétien, then serving as the federal minister of justice, was Trudeau's main lieutenant. No one knew better than Chrétien that history could be an unforgiving taskmaster.

It is a widely accepted truth in Quebec that Trudeau's role in the 1980 referendum campaign was "notorious."[7] Just six days before Quebecers went to the polls, he gave a dramatic speech at Montreal's Paul Sauvé Arena. There, with a stern, confrontational stare, his body language taut and resolute, his index finger stabbing insistently as he lashed out against his separatist adversaries, Trudeau promised that a No vote would be interpreted by the Government of Canada, the leaders of all three federal parties, the nine provincial governments outside Quebec, and all seventy-five Liberal MPs from Quebec as "a mandate to change the Constitution, to renew federalism." "I make a solemn declaration to all Canadians in the other provinces," Trudeau declared, his voice rising, "[that] we, the Quebec MPs, are laying ourselves on the line. We want change and we are willing to lay our seats in the House on the line to have change."[8] It was one of the most electrifying speeches of his political career, and it sent shock waves through Quebec and Canada. When the referendum ballots were counted on May 20, 1980, Quebecers had voted 60–40 to reject René Lévesque's sovereignty-association option. Trudeau's Sauvé Arena speech was credited with having turned the tide.

But what had Trudeau meant by his promise to renew federalism? Had he changed his tune?

As prime minister, Trudeau had made no secret of the kind of political order he envisaged for Canada. He believed resolutely in a strong central government, in the equality of individuals and of provinces, and in official bilingualism through which French Canadians could be *maîtres chez nous* anywhere in Canada. Trudeau had always said that, left to his own devices, he would repatriate the Canadian Constitution and introduce a charter of rights and freedoms. In contrast with a great many of his fellow Quebecers, he rejected any "two nations" conception of Canada, in which Confederation was understood as a pact between English and French Canadians. "I think particular status for Quebec is the biggest intellectual hoax ever foisted on the people of Quebec and the people of Canada," Trudeau said flatly.[9]

So what did he mean when he promised in May 1980 to put his own neck on the block for change?

Université Laval political scientist Guy Laforest is a committed sovereignist whose interpretation of Trudeau's Sauvé Arena speech would directly influence the course of the 1995 referendum debate. In his 1992 book *Trudeau et la fin d'un rêve canadien* (*Trudeau and the End of a Canadian Dream*), Laforest claimed that the self-styled straight-shooter Trudeau had knowingly played fast and loose with Quebecers' sensibilities when he spoke about the need for change. For a full year before his Sauvé Arena speech—a period that included the federal election campaign of January and February 1980—Trudeau had said almost nothing about his own constitutional ambitions. Instead, he watched from the sidelines as two reports, the *Task Force on Canadian Unity* and the *Beige Paper* of the Quebec Liberal Party, transformed the conversation in Quebec about what it would actually mean to renew federalism. Both studies "advocated enshrining Quebec's specificity within the constitution" and as such "gave expression to the conventional meaning of renewed federalism that had, in a certain sense, crystallized in Quebec during the years 1979–80."[10] Pierre Trudeau understood this, according to Laforest; thus his appeal to Quebecers in his Sauvé Arena speech was one of coldly calculated ambiguity. With his vague but impassioned promise to "renew federalism," Trudeau had artfully hijacked the vocabulary of the Quiet Revolution. He had played on the hopes and dreams of Quebecers without any intention of ever realizing them.

In the minds of many Quebec sovereignists, Guy Laforest among them, everything Pierre Trudeau subsequently accomplished on the constitutional file—abetted at every turn by Jean Chrétien—followed from this initial deceit at the height of the 1980 referendum campaign. Trudeau's patriation of the Constitution without Quebec's consent was a betrayal, they say, a fundamental insult to the spirit of Confederation. November 4, 1981, is infamous among Quebec sovereignists as *la Nuit des Longs Couteaux* (the Night of the Long Knives), for that was the night Jean Chrétien and the nine premiers from English Canada hammered out their patriation deal while Quebec premier René Lévesque slept. For Parti Québécois stalwarts like Jacques Parizeau, who would go on to become premier of Quebec and leader of the No side in 1995, these events amounted to treachery, plain and simple. Trudeau and

Chrétien were sell-outs. "You remember the Night of the Long Knives," Parizeau would say. "One day we will have to understand this method of using Quebecers in Ottawa to carry out designs, to achieve things that anglophones would not dare try to achieve on their own. These affairs are nauseating. We remember 1981, we remember the Night of the Long Knives. We are a people. We are a nation. We will decide what's best for us. There is no one in the world who can deny us that right."[11]

—

Poring over his notes for the speech he would give at Verdun, Jean Chrétien was pensive. He knew better than anyone that Jacques Parizeau and his *péquiste* comrades had long memories. He knew that their dream of a sovereign Quebec had been built in part upon a reading of Canadian history that emphasized Quebecers' "humiliation." By plunging into the 1995 referendum debate at the eleventh hour, Chrétien faced a double risk. He might appear to be acting out of desperation, which would be a gift to the Yes side. Worse, he might be accused of pulling the same humiliating stunt that Trudeau had pulled in 1980. Chrétien understood that he would have to walk the knife edge. "I won't make promises that I can't keep after the referendum," he confided to Eddie Goldenberg. "I won't promise constitutional change. I don't want to create the expectations that Trudeau, rightly or wrongly, created in 1980 at the Paul Sauvé Arena, and then find I'm not able to deliver. In the long run, that would be disastrous for the unity of the country."[12]

The prime minister weighed his options. "In 1980," he observed, "Trudeau had used his final intervention to make a dramatic and remarkably personal pitch to the voters. I decided to adopt a more low-key tone in order to concentrate on two substantial issues. First I would assure Quebecers that their province would have a veto power over any future constitutional changes."[13] This was a concession to the established view in Quebec that it had always enjoyed an historic right of veto, despite a 1982 decision of the Supreme Court of Canada to the contrary.[14] "The second issue," Chrétien continued, "the recognition of Quebec as a distinct society, was more fraught with difficulty. Most

Canadians were still highly suspicious that 'distinct society' meant special powers for the government of Quebec. The phrase had become an important symbol for many Quebecers, however, and if it was what they needed to feel more respected and comfortable within Canada, it wasn't much of a problem for me to offer it to them."[15]

The prime minister was correct about one thing. The phrase *distinct society* had by 1995 become a potent touchstone for Quebecers and Canadians alike. But the odds that he could casually toss it out to disgruntled Quebecers in the final days of the referendum campaign and win their loyalty to Canada were long. The truth is that by October 1995 no one, not even Pierre Trudeau, had become more entangled in the thorny politics of *distinct society* than Jean Chrétien. In a sense, *distinct society* was precisely what the referendum was about.

Chrétien had famously been one of three Quebecers to welcome Queen Elizabeth II to Parliament Hill on April 17, 1982, where she signed into law Canada's new Constitution and Charter of Rights and Freedoms. (Pierre Trudeau and André Ouellet were the other two.) A bitterly disappointed René Lévesque, still smarting from the Night of the Long Knives, led a protest march in the streets of Montreal on the same day. The phrase *distinct society* had been in use since the 1960s to highlight what was obvious to everyone, namely that Quebec was unique among the Canadian provinces and that its French language and culture were worthy of recognition and protection. But after the windswept patriation ceremony of 1982, the phrase acquired a powerful new meaning. It distilled a vast and complicated legal conversation about how to "bring Quebec back into the Canadian family"[16] into a deceptively simple question: should Quebec be recognized in Canada's Constitution as a distinct society and thus enjoy a constitutional prerogative to protect its French culture? After 1982, Canadian jurists, scholars, and philosophers would dissect the minutiae of Canada's constitutional predicament with such intensity and elegance as to bring them international recognition.[17] But for many ordinary Canadians, the issues were fairly straightforward. Could Quebec be recognized as a distinct society yet remain a Canadian province like all the others? And if so, would Quebecers, particularly those who did not speak French, still enjoy the rights enshrined in the Charter?

In the years between the patriation of 1982 and the referendum of 1995, the answers to these questions proved elusive, exasperating, and intractable, in that order. As Jean Chrétien himself had predicted, the words *distinct society* came to bedevil virtually anyone who dared utter them. Distinct society was the defining idea of the ill-fated Meech Lake Accord, Prime Minister Brian Mulroney's effort to bring Quebec into the Constitution with "honour and enthusiasm," and it had died in the provincial legislatures of Manitoba and Newfoundland in June 1990. The phrase *distinct society* also appeared in the follow-up Charlottetown Accord, which Canadians and Quebecers rejected soundly in referenda in October 1992. By the autumn of 1995, polls showed that public opinion in Canada had polarized. A majority of Quebecers thought distinct society was the least Canada should offer Quebec. An even larger majority of Canadians outside Quebec believed it was far too much. As former prime minister Joe Clark, the main architect of the 1992 Charlottetown Accord, lamented, "The words *special status* became a code, not to describe the enduring genius of Canadian Confederation, but to imply privilege for Quebec."[18]

Jean Chrétien later suggested that the phrase *distinct society* was never the obsession for him that it had been for his political mentor. "Mr. Trudeau and I differed," said Chrétien. "He insisted there wasn't a single meaningless word in the Constitution. The expression *distinct society* creates a problem. This often happens in politics. Take, for example, same-sex unions. If you call it a *marriage*, you get a lot of opposition, but it doesn't change anything in reality. The problem is with the word. These are battles that create illusions."[19]

Would Chrétien be creating illusions if he went to Verdun and offered to recognize Quebec as a distinct society? He knew as he reviewed his notes that this was not merely a question of semantics. There was also his own political record to consider.

Jean Chrétien was "a founding father of the Charter," as the *Globe and Mail*'s John Ibbitson has observed.[20] As a Quebecer, Chrétien was perfectly willing to acknowledge that Quebec society was distinct. "Everyone knows that I'm French when I speak in English," Chrétien joked at the height of the 1995 referendum. "You don't have to write it in the Constitution!"[21] But as a statesman, he could never agree to a constitutional arrangement in which distinct-society provisions might allow the government of Quebec to override Canadians' Charter rights.

In this respect, Chrétien's position was principled, consistent, and identical to Pierre Trudeau's. And it explains his take on constitutional reform in the years leading up to the 1995 referendum. Chrétien objected to the distinct-society clause in the original (1987) Meech Lake Accord because it appeared within the body of the Constitution in the form of a new Section 2, where, he believed, it could be used to undermine the Charter. During the federal Liberal leadership race against Paul Martin in 1990, he said that he could support an amended Meech, but only if the distinct-society clause was moved to the preamble, where it could do little harm. Two years later, Chrétien supported the Charlottetown Accord because the phrase *distinct society* appeared in an interpretive clause, not in the body of the Constitution.[22] (Not surprisingly, this was also why most Quebec sovereignists rejected Charlottetown and mobilized Quebecers to vote against it.) Chrétien paid a heavy price in Quebec for sticking to his principles in these years, even within his own party. At a 1990 Liberal leadership debate in Montreal, Paul Martin's supporters chanted "*vendu*" (sell-out) when Chrétien explained his position on Meech. After Chrétien won the party leadership, Liberal MP Gilles Rocheleau quit the party in disgust, publicly calling him "Quebec's Judas Iscariot." Such slurs hurt Chrétien deeply.

In his 2007 memoirs, Chrétien recounted a private conversation he had had with Pierre Trudeau in October 1992, just as the country was heading into the Charlottetown referendum. For two-and-a-half hours, the two friends debated the meaning of distinct society over dinner at Toronto's Royal York hotel.

"Jean, there are no words that mean nothing," Trudeau insisted.

"I don't know too many," replied Chrétien, "but these two mean nothing."

Trudeau tried his best to talk Chrétien out of supporting Charlottetown, but Chrétien held his ground. The two could agree only to disagree.

"You're the leader now, not me," Trudeau ended up saying, "so you have to live with some political realities that I can afford to ignore."[23]

Now, in October 1995, with only a week to go in a referendum contest the polls said he was going to lose, Chrétien made a decision that he had dearly hoped he would never have to make. He would go to Verdun and open up Pandora's box. He would make a commitment to recognize Quebec as a distinct society, and he would offer Quebec a veto on constitutional change. Yes, the odds were long, but Canada hung in the balance. It was time to face the music.

Chrétien picked up the phone and called Pierre Trudeau.

"Is it true that we're losing, Jean?" Trudeau asked.

"Yes, we're behind and it's going to be close, but I'm confident we can turn it around if we work hard," Chrétien replied. "I may have to say something you won't like about distinct society and the veto."

"You're in charge," Trudeau affirmed. "Do what you think you have to do."[24]

~

The Verdun Auditorium is an unremarkable barn-like arena on Boulevard Gaétan-Laberge in western Montreal. With its cement floors and wooden benches, it is indistinguishable from hundreds of similar structures that dot the Canadian landscape from Halifax to Whitehorse. Its raison d'être is not politics but heavy-metal concerts and hockey, a sport that has always been celebrated in Canada as a bridge between the two solitudes. It was perhaps fitting that the Canadian prime minister should endeavour to save the country in such a venue.

Word that Jean Chrétien would be speaking at Verdun the evening of October 24 energized the federalist ranks in Montreal as nothing had in weeks. By 7:15 p.m., an estimated 12,000 people had shown up to raise their voices in defence of Canada and cheer on the leaders of the No side. Seven thousand crammed into the arena—a thousand more than it had been built to hold. The rest waited in the rain-drenched parking lot and adjoining streets to watch the proceedings on video screens. Traffic was so heavy that Jean Chrétien, his wife, Aline, and several of his advisors hopped out of their cars and walked the last several blocks through the rain to the auditorium. Along the way, they bumped into federal Tory leader Jean Charest and his wife, Michèle, and together they made their way through the sea of bodies to the side entrance.

"Vive le Canada!" yelled the crowd. The cool, muggy air was heavy with nervous anticipation. "Everyone knew it was to be a crucial night," Jean Chrétien later recalled, "full of high-stakes drama and high-octane emotions."[25] Many of the ordinary Canadians who had turned out, like Montreal businessman Avrum Stark, said that they had been drawn by the grim polling numbers and the suddenly all-too-real possibility that Canada might break up. "It's a very scary and emotional experience for me," said Stark.[26] The prime minister himself, exhausted from anxious days and sleepless nights, seemed to draw energy from the enthusiasm and warmth of the crowd. Some spectators managed to reach through his security detail to wish him good luck. One of them was McGill University student Victor Debbas. "I just shook his hand and I'm proud of it," said Debbas. "The whole idea of Canada is of a multiracial place where people get along, not separate. I don't see why we're splitting up."[27] Grade 11 student Michelle Paiement was one of several students waiting patiently in the rain wrapped in a Canadian flag. "We can't even vote and we're here," exclaimed Paiement. "We are the future of this country."[28] "There's no country in the world like Canada," added France Héroux, a self-styled old-stock Quebecer who had driven down from Trois-Rivières. "Canada is like the promised land for the rest of the world. I'm proud to be a Canadian."[29]

The crowd streamed into the arena, many of them chanting "Ca-na-da!" and "Qué-bec!" and waving Canadian flags and *fleurs-de-lis*. The music of Céline Dion and Robert Charlebois blared on the PA. Short pro-Canada testimonials from Quebec sports stars, celebrities, and ordinary citizens looped on video screens. Some of the younger participants had painted flags on their faces and hair, evoking the atmosphere of a rock concert. The only emotion visible on the faces of older participants was anxiety, some visibly shell-shocked and barely able to keep their composure. Towards the front of the crowd stood federal finance minister Paul Martin and his cabinet colleague Lucienne Robillard, Chrétien's hand-picked liaison on the No committee.

Rally organizers did their best to bring out the star power of the No leaders, with pounding music and intense spotlights. Like prize fighters entering the ring, Chrétien, Daniel Johnson, and Jean Charest were mobbed as they made their way slowly through the crowd to the stage. Camera crews roamed backstage as part of the province-wide television broadcast of the rally. When a cameraman trained his lens on Jean Chrétien just moments before he stepped up to the podium to deliver the evening's first speech, viewers at home caught a glimpse of "near-panic" on his face, as historian Sylvie M. Beaudreau put it. "The cameras revealed what many Canadians feared was only too true, that the federalists were aware they could quite possibly go down to defeat and were making an extraordinary, desperate, and last-ditch effort to do whatever was in their power to prevent this from happening."[30]

The prime minister was greeted by thunderous applause as he took the stage. Behind him was a row of flags—alternating Maple Leafs and *fleurs-de-lis*—flanking a backdrop bearing the slogan of the No campaign, "*La Sépa NON ration?*" (the word *séparation* bisected by the word *non*). Looking out over the crowd, Chrétien's face was a picture of sober intensity. For months, he had been supremely confident, almost cocky. "I'm not scared," he had said over and over. "There's no reason to be scared because I have the best product to offer, Canada."[31] Nothing remained of this blithe certitude. There was no evidence tonight of the famously populist Chrétien, the man of the people, *le p'tit gars de Shawinigan*. He did not smile at the crowd, or feign humility, or gloat. Standing purposefully, waiting for the applause to subside, Chrétien knew that he was standing in the white light of history as few world leaders had, the head of state of a country at the brink. Tonight's speech was about one thing and one thing only: *rester ou partir*, to stay or to go. "As prime minister," he began, "I bear a heavy responsibility . . ."

With those words, it became clear that Chrétien intended to preach not to the converted but to those beyond, to the roughly 15 per cent of Quebecers whose political allegiances were "soft" and whose voting intentions remained undecided. He offered a thinly veiled *mea culpa*. "We are not being asked to choose a government or a premier that we will be able to vote out in four years' time," said Chrétien. "This is not a popularity contest in which certain individuals are better liked than others. It is a fundamental and irreversible choice of a country." Chrétien knew that his public approval ratings in Quebec were abysmal. According to a recent SOM poll, only 13 per cent of Quebecers thought him the most trustworthy leader.[32] There was no point in painting himself as Quebec's saviour. He had to cut right to the heart of the matter, which was saving Canada. "The breakup of Canada would be the failure of a dream," Chrétien insisted. "It would be the end of a country that is the envy of all the world. It would be the failure of a country that is a model for countries in the process of building their own institutions. Canada is built on values that you know well: tolerance, generosity, respect for differences, social justice, and compassion. Quebecers share those values with all other Canadians. Next Monday, we will have to decide if we are prepared to give up on the country that embodies those values better than any other country in the world."

The crowd responded warmly, some of them with tears in their eyes, as the prime minister segued to his own family roots in Quebec. "My friends," he said solemnly, "I am a Quebecer proud of my language, my culture and my heritage. And I am also a Canadian who feels at home in every region of the country. Our ancestors, yours and mine, built a country in which the French language, culture and identity have been able to develop and assert themselves. They built a country in which Quebecers, regardless of any past injustices, now have the tools and the power to fulfill themselves. It's true that this great country is not perfect. It's true that it's a country that must continue to adapt to modern reality; a country that can and must improve further—that is true. But it is a country worth fighting for, worth doing the impossible to preserve."

And then came the moment of truth.

"I have listened to my fellow Quebecers throughout this campaign saying that they are deeply attached to Canada. But they've also been saying that they want to see this country change and evolve toward their aspirations. They want to see Quebec recognized as a distinct society within Canada by virtue of its language, culture and institutions." As the phrase *société distincte* passed his lips, the crowd erupted into cheers. "I've said it before and I'll say it again," Chrétien continued, after a brief pause. "I agree. I have supported that position in the past, I support it today, and I will always support it, whatever the circumstances." Again the crowd erupted into cheers and whistles.

The prime minister concluded his speech with a poignant quotation from former Quebec premier Jean Lesage. "*Le Canada c'est mon pays, le Québec c'est ma patrie*" ("Canada is my country, Québec is my homeland"). Then with a sharp "*Merci beaucoup,* thank you very much!" he stepped back from the podium to let the applause of the audience wash over him. He had ended the speech as he had begun it, seriously, earnestly, a man on the edge. There was no triumphalism in his final waves and nods to the crowd, no relief. His searching gaze and fitful stance gave every impression that he did not know whether his speech had succeeded or failed.

A woman at the front of the stage handed Chrétien two red roses. He grasped the flowers, gave a final wave, and descended the stairs into the crowd.

~

The next morning, Wednesday, October 25, the federal Liberal caucus met in Ottawa. MP Jane Stewart chaired the meeting. She later recalled the dramatic moment when Jean Chrétien appeared at the door. "When I saw him come into the caucus room, my visceral response was dramatic. I started to shake and feel sick to my stomach. The look I saw was one I know, stress and perhaps panic. I felt like crying."[33]

Stewart did not exaggerate. Visibly anxious, emotional, beaten down—this was a Jean Chrétien Liberal MPs had never seen. The mood in the room was sombre, even fractious. Many MPs were beside themselves about the referendum polls, and they blamed the prime minister and his advisors for sidelining them in a disastrous top-down campaign that now threatened the country. "I sympathized with those MPs and ministers who felt they were being forced to stand by and watch their great country fall apart without being able to do anything about it," Chrétien himself later recalled.[34]

Some of those MPs had already read journalist Lysiane Gagnon's devastating *La Presse* column for that morning. The rally in Verdun had been nothing but an "epiphenomenon," wrote Gagnon. "It was too little, too late. Weeks and years too late. The evening brought nothing new. For federalists in Quebec, it was a pathetic admission of weakness."[35] Within hours, Gagnon's words would reverberate throughout Quebec and Canada. As many Liberals anticipated, opposition Bloc Québécois MPs would be only too happy to throw Gagnon's words in Chrétien's face. "At the very last minute, a panicky Prime Minister of Canada has entered the referendum campaign with empty hands," Bloc MP Jean H. Leroux would tell the House of Commons that very afternoon. "It is too little, too late. Quebecers will not be fooled; they will vote Yes next Monday."[36]

The prime minister addressed the caucus. His tone was one of bitter resignation. Nothing remained of the bravado that had carried him aloft through most of the campaign.

Lies and personal attacks had given the separatists momentum late in the campaign, Chrétien fumed, in no small measure because an obliging national press had published "the big pile of shit."[37] It was absurd, he railed. At one point in his speech, Chrétien faltered in mid-sentence, tears welling up in his eyes. "I choked up when I reflected on the indecency of being called a traitor to my people," he later admitted.[38] The prime minister paused and turned from the lectern. Jane Stewart embraced him. Others in the room—Brian Tobin, David Dingwall, David Collenette, Sergio Marchi, Christine Stewart—felt their hearts sink and their eyes water. Never had they seen Jean Chrétien, the famed political brawler, so despondent.

After a few moments, Chrétien regained his composure and continued with his remarks, trying his best to rally his troops in the home stretch of the campaign.

"Remember we live in the best country in the world," he said.[39]

His speech concluded, the prime minister and his caucus filed dejectedly out of the meeting and back to their parliamentary offices. They knew they had but four-and-a-half days to try to avert disaster, to put the missteps of the campaign behind them and appeal to the people of Quebec to think twice about voting to leave Canada.

They put a brave face on the challenges before them, girding themselves for the fight of their lives. But alongside their resolve remained confusion, bitterness, and fear.

How, they wondered, had it ever come to this?

CHAPTER ONE

Ottawa, 1993

As it happened, Jean Chrétien's tearful caucus meeting fell on the second anniversary of his resounding 1993 electoral victory. What should have been an occasion for celebration—the Liberals' biggest landslide since 1949—had become instead a scene of recrimination and doubt.

For two years, the Liberal government had stood idly by and watched as Quebec sovereignists had painstakingly resuscitated the dream of an independent French-speaking state in North America, a dream that even many diehard Quebec separatists believed had died with René Lévesque. Appealing to Quebecers' resentment over Meech and Charlottetown, overcoming their own deep schisms, and producing a roadmap for sovereignty they believed even moderate Quebec nationalists could support, the sovereignists' had exceeded not only Jean Chrétien's expectations but their own.

Some Canadians mused that Chrétien was powerless to stop the sovereignist juggernaut. He was the right man at the wrong time, they said. History was against him. But as the prime minister and his dejected comrades filed out of their gloomy caucus meeting at noon on October 25, 1995, the point was moot. The simple truth was that he hadn't even tried.

~

The federal election of 1993 is best remembered for nearly obliterating the ruling Progressive Conservatives and for ushering in Jean Chrétien's decade-long "friendly dictatorship."[1] The Liberals won 177 out of 295 seats, the outgoing Tories only two. The New Democrats, led by Audrey McLaughlin, were reduced from forty-three seats to nine.

The Liberal sweep was a triumph for Jean Chrétien and the "natural-governing party," but seen from the perspective of national unity, it was an ominous fork in the road for Canada. The sovereignist Bloc Québécois became the Official Opposition with fifty-four seats, all of them in Quebec. The populist Reform Party took fifty-two seats, all but two of them west of Manitoba. The Liberals took only nineteen of seventy-five seats in Quebec—a sea change in Canadian political history, given that every French-Canadian prime minister before Chrétien had won overwhelmingly in Quebec. (The last French-Canadian prime minister before Jean Chrétien was Pierre Trudeau, and in his final election, in 1980, Trudeau had swept Quebec with seventy-four seats.) The rise of Reform and the Bloc revealed that the chickens of regional alienation had come home to roost. All of a sudden, the national conversation was a lot less national.

During the 1993 campaign, Jean Chrétien adopted a "Don't worry, be happy" approach to national unity. "We had made the constitutional status quo an element of our election program," Eddie Goldenberg later recalled. "Mr. Chrétien had made it clear that the Constitution, on a priority list of 100 priorities, was 101."[2] Chrétien sensed that Canadians were suffering from constitutional fatigue and wanted their government to deal with the sputtering economy, unemployment, and the mounting debt crisis. Brandishing his famous *Red Book* to great effect, he offered Canadians a platform of economic reforms that would restructure costly social programs, balance the books, and pull the country out of recession. "If you want to talk about the constitution," Chrétien said on the campaign trail, "don't vote for me!"[3]

Behind this cheeky remark lay Chrétien's bedrock conviction that Quebecers would never vote to break Canada up. "Canadian federalism is more than a form of government," Chrétien would say. "It's also a system of values that allows different people in diverse communities to live and work together in harmony for the good of all. Will independence bring a better form of government for the people of Quebec? In my opinion, no. Will it bring more peace? No. More prosperity? No. More justice? No. Even a better chance for the survival of the French language and culture in North America? Again, no. The fact that Quebec is part of Canada makes a big contribution to Quebec—and to Canada as well."[4]

With the ashes of Meech and Charlottetown still smouldering and the country fresh out of constitutional fixes, Chrétien reassured Canadian voters that federalism could evolve, practically and to everyone's advantage, without reopening the Constitution. This was a lesson that he believed Canadians had learned from Brian Mulroney's roll of the dice. "I thought Mulroney was wrong to have reopened the constitutional file," Chrétien later recalled. "In general, I felt that changing the Constitution is a distraction from dealing with the practical issues of the day, something to be undertaken only when all other options have failed."[5] In this sense, Chrétien had imbibed one his mentor's most famous dictums. "Canada is a success, looking for a problem," Pierre Trudeau liked to say. "We are a united people divided by our leaders."[6]

On one level, Jean Chrétien's instincts heading into the 1993 campaign proved correct. The Canadian economy was indeed in the tank, and Canadians were almost uniformly anxious about it.[7] Terms like *globalization, outsourcing,* and *debt clock* entered the Canadian lexicon for the first time. Everyone understood that the reforms necessary to retool the Canadian economy were structural. That meant they were going to hurt.

But Chrétien's refusal to talk about the Constitution played into the hands of Quebec sovereignists, who spoke of little else. Foremost among them was Lucien Bouchard, the former Mulroney Tory who had launched the Bloc Québécois in 1990 and personified its meteoric ascent in federal politics. Bouchard had no formal platform document, no *Red Book,* in 1993. He didn't need one. He agreed with Chrétien that Canada's endless constitutional wrangling was a dead end but interpreted this to mean that Quebecers had no choice but to chart an independent course. His campaign objectives were straightforward: he would promote Quebec sovereignty, prepare English-speaking Canada for the inevitable, and defend Quebec's interests in Ottawa in the meantime.[8]

Sensing that the Tories were a spent force, Bouchard aimed his formidable rhetorical skills at Chrétien, who, he liked to say, "represented everything I abhorred about politics."[9] Out on the hustings, Bouchard was merciless. "Each time Quebec gets a good slap in the face, if you scratch a little, you'll find Jean Chrétien," he told Quebec voters.[10] "Chrétien cannot claim, as Trudeau did, to represent Quebec. For Québécois, the most decisive thing to come out of the dual failure of Meech and Charlottetown has been this: English-speaking Canadians, out of respect for their own national identity, out of loyalty to their vision of Canada, have refused to make any concessions to Quebec."[11]

Many Canadian anglos scratched their heads in wonder at Bouchard's sweeping claims, but many francophone Quebecers seemed to be receptive. In 1991, the upstart Bloc had claimed the loyalty of only 18 per cent of Quebecers. Yet on election night, October 25, 1993, the party took an extraordinary 49 per cent of the popular vote in Quebec. Exit polls showed that Quebecers' attitudes towards sovereignty directly influenced their votes, and that those attitudes were "strongly correlated" with their personal feelings about Bouchard.[12]

Whether or not Quebecers bought Bouchard's particular diagnosis of Canada's constitutional ills, they handed the Bloc virtually every francophone seat in the province, putting in motion an inexorable challenge to the rest of Canada. "Within two years, a referendum on sovereignty will ask Québécois to cut the Gordian knot," Bouchard announced in the aftermath of the election. "This will also be the moment of truth for English Canada."[13]

~

Lucien Bouchard once mused that when historians turned their thoughts to the 1995 Quebec referendum, Premier Jacques Parizeau would occupy centre stage. "I'll be a footnote," he said.[14] No sound bite better encapsulates the deep and ultimately irreconcilable contradictions Bouchard had come to personify in the mid-1990s. Many francophone Quebecers revered him as a principled and dedicated servant of their national hopes and dreams. An equal number of English Canadians thought him a fickle and ambitious megalomaniac whose claims to modesty were transparently false.

Lucien Bouchard was born in Saint-Cœur-de-Marie, in 1938, and raised in Jonquière in the Saguenay region of Quebec. Like Jean Chrétien, who was born almost five years earlier in Shawinigan, north of Trois-Rivières, Bouchard came from a family whose origins were humble, isolated, and rooted deeply in traditional Québécois culture. Bouchard's mother, Alice Simard, once famously told a journalist that she had no opinion of English Canadians because she had never met any. Like Chrétien, Bouchard earned a law degree from Université Laval and—also like Chrétien—he did not learn English until he was well into adulthood. In contrast with the populist Chrétien, who projected a gregarious and self-effacing *habitant* persona, Bouchard came across as a priestly antiquarian and a loner. In this respect, he was much like Pierre Trudeau—introspective, intense, self-contained, a man who conveyed the impression that he took his greatest pleasure in the company of books rather than people. As with Trudeau, Bouchard's commanding physical presence, brooding good looks, and love of language would give him an almost professorial standing among his allies and followers. But in contrast with Trudeau's cultivated cool, Bouchard had a volatile temperament that erupted regularly into incendiary rages. He was easily humiliated, as he admitted himself, and he wore his torments on his sleeve. When Lucien Bouchard fumed about the humiliation Quebecers suffered at the hands of English Canadians, it was not political posturing. His humiliations and Quebecers' were inextricably linked, and he felt both intensely.

Politically, Bouchard had sampled the entire buffet available to Quebecers of his generation. He joined the Parti libéral du Québec (PLQ) in the 1960s but defected to René Lévesque's Parti Québécois in 1971, in part because of his distaste for the Liberals' handling of the 1970 FLQ crisis. Much to the disbelief of some of his sovereignist friends, Bouchard agreed to write speeches for his old law-school friend Brian Mulroney in the lead-up to the 1984 federal election. Some of Mulroney's most memorable campaign appeals to Quebecers, including his promises to right the wrongs of Trudeau's 1982 repatriation, were, in fact, penned by Bouchard. After Mulroney's landslide victory, the Tory leader rewarded Bouchard by appointing him Canada's ambassador to France. Once he had returned from Paris, in 1988, Bouchard was persuaded by the prime minister to run as a Tory in a Lac Saint-Jean by-election. He won handily, joining the cabinet as Mulroney's Quebec lieutenant and later as minister of the environment. Though Bouchard's reputation as a passionate Quebec nationalist never flagged, Canadians could have been forgiven for believing that his rehabilitation as a federalist was complete.

Then, seemingly out of nowhere, on May 22, 1990, as the clock ticked down on the June 23 deadline to ratify the Meech Lake Accord, Bouchard made the dramatic announcement that he was resigning from the cabinet. Without a word to anyone on the inside, he severed all connections with the Tory party and with Brian Mulroney personally.

To this day, the circumstances surrounding Bouchard's resignation remain in dispute, including the basic question of whether he quit or was fired. The pretext for the breach was Mulroney's eleventh-hour decision to renegotiate Meech on the basis of recommendations made by Bouchard's cabinet colleague Jean Charest. Bouchard claims that his position on Meech never wavered throughout 1989 and 1990. He always insisted that the accord had to be accepted *as is*—that is, as written and endorsed by the eleven first ministers in 1987.[15] Yet it was Bouchard himself who had asked the "brilliant young lawyer" Charest to strike up a special committee when it became clear that the original accord was at risk of not being ratified in some of the provincial legislatures.[16] How Bouchard could later claim to be outraged by the Charest Report remains a mystery to both Charest and Mulroney. But outraged he certainly was. "I could not believe my eyes," Bouchard later wrote. "The strategy and positioning of the government of which I had been a part for more than two years had finally been revealed to me: The 1987 accord had been downgraded to nothing more than a negotiation paper accommodating the shopping list of each of the other provinces." Jean Charest could not believe his eyes, either. He heaped scorn on Bouchard, calling his resignation "meticulously planned treachery."[17] An equally bitter Brian Mulroney swore that he would never forgive Bouchard for stabbing him in the back at such a critical moment in Canadian history, and he never has. "He had fabricated every word of his story," Mulroney later wrote of Bouchard's high-minded rationalization for quitting the government. "He had conspired with [Jacques] Parizeau at least two weeks beforehand to betray me."[18]

Freed of his obligations to his federalist friends, Bouchard retreated into the world of the Quebec sovereignists. He was not alone. When Meech died, on June 22, 1990, a group of five disaffected Quebec MPs—Benoît Tremblay, Gilbert Chartrand, Nic Leblanc, Louis Plamondon, and François Gérin—followed Bouchard out of the Tory party, intent on fashioning some new enterprise dedicated solely to the interests of Quebec. They were joined in short order by two Liberal MPs from Quebec, Jean Lapierre and Gilles Rocheleau, who were equally disillusioned by the loss of Meech but who also held their own leader, Jean Chrétien, in contempt. "I feel sad, humiliated and betrayed," warned Lapierre. "For those who thought that Meech was too much, take note that from now on it is not enough."[19]

Thus was born the Bloc Québécois, which, in only three years, would channel the dreams and resentments of disaffected Quebec voters into such a potent political coalition that it would, in 1993, form Her Majesty's Loyal Opposition. Every step of the way, it was Bouchard himself who played the leading role, powerfully articulating the *Bloquistes'* vision, piloting his new party to ever more commanding heights, and readying his troops for the referendum battle that would, as he liked to say, lance the constitutional abscess once and for all. "The sovereignist avant-garde will displace yesterday's federalist allies," Bouchard said. "The Bloc will be the enveloping wing of the sovereignist advance. For a change, we will be united rather than divided: sovereignist in Quebec, sovereignist in Ottawa. A referendum on sovereignty is a prerequisite to the success of this strategy. Nothing can exempt Québécois from making their decision."[20]

Bouchard's instincts for the aspirations and agonies of Quebecers proved impeccable, then and later. Quebec was his *patrie*, his homeland, and he had absorbed its cultural and political rhythms by osmosis as well as by careful study. "They feel they form a nation," Bouchard would say of the Québécois, "one that is predominantly francophone, to which they pledge their primary loyalty. They have long recognized in the various elements that make up a state the attributes of a country: state, territory, loyalty, people, and culture."[21] He was correct about this, of course. And when he was not trying to score cheap political points, he would quietly acknowledge that many of his nominal adversaries saw themselves as citizens of that same nation. "We must never forget that Quebec federalists are nationalists like us," Bouchard told journalist Paul Wells in 1994. "That they share the same notions. That there is no difference, fundamentally, between the nationalism of Robert Bourassa and that of Jacques Parizeau. That both of them—and René Lévesque, Jean Lesage, Daniel Johnson Sr.—wanted Quebec to develop as its own collectivity."[22]

Bouchard's great gift—what so many Quebecers came to love about him during the referendum campaign—was his ability to articulate a prudent, achievable sovereignist vision for Quebec, in which everyone could find a place and make a contribution. There was no hint of radicalism in anything he said or wrote, nothing intimidating, nothing even to suggest that one country would have to be broken up to give rise to another. "Quebec will be what we make it," said Bouchard. "We have the tools to form a dynamic country with a window on the world: an efficient economic structure, a modern government, a responsible and hardworking population, natural resources, the capacity to adapt with flexibility and cohesion to the globalization of the economy. Everything depends on our solidarity, energy, and collective discipline. In other words, everything depends on us."[23] After the achievement of sovereignty, Bouchard assured Quebecers, they would sit down amicably with English Canada and negotiate a new bilateral treaty, along the lines of what he called *le modèle européen* (the European model).[24] "Our mutual interests will require us, Canadians and Québécois, to define in a responsible way, from the point of view of our respective sovereignty, the relationship that geography, economics and history are asking us to preserve."[25] There was nothing to fear in such a future, he said, for either side. "Quebec sovereignists do not consider Canada an enemy."[26]

Bouchard would repeat this beguiling message, without variation, until the day Quebecers cast their referendum ballots. "The negotiations [with Canada] will be done with extraordinary calm," Bouchard told a Yes rally in mid-October 1995. "It will be done with serenity. Because we have the weight of the people we won't need to yell. We only need to talk."[27]

~

These heady appeals to Quebecers' sense of nation resonated deeply, but as Bouchard had recently defected from the Mulroney Tories, his leap of logic from nationalism to outright secessionism was less sure-footed and, ultimately, less convincing. Yes, Quebecers enjoyed many of the attributes of nationhood, but was it really the case, as Bouchard claimed after the death of Meech, that Quebec "is, in fact, a country that is being artificially kept within the Canadian country"?[28] Some hard-line Quebec separatists expressed doubts about Bouchard's *souverainiste* convictions, then and later. So did many Quebec federalists and an even larger number of English Canadians. They wondered, not without justification, whether Bouchard believed such statements himself. *Toronto Star* columnist Richard Gwyn, for example, dismissed Bouchard as a "bolter" for his apparent lack of loyalty to either people or principle. "Bolters don't think," wrote Gwyn. "They just rear up and head off."[29] Less sympathetic observers called him a shameless opportunist, a dangerous demagogue, and worse.

Bouchard got himself in even hotter water with English Canadians when he presumed to speak for them. In marked contrast to some of his worldly and well-travelled compatriots—Pierre Trudeau and Jacques

Parizeau, for example—Bouchard had not set foot outside Quebec until he was an adult. Until then, English Canada was for him a *terra incognita*, a place he had only ever read about. His instincts for the country that lay beyond his home province were thus not only poorly developed but also skewed towards old-fashioned stereotypes. "English-speaking Canadians condemned Meech," Bouchard wrote in 1994, "because it threatened the idea they had of their country. The country they carry in their minds and hearts is the present Canada, in which English is clearly predominant and which admires and is nostalgic for the British Crown, institutionalized and personified in a central state."[30] *Nostalgic for the British Crown? Central state?* Many Canadian anglos were rightly incredulous. The last serious national conversation about Canada's British connection had been the flag debate of 1964. And as every prime minister since Lester Pearson could attest, a steadily lengthening list of provincial prerogatives, many of them originating in Quebec, had taken Canada far further down the path of decentralization than some would have preferred to go.

More than this, there was something mischievous and uncharitable about Bouchard's ill-informed generalizations. For the many English Canadians who had voted for federal parties led by Quebecers, supported official bilingualism and Charter-based language rights, enrolled their kids in French immersion, and celebrated a tolerant and inclusive Canada they believed was the envy of the world, Bouchard's words savoured strongly of propaganda. When he presumed to tell Canadians that the "natural incompatibility" of Canada and Quebec "prevents common economic policies and an authentic national enterprise," they wondered if he was describing the Canada of their grandparents or of Hugh MacLennan's 1945 novel *Two Solitudes*, a Canada yet to be transformed by the Quiet Revolution.

Indeed, Bouchard's limited appreciation of Canadian anglos made his own work as Bloc leader more challenging, since he felt an obligation to acquaint them with the mysteries of modern Quebec. "English-speaking Canadians need to know the intensity, determination, and objectives of the sovereignist vision," Bouchard wrote in 1994.

"Someone has to tell them that, contrary to the reassuring speeches from official sources, Quebec has not been anaesthetized. There is broad consensus for a referendum on sovereignty. If we were to keep our Canadian friends in ignorance or under a false sense of security, we would be setting them up for some nasty surprises. They must be prepared for a referendum whose outcome will be favourable to sovereignty."[31] *Anaesthetized*? In the face of such condescension, many anglos rightly wondered how many "Canadian friends" the Bloc leader actually had left. But there was a larger issue. When Bouchard claimed that there was "broad consensus for a referendum," was he not obscuring the hard reality that there was no consensus within Quebec on sovereignty itself? Even after the Bloc's 1993 election triumph, poll after poll showed that only 43 to 45 per cent of Quebec voters supported "sovereignty" and an even more paltry 35 to 38 per cent supported "independence."[32] Given that a sizeable majority of Quebecers still appeared to prefer Canada to any sovereignist alternative, English Canadians' sense of security was patently neither ignorant nor false.

Bouchard's most serious misreading of Anglo-Canadians—one that would have an incalculable impact on Quebecers as they considered their referendum options—was to imagine that they somehow formed a coherent political entity independent of Quebec. "If there is a people," Bouchard told Quebecers repeatedly, "it's English-Canada because they too have built between themselves deep links of solidarity, great emotion and the country they share they feel in their hearts."[33] To be fair, this deceptively simple idea was not Bouchard's alone. After the death of Meech, in fact, it crystallized into the acronym ROC, meaning the "rest of Canada" or "Canada outside Quebec," thus becoming part of the country's constitutional shorthand. The simplicity of the concept was deceptive because, as constitutional authorities like Professor Alan C. Cairns took pains to remind Canadians throughout the 1990s, *there was no Canada without Quebec*. "The Rest-of-Canada," said Cairns, "enjoys only a shadowy existence. It is the empty chair at the bargaining table. The structural reason for this absence of voice and incapacity for introspection is obvious. The

Rest-of-Canada has no institutional or constitutional existence, and thus has no one with authority to speak for it. It is headless and therefore officially voiceless."[34] Most ordinary Canadians were not reading the growing mountain of academic literature on the constitutional impasse, of course. They didn't have to. A ubiquitous bumper sticker said it all: "My Canada includes Quebec."

Some of Bouchard's federalist critics, Jean Chrétien among them, accused him of conjuring up the spectre of a united, arrogant, and ultimately obdurate English Canada to win the hearts and minds of undecided Quebec voters. There is certainly some truth in this claim. Bouchard routinely asserted in one breath that English Canada had callously torpedoed Meech and in the next that if Quebecers did not support the push for sovereignty, the same English Canada would happily trample their rights again and again. But the historical record suggests that Bouchard actually believed what he said about the unity and purpose of English Canadians, and that once he became the leader of the Bloc Québécois, his essentially binary conception of Canada versus Quebec was genuine.

In this sense, Lucien Bouchard projected his own deeply personal experience of Quebec nationalism onto the rest of Canada: Anglo-Canadians would respond to Quebec sovereignty, he believed, exactly as he would do in their place. In so doing, he handed Quebecers—even disillusioned federalists—a powerful incentive to play hard ball with English Canada, without reservation or remorse, just as he had done with his old friend Brian Mulroney.

~

"By the time I arrived in Ottawa in 1993," Reform Party leader Preston Manning later reflected, "I had long considered ways to cope with the threat of secession."[35]

Such certitude could only have struck Prime Minister Jean Chrétien as cold comfort, coming from the man who had come to personify the Anglo-Canadian stereotype that Lucien Bouchard found so loathsome. The unilingual Manning was fed up with Quebec's special pleading and the feds' kowtowing to it. His grassroots contact with thousands of Canadians gave him "a better grasp than any other federal leader on the growing frustration in the rest of Canada," he later claimed. "It was not just the future of Quebec that was being decided by the Quebec referendum but the future of all of Canada, and Canadians in the rest of Canada wanted a say."[36] Manning had resolutely opposed the Meech Lake and Charlottetown accords, arguing that the granting of distinct-society status to Quebec violated the bedrock principle of the equality of the Canadian provinces. If Quebecers could not abide by the rules of democracy, he stated bluntly in 1994, then "Quebec and the rest of Canada should openly examine the feasibility of establishing a better but more separate relationship between them."[37] Jean Chrétien drew the obvious conclusion. "My suspicion," said Chrétien, "was that Manning knew he could never become prime minister of Canada because of Quebec and, consequently, that he wouldn't have been terribly sorry to see it leave the federation."[38]

Preston Manning's ascent in federal politics had been as meteoric as Lucien Bouchard's, yet another by-product of the collapse of the Mulroney Tories. From a meagre one-seat foothold in the federal parliament, won by Deborah Grey in a 1989 by-election, Reform vaulted to fifty-two seats in the election of 1993. Reformers took almost 19 per cent of the popular vote—5 per cent more than the *Bloquistes*—but owing mainly to vote-splitting came up two seats shy of second place. They wanted to form the Official Opposition so badly they could taste it. "People aren't concerned about Quebec to the degree they are concerned about taxes, their jobs, the economy, criminal justice and health care," said Deborah Grey, whom Manning appointed deputy leader in 1993. "With Lucien Bouchard having abdicated the throne to go off referenduming, we will be in that [Official Opposition] position even more legitimately."[39]

As with the Bloc, the public face of Reform was the face of its leader. Born in Edmonton in 1942, Preston Manning had emerged fully formed on the federal scene in the 1980s as a homespun populist, fiscal conservative, and self-styled evangelical Christian. The son of Ernest

Manning, "Bible Bill" Aberhart's long-serving successor as premier of Alberta, Preston had a political pedigree so far to the right of Canada's then-dominant left-liberal consensus that many Canadians thought him an extremist. In marked contrast to Lucien Bouchard, who had dabbled freely in Quebec politics, Manning had never detoured from the true-blue conservatism he inherited from his father. By the end of Canada's centennial year, 1967, when many other Canadian twenty-five-year-olds were turning on, tuning in, and dropping out, Manning had already run as a Socred for a seat in parliament, co-authored a white paper for the Alberta government, and joined his first free-market think tank. He was, in the parlance of the day, a square. When Manning took his seat in the House of Commons for the first time in 1993, Reform was already known to Canadians as a party of "doctrinal rigidity."[40] It was a label its MPs did not dispute.

The Reform platform included massive cuts to government spending, particularly on welfare, an elected (Triple-E) Senate, major deficit and debt reduction, repeal of the Tories' hated GST, support for NAFTA, and a smattering of "socially conservative" policies including opposition to the extension of gay rights. Above all, Reformers demanded that "the West wants in"—into Ottawa, into the national conversation, into a political culture they perceived as favouring soft liberal centralizers in general and pampered Quebec nationalists in particular.

Preston Manning's position on the Constitution was categorical, then and later. If it were up to him, he would offer Quebec a federalist alternative to the status quo by decentralizing Canada on a vast scale. Quebec nationalists would get most of the powers they wanted, but so would the rest of the provinces. "The status-quo federalists have lost the last three contests in Quebec," Manning said in late 1994. "We won't attack. We will just present our own positive view: that there is a better federalism than what we've got now and that there is public support for it outside Quebec."[41] Stephen Harper, Manning's point man on the unity file and one of only four Reformers who in 1995 could speak French, would carry Reform's tough-love approach into Quebec during the referendum debate. The message never varied.

"Canadians told us they want Canada to be a balanced and equal federation," Harper told Montrealers two weeks before the 1995 referendum vote. "There will be no special status, formally or informally for Quebec or any other province."[42] Such pronouncements were guaranteed to alienate both Quebecers and the many English Canadians who sought some kind of accommodation with Quebec. Even old-style Alberta Tories like *Globe and Mail* editor-in-chief William Thorsell were put off by Reform's intractability. "The [Bloc Québécois] succeeded in 1993 because people like Mr. Manning prevailed," an exasperated Thorsell wrote in December 1994. "Mr. Manning will not be prime minister indeed."[43]

Oddly enough, most Quebecers, Lucien Bouchard included, politely ignored the Reform Party. Their fight was not with Preston Manning. In the thousands of pages of newspaper copy generated by the referendum debate in Quebec, Reform was hardly ever mentioned. When either Preston Manning or Stephen Harper made public appearances in Quebec, which was not often, he was little more than a sideshow. Pascale Gemme, a Sherbrooke man who attended a small street protest when Manning visited his city in October 1995, spoke for many Quebecers. "In a way we could be happy that he's here," said Gemme sardonically of the Reform leader, "because he can help the *Oui!*"[44]

Manning knew, of course, that for Quebecers he was beyond the pale. He later wrote this colourful description of his being *non grata*: "Have you ever been at a neighbourhood barbecue when a family feud breaks out and no one quite knows what to do? You are standing there in line to get your burger and drink, just minding your own business, when all of a sudden the Bouchards and the Chrétiens from down the street (they're related, you know) start going at it. Someone in the family wants a divorce, and every member of the family is getting in on the act about whose fault it is and who did what to whom, including what Uncle Pierre did to Aunt Renée in 1982. The voices are getting louder and louder so nobody else can hear or say anything, and the chairman of the barbecue committee keeps saying 'Order, order,' but nobody's listening. In your heart you'd like to help, but you're not sure how, and they don't want anyone to 'interfere,' so about all you can do is look busy fixing your burger and trying to stay out of it."[45]

Consigned to the sidelines, looking busy and fixing their burgers, Manning and Harper would in 1995 play the only role available to them, as federalist *agents provocateurs*. They would press Jean Chrétien at every step of the referendum campaign to take a firm and unambiguous stand against the sovereignists, whether this meant challenging the constitutionality of unilateral secession, or confronting legal arguments about the territorial integrity of Quebec, or determining whether 50 per cent plus one vote was enough to decide the referendum, or contradicting sovereignist promises that Quebecers could continue to use Canadian passports and the Canadian dollar after separation. And press they did, again and again, attacking what they saw as Chrétien's do-nothing strategy at every turn. In the House of Commons, where this battle played out almost daily, Chrétien did his best to bob and weave. It frequently fell to his no-holds-barred deputy prime minister, Sheila Copps, to deploy government countermeasures. "[Calgary West MP Stephen Harper] is on very dangerous ground," a fiery Copps told the House in December 1994, "when at a very crucial point in Canada's history he and his leader and other members of his party are more intent on attacking the federal government than on attacking the separatists."[46]

In January 1994, Preston Manning had his first private meeting with Jean Chrétien. The question of Quebec inevitably came up. Manning pitched the idea of "reforming federalism" but was stonewalled by the prime minister's "mantra" that the only option available after Meech was "routine federal-provincial negotiations." When Manning expressed the view that the government's lacklustre platitudes were no match for Lucien Bouchard's "separatist dream," the prime minister simply shrugged.

"I left this meeting on cordial terms with Chrétien," said Manning, "but with the sinking feeling that he really had no forward-thinking strategy for combating separatism."[47]

~

Appearing not to have a strategy is, of course, a strategy.

Since retiring from public life, Jean Chrétien has revealed that he was persuaded by his inner circle to stay in the weeds in the lead-up to the 1995 referendum vote. "Going into the campaign, my advisors had convinced me that I should limit my participation," he recalls, "even though a low-profile strategy ran against my political instincts and my competitive personality. I reluctantly went along."[48]

Canadians know Jean Chrétien as a smart, savvy, and supremely self-confident individual. They know that he would heed the advice of men like Jean Pelletier, Eddie Goldenberg, and John Rae—over a two-year period and on a matter of grave national importance—only if he thought it was good advice. When Chrétien took power in October 1993, he was a thirty-year veteran of Canadian politics, he had held every major cabinet portfolio, he commanded a huge majority in the House of Commons, and he faced a weak and divided opposition. In almost every other policy area, he and his ministers could write their own tickets—as they later demonstrated by slaying the deficit and introducing sweeping reforms to social programs. "It is hard for most Canadians to remember how bleak our days looked at that point in our history," Chrétien has recalled. "To be frank, Canada was in terrible shape—exhausted, demoralized and fractured."[49] Canadians voted for Chrétien because they wanted him to act, and they gave him the mandate to do it.

But Quebec was different, much different. Chrétien had refused to campaign on the Constitution, and Quebecers had punished him for it, voting overwhelmingly for *Bloquistes* and very nearly evicting him from his own seat in Saint-Maurice. Even after the election, the prime minister plainly did not want to appear obsessed with Quebec, as Pierre Trudeau and Brian Mulroney had been. The reason was obvious, and he did not need to hear it from his advisors: in the high-stakes contest for the hearts and minds of Quebecers, he wasn't holding many good cards.

The truth was that the prime minister was himself a liability. "Unlike Trudeau fifteen years earlier," Eddie Goldenberg recalls, "Chrétien in 1995 was not popular in Quebec. He had been demonized for years because of his role in the patriation of the Constitution and his position on the Meech Lake Accord. That demonization had come from all quarters."[50] It bears repeating that Chrétien was so little trusted in francophone Quebec that Lucien Bouchard could impugn his character, and even his patriotism, without fear of reprisal. Chrétien's "stubborn refusal" to reopen the Constitution, as one academic observer put it, did nothing to mitigate this distrust.[51] Nor could he fall back on fiscal federalism and bribe Quebec to stay in Canada. Facing a $40-billion deficit and a $500-billion debt, Chrétien had "far fewer carrots" to offer Quebec than Trudeau had had in 1980, as a *Globe and Mail* editorial noted. He could not propose new spending because "there is no money."[52] Threats of economic reprisals after separation were yet another dead end. As Osgoode Hall professor Patrick J. Monahan liked to remind Canadians, "a sovereign Quebec would remain part of the continental trading system regardless of the attitudes of Canadian politicians."[53]

When it came right down to it, what lay behind Jean Chrétien's strategy of having no strategy was numbers—endless streams of numbers, endlessly extrapolated by the country's growing army of pollsters, demographers, and armchair mathematicians.

The overriding assumption of the prime minister and his advisors heading into the referendum was that the core federalist vote in Quebec—the 60 per cent won by Trudeau in 1980 and sustained more or less consistently ever since—would hold.[54] Time was on their side, or so said the experts. "Quebec's aging population has doomed separatism," Carleton University economist John Samuel announced in the fall of 1994, after observing that the number of Quebec voters under forty had been dropping since 1980. "Based primarily on demographic factors," he concluded, "the movement of separatism is fast fizzling out in Quebec and will soon die."[55] A December 1994 SOM poll confirmed that the over-forty-five crowd did indeed tend to be more conservative and leery of separation.[56] A 1995 study by McGill political scientist Maurice Pinard showed that support for sovereignty among university-educated young francophones had declined by roughly 15 per cent since the last referendum.[57] In January 1995, *Toronto Star* columnist Richard Gwyn added his voice to the chorus of number-crunchers. According to Statistics Canada, wrote Gwyn, the population of Quebec had just fallen below the threshold level of one-quarter of Canada's overall population. "Most probably," he concluded, "we can win the referendum without being generous."[58]

To be sure, the numbers were endlessly fascinating. Watching the polls was at least as interesting to Canadians in 1995 as watching the politicians. But as Jean Chrétien and his team were about to learn the hard way, demography is not destiny. People change their minds. They evolve. They can be won over by new ideas and charismatic personalities, by elegant arguments and also by artful manipulation. All of these forces would be put in motion in the course of the referendum debate.

Sovereignists like Lucien Bouchard were every bit as obsessed with numbers as their federalist adversaries, but never were they slaves to them. The *Bloquistes* knew that they had strategic advantages that could not be quantified, including control over the timing of the referendum, a dispirited and anxious electorate, Official Opposition status in Ottawa, and a prime minister who seemed intent on making their job easy for them. It would take hard work to massage the numbers into a majority vote for sovereignty, but with the right sort of referendum question, the right team, and a little luck, they believed they could prevail.

In politics, momentum is everything. Within months of the Bloc's electoral triumph in Ottawa, pollsters began projecting a Parti Québécois sweep in the provincial election scheduled for September 12, 1994. The essential elements of Bouchard's victory scenario—"sovereignist in Quebec, sovereignist in Ottawa"—were coming into view.[59]

The sovereignists had every reason to imagine that the momentum was all on their side.

CHAPTER TWO

Quebec City, 1994

In the autumn of 1995, Quebec premier Jacques Parizeau was sixty-five years old. He had spent a political lifetime advancing the idea of a sovereign Quebec, and he knew that whatever the outcome of the October 30 vote, the referendum would mark his last chance to realize his grand dream.

Until he became premier, Parizeau was not well known outside his home province. This relative anonymity was a gift to his Canadian critics. By the time he was in his sixties, Parizeau's stodgy appearance, mannerisms, and speech made him an object of easy satire. The *Globe and Mail*'s John Gray compared him to the P.G. Wodehouse character Jeeves, "on whom he apparently models his impeccable but curiously dated English."[1] Thanks to irreverent columnists and cartoonists, Canadians learned that Parizeau's Boy Scout nickname had been *Belette Vibrante* (Vibrant Weasel), that he bore a striking resemblance to Rich Uncle Pennybags, the Monopoly man, and that he never spoke to anyone, including his closest advisors, using their first names or the familiar *tu*. No Quebec separatist had much of a chance of endearing himself to the citizens of the country he was working to destroy, of course, but these sorts of caricatures made Parizeau easy to lampoon. "He is fond of irony and underlines it with deep laughter," noted one American observer, "but the dominant impression is of the former professor imparting a lesson."[2] Compared to the hot-blooded Lucien Bouchard,

Jacques Parizeau was a cold fish.[3] Canadians outside Quebec tended to distrust Bouchard because they saw him as an opportunistic dilettante. They distrusted Parizeau, too, but for the opposite reason. He was widely perceived as an opportunistic hardliner.

Within Quebec, however, Parizeau's talent was legendary. And despite his lack of conventional charisma, as he put it himself, he was extremely popular. He held a PhD from the London School of Economics, and as one of the province's leading economists during the Quiet Revolution, he had been present at the creation of the modern Quebec state. In the 1960s, he played a leading role in the breakneck modernization of the provincial economy, including the epochal nationalization of Hydro-Québec. He worked alongside René Lévesque in the 1970s to build the Parti Québécois into a provincial contender and was named minister of finance in the first PQ government, elected in 1976. Lucien Bouchard's relationship with Jacques Parizeau was never close, and sometimes it was openly fractious. But this did not prevent the younger man from seeing in the elder a Québécois nation-builder of almost unequalled stature. If Parizeau had followed "the beaten path of federalism," Bouchard observed, he could have been governor of the Bank of Canada, even prime minister of Canada. "Everything was within the grasp of his talent, education, background, and perfect bilingualism."[4] Instead, Parizeau achieved unrivalled supremacy in René Lévesque's government. "Parizeau, who sat in Duplessis's former office, made fifty decisions a day, and did the governing," said Bouchard. "The government held no secrets for Parizeau, for the simple reason that he had designed most of the system himself. He played it for all it was worth, like [violinist Yehudi] Menuhin on a Stradivarius, even choosing the score."[5]

Parizeau later recalled the moment when he realized that he was a Quebec sovereignist. The year was 1969. He was taking a three-day trip by train from Quebec City to a conference in Banff, Alberta, spending his days in his private berth writing the paper he had been invited to give. "It started as a federalist paper but the conclusion was clearly sovereignist," said Parizeau. "It seemed so obvious after so many years that we couldn't go on divesting Ottawa of its power, its money. We were very successful in doing that. God, we were good!"[6]

Parizeau thought René Lévesque's idea of sovereignty-association was a weak substitute for outright sovereignty, but he played the good soldier and campaigned for the Yes side during the 1980 referendum. In 1984, Lévesque took a giant step back from the dream of independence and agreed to work with Prime Minister Brian Mulroney on a new constitutional deal for Quebec within Canada. Lévesque called the gesture a *beau risque* (beautiful risk), but Parizeau saw little beauty in it. He quit Lévesque's cabinet over the issue, announced his resignation from politics, and added "principled sovereignist" to his already distinguished résumé. Three years later, with Robert Bourassa's Liberals back in power in Quebec City and Lévesque dead from a myocardial infarction, Parizeau re-entered the political arena and was acclaimed as leader of the PQ. He lost the election of 1989 to Bourassa, and lost badly, but that was before Meech and Charlottetown had torpedoed Quebecers' hopes that Canadian federalism might be renewed. By the time the Liberals were forced to seek a new mandate, in 1994, Parizeau's sovereignist ambitions had an entirely new lease on life.

Like Lucien Bouchard, the self-styled "technocrat" Jacques Parizeau understood the importance of appealing to Quebecers' idealism as well as their pragmatism. "The desire for an independent Quebec is not based only on rational arguments, cost and benefits analyses, and hopes of higher living standards," Parizeau has written. "First and foremost comes the desire of a people or a nation to assume full responsibility for itself, to live together and prepare a shared future, and to build on the pride of a shared history."[7]

Although, ironically, Parizeau's unfiltered rhetorical jabs and snappy one-liners would occasionally land him in hot water, he had a reputation for being inordinately cautious about what he said in public and how he said it. Even more than Lucien Bouchard, he was a genuine wordsmith, in both French and English, which helps to explain why even his own followers thought his speeches sounded too well-rehearsed, or too brainy, or just plain smug. Parizeau would be accused by his opponents during the

1995 referendum campaign of using loose language as a form of political cover, but to this day he dismisses such charges.[8] Parizeau could be snarky ("Canadians love Quebec, yes, but the way you love a postcard. They say: be beautiful and shut up").[9] But he also loved to laugh, even at himself. He took full responsibility for his own remarks, seldom dissembled or apologized, and regularly interceded in fiery parliamentary debates with appeals for everyone to keep calm.[10] Parizeau's unguarded remarks at the conclusion of the 1995 referendum campaign would become infamous, to be sure. But during the sovereignty debate, with the future of Canada at stake and emotions running high, he was at pains not to let sovereignist passions rage out of control.

In sharp contrast with many of the left-leaning stalwarts of the Parti Québécois—"the long hair and mutton-chopped post-hippie generation of Quebecers who smoked pot and listened to Beau Dommage"[11]— Jacques Parizeau has always evinced a conservative's fondness for pomp and ceremony. Never has he missed an opportunity to build national symbols into his vision of an independent Quebec. He was delighted when, in 1968, the Quebec legislative assembly was renamed the Assemblée nationale du Québec (National Assembly), and he has only ever referred to provincial premiers by the designation *premier minis-tre*. When he became premier himself, he took great pleasure in being treated by foreign dignitaries as a de facto head of state, particularly when he visited Paris. It was Parizeau who designated the Tudor house at 1080 Avenue des Braves in Quebec City the official premier's residence, still affectionately known as the Élisette, a neologism combining Parizeau's wife's given name, Lisette, and the Élysée Palace, the official residence of the French president.

As they readied themselves for the election of 1994 and what they promised Quebecers would be a referendum campaign the following year, Parizeau and the PQ national executive laid out their blueprint for sovereignty in the booklet *Le Québec dans un monde nouveau* (*Quebec in a New World*). A sovereign Quebec, they wrote, would be one in which all taxes imposed on Quebecers would be collected by the government of Quebec, all laws would be passed by the Quebec National Assembly, and all international treaties would be ratified by it.[12] It was Parizeau's love of ceremony that gave the otherwise staid document its Founding-Fatherly tone. The first step in the achievement of sovereignty would be the submission to the National Assembly of a "solemn declaration stating Quebec's wish to accede to full sovereignty."[13] After that, a Quebec constitution would be drafted, an economic association with Canada negotiated, and an independent seat at the United Nations sought.

Clearly, Parizeau grasped something that few other sovereignists appear to have considered at the time: the popular legitimacy of the new republic of Quebec would depend on the potency of both its national symbols and its founding myths. *Le Québec dans un monde nouveau* concluded with a flourish from Parizeau's own pen. "We must keep our appointment with destiny."[14]

~

Daniel Johnson Jr. took over as premier of Quebec on January 11, 1994, following the resignation of Robert Bourassa. The scion of one of Quebec's leading political families, Johnson seemed literally born to greatness. His father, Daniel Sr., had served as Quebec's last Union Nationale premier between 1966 and 1968, while his brother, Pierre-Marc Johnson, served briefly as PQ premier in 1985 in the wake of René Lévesque's resignation. Daniel Jr. held a PhD from the University of London and an MBA from Harvard. His ascent in Quebec business circles had taken him, at the age of thirty-three, to the rank of vice-president in Paul Desmarais's Power Corporation. During the 1980 referendum campaign, Johnson campaigned aggressively for the No side, making more than thirty-five stump speeches and greatly impressing provincial Liberal leader Claude Ryan. Johnson entered Quebec politics as a Liberal MNA in 1981. When the Liberals were returned to power in 1985, he served as Premier Bourassa's minister of industry and commerce, and later as president of the Treasury Board. Outside Quebec, he became known as "Robert Bourassa's bloodless number-cruncher."[15]

Johnson's inheritance from Bourassa was a politically exhausted mélange of federalist constitutional initiatives sugar-coated with nationalist rhetoric. As premier, Johnson decided he would break decisively with Bourassa and position himself as a proponent of flexible federalism, much as Jean Chrétien was doing at the federal level. When Johnson named his cabinet, he assumed the intergovernmental-affairs portfolio himself, an important symbolic gesture. "After Quebecers have rejected separation," he said, "we must relearn how to conduct constitutional reform in a less spectacular and more evolutionary manner. The practice of constitutional negotiation must not persist as a high-stakes game which monopolizes the public agenda. It will certainly call for less stomping and more statecraft."[16] Columnist Robert Sheppard of the *Globe and Mail* remarked sardonically that Johnson's approach was good for Canada because he "holds the notion of constitutional change as if it were a bag of kitty litter: useful in its own way, but not something to bring to every public occasion."[17] Interestingly, Jacques Parizeau also claimed to be impressed with Johnson's candour, since it brought clarity to the public debate. "The people of Quebec will have to choose their destiny," said Parizeau. "Quebecers will choose between two political options: separation and political union."[18]

Johnson had a confident and assertive debating style, which would prove a great asset during both the provincial election of 1994 and the referendum campaign the following year. And yet his speeches, even his casual remarks, conveyed no great emotional attachment to Canada. Never, for example, did he publicly defend the 1982 Constitution, and on at least one occasion he looked "uneasy" when federalist Quebecers broke into "O Canada."[19] When he assumed the premiership, Johnson was asked why he was not a sovereignist. "As the [Quebec] economy opens," he replied, "as we become citizens of the world, it appears to me wrong that we should put up new borders, new frontiers and thus reduce ourselves to a small geographical area."[20] There was no mention at all of Canada. Whenever Johnson did allude to the country beyond Quebec, it was almost always as a dollars-and-cents proposition from which Quebecers drew considerable advantage. "The share that we gather as members of the Canadian political and economic union far outstrips our contribution to the system," he told Montrealers in August 1994.

"We benefit as Quebecers from that union. On the face of it, how can separating be an improvement?"[21] Even now, it is hard to tell whether Johnson made such anodyne statements to appeal to recalcitrant voters or because he believed them himself. On one point, however, he was unequivocal and in complete agreement with Jacques Parizeau: the matter of Quebec's political future was for Quebecers alone to decide.

~

The 1994 provincial election was hard fought but "remarkably uneventful," as one observer put it.[22] Jacques Parizeau and the Parti Québécois ran on the slogan *"L'autre façon de gouverner"* ("The other way of governing") rather than an expressly sovereignist platform. Federal Tory leader Jean Charest was one of many Canadians to accuse Parizeau of cynically trying to mask his true intentions. "The Péquistes, true to form, buried the separatist option to get themselves elected," Charest later wrote. "They chose instead to focus on other, very negative themes. They attacked the government."[23] It is true that Parizeau's inner circle advised him to play it safe and not dwell upon sovereignty, but the irrepressible PQ leader often did exactly the opposite out on the campaign trail. He could not help himself. At an August 1994 rally at Gaspé, for example, Parizeau told local fishermen that the only way to protect their fish stocks was to have a sovereign Quebec. In Gatineau, Parizeau addressed a group of PQ supporters. "We will need you once again next year, because next year there is going to be a referendum," he said. "It's not because we will have elected a Parti Québécois government in 1994 that we will automatically win the referendum in 1995. We are going to have to work hard to win the referendum in 1995."[24]

For his part, Daniel Johnson played the best card he thought he was holding: Quebecers' private worry that a Parti Québécois government would propel them too precipitously towards independence. "The PQ strategy is to provide the illusion that by voting for them, you're not voting for a party that will initiate separation when it's elected," warned Johnson. "There are contradictions, paradoxes, make-believe appeals to people's gullibility in the PQ platform. These people will say anything."[25]

Pre-election polls showed that Quebec voters were, in fact, far from gullible. In the time-honoured Canadian tradition of throwing the bums out, many had grown tired of the Liberals and simply wanted a change. A majority thought good government rather than sovereignty would be the top-of-mind issue for them when they cast their ballots. Significantly, a majority of Quebecers approved of Parizeau's proposal to hold a referendum on sovereignty even though the number of decided Yes voters remained stalled at 37 per cent. Much as it baffled some English Canadians—CBC-TV news ran a fifteen-minute panel hoping to "explain the contradictions"[26]—this was Quebec democracy at work. Sovereignty was plainly less popular than the Parti Québécois, just as it had been in the 1970s when roughly 10 per cent of Quebec francophones had voted for René Lévesque without supporting sovereignty-association.[27] The trick for Daniel Johnson and the Liberals this time around was to work their anti-separatist strategy without insulting the intelligence of Quebec voters.

When the ballots were counted on the evening of September 12, the results surprised nearly everyone. The Parti Québécois won the election, taking seventy-seven seats to the Liberals' forty-seven. But seen from the vantage point of Quebecers' pre-election expectations, Daniel Johnson won a victory of his own. The PQ managed to win only 44.7 per cent of the popular vote versus the Liberals' 44.3 per cent. More than 4 million Quebecers had voted, but the margin of victory for the PQ was less than 15,000 votes. These results shocked even the PQ's own pollster, Michel Lepage, who had predicted right up to election day that his party would win eighty-five seats and roughly half of the popular vote.[28] Some voices outside Quebec asserted, with obvious relief, that the results had "shattered the party's self-confidence."[29] But this was surely an exaggeration. Parizeau's victory put him "*en route vers le pays*" ("en route towards a country"), in the words of the Quebec daily *Le Soleil*, and that was really all that mattered.[30] Asked on election night whether he was disappointed by the returns, Parizeau replied, "Of course not, we won."[31]

Parizeau celebrated his victory with a speech to a thousand *fleurs-de-lis*–waving PQ supporters, assembled at the Capitol Theatre in

Quebec City. He wasted no time getting to the subject of a referendum. "My friends," said Parizeau, "we will present to Quebecers something once we have put all the cards on the table. We will ask them the question that will make a people into a country. We will go forward to a new chapter in our history."[32] The premier-elect knew the polls, and he knew that harnessing a majority of Quebecers to his sovereignty option within a year was going to be a challenge. But that was his promise to the people, and he intended to keep it. Asked whether he would oppose the feds and the other provincial governments in his day-to-day work as premier, Parizeau was direct. "I don't want to oppose the system," he said. "I want to get out of it. I'm not interested in going on with sterile battles. I want to leave."[33]

Lucien Bouchard took the stage after Parizeau's victory speech. He was greeted by a thunderous ovation—evidence, if any was needed, that his appeal among sovereignists had already far surpassed Parizeau's. The "dominoes of the federal regime are falling one after the other," a subdued Bouchard told the crowd. "We are now called to a mobilization of our energy and a closing of ranks around an idea that is both simple and strong: Quebec must become a normal country. We have to prepare the historic rendezvous to which Quebecers will be invited."[34]

Bouchard had already begun recalibrating the relationship of the Bloc to the Parti Québécois. On the one hand, he welcomed a sovereignist government in Quebec City. "We will feel less lonely on the other side of the Ottawa River," he said. "The federalists will now have to break their silence. We will now have two teams to demonstrate the cost of federalism."[35] But he was at pains to show that the Bloc Québécois was not merely the handmaiden of the new PQ government. *Bloquistes* had their own agenda, their own responsibilities. Canada, for example, would have to be brought into the debate about Quebec's future. "This debate will not be confined to Quebec," said Bouchard, "because it does not interest only Quebec. One of the direct consequences of this debate will be to affect the integrity of Canada as a country. And I don't know of any country in the world, of any federal government, that wouldn't bother about that."[36]

As for Daniel Johnson, his unexpectedly strong showing in the election meant that he could keep his job as Liberal leader. "Even after nine long years of power, at the end of a long recession that hit all our citizens in every region of Quebec, the number of votes we got is almost as high as that of the Parti Québécois," Johnson told a crowd of his own supporters. "I intend to take on the role of leader of the opposition with vigour, with seriousness and with diligence."[37] The morning after the election, a forthright Johnson warned Parizeau that Quebecers regarded his promise of a timely referendum as binding. Like Jean Chrétien, Johnson knew that the current polling numbers did not favour a Yes vote. But he also knew that the No side—which was now his to lead—had little to offer Quebecers in lieu of the flexible-federalism status quo. "One would be misreading the mood of the rest of Canada and other [provincial] governments," said Johnson, "if we thought that significant, substantial, momentous constitutional offers were in the offing. That has been made fairly clear."[38] Johnson knew that the longer the sovereignists waited to hold their referendum, the better grew their chances of winning it. He tried to ease the worried minds of Canadians outside Quebec. "To all other Canadians, I tell them that I am quite confident that we can constructively go on forward in the future for many, many years to come. And I ask them to show that same degree of confidence that I have in the future of this relationship and this partnership we all have together."[39]

The biggest surprise on election night was the extraordinary success of Mario Dumont's upstart Parti Action Démocratique du Québec (ADQ). Although the ADQ won only one seat—in Dumont's own riding of Rivière-du-Loup—it took 6.5 per cent of the popular vote (fully 10 per cent of the popular vote in the eighty ridings in which it ran candidates). The ADQ offered Quebecers what it called an *autonomiste* rather than a *souverainiste* platform: sovereignty was desirable, but it was a distant second priority behind fixing the Quebec economy and not nearly urgent enough to warrant a year-long referendum campaign.

The twenty-four-year-old Dumont had been head of the youth wing of the Quebec Liberal Party while attending Concordia

University. He had broken with Robert Bourassa to campaign against the Charlottetown Accord, after which he, Jean Allaire, and other high-profile Liberal nationalists defected to form the ADQ. Dumont himself was a mystery to the many Canadians for whom maturity and experience were the cardinal political virtues. "The Mario Dumont phenomenon continues to amaze me," wrote Montreal *Gazette* columnist Don Macpherson. "He's the only elected member of a fledgling third party. He is not a good public speaker, firing rapid, nervous, machine-gun bursts of empty clichés emphasized by constant, jerky hand gestures."[40] What made Dumont a phenomenon was simple math. His soft-separatist message had struck just the right chord with a quarter-million Quebec voters, which, given the almost-even split in popular support for the two leading parties, might make or break a future vote on sovereignty.

In the weeks and months after the election, the ADQ's young leader would make a great show of resisting the seduction strategies of the PQ and the Bloc.[41] But, of course, Jacques Parizeau and Lucien Bouchard could add. If Monsieur Dumont really carried 6.5 per cent of the Quebec electorate in his back pocket, then the Yes tent would have to be built big enough to include him.

～

Back in Ottawa, Prime Minister Jean Chrétien saw an opportunity in the weaker-than-expected victory of the sovereignists and used a nationally televised speech to spin the results to his own advantage. "Throughout the election campaign," he said, "the Parti Québécois and its leader repeatedly stated that this election was about a provincial government, nothing else. Tonight, I am convinced that in the coming months, Quebecers will once again demonstrate their profound attachment to being a full part of Canada."[42] In private, Chrétien's emotions were less restrained. He later recalled being "infuriated by Parizeau's declaration on the night of his victory that Quebecers wanted to become 'a normal people in a normal country.'" Was it "normal," fumed Chrétien, "to want to split up a country that had been built on respect for values such as tolerance, generosity, and openness? To separate from a country that had allowed people of different ethnicities and languages to live together in a peaceful, democratic, and free society? To give up on a country that the United Nations had put first in terms of quality of life?"[43]

One of Chrétien's advisors was asked how the feds would approach Parizeau's promised referendum. "Obviously we have a strategy," said the advisor, "but it's not a very elegant or sophisticated strategy. It's to stick to the agenda of the national government and not let the election of a provincial government overly influence us."[44] The government's oft-repeated message to Canadians was to stay calm, measure their words, and not allow themselves to be suckered into the kind of Quebec-bashing that might boost the pro-sovereignty vote. "One of the things that Mr. Parizeau and Mr. Bouchard would love is to get into a good fight with Canadians," observed deputy prime minister Sheila Copps. "They would love to have Canadians across the country sniping at them. I think one of the big challenges for us over the next ten months is to stick to our agenda and to show Quebecers that we have an agenda that works and not to fall into the trap of responding to what will no doubt be some fairly heavy insults and jibes directed towards Canada."[45]

Reform leader Preston Manning responded to the victory of the PQ by taking aim, as usual, at Jean Chrétien. "I think it's important for the federal government to remember that there are nine other provinces," Manning said on election night. "There is a vast frustration on the part of a lot of Canadians. They don't want economic, social and political reforms hung up simply because of the election of a PQ government in Quebec."[46] Stephen Harper, on the other hand, took a page out of the Liberals' own playbook and advised Canadians not to let themselves be drawn offside. "If we stand in the fear that we'll lose the country," said Harper, "we could lose it anyway. I certainly think that Mr. Parizeau will be pro-active. It's important the rest of the country doesn't try to get goaded."[47] The premiers weighed in with similar even-tempered messages. Yes, Jacques Parizeau had won a mandate to govern, but this did not mean that he could now lead Quebec out of Canada. "Most of us feel that with a strong opposition in the legislative assembly in Quebec now," observed Saskatchewan premier Roy Romanow, "it's not going to be an easy ride getting this so-called solemn declaration passed."[48] New Brunswick premier Frank McKenna had this sage advice for Canadians: "Take a Valium, stay calm."[49]

English-Canadian editorial responses to Parizeau's election were for the most part bluntly worded but not incendiary, even in the West. "The arrogant Parizeau now finds himself about to lead a province that can't bring itself to vote for separation from the rest of Canada," said the *Vancouver Province*. "A firm 'No' to Parizeau's demands is all that is needed—especially from Prime Minister Jean Chrétien."[50] Writing in the *Globe and Mail*, Alberta historian David J. Bercuson announced grimly that "sooner or later a majority of English-speaking Canadians will come to the conclusion that the secession of Quebec has become unavoidable."[51] Writing in the *Toronto Star*, the Montreal-based historian Desmond Morton—one of the few Cassandras to perceive early on that the referendum was going to be a hard fight—reminded Canadians that Quebec's new premier was too close to his dream of sovereignty to pursue it in half-measures. "Having set independence as his goal," wrote Morton, "Parizeau won't be slow or intellectually squeamish about getting it. He will be merciless, unscrupulous and single-minded, and he will find sympathizers, collaborators and agents wherever he needs them."[52]

One indicator that the PQ victory did not appear to represent an existential threat to Canada was the "euphoria" in financial markets the next day.[53] The Canadian dollar rose 1.05 cents, its largest one-day advance in six years.[54] *Separatists in Quebec City?* Not a problem, the world's currency traders seemed to be saying. *Business as usual.*

Twenty-four hours after the election results were announced, having taken stock of the national and international reaction, Jean Chrétien went on the offensive. Financial markets had not punished Canada, which was "very good," said the prime minister. "For me, the result of yesterday, short of victory for Mr. Johnson, was the best I could hope for. The reaction of the Canadian people and the premiers has been very good." Asked if he was planning to reopen the Constitution in light of the sovereignist victory, Chrétien answered with a blunt "No." Parizeau's win relieved the prime minister of any temporizing he might have experienced on the lingering question of the Constitution, which in turn clarified the national-unity debate and bolstered his own confidence. "It is very clear to me that the Parti Québécois doesn't want to change the Canadian constitution," said Chrétien. "Their purpose is to leave the country, not to change the constitution."[55]

The prime minister was feeling so bullish in the days after the PQ victory, in fact, that he offered Jacques Parizeau a dare: why did he not hold his referendum before July 1, 1995, so Quebecers could reject sovereignty and Canadians could celebrate "a great Canada Day"?[56]

~

Jacques Parizeau's new PQ government was sworn in on September 26, 1994. Even Quebecers who were not especially enamoured of his separatist agenda congratulated the premier on the high quality, and especially the regional balance, of his cabinet. Parizeau himself referred to the twenty members of his new executive as having *"le goût du pays"*— the taste of the country.[57] Louise Beaudoin, once a young protégé of René Lévesque, was named minister of intergovernmental affairs, which meant liaising with the Bloc Québécois and locking horns with the Chrétien Liberals. Richard Le Hir, a former head of the Quebec Manufacturers Association (QMA), was appointed minister of restructuring, which implied managing the nuts-and-bolts of the transition to sovereignty, particularly as it affected Quebecers working in the federal bureaucracy. PQ veteran Bernard Landry was named deputy premier, minister of international affairs, and minister responsible for French-speaking communities, which taken together signalled that he would serve as Jacques Parizeau's man abroad. Jean Campeau, a former head of Domtar and of the Caisse de dépôt et placement de Québec, was named minister of finance. Together, despite their many differences, Campeau, Le Hir, Beaudoin, and to a lesser extent Landry would serve as Parizeau's right-hand men and women, and later as his referendum brain trust.

Parizeau clearly understood the importance of statesmanship as his thoughts turned from the election to the referendum. He resolved to stand before Quebecers, Canadians, and all the world, not as a parochial *chef* but as a leader of national and international stature. His first address to Quebecers as premier invited them, irrespective of their political allegiances, to become founders of the new Quebec state. "The time for partisan battles is over," said an exuberant Parizeau after his swearing-in ceremony. "After the referendum, once sovereignty is achieved, everyone will return to their party. Each and every [Quebecer] will propose their vision of a sovereign Quebec. Sovereignty does not belong to us [the Parti Québécois]. We do not have a monopoly over it. Sovereignty belongs to all Quebecers."[58] Parizeau's message to non-Quebecers was to have faith in Québécois democracy. "We are fully aware of our responsibility, as a government proposing sovereignty to its people, of keeping this debate in the confines of a civilized, democratic, if heated, debate," he said.[59] Asked whether his 1995 deadline for a referendum was firm, the premier was categorical. "That's exactly it," he said. "What you see is what you get. I am telling you '95. The horizon is '95."[60]

It was a heady time for Jacques Parizeau, to say the least. And yet, in one important sense, he had already begun losing control of the referendum process that he had waited so long to initiate. Bloc leader Lucien Bouchard had stated publicly on election night that the PQ's share of the popular vote was "a little less than I expected."[61] In the days that followed, he made it known that he was more than a little disappointed with the election results and, moreover, that he was not prepared to fight a referendum battle he could not win. During a scrum outside the House of Commons on September 19, Bouchard was asked about Chrétien's "dare" that the referendum be held before July 1, 1995. "Why is Mr. Chrétien so enthusiastic about a premature referendum?" Bouchard countered. "Because he thinks he could win it. What Mr. Chrétien would like is to have Quebec weakened and divided by a referendum that we would lose, so that he could go on and continue the job [of betrayal] he did to René Lévesque in 1981. He will not have that pleasure." Asked repeatedly whether he felt bound to Jacques Parizeau's

1995 referendum timetable, Bouchard left the unmistakable impression that he did not. What mattered was not timing but prevailing. "Winning is the essence of everything in politics," he said. "There's only one word to recall from what I said: *win*. There is no way that sovereignists will engage in a losing referendum. It would be impossible to win a referendum today."[62]

Jean Chrétien recognized immediately that a crack had opened in the sovereignist ranks. He wasted no time driving a federalist wedge into it. "I'm amazed that not a week after the election is over, Mr. Bouchard is asking Mr. Parizeau not to keep his word," said Chrétien. "I think Mr. Parizeau will keep his word."[63] A bemused Paul Martin, Chrétien's finance minister and a fellow Quebecer, piled on, mocking what he saw as the sovereignist leaders' oversized egos. "I think that it's pretty clear that Mr. Bouchard and Mr. Parizeau both have the same ambition and that's to live in a presidential palace in Quebec City," he said drily.[64]

～

Premier Parizeau was unmoved.

The achievement of sovereignty was like a hockey game, he liked to say.[65] The first period ended with the 1993 electoral triumph of the Bloc Québécois in Ottawa. The second ended with the victory of the Parti Québécois. Team Sovereignty was in the lead heading into the third and final period—the referendum campaign itself—and despite the persistently low numbers of committed Yes voters, it still had momentum on its side. All that was needed to eke out a victory was teamwork, good strategy, and, above all, the will to win.

As captain of the team, Parizeau felt an obligation to play a gentlemanly game. But this did not mean that he was above using his elbows in the corners.

CHAPTER THREE

Sovereignty for What?

Jacques Parizeau's unassailable conviction that Quebec would be better off without Canada was genuinely baffling to many English Canadians. Why would Quebecers want to abandon a country widely acknowledged to be one of the best in the world, a country in which they exerted disproportionate influence and enjoyed disproportionate material advantage?

India-born Gurbax Singh Malhi, Liberal MP for the southern Ontario riding of Bramalea-Gore-Malton, spoke for many old-stock and new Canadians alike. "Canada is consistently rated as one of the best nations in the world in which to live," Malhi observed in 1995. "All around the globe are people who yearn for the rights and freedoms, not to mention the peace and personal security, we enjoy as Canadians. We are incredibly fortunate to live in a country founded on the principles of freedom and democracy. As an immigrant to this great country I find it hard to believe anyone, let alone descendants of the first Fathers of Confederation, would ever consider leaving it. Quebecers should take a good hard look at the state of other countries around the world before they decide to separate from this one."[1] This sentiment would be articulated ceaselessly by English Canadians over the course of the referendum debate—in parliament, in newspapers and other media, in university common rooms and pubs, on shop floors, around dinner tables, anywhere people congregated. It was a constant refrain, a chorus of incredulity.

It was not as though French Quebecers were marginalized in the corridors of power. "The French fact has become a reality in Ottawa. Francophone Quebecers occupy the highest positions in the administration. The Governor-General of Canada is an Acadian; the Chief Justice of the Supreme Court of Canada is a Quebecer; the Clerk of the Privy Council, the highest-ranking civil servant, is a Quebecer; the Minister of Finance is a Quebecer; the President of the Export Development Corporation is a Quebecer; the Minister of Foreign Affairs is a Quebecer; and the Prime Minister is a Quebecer."[2] The words were Jean Chrétien's, but they, too, were repeated endlessly, and from both sides of the linguistic divide.

Indeed, language itself—the *sine qua non* of Quebec's struggle for *la survivance* and the moving force behind all recent efforts to make Quebecers *maîtres chez nous*—had by this time lost much of its historic edge. "Young people in Quebec might not be aware of the progress," Jacques Parizeau liked to say, "but for people of my generation the contrast between before and after Bill 101 is staggering."[3] He was correct about this. By the time Parizeau became premier in 1994, Bill 101 (La Charte de la langue française), the provincial law mandating French as the working language of Quebec, was approaching its twenty-year anniversary. Years of legislative and legal wrangling had produced "a hard-won language peace," as one observer put it, though *language ceasefire* was probably a more fitting term.[4] In 1995, there remained significant pockets of resistance to Quebec's linguistic status quo—the English-rights group Alliance Quebec and the French-rights Societé Saint-Jean-Baptiste, most notably.[5] But in contrast with the 1980 referendum battle, language would not emerge as a prominent issue in 1995, evidence that Jacques Parizeau and Lucien Bouchard knew that it had lost its political salience. "We won the [language] battles," federalist Quebecers would say routinely in 1995. "We already have cultural security, the protection of French."[6] Many sovereignists agreed. "We are more secure," said Richard Martineau, managing editor of the weekly newspaper *Voir* in

Montreal, citing Bill 101 as the reason. "We no longer feel threatened. Let's face it, francophones have all the power in Quebec."[7]

~

Canadian Anglos perceived other flies in the sovereignist ointment. One was the seemingly obvious fact that the Canada-Quebec binary evoked by hardliners on both sides—the "two solitudes"—had little basis in the lived reality of the country.

Thoughtful Canadians had come to know Canada as a complex and diverse society, shot through with the myriad personal entanglements of family, school, work, and leisure. According to the 1991 census, 18 per cent of Quebecers were not francophones, but 15 per cent of Canadians living outside Quebec were. Of the 800,000 English Canadians who lived in Quebec, 58 per cent were bilingual, compared with only 31 per cent of francophones. More than a quarter of married Quebec anglos had francophone spouses, and among young newlyweds the proportion was even higher.[8] Quebecers whose first language was neither French nor English, the so-called allophones, represented 10 per cent of the provincial population (and fully 30 per cent of the population of Montreal). And like most of the anglos who stayed in Quebec after the Lévesque-era exodus, the allophones had made their peace, however grudgingly, with the province's language laws. In the lead-up to the referendum, a group of Anglo-Quebecers dubbed "angryphones"—author Mordecai Richler, columnist William Johnson, and broadcaster Howard Galganov, most notably—blasted the sovereignists' "demonization of *les Anglais*" and skewered their "lamb lobby" of anglo appeasers.[9] But the truth was that there were few non-francophone Quebecers left to convert to the cause of defeating sovereignty. A near-monolithic 93 per cent of anglophones and 79 per cent of allophones intended to vote No.[10]

An even larger proportion of the roughly 70,000 aboriginal people living in Quebec—over 95 per cent—wanted no part of the PQ's sovereignty plan, either.[11] Jacques Parizeau and his native affairs spokesperson David Cliche insisted that Quebec's existing borders were inviolable, and hence native people living within the province would secede along with other Quebecers after a Yes vote.[12] But this was not how aboriginal leaders understood the situation. Matthew Coon Come, Grand Chief of the Quebec Crees, was the most outspoken. He stated repeatedly during the referendum campaign that his people had every right to stay in Canada if Quebec voted to separate, and that they might take two-thirds of the province with them.[13] "There will be no annexation of ourselves or our territory to an independent Quebec without our consent," said Coon Come flatly.[14] "We will not allow our rights to be determined in 1994 and 1995 by the descendants of those who characterized us as savages, wild creatures, squatters and heathen."[15] Quebec Assembly of First Nations grand chief Ghislain Picard agreed.[16] So did Joe Norton, chief of the Kahnawake Mohawk. "I believe in separatism," said Norton. "I believe in *Mohawk* separatism if there is such a thing as separatism."[17]

As for French-speaking Canadians living outside Quebec, they, too, were almost uniformly hostile to Jacques Parizeau's sovereignty proposal. "Separation would result in the worst geopolitical setback for French in North America since [the Conquest of] 1759," said Ontario francophone MP Paul De Villers.[18] Robert Thibault of the Acadian Federation of Nova Scotia agreed. "The effect [separation] will have on francophones outside Quebec, I think, would be, in the long term, devastating," he observed.[19] Organizations representing francophones living outside Quebec would be among the first to volunteer for the No side in the referendum campaign. "We believe in the future of the Canadian francophonie," said a Fédération des communautés francophones et acadienne statement released in early 1995. "We urge our Quebec compatriots to say No in the referendum and to remain united with us in the pursuit of these objectives."[20] (Predictably, Quebec sovereignists were not impressed. "Our message to francophones outside Quebec is clear," said Bloc Québécois official-languages critic Suzanne Tremblay. "Let us make our own decision. Don't stick your noses in our business."[21] This blunt censure demoralized Franco-Ontarian activists like Pierre Pelletier. "We are being told by these people that we are dead," he said bitterly.[22])

The perennial riddle—*What does Quebec want?*—was all the more baffling to outsiders in light of Quebecers' own apparent affection for

Canada. A CROP poll taken after Jacques Parizeau's election victory showed, for example, that 82 per cent of Quebecers agreed "completely" or "generally" that "Canada is the best country to live in." The same proportion, 82 per cent, agreed with the statement "Quebecers should be proud of what French and English have accomplished in Canada."[23] Not surprisingly, non-Quebecers expressed similar sentiments in similar numbers. In stunning contrast to the "tough-love" stereotype of English Canadians evoked by Lucien Bouchard and personified by Preston Manning, 80 per cent of Canadians outside Quebec told pollsters that "it is important that Quebec remain in Canada." And contrary to the sovereignists' claim that a No vote in the referendum would mean a humiliating retreat into the pre-Meech status quo, fully 81 per cent of Canadians outside Quebec believed that a No vote would mean that "Quebecers want change but just don't want independence."[24]

Alas, Quebec sovereignists were not wrong in supposing that anti-French sentiment persisted on the fringes of English Canada. Since the election of the Chrétien Liberals in 1993, thirty-four members of the federal parliament had tabled petitions from their constituents requesting that French be terminated as an official language of Canada. The total number of petitions presented to MPs—virtually all of them spearheaded by the Alliance for the Preservation of English in Canada (APEC)—was seventy-four, and each petition carried an average of sixty-five signatures. Of the thirty-four MPs to table, twenty were Liberals. Thirteen were Reformers, including Stephen Harper. Some Liberals, including Lyle Vanclief and Don Boudria, believed that it would be undemocratic not to table petitions from their constituencies, regardless of whether they agreed with the proposed content. Yet at least ten Liberals refused to table such petitions precisely because of their strong stand in favour of official bilingualism.[25]

In matters of the heart, it is a short jump from confusion to frustration, and then to anger. So it was for many Canadians who did not appreciate Quebec sovereignists working to break up their country. Peter C. Newman, the venerable author and former editor-in-chief of *Maclean's*, captured the public mood in 1995. "Messieurs Bouchard and

Parizeau are intelligent and suave ambassadors for their cause but they are also true believers," Newman wrote, "and some of their revolutionary ideas are strictly Looney Tunes. Their basic tactical and strategic error is to believe that Canadians outside Quebec will accept the splitting asunder of their country with cool equanimity. It's not going to happen."[26] The famously patriotic folksinger Stompin' Tom Connors agreed. "It seems to me that Mr. Parizeau and his separatist friends are planning to play Russian roulette with the people of Quebec for as many times as it takes to spin the chamber of his pistol until that one bullet of destruction is finally fired," he said.[27] Conrad Black, the newspaper magnate who in the 1960s had been so enamoured of Quebec that he moved there and became fluent in French, dismissed the sovereignists out of hand in 1995 in the American journal *Foreign Affairs*. "I expect that Parizeau's attempt to back into independence via a spurious referendum on sovereignty within Canadian confederation will be rejected as a scam," wrote Black, "probably by the Québécois or, if necessary, by the countries with which Parizeau would seek to exchange embassies."[28]

Tired though they were of constitutional bickering, the great majority of English-speaking Canadians believed themselves to be well-intentioned and accommodating when it came to Quebecers' place within a united Canada—*as long as Quebec was not granted powers the other provinces did not have.* Professor Alan C. Cairns cogently summarized "the ROC perspective" in 1994. "Quebec and French Canada have already been accorded a generous response," wrote Cairns, "by federalism, by the Official Languages Act, by the language clauses of the Charter, by virtual monopolization of the office of prime minister in all but one of the past twenty-four years, and by the perception that Quebec has been an excessively favoured recipient of federal bounty. ROC [does] not view Quebec as an exploited, impoverished community whose plight elicit[s] sympathy, but [sees] it as a fully integrated, thriving provincial member of the established system."[29]

Although they were seldom surveyed on the question—presumably because pollsters thought it odious—it is evident that English-speaking Canadians were skeptical about the kind of society sovereignists like

Jacques Parizeau envisaged for Quebec. Like many uncertain Quebecers themselves, in fact, they wondered, *Sovereignty for what?*

Some prominent English Canadian intellectuals—McGill University philosopher Charles Taylor and York University political scientist Reg Whitaker foremost among them—understood the sovereignist movement as working towards an enlightened, outward-looking, and multi-ethnic society that would be the envy of liberals everywhere. In defending Quebec's claims to progressiveness, they pointed to the province's path-breaking 1975 Charte des droits et libertés de la personne (Charter of Rights and Freedoms), to Quebecers' commitment to social welfare, economic rights and public education, and especially to the ethos of inclusiveness the *péquistes* had sought to inculcate within their own ranks.[30] Anne Michele Meggs, an Ontario-born anglophone who abandoned federalism altogether to join both the Bloc and the PQ, spoke especially eloquently of the sovereignists' utopian vision. "Quebecers will be better off in a sovereign Quebec because in achieving that status they will have passed through a profoundly significant process of collective self-affirmation," Meggs wrote in 1995. "They will have chosen to give themselves and the state that represents them the powers required to ensure that Quebec can flourish as a model of modernity, solidarity, openness and tolerance."[31]

Other English Canadians, however, likely a majority, were not persuaded. They perceived in the sovereignists' emotional appeals to French Quebecers evidence of ethnic nationalism, xenophobia, and even racism.[32] "Mr. Bouchard and Premier Jacques Parizeau talk of 'our people' and 'we' and '*le peuple Québécois*,'" observed *Globe and Mail* correspondent John Gray, "and when they do so they are not thinking of the hundreds of thousands of recent immigrants or even those who have been here for much, much longer but whose mother tongue is not French. Both men find it natural to draw the dividing line in their society between those who are 'old stock Quebecers' and those who are not."[33] Montreal *Gazette* columnist (and bilingual Anglo-Quebecer) William Johnson was more caustic. "For three decades," Johnson wrote in 1994, "Quebec's provincial leaders have shared a common political vision: Quebec as a French ethnic state."[34] With a sovereignist government in Quebec City, Johnson warned, the time had come for English Canadians to wake up, jettison their sentimental illusions about Quebec nationalism, and realize what dark forces they were up against.

In the fall of 1994, few Canadian anglos were prepared to adopt the fighting words of angryphones like William Johnson. But many, even in Canada's ivory towers, quietly wondered whether he had a point. If the PQ and the Bloc were so committed to building a modern, multicultural society, why did they not do so within the modern, multicultural state of Canada?

～

The sovereignist answer to this question—one that resonated powerfully among many non-sovereignist Quebecers as well—lay in the pattern of rejection that had coloured Canadians' constitutional manoeuvres since the referendum of 1980. For over a decade, reasonable Quebecers had sought an accommodation with the rest of Canada. Though they had felt the sting of *la Nuit des Longs Couteaux* and of Pierre Trudeau's 1982 patriation victory, they did not give up on reforming Canadian federalism. On the contrary, Quebecers returned to the bargaining table in the best of faith, first under the auspices of René Lévesque's *beau risque* and later as ungrudging participants in the Meech Lake process. Yet even the minimalist concessions of Meech proved unacceptable to Canadians outside Quebec in 1990, and so did the even more diluted compromises of the Charlottetown Accord two years later.

"The rout of Meech was more than a failure of negotiations," Lucien Bouchard would say. "Banished eight years earlier from the constitutional family, Quebec was now being told, when it was making every effort to be readmitted, that it must continue stagnating in constitutional limbo. Many communities would be angry for much less."[35] This idea, that well-meaning Quebecers were the victims of a persistent pattern of arrogance and indifference from Canadians elsewhere, was widely held in Quebec nationalist circles. Its impact on the thinking of ordinary Quebecers is impossible to exaggerate. As one exasperated Yes voter put it at the height of the 1995 referendum debate, "We voted no in 1980 and it didn't work. We elected Trudeau and it didn't work. We went along with the rest of the country and elected Mulroney. We voted No in the 1992 referendum, just like the rest of the country. What else do we have to do? Disappear?"[36] Some English Canadians sympathized unreservedly with Quebecers' feeling of rejection. "The saddest part of this whole impasse," lamented University of Regina sociologist John F. Conway in 1994, "is that a resolution has always been within our grasp, but English-Canadians have never mounted sufficient political will and good faith to seize the many missed opportunities."[37]

Premier Jacques Parizeau had a golden opportunity to address these concerns in late November 1994 when, just weeks after his election victory, he visited Toronto. It was his first trip outside Quebec since taking office. Accompanied by an entourage that included his wife Lisette Lapointe, intergovernmental-affairs minister Louise Beaudoin, and numerous staffers and security people, Parizeau orchestrated the one-day trip as he would a state visit. He claimed before leaving Quebec City that he wanted to use the trip to "explain Quebec sovereignty to the rest of the country."[38] But he came packing grudges instead of olive branches, and in less than twenty-four hours managed to alienate Ontarians almost completely.

The first scheduled stop on Parizeau's visit was a private meeting with Premier Bob Rae. Though fluently bilingual and a Meech supporter, Rae was no pushover when it came to national unity. He neither liked nor trusted Parizeau, and he well knew that the target audience for any pronouncements the Quebec premier might make in Ontario would be voters in his home province.[39]

In the days before he arrived in Toronto, Parizeau had discussed his intentions frankly with members of the city's press corps. His message: Quebec was likely going to become sovereign within a year, and there was nothing Canadians could do to stop it. There was no point in dancing around the issue. "You're a Canadian or you're not," said Parizeau. "And that's fine. But it's about time we say it to each other. This thing has to be settled."[40] Parizeau said he hoped to preserve the historic trade linkages binding Quebec to Ontario. "We are neighbours forever," he observed.[41] But he also made it clear that he had no intention of appealing cap in hand to Premier Rae or anyone else for special dispensations. Canadians, he said, had nothing left to leverage. They could not prohibit Quebec's use of the Canadian dollar, nor would international trade rules allow them to threaten Quebec with economic sanctions. Asked to gauge the public mood, Parizeau spoke bluntly. "I find the Quebec bashing has gone a bit too far over the last few years," he said. "If you look at everything that is widely read about Quebec you get the impression that we are some awful horde of intolerant racists. No, no, let's not get excited. We are not like that. It's not true."[42]

Parizeau met with Bob Rae at Queen's Park the morning of November 22. Their forty-five-minute conversation was forthright, even confrontational. "I can't pretend that this was just an ordinary meeting between two premiers," Rae later conceded. "We were both polite, we didn't come to blows, but it was extremely direct." Rae's overriding impression was that Parizeau had sorely underestimated the passion many Canadians felt for their country. "We are talking about the future of Canada," Rae told Parizeau. "We are not talking about an economic space. We are not talking about transfer payments. We are not talking about statistics or numbers. We are talking about a country for which people have fought and died over 125 years and about which there is a great deal of passion in all parts of Canada, including Quebec." The chilly meeting ended with the two premiers agreeing only on the rules of engagement. "What I said to Mr. Parizeau," said Rae, "was 'If you feel you've got a mandate to break up the country, prove it. Go out to the people and make your case, and I'll make my case.'"[43]

Parizeau's next stop was the Canadian Club, an elite group of Toronto business and legal professionals. Again he raised the spectre of Quebec-bashing. "I am truly saddened to say that respect for Quebec and Quebecers has been a disappearing feature of Canada's life," Parizeau lectured the group. "It has become customary in Canada to portray Quebec as an inward-looking and intolerant society. I think the most ludicrous accusation concerns the 'ethnic nature' of Quebec. It's now widely held, from Saint John to Victoria, without any doubt, that 'up there in Quebec, if your ancestors don't come from France you're toast.' This may come as a shock to you, but Quebec society is quite close to being *blind* to ethnicity."[44] Parizeau concluded his remarks by invoking a powerful analogy. "This Quebec problem is like a never-ending visit to the dentist," he told his audience. "Quebec wants more powers, more autonomy. You never say yes, and the drilling doesn't stop."[45]

Torontonians knew provocation when they heard it, especially when it knocked twice in two days. "By wrapping himself in the flag of ethnic pride, by caricaturing Canadians as bloody-minded neighbours, Parizeau is positioning himself as Quebecers' true savior on the eve of the referendum," fumed a *Toronto Star* editorial.[46] *Globe and Mail* columnist Robert Sheppard agreed. "Mr. Parizeau's apparent intention [is] to cloud the [sovereignty] debate these past few days by reacting with outrage to every slight provocation and by attempting to advance a campaign that portrays Quebec as a 'victim' of English-Canadian prejudices."[47] An unusually combative Richard Gwyn suggested that Parizeau's barbs were born of desperation, nothing more. "Next year's referendum has been lost already—by the separatists," he wrote. "Only malignant stupidity by the rest of us could alter this result."[48]

Ignore Premier Parizeau and he would go away, Toronto's pundits agreed. The only people with any real cause to take offence at his bons mots were dentists.

CHAPTER FOUR

Noui

Jacques Parizeau's tough talk during his Toronto visit, he later revealed, had been both intentional and tactical. "The entire referendum strategy," he noted, "was based on the notion that negotiations with Canada, which were inevitable on some issues and desirable on others, had to be conducted under conditions in which Canada was not in a position to refuse to negotiate, and in so doing, prevent Quebecers from achieving sovereignty if that was what they wished. *It was vital to avoid depending on Canada's good will, since that good will would only be present if Quebec did not depend on it.*"[1]

Parizeau faced an altogether different sort of challenge within Quebec, where support for sovereignty remained soft and morale at Parti Québécois HQ was correspondingly low. Speaking at a gloomy meeting of the PQ national executive in November 1994, Parizeau warned his troops that a defeatist attitude would surely sabotage the separatist cause. He did not pull his punches. "I'm a bit appalled by this pessimism," he said. "I'm appalled because it's as though you lack confidence in yourselves. We can defeat Jean Chrétien, we can conquer fear, we can dispel the legitimate doubts of our fellow citizens. But if we allow pessimism to triumph, we may as well pack our bags and forget about it. If you yourselves are not convinced that we will, next year, make Quebec into a country, then we will not, next year, make Quebec into a country. You must yourselves be convinced."[2]

Parizeau knew why his comrades were pessimistic, of course. It was no great mystery. Rosy polling numbers during the provincial election campaign had hinted that the Parti Québécois might be able to win a referendum in 1995 entirely on its own terms—that is, with a straightforward question on independence and without concessions to the "soft nationalists" in the Bloc and the ADQ. But it was not to be. Majority support for outright independence remained out of reach.[3] Parizeau himself would have preferred a simple referendum question: *Do you want Quebec to become sovereign?* He was no more interested in sovereignty-association as premier than he had been as René Lévesque's right-hand man, if by *association* some kind of umbilical tie to Canada was implied. But Parizeau was shrewd. He knew that it would be better to win a referendum on an ambiguous question than to lose on an unambiguous one. Lucien Bouchard was right about this.

Having won only 44.7 per cent of the popular vote in the provincial election, moreover, Parizeau had to acknowledge as well that the *péquiste* vote alone could not carry the Yes side to victory. Lucien Bouchard had been right about this, too. The PQ would have to broaden its appeal, targeting nationalists in the ranks of the provincial Liberals, the ADQ, and even the federal Tories. The trick, as Parizeau told his national executive, was to promote this necessity as though it were a virtue. "We should rejoice in the fact that around us, other people, other parties, have their own vision of what a sovereign Quebec should be, visions that are sometimes contradictory to ours," said the premier. "Right now we are at a dead end, prisoners of a vision of Canada that Quebecers do not share. But the fact remains that our adversaries are very much afraid of what we are about to build."[4]

Thus was born Parizeau's "rainbow coalition" strategy, through which a broad cross-section of Quebecers might be emboldened to vote Yes even if they were not enamoured of the PQ. (The phrase *rainbow coalition* he borrowed from the 1984 campaign of U.S. Democratic presidential candidate Jesse Jackson.) "Many people hesitate to take the step [towards sovereignty] because they don't know what they will find," said Parizeau. "We must tell them that after, they will find Quebec democracy. Many parties, many programs, many prospects for the future. We must say this to Quebecers and say it to members of other political parties."[5]

~

Who were these soft nationalists, exactly? And where did they stand on sovereignty?

According to Quebec pollsters, in 1995 roughly 40 per cent of Quebecers self-identified as sovereignist and another 40 per cent as federalist. The "soft middle" included the remaining 20 per cent or so of the Quebec electorate, voters who were not separatists but who might be open to sovereignty if it were bundled with some kind of economic or political union with Canada. Since neither side in the sovereignty debate saw much point in preaching to the choirs of the other (the "Hard Yes" and "Hard No" voters), the battle for the hearts and minds of Quebecers in 1995 would centre almost entirely on these undecideds—those whom the Quebec press imaginatively called *Noui* voters. This was the overarching strategic priority of both sides. Little else mattered.

Quebec pollsters called the undecideds butterflies because "they are hard to identify and hard to catch."[6] According to Michel Lemieux of Léger and Léger, they tended to be people with little education, low incomes (between $20,000 and $40,000 a year), high levels of household debt, and little interest in—or knowledge of—politics. "We've done polls trying to pierce their mythology," said Lemieux of the undecideds. "It's very complex. They also happen to be the most difficult to poll. There's no magic question to reach them, no kind of political maneuver. They don't belong to any kind of organized group they would follow."[7] Perhaps the most significant demographic characteristic of the undecideds was that fully two-thirds of them were women.

Middle-aged Montrealer Louise Plamondon was typical of the undecideds. "Some days I listen, or I read a paper," Plamondon told the CBC's Hana Gartner. "When I [am] the more reticent it's when they talk to my reason, when they talk to my intelligence. Sometimes I say: Gee, there's a risk, and am I going to be able to live with that risk? Am I going to be able to face it? To face the outcome of the referendum? So that's why I want to read everything before I take my decision." Jean Kerwin, another undecided, agreed. "I'm not sure what I'm going to be doing at all," he said. "It's just so confusing. Do we have to change our own postal services? How about the money? How about the government? Do we have to invent a new government? What's going to happen? Is it going to make us so poor or is it going to make us so rich?"[8]

Veteran pollster Jean-Marc Léger believed that with only the slightest nudge from the federalist side, most undecideds would fall backwards off the fence. "That's all they need to vote No," Léger observed. "They need a little hope that there is a place for devotion to Quebec in the Canadian federation. If the No side could just give a little hope to the people who are going to vote No, of possible change, not necessarily a constitutional conference but a possible change, an improvement in the condition of Quebecers, it's certain people would vote No."[9] Léger's suggestion that federalism was the default position of the undecideds made sense in the light of recent Quebec history. René Lévesque had lost the 1980 referendum by 20 per cent and, with the exception of the immediate post-Meech period, polls ever since had shown undecided Quebecers erring on the side of the status quo.

But *certain* is a big word in the close-but-no-cigar world of polling. Not everyone agreed with Jean-Marc Léger's confident analysis of the *Noui* vote (but because he was a prominent media commentator and his firm, Léger and Léger, was officially neutral in the sovereignty debate, his voice was highly influential). One of the hired guns for the No side, pollster Grégoire Gollin of the firm Créatec-Plus, was more circumspect. He estimated that perhaps as much as one-quarter of the Quebec electorate was on the fence and, moreover, that these people were so genuinely conflicted as to make them "legendary ambivalents." Their nationalist idealism, Gollin suggested, was at odds with their feelings of economic vulnerability. "It is an unstable equilibrium between two basic needs," he observed. "One is the need for identity and the other is the need for security."[10]

As noted above, the centrality of polling to the 1995 referendum campaign cannot be overstated. In 1995, there were thirty-two polling companies in Quebec, and in the lead-up to the October referendum vote they were surveying Quebec voters practically daily.[11] Pollsters themselves joked that no Quebecers remained who had not been interrogated about their views on sovereignty. This obsession with numbers is why the undecided *Noui* vote emerged as the single most important moving force in the referendum campaign. Everything followed from this strategic reality. Jacques Parizeau, Lucien Bouchard, Daniel Johnson, and Jean Chrétien knew that they had to act and speak as though they were reaching out to all Quebecers. But beneath this thin, calculated veneer of inclusiveness, they were, as methodically and as tirelessly as possible, targeting the only Quebec voters they had a chance of converting—economically insecure, apolitical, mostly female undecideds, Quebecers who happened to be demographically the least like the politicians themselves.

When the leaders of the Yes side offered Quebecers soothing nostrums about the great potential of the Quebec economy after the achievement of sovereignty, they were not trying to reach editorial writers or university economists or bank presidents. They were trying to reach the butterflies. And when the No side countered, evoking fearsome doomsday scenarios for the Quebec economy after a Yes vote, they were playing exactly the same game.

Both sides understood, in short, that on referendum day it would matter very little what the chattering classes thought of their ideas. What mattered was how those ideas struck the classes that did not chatter at all.

～

For Jacques Parizeau, who now had the levers of provincial power at his disposal, reaching the undecideds meant not merely offering winning ideas. It meant fashioning a referendum process that would itself do the work of conversion. "It won't be a simplistic operation," Parizeau said after a two-day PQ strategy session. "It is a strategy to rekindle what must be rekindled."[12] His critics understood precisely what he was up to. Indeed, many had anticipated him. "What all this warm, fuzzy talk

boils down to," observed Don Macpherson of the Montreal *Gazette,* "is
that the government intends to mount a publicly-funded operation to
condition Quebecers to vote Yes in the referendum. It will involve them
in the sovereignty project so that they become more comfortable with
sovereignty, develop an emotional investment in it, identify with it and,
ultimately, embrace it."[13]

Parizeau's rainbow-coalition strategy was the brain-child of one
of his closest and most creative political advisors, Jean-François Lisée,
a former journalist, Governor General's Award–winning author, and
committed sovereignist. (At the time of writing, winter 2014, Lisée
was serving as minister of international relations, la francophonie,
and external trade in the PQ government headed by Premier Pauline
Marois.) Like Parizeau, Lisée would in 1994 have preferred outright
independence to any political or economic union with Canada. But,
also like Parizeau, he was pragmatic. "Political life in Quebec has been
flooded with surveys for 40 years," Lisée observed, "and we know there
is no majority for independence in Quebec and no majority for the current federalism. Only two majorities are possible: renewed federalism or
the sovereignty of Quebec with an association, in one form or another,
with the rest of Canada. To try to reduce Quebecers to either the current
federalism or secession without any desire for an agreement [with the
rest of Canada] is to reject their political reality and their political will."[14]
The two other staffers to whom Jacques Parizeau had entrusted referendum strategy—chief of staff Jean Royer and deputy minister Louis
Bernard—needed no convincing. They agreed with Lisée that achieving
sovereignty would be an act of statesmanship, not of partisanship.

On November 29, 1994, Parizeau gave his inaugural address to
the National Assembly. (In contrast with throne speeches delivered
elsewhere in Canada, the premier himself rather than Lt.-Gov. Martial
Asselin read the text.) Anticipated as "perhaps the most important
inaugural address in Quebec's contemporary history," the speech
was televised throughout Quebec.[15] The premier was upbeat and
animated, and he had good reason to be. A fresh CROP poll put PQ
support at 51 per cent, while a Léger and Léger poll showed support

for sovereignty at 45.7 per cent.[16] Parizeau had the wind at his back. There was speculation that he might unveil his "solemn declaration" right then and there.

It didn't happen. The great bulk of Parizeau's speech—fifteen of eighteen pages—concerned bread-and-butter issues including job creation and regional development. On the question of sovereignty, the premier was long on vision but unexpectedly cagey on specifics. "To every Quebecer I say: It will be beautiful to have our country," said Parizeau. "It will be worthy to be masters in our own house." The premier took aim at the undecideds. "What is holding Quebecers back?" he prodded. "It isn't the Rockies. It isn't because they share the project of Jean Chrétien and Clyde Wells of a Canada that files off a bit more each day of what distinguishes Quebec."

The PQ government would be tabling a document in a few days' time, Parizeau continued, one that would serve as "the basis for popular participation" in the referendum process. "We intend to propose to Quebecers a new, innovative method by which they can speak out. We will reach out to them in their homes so that they can express both their hopes and their fears, their ambitions and their hesitations. Let's put everything on the table. The unknown frightens when it is kept in the dark. In daylight, we will see better." The premier reiterated his mantra that the Parti Québécois did not claim a monopoly on Quebec sovereignty, concluding with a shot across Daniel Johnson's bow. "I have little hope of convincing [Johnson] personally to achieve sovereignty with me. But through him, I extend a hand to each and every federalist or undecided Quebecer."[17]

Why had Parizeau not simply tabled his referendum plan? Three theories emerged. One was that the premier wanted to add drama and suspense to the process. Another was that he had been reading the polls, which still showed that Quebecers thought the economy—and not sovereignty—was the most important issue. The third, as Université de Montréal political scientist Stéphane Dion put it, was that "he wants a big fish, a non-sovereignist, to head [a] public commission and was having last-minute problems settling details."[18] Already the tone of English-Canadian press coverage of Parizeau was one of exasperation.

"He might try tactical shenanigans with the referendum itself," pronounced the *Ottawa Citizen*, "adjusting the date to Péquiste convenience, or somehow rigging the question. But these would be more or less desperate acts of a leader heading for defeat. Parizeau's only honest course is to try to convince the unconvinced, the majority who do not want to make Quebec an independent country. He will have to make Confederation seem so dreadful, and independence so alluring, that more than half the voters in Quebec will be ready to call themselves separatists on the day of the referendum."[19]

For his part, Daniel Johnson mocked Parizeau's attempt to draw provincial Liberals into the PQ's sovereignty process. "Extend your hand to what?" Johnson chided the premier in the National Assembly. "Just to pull you in the water? Or you have to count your fingers, possibly, after you've shaken hands. Taking the hand to lead where? To separation, to the breakup of this country? I will not extend my hand to break up this country."[20] Johnson put Parizeau on notice that Quebecers would not tolerate a convoluted referendum process designed to wear them down and win their acquiescence. "The government doesn't have the mandate to trigger a slow separation without having been authorized in advance democratically," said Johnson. "Until Quebecers give him a mandate, he must play by the rules of the game."[21]

Johnson was under no illusions that he could, like Jean Chrétien, remain aloof from the sovereignty debate. He knew that he would at some point have to offer Quebecers a credible alternative to separation, assuring them that a No vote would not be interpreted in the rest of Canada as an affirmation of the status quo. Canada was not perfect, said Johnson. "But it isn't the gulag, to repeat the words of René Lévesque. So, should we break up one of the most enviable countries in the world because we are not satisfied with the constitutional arrangement? Courage isn't slamming the door but [sitting] down with people who do not share all of our views but who still want to make compromises."[22] Canadian federalism could evolve, insisted Johnson. "To separate because of our grievances with federalism would be like amputating a leg in order to heal a sprained ankle."[23]

Jean Chrétien and Daniel Johnson had already held their first meeting to plot strategy for the federalist side. "They are trying to converge on a reasonably harmonized organization and storyline as quickly as they can," said one Chrétien insider after the secret November 1 tête-à-tête.[24] The prime minister agreed from the outset to play "second fiddle" to Johnson during the referendum campaign. He acknowledged that Johnson's solid connections to former Liberals in the ADQ and also to federal Tories meant that he was far better positioned to appeal to the soft nationalists Parizeau was chasing.

Chrétien believed that the best thing he could do for national unity was not to obsess about it. "In the next seven months, we will have to face, again, a referendum in Quebec, but I'm telling you, I'm happy," he told Liberals at a $500-per-plate Toronto fundraiser on November 29. "We'll turn the page. If we stick together, if we show this country can work, if we keep giving the Canadian people the kind of government they deserve and want, I'm telling you that by the end of next year, Canada will be united and we will make this country ready for the twenty-first century."[25] Speaking in English, Chrétien acknowledged his own obligation. "The first responsibility of the Prime Minister of Canada is to ensure the unity of the country," he said. "And you can be assured that I will continue to do that in the months ahead. All my years I have stood up for Canada in Quebec. And I have stood up for Quebec in the rest of Canada. And I am not about to stop now."[26] Chrétien then spoke in French. "I will make the case for Canada by concentrating on providing good government, on promoting jobs and economic growth and the real issues that Canadians and Quebecers in every province care about. They don't want quarrelling and continued talk of the Constitution."[27]

～

"The referendum battle has begun," Lucien Bouchard announced to a Bloc Québécois rally in Beaupré on 28 November. Now the party had to "create the winning conditions."[28]

Bouchard was wrapping up a weekend strategy meeting of the Bloc's general council. He and his closest advisors agreed that, with Parizeau at the helm of the Yes side, the best contribution Bloc MPs could make to the cause of sovereignty would be to hammer Jean Chrétien in the House. They would use their power as the Official Opposition to expose how government policies worked against Quebec. And they would be relentless in their efforts to "bait" the prime minister on his intentions for the campaign. "The ideal situation would be that [Chrétien] be forced to take the mask off right away," said Bouchard, "because federalists in Quebec don't seem to be aware of the major offensive being prepared by the federal government."[29] The Bloc leader believed that, given the debt crisis facing Ottawa, Chrétien would have no alternative but to centralize power there. Cutting social spending and slaying the deficit would inevitably weaken the power of Quebec's National Assembly and alienate voters. "It's a very important debate which we are following closely," said Bouchard, "and it is closely tied to the strategies and the timetable of the referendum in Quebec. That's why I don't believe we should telegraph to Ottawa the referendum date. The less they know about the date, the better. And the less we rush ourselves, the better off we will be."[30]

Interestingly, Bouchard also confided to Bloc members that he was worried that the presence of a sovereignist party in Ottawa might actually work against a sovereignty vote. "People must not think that by voting No that they'll always have an insurance policy in Ottawa and there will always be a Bloc in Ottawa," he said.[31] Bouchard knew that Quebecers' appetite for independence was weak, so he altered his message to them, adopting what the English-Canadian press called "the fear factor."[32] Quebecers had to know, Bouchard said, that if they were to reject sovereignty, they would lose their leverage in negotiations with the federal government. "You have to make a decision on your fears," said Bouchard. "Many Quebecers will vote Yes so as to avoid that a No vote would weaken Quebec."[33]

Two days later, on Tuesday, November 29, 1994, Bouchard was quietly admitted to Saint-Luc Hospital in Montreal with what doctors believed was thrombophlebitis in his left leg. Two days after that, shocked Quebecers and Canadians alike awakened to the news that

Bouchard was, in fact, in serious condition in hospital after having his leg and much of his hip amputated. The medical explanation was ghastly: a clot in Bouchard's leg had become infected with necrotizing fasciitis-myositis ("flesh-eating disease"), a deadly condition in which the streptococcus-A bacterium burrows beneath the skin and eats away at fat and muscle tissue. Bouchard's doctor, Michel Poisson, chief of microbiology at Montreal's Hôtel-Dieu hospital, reported that although surgeons had removed flesh from Bouchard's hip to his chest cavity, it would take up to two more days to determine whether the spread of the infection had been halted. "Sometimes the infection progresses even after amputation," said Poisson, "because it's infected a small part of the throat or somewhere else in the body. Unfortunately, it's fatal in 40 to 60 per cent of cases."[34]

Bouchard's comrades in the sovereignist camp were horror-struck. "My wife and I have just learned the terrible news about Mr. Bouchard, my friend," said a shaken Jacques Parizeau. "Our first thoughts are for Audrey and the children and for himself. All I can really say in front of the cameras is to say to my old friend, hang on. Show the same courage that you've shown so often in the past. And I hope that soon it will just have been a very bad dream. Hang on, old friend."[35] Bouchard's political adversaries were equally gracious. "My only thoughts are for Lucien Bouchard's family and friends," said Quebec Liberal leader Daniel Johnson.[36] Prime Minister Jean Chrétien issued a statement from Paris. "At moments like this," it read, "we put political differences aside to express our personal solidarity with the suffering of a fellow human being."[37] Other federal politicians, including Reform Party leader Preston Manning, offered similar well-wishes and prayers. Canadian political life ground almost to a dead stop. Veteran reporters of the Ottawa beat commented that they had seldom seen such a sombre mood in the halls of parliament. "This wasn't manufactured for-the-cameras emotion," they agreed. "Everyone felt caught in the drama going on at Saint-Luc Hospital in Montreal."[38]

In Quebec, the outpouring of public affection for Bouchard—as familiar to ordinary Quebecers as any living public figure—was instant, massive, and mostly non-partisan. Saint-Luc's Hospital and the office of the Mouvement souverainiste du Québec received sympathetic notes, flowers, and gifts in the thousands. Vigils were held, candles lit, cards signed, tears shed. Bloc Québécois strategists led by house leader Michel Gauthier and whip Gilles Duceppe would not speculate on what the loss of Bouchard might mean for the future of the party and the sovereignist movement. The prospect was unthinkable. The vacuum Bouchard's death would leave in the organization he had founded and still personified would be immense. For *Bloquistes*, as for Bouchard's family and friends, time stood still.

Then at noon on Saturday, December 3, Bouchard's medical team convened a press conference to announce that he had been removed from the critical list. His life was no longer threatened. Though he was still in the ICU, Bouchard's fever and swelling were receding. Antibiotics had the infection under control. Recounting their patient's courage and strength through three emergency surgeries, the doctors acknowledged with visible exhaustion and relief that the Bloc leader had survived a terrible ordeal. He would, of course, face a long road of recovery and rehabilitation, but the worst was now behind him. "Considering the strength of character of Mr. Bouchard," observed Dr. Patrick D'Amico, "I'm sure he will be able to return to public life—probably three or four months after he gets out of hospital."[39]

Cardiologist Pierre Ghosn then read aloud a note Bouchard had scribbled the day before. It said *"Que l'on continue—merci"* ("Let us carry on—thank you"). Though seemingly intended as a private gesture of gratitude for his medical team, in the context of the looming sovereignty debate the message quickly assumed an almost otherworldly political significance. From the clutches of a unimaginably terrifying, almost medieval, scourge, Quebec's most popular sovereignist politician had had the presence of mind to tell his loyalists to carry on with the struggle. A photograph of Bouchard's scribbled words was published in Quebec newspapers. A banner reading *"Que l'on continue"* was hung on the façade of the building across from his hospital room. Biblical analogies were invoked. Fearing perhaps that too much heady symbolism might be counterproductive, Jacques Parizeau counselled a little perspective. "We're faced here with a friend who came out of the abyss," said the premier. "It's a superb message of life. I don't want to connect in any way anything political to what has happened in the last 24 hours."[40]

Word that Bouchard was likely to survive his ordeal spread quickly throughout his home province. As *Le Devoir* publisher Lise Bissonnette intimated, the sound of Quebecers exhaling was practically audible. "Why had Quebec held its breath during the worst hours for Mr. Bouchard?" asked Bissonnette. "The void that suddenly opened in the political debate, on the threshold of a year of decision, made one dizzy. But everywhere, with striking unanimity, rose words of real affection for someone close whom no one could think of losing."[41] Even some of Bouchard's avowed federalist adversaries agreed. Quebecers, wrote Montreal *Gazette* columnist Don Macpherson, saw in Bouchard "someone who placed principle and honor ahead of career. In his candor, his willingness to admit at least the political weaknesses and mistakes of his movement, they recognized their own imperfections and humanity. And so they accorded him the rare honor for a politician of referring to him familiarly, by his first name alone. They knew him simply as Lucien."[42] "People who empathized with him and his family through the hours when they thought he was lost to this world will never be able to see him entirely as just a politician," added *Gazette* columnist William Johnson. "They have forged a bond with the human, vulnerable man that will never entirely dissolve."[43]

Le Devoir's front-page headline for December 5, 1994, announced "He is Out of the Woods," without even mentioning who "he" was. Federalists across Canada drew the obvious conclusion. For many Quebecers, Bouchard's miraculous recovery had generated a powerful mystique, and that would not make their job of defeating a Yes vote any easier. *Globe and Mail* columnist Robert Sheppard noted that Bouchard's legendary status now extended beyond Quebec. "I can't pretend that Lucien Bouchard is well-liked in English Canada," said Sheppard. "In fact, he is heartily mistrusted and generally viewed as haughty and perversely partisan. But the fact that the entire country was prepared to mourn and honour him as a fallen Canadian should not be undersold. English Canada has not been able to offer up a mythical counter-hero to Lucien Bouchard and probably never will."[44] Chantal Hébert, Ottawa bureau chief of *La Presse*, agreed, emphasizing Bouchard's past contributions to Canadian life. "His pride at Canada's peacekeeping role, his stand for official bilingualism, his fight to keep the CBC and other cultural agencies financially healthy and his insistence that Canada's social safety net be maintained have reminded Quebecers and other Canadians that, to have a country worth its salt, one must be ready to defend its values," wrote Hébert. "Bouchard's actions on this front have contributed to make him, a committed sovereignist, a somewhat tolerable leader of the Official opposition for many Canadians. No one else in the Bloc could pull this off."[45]

A special meeting of the Bloc caucus was called to discuss how the party would continue for the three or four months with Bouchard absent. It was agreed that, in the House of Commons, the job of taking the fight to the Chrétien Liberals would fall to his lieutenants, Michel Gauthier and Gilles Duceppe.

Among Quebec sovereignists more generally, Bouchard's survival against such great odds seemed to catalyze a new optimism. Jacques Parizeau's emotional statements of solidarity with Bouchard had undercut his pompous public persona, for example, and helped to humanize him. There was talk as well that the crisis had "cleared the air" between the Parti Québécois and the Bloc, where tensions about who was to lead the Yes campaign had been left unresolved.[46]

Some in the federalist No camp whispered the hope that perhaps Bouchard's brush with mortality might prompt him to quit politics, which he had always said was a thankless but necessary chore. Before long, however, it was clear that the political winds were blowing in the opposite direction. No sooner was Bouchard back on solid food than he was plotting strategy and issuing instructions from his hospital bed via his chief of staff, Gilbert Charland. "I can't presume to speak for him," said Charland, "but based on the conversations we've had, he doesn't look like a man who wants to quit politics."[47] Even worse for the federalists, Bouchard's ordeal had served to bring him and Parizeau closer together personally. "One could feel that beyond their character differences and their inability to really communicate," observed Jean-François Lisée, "there was a new bond, a complicity, that had formed between them."[48]

Lucien Bouchard was well enough early on Tuesday, December 6, to consult by phone with Jacques Parizeau.[49] The main topic of conversation was the tabling of the PQ's referendum plan in the Quebec National Assembly, scheduled for that very morning. Word that Parizeau was not going to postpone his presentation in the legislature gave Quebec sovereignists a huge lift, since the premier's calculated efforts to build suspense into the process had been met by a chorus of criticism from federalists that he was merely stalling.

That the premier had Bouchard's blessing on that auspicious morning was a windfall worth savouring. "We prepared all this together," said Parizeau. "It's been months that Mr. Bouchard and I have been working together, refining the strategy and the evolution of things. We had a series of meetings together. We are in total agreement."[50]

CHAPTER FIVE

Clever, Quite Clever

In the days leading up to his inaugural speech, Jacques Parizeau had promised Quebecers that his referendum plan would be "clever, quite clever." One very long week later—the week Lucien Bouchard had spent fighting for his life—an impatient Daniel Johnson challenged Parizeau to get on with it. "I am still waiting for the Prime Minister to give us the details," Johnson told the National Assembly. "He remains unclear. He is always clever, but never clear."[1]

Johnson got his wish on December 6. At 10:10 a.m., Premier Parizeau rose in the National Assembly to table French and English versions of his draft bill, *Avant-projet de loi sur la souveraineté du Québec* (*An Act Respecting the Sovereignty of Quebec*). Dressed in a tailored black three-piece suit, white shirt, and red tie, Parizeau was impeccably groomed for the Radio-Canada cameras that were broadcasting the day's historic proceedings live. Leaving nothing to chance, he read from a prepared text, formally introducing his draft law, as well as a supplementary document entitled *La Participation des citoyens au projet de souveraineté* (*Citizens' Participation in the Project of Sovereignty*). Parizeau's tone and his bearing were sober and statesman-like. He did not smile, or break stride, or speak extemporaneously. Throughout his remarks, the National Assembly maintained a respectful silence. When the premier concluded and took his seat, after only five minutes, his Parti Québécois colleagues rose to give him a hearty standing ovation.

The entirety of Parizeau's seventeen-section draft bill fit onto a single sheet of paper. The text itself was not complicated. Section One comprised five words: "Quebec is a sovereign country." Section Two authorized the government of Quebec to conclude an agreement on "economic association with Canada." The third section provided for the drafting of a constitution for Quebec, including a charter of human rights and freedoms, guaranteed protections for English-speaking Quebecers and "Aboriginal nations," and the creation of a Superior Court of Quebec. Other sections set out the institutional terms of the transition to sovereignty, including the transfer of federal public services, pensions, and Quebec's share of the federal debt. According to the draft bill, Quebec citizenship would be automatic for any Canadian living in the province at the time Section One came into force. The currency of Quebec would be the Canadian dollar. Quebec would negotiate its own treaties and therefore seek membership within the Commonwealth, La Francophonie, NATO, NORAD, NAFTA, and GATT. Canadian laws would remain in force until Quebec's own legal and judicial apparatus could be established.

Sections Sixteen and Seventeen set out the terms by which the draft bill would become the law of the land:

16. This Act comes into force one year after its approval by referendum, unless the National Assembly fixes an earlier date. However, Sections 2, 3 and 15 [empowering the government to begin negotiations with Canada] come into force on the day following the day this Act is approved by referendum.

17. This Act shall be submitted to a referendum. This Act may not come into force unless a majority of the votes cast by the electors in a referendum held in accordance with the *Referendum Act* on the following question are cast in the affirmative: "Are you in favour of the Act passed by the National Assembly declaring the sovereignty of Quebec? YES or NO."

Question Period followed Parizeau's tabling of the draft bill. Focused and well-briefed, the premier controlled the debate brilliantly, using his allotted floor time to pitch his sovereignist vision directly to Quebecers. "The sovereignty of a country belongs to everyone and it does not belong to any political party," said Parizeau, after reading aloud several sections of the draft bill. "We will invite everyone in the National Assembly and outside of the National Assembly, to participate in this exercise. We need all those interested in the future of Quebec to come to discuss these things."[2] Having deftly stacked the visitors' gallery with *péquistes*, including his own wife, Lisette Lapointe, the premier beamed happily when it erupted in cheers of "Bravo!" and "Congratulations!" The Speaker's stern warnings about the need for silence in the gallery could not dampen the high spirits of the morning.

With raw emotion now visible on his face, Parizeau announced what everyone knew was the crowning achievement of his life in politics. "Let me again quote from this draft law," said the premier. "It contains a preamble that will be a declaration of sovereignty. The page is blank, and below it, we read: 'The *Declaration of Sovereignty* will be drafted on the basis of suggestions that will be made during the process of information and participation which will be held on the draft law. It will set out the core values and key objectives we want to give the Quebec nation once it has acquired the exclusive power to make all laws, levy all taxes and conclude all treaties.'" Again the visitors' gallery burst into hearty applause. "Bravo! Bravo!" Again the speaker called for silence. "We invite as many Quebecers as possible to participate in the writing of this *Declaration of Sovereignty*," the premier concluded.[3]

If the text of Parizeau's draft bill was straightforward, the process by which he proposed to achieve sovereignty was not. Indeed, the premier's plan to build public consultation into the referendum process was "clever," as he had put it himself, precisely because it side-stepped Quebec's rigorous *Referendum Act* without actually violating it. As the premier himself explained, fifteen regional commissions would be created. Headed by prominent citizens, not all of them necessarily politicians or even sovereignists, the commissions would consult with

Quebecers—and only Quebecers—starting in February 1995. They would report their findings to the government the following month. The draft bill would then be amended by a committee of the National Assembly, after which the final legislation would be put to a province-wide referendum.

On the surface, the plan appeared to put sovereignty on an extremely fast track. But the question on everyone's lips—*When would the referendum be held?*—remained unanswered. Nothing was said or even implied in the draft bill about the date of the referendum, nor did Jacques Parizeau give any indication as to his intentions. The rules governing the timing of referenda were clearly stated in Quebec's *Referendum Act*: the National Assembly would have thirty-five hours to debate the bill in question, a writ for the referendum would be issued eleven days later, and the campaign itself would not exceed thirty-five days. The catch was that the clock would start only after the government had announced a referendum date. As Jacques Parizeau well knew, without a fixed date there were no fixed rules governing the work of his sovereignty commissions—or even the length of the consultation period. The government was free to delay the announcement of a referendum date indefinitely, which meant that it could massage the consultation process itself to build majority support for a Yes vote.

Watching Parizeau present his historic *projet de souveraineté* from across the main aisle of the legislature, opposition leader Daniel Johnson knew that he had to respond with something powerful, something quotable. "Reading the documents that the Prime Minister has just tabled," said Johnson, "one can already see that this is a sad day for democracy in Quebec."[4] Johnson protested the premier's plan to launch his consultation process without debate in the National Assembly, but he knew that Parizeau was within his rights under Quebec's law on parliamentary commissions to do this. He also knew that procedural nit-picking would hardly win the hearts and minds of Quebecers. So he hit hard—and repeatedly—where he believed Parizeau was most vulnerable. He accused the premier of trying to seduce Quebecers into sovereignty when a majority of them had no desire to see Quebec leave

Canada. "Today we see the Prime Minister," said Johnson, "as PQ leader and head of government, using our institutions to invite Quebecers to a single task: write a declaration of sovereignty. How can Quebec federalists participate in drafting the *Declaration of Sovereignty*? Why not go immediately into a referendum to see if Quebecers share this vision? And why not ask the one obvious, concrete, practical question Quebecers expect: Yes or No, Quebec should be a separate country from the rest of Canada?"[5]

Johnson did not relent. He hammered Parizeau with charges of "sophistry and cunning." But on this auspicious day at least, nothing could dent the premier's cheery optimism or knock him off his script. Of course there would be Quebecers participating in the consultations whose views were not those of the government, Parizeau conceded. "But it's great! That's what we want, that's all we need to do, we Quebecers, to adopt this law in the National Assembly, and then to hold a referendum to ask the people of Quebec as a whole if they agree to implement it."[6]

⁓

Despite Jacques Parizeau's first-round victory in the National Assembly, it was immediately evident that he had ceded a good deal of conceptual ground on his *projet de souveraineté* to Lucien Bouchard and his own like-minded advisors. Nothing remained of his "solemn declaration," nor of his proposal to initiate negotiations right away with Ottawa over the transfer of federal powers to Quebec. The novel idea to hold public hearings had come from Jean-François Lisée, who believed that it was necessary to "give visibility and substance to sovereignty in a process of popular solidarity."[7] It was also Lisée's idea to place responsibility for the writing of the *Declaration of Sovereignty* in the hands of Quebecers. Parizeau reportedly liked both suggestions. It was true that they marked a detour on the road to independence, but they did not violate his bedrock principles. The premier was not asking Quebecers for a mandate to negotiate sovereignty-association, as René Lévesque had done in 1980. He was asking them to vote for sovereignty before any negotiation with the rest of Canada had begun. This was the issue over which Parizeau had broken with Lévesque. Never would he place the decision about Quebec's sovereignty in the hands of anyone other than Quebecers.

Parizeau gave a televised speech the same evening he tabled his draft bill, December 6. Canadian federalism was a dead end, he said. "The more time goes by, the more the Canadian majority is determined to act as though there is but one nation in Canada, as though all provinces are equal. This is the Canada of tomorrow. Do we want to be part of it?"[8] Again the premier appealed to all citizens of Quebec. "From this day forward, Quebecers will have the opportunity to open a new chapter in the history of Quebec," said Parizeau. "The draft bill means the document is yours. Yours to modify. Yours to shape the way you see fit. I now call upon each and every one of you—as one—to build our country: Quebec."[9] As he had in the National Assembly, the premier held up a blank page, saying that it would later contain Quebec's declaration of independence. "It might begin with the words 'We the people of Quebec,' or perhaps in these terms, 'The citizens of this nation,' or any number of ways. I'll leave it up to you to find them. This blank page is yours to complete. It's a call to duty to give the very best of ourselves."[10]

Daniel Johnson gave his own televised speech immediately after Parizeau. He dismissed the premier's proposed commission hearings as a "propaganda exercise" and boldly announced that he and his Liberal Party would boycott them. "Even if everyone is invited," asked Johnson, "how can it be imagined that Quebecers who do not share the idea of separation from Canada will participate in the exercise? How can federalist Quebecers participate in drawing up a declaration of sovereignty?"[11] The estimated $2-million price tag for Parizeau's commissions, Johnson added, amounted to government spending on a transparently partisan agenda. It was a travesty.

The next day, December 7, Parizeau took Johnson to task in the National Assembly for boycotting the commissions. "What does the leader of the opposition fear when he says that we are trying to prevent him from expressing his point of view?" asked the premier. "Why sulk like that? Why can we not discuss these questions in a correct, civilized, parliamentary manner?"[12]

Johnson would have none of it. Before the National Assembly could vote on the draft bill, he led the Liberals out of the chamber in protest. "We refuse to be accomplices to this frame-up job," said Johnson. "Why not submit to Quebecers all the options that are available to Quebecers instead of insisting on framing and limiting the debate to a declaration on sovereignty?"[13] Two days later, the Liberals escalated their attack on the government, tabling a motion of censure in the National Assembly. The motion described the government's sovereignty scenario as undemocratic, disrespectful to Quebecers, and misleading because it avoided the only relevant question, "Are you for or against the separation of Quebec from Canada?"[14] To no one's surprise, the PQ used its majority to defeat the Liberal motion, 52–42.

One of the MNAs who voted against the Liberal motion was Mario Dumont. Initially, the ADQ leader's response to Parizeau's draft bill had been decidedly chilly. He was present in the National Assembly when Parizeau tabled his plan, but he did not applaud the premier. "I want to see whether it's a platform or a trap," Dumont said bluntly after the session.[15] Two days later, the ADQ leader announced that his party would co-operate with the work of the commissions, but only if Jacques Parizeau met several conditions. These included ADQ input on the selection of the heads of the commissions, the distribution to all Quebec households of all parties' constitutional proposals, and a commitment from the premier that non-separatists would be welcomed without prejudice into the consultation process. Dumont favoured another round of constitutional talks with the rest of Canada, but this he knew he was not going to get. After several days of behind-the-scenes manoeuvring, the premier acceded to every one of Dumont's conditions—evidence of how valuable Parizeau and his people believed ADQ voters were to the Yes side.

Asked whether he would now be following Dumont's example and participating in the commissions, Daniel Johnson scoffed. "This is not expanding the discussion," he observed. "It is really an agreement between two separatists, Jacques Parizeau and Mario Dumont. They are both of the same mind and there is no room for people who want to indicate to the commission that separation doesn't make sense."[16]

~

Quebecers' responses to Parizeau's *projet de souveraineté* varied.[17] They knew the premier as the most committed of separatists, a man unlikely to squander a PQ majority in the legislature on any cause less hallowed than the independence of Quebec. But by framing his province-wide dialogue on sovereignty without reference to Quebecers who opposed independence, had he, as Daniel Johnson charged, undermined democracy? Léon Dion, an éminence grise of the Quiet Revolution (and father of federalist Stéphane Dion), believed so. "On a purely legal basis," observed Dion, "the law is not being broken, but the content of the draft bill does not respect fairness in terms of the right to a free debate in a democracy."[18] Nonsense, said Laval professor Guy Laforest; Parizeau was merely playing the hand he was dealt. "If there's anything illegitimate," said Laforest, "it was the way the Canadian constitution was repatriated in 1982."[19] *Péquiste* standard-bearer Camille Laurin agreed, observing that it was "perfectly natural and logical to start with a draft bill and to go to the population and ask for their opinions."[20]

Editorials in the French-language press were not quite so generous. "The PQ is trying to anesthetize the entire population of Quebec," said a *Le Soleil* editorial flatly.[21] "Federalists are being invited to lock themselves into a process chosen exclusively by the Parti Québécois and that amounts to a hijack of parliamentary institutions," added Jean-Jacques Samson of the same paper.[22] "Let's get serious," wrote Alain Dubuc at *La Presse*. Given that the majority of Quebecers opposed sovereignty, the premier's commissions would be little more than "PQ fan clubs."[23] Some francophone pundits, including *Journal de Montréal* columnist Michel C. Auger and political scientist Daniel Latouche, cautioned Quebecers not to rush to judgment on Parizeau's methods—or his principles. "You may not be overly excited about the process and the idea of consulting everybody and nobody at the same time," wrote Latouche. "But I have a really hard time with people who slam the process for being illegitimate."[24] Others, however, expressed astonishment at the premier's fancy footwork. Parizeau had always been "a radical *indépendantiste*," wrote Lysiane Gagnon, "eager to be frank and direct about the real meaning of separation. For 20 years he showed nothing but contempt for the soft-selling strategy of his predecessor, René Lévesque. The backtracking is spectacular."[25]

Predictably, the English-language Montreal *Gazette* led the charge against Parizeau's *projet de souveraineté*, pronouncing the premier clever indeed but "masterfully deceitful." It was "appalling," said a *Gazette* editorial, "that the Parti Québécois government appears to want to achieve [sovereignty] by misleading, manipulating and tricking Quebecers."[26] Parizeau's plan was a "tissue of deception," wrote *Gazette* editor-in-chief Joan Fraser.[27] Columnist Don Macpherson called the premier's draft bill "a masterpiece of subtle political propaganda and psychological manipulation."[28] Hubert Bauch was even more emphatic. "What Parizeau launched yesterday is the biggest power play in Canadian history since confederation," he wrote, "but in the end it all comes down to a mind game in which the winning answer will be dictated by the winning question."[29]

In English Canada, responses to the PQ's *projet de souveraineté* were almost uniformly hostile. Many Canadians who had given Jacques Parizeau the benefit of a sizeable doubt—hoping that he would lead Quebec responsibly and do nothing precipitous to destroy Canada—saw nothing but treachery in his draft bill and promptly gave up on him. Parizeau was "totally unrealistic," asserted Ontario premier Bob Rae. "He is not in a position to give assurances about what is going to happen to the Canadian dollar, about what's going to happen to people's passports, about what is going to happen to people's pensions."[30] Premiers Frank McKenna, Roy Romanow, Gary Filmon, Ralph Klein, and Mike Harcourt made similar statements, stressing that there was "no constitutional mechanism for any province to separate."[31] A *Globe and Mail* editorial charged that "the new plan of the Parti Québécois to detach Quebec from Canada" bore "an aura of fantasy and a ring of hollowness."[32] *Globe*

columnist Andrew Coyne called the draft bill "almost comically dupli-
citous" and cautioned the "useful idiots" in the premiers' offices not to
appease Quebec with Parizeau's knife at their throats. "It is no more legitimate for secessionists to claim title to Quebec than to the Rideau Canal,"
fumed Coyne. "*It doesn't belong to them.*"³³

Pollsters weighed in. On December 9, a SOM survey conducted
for *La Presse* and Radio-Canada found that 55 per cent of Quebecers
approved of Parizeau's promised referendum, but only 43 per cent
approved of his draft bill on sovereignty. Fully 68 per cent of Quebecers
thought federalists should participate in the consultation process—a
number that struck Daniel Johnson as dispiriting, since he had
announced his decision to boycott the hearings before consulting his
own pollsters.³⁴ A second SOM poll published a week later estimated
the spread between Quebecers who would vote Yes for "sovereignty"
but not for "independence" at 5 per cent.³⁵ Beyond Quebec, meanwhile,
attitudes appeared to be hardening. An Angus Reid/Southam News poll
showed that Canadians outside Quebec were unwilling to let Quebec
decide its relationship with Canada unilaterally. Fifty-six per cent said
they would oppose any formal economic association between Canada
and Quebec, 59 per cent said Ottawa should be tough in negotiations
with Quebec "even if it means the issues won't be resolved for a long
time," and 55 per cent said such talks should not even begin before
Canadians had approved of them in a national referendum.³⁶

Person-on-the-street interviews in Quebec echoed the pollsters'
findings. "It's too confusing for the average person," said forty-one-
year-old Châteauguay resident Colleen O'Connor. "Why do they
need to adopt a law on sovereignty first and then hold a referendum?
It should be the other way around."³⁷ Thirty-six-year-old Christine
Smith of Westmount was critical of the proposed referendum question.
"There's too much ambiguity in it," said Smith. "If there's any ambiguity
in the question, people won't be satisfied."³⁸ Eduardo Pereira of Pointe-
Claire agreed. "I think this is crazy," he said. "They're going to adopt
a law by themselves which is going to affect everyone—francophones
and non-francophones—without consulting us. I think they're going

too far. It looks like a dictatorship."[39] René Rénaud, a sixty-eight-year-old francophone from Hochelaga-Maisonneuve, in contrast, liked what he saw. "Mr. Parizeau wants everyone to participate in the debate," said Rénaud. "I think the process is democratic and quite clear to me. This whole issue is not a question of breaking away from Canada, but creating our own state and republic."[40]

Anglophone-rights organizations led by Alliance Quebec decided to follow Daniel Johnson's example and boycott the commissions.[41] (This was a decision Jacques Parizeau pressed hard and often to get them to reconsider. "I regret Alliance Quebec refuses to participate," he would say. "The anglophones of Quebec, I've said in the past, they are us. Look, we might disagree on a number of things and often, but we belong to the same society. I will never give up, never.")[42] The Cree Grand Council of Quebec, led by Matthew Coon Come, announced not only that it would boycott the process but also that it would hold its own hearings to determine how Crees would together resist a declaration of sovereignty. The Inuit of Quebec also said that they would boycott the process. "If Quebec opts for sovereignty," said Inuit leader Zebedee Nungak, "the future of Nunavik will not be decided by Quebec or by the rest of Canada, but by the Inuit who are the residents of this territory."[43] At a special general meeting of the Assembly of First Nations, aboriginal leaders demanded unanimously that Ottawa "fulfill its historic treaty, fiduciary and constitutional obligations to protect and promote the rights of First Nations in Quebec and Labrador." Native people across Canada, they insisted, "will not permit the historic links and relationships between the first nations inside and outside Quebec to be infringed or severed."[44]

Some civic organizations in Quebec took the position that they would not participate in Parizeau's hearings but their members were free to do so. They included the Union des producteurs agricoles (farmers' union), the Quebec Chamber of Commerce, the Conseil du patronat (employers' council), and the Quebec Manufacturers Association.[45] "Ethnic" organizations whose leaders initially said that they would not participate in the hearings included the Quebec branches of the

Canadian Jewish Congress, the National Congress of Italian Canadians, and the Hellenic (Greek) Congress of Quebec. Pressure from within the membership of all three groups later drew them into the consultation process, however, presumably as a hedge in the event of a sovereignist victory.[46] Pro-sovereignist groups whose support for the PQ's *projet de souveraineté* was a foregone conclusion included the Societé Saint-Jean-Baptiste, the Union des artistes, the Union des écrivains et écrivaines (writers' union), the Conseil québécois du théâtre (Quebec Theatre Council), and Quebec's two largest labour unions, the Confédération des syndicats nationaux and the Fédération des travailleurs et travail-leuses du Québec.

~

The morning Parizeau tabled his draft bill, Prime Minister Jean Chrétien was in Europe and keeping mum on the drama unfolding in Quebec. Back in Ottawa, however, his cabinet was holding its weekly Tuesday morning strategy session as usual. Chrétien advisor Eddie Goldenberg later described the impact of Parizeau's draft bill as a bombshell. "As the news of his draft legislation spread in the room," said Goldenberg, "ministers were visibly shaken and some seemed almost panic-stricken. Until then, the reality of what Parizeau was up to had not yet fully sunk in for some federal ministers, especially for those from outside Quebec, many of whom were quietly unhappy with a seemingly perpetual focus by Chrétien on Quebec problems. Now they wanted to act immediately, but had no idea what to do."[47] Goldenberg left the meeting discreetly and had the Commons operator place a call to Chrétien. The prime minister offered his troops encouragement. "Tell them not to panic and not to worry," said Chrétien to Goldenberg. "This is just another one of Parizeau's tactics. We have beaten the separatists before and we will beat them again."[48]

Liberal MPs trooped into the House of Commons knowing full well that the Bloc Québécois would use its Official Opposition status to champion the PQ cause. Bloc whip Gilles Duceppe was only too happy to introduce the subject of Parizeau's draft bill on sovereignty. "What distinguishes this process is its clarity and openness," said Duceppe. "We hope that the Quebec members of the Liberal Party of Canada will respect this process and that they will accept the invitation of the Quebec government to participate in the consultation exercise."[49]

During Question Period, it was not the Bloc but Reform that put the screws to the Liberals. "Does the Government of Canada agree that the draft act respecting the sovereignty of Quebec is beyond the legal powers of the government and Assembly of Quebec?" asked Preston Manning.[50] With Jean Chrétien absent, it fell to deputy prime minister Sheila Copps to respond. "The Government of Canada has every confidence that the people of Quebec, when given the chance to vote on the real question of whether they want to become a part of a separate country or whether they want to stay in Canada, will vote an overwhelming yes to Canada," said Copps. "The premier of Quebec has no right to put a bill before the people when the people have not chosen the route of separation."[51] This was not good enough for Manning, who repeated his question word for word. "Mr. Speaker, it is unfortunate that the leader of the Reform Party is playing Jacques Parizeau's game," an exasperated Copps replied. "We do not intend to play that game. We intend to ask the people of Quebec a very clear question: Do you want to stay with Canada or do you want to separate? That is the question they will be voting on in the referendum."[52]

Jean Chrétien, en route home from his European visit on December 7, offered his first public reaction to Parizeau's sovereignty plan during a stopover in Newfoundland. To the astonishment of the journalists travelling with him, the prime minister had just dropped out of his Canadian Armed Forces plane using an emergency ladder from the cockpit because he had grown impatient waiting for the airport to find a stairway long enough to reach the cabin doors. "For me, it is a very surprising move that they will do something so desperate because it's not democratic," said Chrétien of the PQ referendum plan. "And the only thing I'm asking is very simple, is a clear, honest question, 'Do you want to separate from Canada?' That's easy. It's a few words, it's clear, no ambiguity and they vote."[53] The prime minister was asked directly whether he would hold a federal referendum. "I don't think it's needed," he replied. "We will see."[54]

The debate in the House of Commons raged again the next day, as MPs familiarized themselves with the terms of Parizeau's draft bill and marked out their parties' turf. Liberals attacked Jacques Parizeau's plan as an "ill-advised adventure" and a "bit of trickery."[55] Bloc MPs countered with rousing endorsements of the Quebec premier and his "deep respect for democratic principles."[56] Bloc house leader Michel Gauthier and whip Gilles Duceppe jousted with intergovernmental-affairs minister Marcel Massé on the question of Quebecers' fundamental loyalties. ("They built this country with their daring, ingenuity and courage," said Massé, always a skillful stickhandler, "and not even a premier will hoodwink them into throwing in the towel and pulling out of Canada.")[57] Preston Manning and Stephen Harper continued to badger Sheila Copps on the legality of the referendum process, prompting Copps to caution them against abetting the sovereignists in the destruction of Canada.[58] When the dust settled, Liberals and Reformers could agree only that federalists should follow Daniel Johnson's example and refuse to participate in Parizeau's commissions, a view also shared by Tory leader Jean Charest. "They have no option to offer Quebecers," observed Gilles Duceppe of the bickering federalist parties. "They don't even agree between themselves."[59]

As Preston Manning had perhaps hoped, Sheila Copps's reluctance to address the constitutionality of the PQ's *projet de souveraineté* hinted strongly that the government did not know how to respond to the sovereignist threat. Canadians took notice. The feds' response to Parizeau's referendum strategy, wrote Claude Charron, columnist for *7 Jours*, had *"l'air d'une poule sur glace"* ("the look of a chicken on ice").[60] "Chrétien's referendum Plan A is to hope that Quebecers don't vote Yes," observed Don Macpherson of the Montreal *Gazette*. "But he'd better come up with a better Plan B, just in case they do."[61] Macpherson's *Gazette* colleague William Johnson called Copps's response to the separatists pathetic. "Any unilateral declaration of independence, with or without a referendum, is unconstitutional, revolutionary, and must be opposed by all legitimate means by the government of Canada," he wrote.[62]

Jean Chrétien returned to the House of Commons on December 8, well aware that he had to take decisive ownership of the national-unity file. *Bloquiste* Michel Gauthier asked the prime minister whether he believed that "holding a Canada-wide referendum on Quebec's constitutional future means denying Quebecers the right to decide their own future for themselves."[63] Chrétien came out swinging. "We want only one thing," he said, "a referendum as soon as possible in Quebec, under Quebec's *Referendum Act*, where they will not play tricks but be honest with the people and ask Quebecers whether or not they want to separate from Canada."[64]

Preston Manning asked the prime minister to comment on Jacques Parizeau's offer to make Quebecers dual citizens of Canada. Again Chrétien responded forcefully. "Citizenship of Canada will be determined by the Parliament of Canada not by the Parliament of Quebec," he said. "Mr. Parizeau's proposition is funny. He wants to keep all the good things that Canada has provided for Quebec. Quebec should stay in Canada. That is my answer." The Reform leader remained unimpressed. "I think Parizeau's game is to take initiatives—including illegal initiatives—and trust the national government will do nothing but sputter and fume," said Manning. "And the federal government is playing exactly that game."[65]

It was true that Chrétien and his top ministers were unwilling, in these early days, to pronounce on the legality of the PQ sovereignty initiative lest they be perceived as undermining the democratic rights of Quebecers. This may have disappointed outspoken legalists like Preston Manning, William Johnson, and Andrew Coyne (whose hard line on the constitutionality of Quebec secession would in 1998 be rejected by the Supreme Court of Canada). But seen in retrospect, this decision made sense. Chrétien and his advisors were shrewd not to rush to judgment and risk handing the PQ its strongest case of all for leaving. Daniel Johnson was already facing enormous pressure to renounce his decision to boycott Parizeau's commission hearings. Polls showed that most

Quebecers thought he had acted precipitously. His own brother, former PQ premier of Quebec Pierre-Marc Johnson, had gone on record as saying that he thought Parizeau's referendum proposal was legitimate.[66] Daniel Johnson put the best spin he could on the backlash. "We are not isolated," he insisted. "We're excluded. And we're excluded with, at last count, about 60 per cent of the population."[67] Jean Chrétien had no wish to find himself similarly excluded.

But it was not true that the federal Liberals were merely sputtering and fuming over what they perceived as the sovereignists' beguiling lies to Quebecers. On the contrary, by the end of the week in which Parizeau had tabled his draft bill, Ottawa's position had emerged almost fully formed—and it was being articulated with confidence and consistency by the prime minister. Asked by Bloc MP Maud Debien whether he recognized Quebecers' right to decide on the wording of their referendum question, for example, Chrétien was forthright. "Quebec federalists have the right to have a say in the wording of the question," he said, "so that it is plain and clear. The rest of Canada is also entitled to a question that is plain and clear. Just think of the number of people who are presently refusing to participate because of the ambiguity, the trickiness. They are trying to trick people, they are using gimmicks."[68] Questioned about Jacques Parizeau's plan to formulate an economic association with Canada, the prime minister was even more categorical. "That is not up to Quebec to decide," he said. "Canada will decide. [The draft bill] says they will keep their Canadian citizenship. This is not up to the Government of Quebec to decide. The Parliament of Canada will decide. It says they will use Canadian currency. The Parliament of Canada will determine interest rates, not the Government of Quebec."[69]

Where Chrétien was at his best, right from the outset, was on the fundamental question of Quebec's place within Canada. "I have no mandate to discuss [sovereignty] with anybody," he said flatly. "I have been elected to protect the whole of Canada and I am the prime minister of all Canadians, including all those who live in Quebec. And I will fight for Canada. I have always done it and I will do it again and we will win again."[70] Though it was not immediately apparent to Chrétien's critics, this simple assertion—*I have no mandate*—proved to be a master stroke. As he would do throughout the referendum campaign, the prime minister refused to debate the sovereignists on their own terms. As far as he was concerned, the Quebec–Canada binary, so casually evoked in Jacques Parizeau's draft bill and his appeals to Quebecers, existed only in the overwrought imaginations of the separatist minority. There could be no discussion of a new relationship between a sovereign Canada and a sovereign Quebec. *There was no Canada without Quebec.* "That's one of the questions that they [sovereignists] will have to answer," Chrétien liked to say. "With whom will they negotiate?"[71]

In the end, it took Chrétien and his advisors just under two weeks to work through the legal and constitutional implications of Parizeau's *projet de souveraineté*—an eternity in politics, to be sure, but hardly an eternity for the lawyers advising the prime minister on a provincial law that envisaged the breakup of Canada. By December 18, 1994, Chrétien's position on the constitutional status of the PQ's sovereignty option was unambiguous. "It's completely illegal and non-constitutional," said the prime minister in a televised interview. And it demonstrated that Jacques Parizeau "does not have the guts to ask the very clear, short question: Do you want to separate from Canada?"[72]

In the meantime, the man who had ignited this national furor was entirely at his ease. "They're becoming agitated in the House of Commons," said Jacques Parizeau, "saying, 'It's *ultra vires*' and that 'They don't have the constitutional right to apply this law.' Well, they're discovering that a little late. The legitimacy that these people in Ottawa are questioning is drawn from the people itself. It is the Quebec people, by virtue of their own laws, which will decide their own future."[73]

~

On December 10, 1994, just days after tabling his draft sovereignty bill, Jacques Parizeau granted the *Los Angeles Times* a feature interview. Conducted in English by the *Times*'s man in Canada, Craig Turner, the conversation took place in Quebec City. Parizeau spoke candidly about his dream of making Quebec a French-speaking country, free to define its own future. Asked whether he would honour his promise to hold his referendum in 1995, Parizeau replied in the affirmative. When Turner pressed him on whether it would come in early or late 1995, the premier became testy. "On the path of history," he replied, "who gives a damn?"[74]

Asked how he planned to achieve a majority vote for sovereignty—given that no Quebec leader had ever managed to do so—the premier gave an unscripted answer that would jolt Canadians and resonate for the remainder of the referendum campaign. "I can't say [that] I'm a superb tactician and I'm sure I'll get beyond 50%," said Parizeau. "Other people will have to comment on how skillful I am. But it's now a question of tactics and strategy. Get me a half-dozen Ontarians who put their feet to the Quebec flag, and I've got it."

The premier was alluding to the desecration of the Quebec flag by a small group of Brockville, Ontario, residents five years earlier—a painful incident that had been seared into Canadians' and Quebecers' consciousness by endlessly recycled television clips. Was Jacques Parizeau really saying that he intended, as a matter of referendum strategy, to provoke Canadian anglos into the kind of anti-Quebec antics that would sour Quebecers on Canada? Absolutely, warned Quebec Liberal MNA Lawrence Bergman. "When the polls show that you're weak, of course you look up your sleeve for a bag of tricks," said Bergman. "Obviously he'd like to provoke nasty situations but that's the sign of someone who is not confident. When you have to hope that people are going to jump on your flag, well, that's the level of debate he wants to have."[75]

By the end of week one of the unofficial referendum campaign, Canadians—outside French-speaking Quebec at least—were in virtually unanimous agreement that Premier Parizeau had proved himself too "clever" by half. He had tabled a bill declaring the sovereignty of Quebec before the people of his province had even given him a mandate to separate. He had laid out a transition plan that made the destruction of Canada look painless, practical, and inevitable. And he had played directly into Canadians' suspicion that he was prepared to sweet-talk Quebecers into sovereignty at any cost, even if this meant making scapegoats of English Canadians.

None of it mattered in the least to Jacques Parizeau, of course. He had long since stopped caring what Canadians outside Quebec thought about his dream of independence. "What Quebec wants," mused the premier, "Quebec will say in 1995."[76]

CHAPTER SIX

Sovereignist Setbacks

On February 22, 1995, Lucien Bouchard entered the House of Commons for the first time since his near-death experience with necrotizing fasciitis-myositis. He returned to public life with a leg prosthesis and crutches, for which he had undergone weeks of intense physiotherapy. "I'm lucky," he said of his ability to manoeuvre on his prosthesis. "I have a good stump, they told me I have a good stump. And I am in great, great physical shape."[1] Contrary to some observers' expectations that his brush with mortality might mark the end of his political career, Bouchard said that it had, in fact, focused it. "Politics seems more important than ever to me now," he reflected. "I've come a long way, I've been at death's door. When you have come through that, you have a profound sense of the fragility of human life, how time is meted out to us. On the other hand, you say to yourself, 'The time that I am given, I will utilize it to the maximum for the things that really matter.'"[2]

Bouchard's return to politics was a national event, and both he and Canadians were eminently gracious about it. A month earlier, Bouchard had been photographed publicly for the first time since losing his leg. The photo, which showed him struggling to master his crutches, had made the front pages across Canada, accompanied by well-wishing captions like the *Globe and Mail*'s "Welcome Sight." A good many Canadians who abhorred Bouchard's politics could not help but marvel at his courage and fortitude. "It's good to have Lucien Bouchard back on the job," said the Montreal *Gazette*. "He looks a little thinner, a little older. His fight for life and to cope with the loss of a limb has taken a heavy toll. In his eyes, you can see a man who has travelled where few of us have been."[3]

Bouchard himself acknowledged that it would not be easy returning to the political ring after Canadians had been so kind to him while he was hospitalized. "I had discovered before that there is a lot of compassion and human values in Canada as there is in Quebec," he observed. "We are close, you know. We share really common values on the human aspects. This was quite a confirmation, it was really moving for me. I was touched."[4] The Bloc leader later recalled that even Jean Chrétien had called him during his convalescence to express his sympathies. "I was sitting at my home one night with Audrey, play-ing cards," he recalled, "and then the phone [rang] and the someone said, '*Le premier ministre.*' I said, 'Okay, Parizeau is calling me.' I was listening for Parizeau's voice. And then it was Jean Chrétien. He was very friendly, very nice."[5]

Coming as it did during the initial wave of debate on the PQ's *pro-jet de souveraineté*, Chrétien's personal kindness did nothing to alter Bouchard's opinion of his politics. "Mr. Chrétien is behaving like some-one who is sure of winning the game," said Bouchard, "so he thinks he doesn't have to take risks, get personally involved. I think at some point he will have to get involved. I would like him to come into Quebec and make a lot of speeches on the separatists." Nor did Bouchard's newfound affection for English Canadians change his sense of their relationship with Quebecers. "If we sit down to talk about the Constitution," said the Bloc leader, "about collective solutions, everything breaks down. We cannot deliver. It's a paradox. I'm sorry about it and I'm quite surprised. There is some incapacity in English Canada to recognize the fundamen-tal [fact] that we Quebecers would like to be recognized as a people, as a nation, *comme un peuple.* So we are here again in the same tough spot."[6]

There was high drama in the House of Commons the afternoon of February 22, as the leaders of all of the parties rose to offer their good wishes to the returning Bouchard. "On behalf of all members of this House," said Prime Minister Chrétien, "I wish to extend a very warm welcome to the Leader of the Opposition. All members of this House and all Canadians salute the courage and determination shown by the Leader of the Opposition throughout his recent ordeal. Since it is one of his fondest wishes, I would like to say to the Leader of the Opposition, on behalf of all members of this House: Welcome back to the shop."[7] Preston Manning and NDP leader Audrey McLaughlin expressed similar sentiments.[8]

Lucien Bouchard then rose to speak. "These past two months have taught me something about this House and its members," he said. "They taught me that one can get homesick for this place. I return here with feelings of gratitude, with pride and confidence. I wish to mention the courtesy and understanding shown by the Prime Minister. His heart is in the right place." Bouchard expressed his genuine gratitude for the ministers, MPs, and ordinary Canadians who had supported him with their messages of encouragement. "I was able to observe how compassionate and generous our fellow citizens from English Canada can be," he reflected. "Who would not have been moved by their expressions of sympathy?" The Bloc leader concluded his lengthy speech with a wry *en garde* to his political adversaries. The "cut and thrust of parliamentary debate," he said, would inevitably fuel the old passions on both sides, and he, for one, relished the opportunity to rejoin the debate. "I was a little worried earlier that the Prime Minister's kind words would have a disarming effect on me," he conceded. "I am aware that I will have to revert to a more robust approach in my first questions to the Prime Minister later on."[9]

Jean Chrétien needed no convincing. Just days before his return to the House of Commons, Bouchard had appeared on the popular Quebec television show *Le Point*. There he reiterated the case he had been making from the outset: a No vote in a referendum would be disastrous for Quebec. Sovereignists simply could not allow it. "Quebec would be saying," argued Bouchard, "'Well, we've had a lot of tough blows from the federal government but we think that Jean Chrétien is right.' We would be saying to Jean Chrétien, 'Look, you've hit us a lot, Jean Chrétien, but hit us again. Go on. We like it.' Are we going to do that? No."[10] Before leaving the set of Radio-Canada's *Le Point*, Bouchard put Quebecers themselves on notice. It was now or never. "This is the last battle for the Bloc," he said. "If sovereignty is definitely rejected, which I doubt, you have to question the future of the Bloc Québécois."[11]

Bouchard's words were as formidable as ever, but even more worrisome for Jean Chrétien was the messianic adulation the Bloc leader's brush with death had brought him among many ordinary Quebecers. Some people seemed to think that "God had spared his life because he had been chosen for a great historic purpose," the prime minister observed. "Even the way he walked with his cane kept the myth alive in the consciousness of Quebecers."[12]

~

Lucien Bouchard was not the only member of parliament given a special welcome in the House of Commons on February 22. Nine days earlier, the Liberals had swept three federal by-elections, two in Quebec and one in Ottawa. Prime Minister Chrétien thus had the privilege of escorting three new government MPs—Lucienne Robillard, Denis Paradis, and Mauril Bélanger—into the House on the very day that the Bloc Québécois leader made his triumphal return. This was no mere coincidence. Since calling the by-elections in December, the prime minister had done everything in his power to cast them as a mini-referendum. "This victory is a clear indication that the federalist forces are poised to win the Quebec referendum," Chrétien crowed on election night. "We now have an indication of how the people of Quebec will respond on referendum day: they will say no to separation."[13] Lucien Bouchard called the by-election results merely "disappointing," but, in fact, they were nothing short of ominous for the Bloc Québécois.[14] The loss of the Bloc seat in the Quebec riding of Brome-Missisquoi reduced the caucus from fifty-four MPs to fifty-three—just one seat more than the Reform caucus.

More than this, the Liberal victories stalled the sovereignists' momentum in the referendum campaign just when they could least afford it. In the weeks since Jacques Parizeau had tabled his draft bill on sovereignty, things had not gone his way. There were rumours, later confirmed, that private differences between Parizeau and Bouchard were threatening to flare into a public breach. The question of referendum timing was especially thorny. Among sovereignists, Parizeau made no secret of the fact that he wanted to fix a date. "'It is certain that Quebecers would rather not have to settle this painful question," he told his top aides. "If you do not give them a deadline, they will not make their decision. We will not be able to mobilize without a deadline."[15] Bouchard, on the other hand, wanted the premier to adopt the Bloc position, namely that there should be no referendum vote at all if winning conditions could not be established.[16]

Daniel Johnson's early efforts to assemble his No team, meanwhile, had the intended effect of heightening Quebecers' worries about the economic and social uncertainties of sovereignty. On January 9, Johnson announced that sixty-five-year-old Michel Bélanger would head Le Comité des québécois and québécoises pour le Non, a joint committee of the federal and provincial Liberals. Bélanger—a former president of both the Bank of Canada and the Montreal Stock Exchange—had in 1990 co-chaired the Bélanger-Campeau Commission with Jean Campeau (now serving as PQ finance minister) and was highly regarded by Quebec federalists. But his roots were in Quebec's "big nationalist family," as one observer put it, and he considered sovereignty "feasible but not desirable."[17] "The job of the No committee essentially is to be on the attack," said Bélanger, "to ask questions [of the sovereignists], to say, Why did you do this? What would be the benefits? How would you explain this?"[18]

Nor was Parizeau's position strengthened when, in December 1994, the youth wing of the Parti Québécois formally adopted a referendum question of its own. The question read: "Do you want the government of Quebec to proclaim the sovereignty of Quebec in conformity of the law declaring sovereignty or that it proclaim Quebec's adhesion to the Canadian federation in conformity to the 1982 constitutional law?"[19] According to Éric Bédard, president of the PQ youth group, the intent of the new question was to strengthen the sovereignist position by reminding voters that Quebec was not a signatory to the 1982 Constitution. But optics mattered. A challenge from within the PQ family over the wording of the referendum question did nothing to shore up the premier's authority. Parizeau put the best face he could on the situation. "The suggestion of Parti Québécois youth to change the issue and ensure that the issue is a choice between sovereignty or the constitutional status quo, as advocated by the Leader of the Opposition, is interesting," he told the National Assembly. "I'm not saying necessarily that, ultimately, that's what we will choose, but the debate is engaged. I'm all ears regarding alternative proposals like this."[20]

Jacques Parizeau's pledge to heed all Quebecers was tested early in the new year when Guy Bertrand, a committed separatist and one-time PQ leadership hopeful, called the party's sovereignty strategy not merely unconstitutional but "suicidal and doomed to failure." "The dream won't be achieved and we have to stop digging in our heels," Bertrand told the newspaper Le Soleil. "To get out of Confederation, you have to have the agreement of all partners. Are we going to lead the people into an adventure saying, 'Jump on the boat in hopes that there won't be any waves'?"[21] Bertrand, well known to Quebecers as a "flamboyant" lawyer with a taste for the media spotlight, suggested that the PQ table a referendum with nineteen questions, followed by a 400-day period of negotiation with the rest of Canada. Parizeau offered no public comment on Bertrand's proposal, but back in Ottawa, the prime minister and his top ministers were delighted. "They gave me hell because I said that!" exclaimed an incredulous Jean Chrétien.[22] "People expect us to indicate that the federation has been very good for Quebec," added Marcel Massé, "but if you have a separatist like Mr. Bertrand who starts to think in depth and comes to that conclusion, then it's much more believable."[23]

Then came the Bourgault incident. In mid-January, Université du Québec professor Pierre Bourgault, a veteran péquiste serving as special advisor to Jacques Parizeau, ignited a firestorm across Canada by intimating that if the referendum vote split along linguistic lines, this result might provoke a violent backlash in Quebec. "If a vast majority of franco-Quebecers vote Yes and are prevented from doing it because the English vote against," Bourgault was quoted as saying, "then it's a dangerous situation." Asked to elaborate, he replied, "It's not difficult to understand. Do I have to explain it to you?"[24]

Some Montrealers were quick to judgment, casting Bourgault's comments as a veiled threat against non-francophones in Quebec. "Bourgault's comments indicate that ethnic and xenophobic nationalism can still be found beneath the surface in this debate," said Stephen Scheinberg, national vice-president of B'nai Brith and a professor of history at Concordia. "The anglophone community has as much at stake and historical claim to this province as any Quebecer. Denying complete legitimacy to their vote is racist. There should be no place among Premier Parizeau's advisors for racists."[25] Veteran *Journal de Montréal* columnist Jean-V. Dufresne argued that Bourgault's words smacked of "intolerance, provocation and blackmail" but were in keeping with some of Parizeau's recent statements. "The premier says he is frankly hoping that a bunch of numbskulls from Kingston are going to trample on the Quebec flag, since that would help win the referendum," railed Dufresne.[26]

At first, Jacques Parizeau was nonchalant about Bourgault's comments. But as the media frenzy escalated, the premier had little choice but to distance himself from his old friend. "As he has often repeated himself," said Parizeau, "Mr. Bourgault isn't a spokesman for the government or for the premier, therefore his remarks are his own and don't in any way commit the government of Quebec."[27] Liberal MNAs in Quebec demanded that Parizeau fire Bourgault. In Ottawa, Jean Chrétien saw a political opportunity and took it. "Everyone has the right to vote," said the prime minister. "I don't see why we would exclude people from a vote like this. If you don't want anglophones to vote, don't let them vote and explain why. If they do vote, they're citizens like everybody else."[28] Finally, on January 19, the Parti Québécois announced that Bourgault had resigned so that, as Parizeau himself put it, the referendum debate could "proceed in serenity and calm."[29] The incident had proved "awkward" for both Bourgault and him, the premier conceded, but more than this, it carried a huge risk that the PQ might lose control over the debate it had been so careful to frame. "Could everyone keep their shirt on and hold on to their horses?" asked Parizeau. "We are engaging in Quebec in the present time in what is probably the most remarkable democratic exercise that we have attempted to define our future. I don't want people throwing all kinds of rocks into the situation we are trying to set out."[30]

It later came to light that Bourgault had not volunteered his statement but, in fact, had responded to a direct question from Canadian Press journalist Don MacDonald. A transcript of the conversation was published.

> *MacDonald:* If the referendum is rejected by a thin margin and, in the end, it's anglophone Quebecers and allophones who have rejected the referendum, do you think there's the risk of a backlash among francophones or would that create a dangerous situation?
> *Bourgault:* Yes, that could create a dangerous situation.
> *MacDonald:* Why?
> *Bourgault:* You know, because you're telling me.[31]

Bourgault later admitted that he had been "trapped like an amateur" in the interview.[32] MacDonald was not persuaded. "Bourgault has been dealing with the media since the 1960s," he observed. "He's a communications professor. He's way past being trapped by a reporter."[33] Bourgault expressed remorse for the trouble he had caused Parizeau, but added that the premier should never have "caved into the pressure from the English."[34] Several weeks later, Bourgault was asked his opinion of polls showing that virtually all Quebec anglos were planning to vote No. "At 80 per cent, I call that a xenophobic vote," Bourgault replied. "At 97 per cent, I call that a straight racist vote."[35] After this remark, the heat on Bourgault was so great that he decided to leave active political life after thirty years. "Each time I open my mouth, I create embarrassment," he lamented.[36]

No sooner had Bourgault resigned than Bloc MP Philippe Paré, a former schoolteacher and a founding member of the PQ, stepped onto the same minefield. "Just for once," Paré asked one of the sovereignty commissions, "couldn't you let the next referendum be decided by old-stock Quebecers?"[37] Lucien Bouchard immediately fired Paré from two Bloc Québécois referendum committees, saying, "Quebec is an open society and all citizens, without any distinction whatsoever, should take part in the debate concerning our common future."[38] Then, in early March, another highly respected sovereignist, Jean-Marc Léger (not to be confused with the pollster of the same name), publicly urged non-francophone Quebecers to exempt themselves from the referendum process. "It's a delicate situation and they should think twice about voting," said Léger. "It's an invitation to all those people who don't really feel integrated here to generously abstain, especially when we're dealing with such an important consultation."[39] Predictably, such comments from high-profile Quebec nationalists breathed new life into the old accusation that behind the sovereignists' warm words of inclusion lay ethnic tribalism and xenophobia. The English-Canadian press exploded with editorial reproaches bearing titles like the *Toronto Star*'s "Separatist Racism."[40] "In some separatist circles," warned the Montreal *Gazette*, "people are succumbing to their worst instincts and looking for scapegoats for a referendum loss."[41]

~

Pierre Bourgault and his ilk may have been pebbles in Jacques Parizeau's shoe, but the premier's real problem—the one that put his entire referendum plan at risk—was that the sovereignty commissions were having no effect on his polling numbers.

The hearings had begun promisingly enough. Eighteen commissions had been struck, three more than had originally been envisaged. Sixteen of these were regional, one dealt exclusively with the concerns of Quebec youth, another with the elderly.[42] The commissioners were a mix of PQ and Bloc Québécois officials and local VIPs, all of them appointed by cabinet decree and reportedly vetted by Jacques Parizeau.[43] The premier scored a major coup when Marcel Masse and

Jean-Paul L'Allier agreed to head two of the commissions. Masse, a former Mulroney cabinet minister (not to be confused with Liberal Marcel Massé) headed the Montreal commission; L'Allier, the sitting mayor of Quebec City, took charge of the commission for his city. Both men were avowed nationalists who had entered politics during the Quiet Revolution, yet both were seen in English Canada—until they accepted Parizeau's offer at least—as federalists.[44] (A *Toronto Star* editorial noted that the appointment of Masse to one of Parizeau's commissions outed him as a "closet Quebec sovereignist.")[45] Camille Laurin asked McGill philosopher Charles Taylor to serve on the Montreal commission, but he declined.

The hearings ran as scheduled between February and March 1995 and were, as the premier had hoped, extensive. The commissioners presided over 388 public meetings, heard from 53,500 Quebecers, and received 4,595 written memoranda. Some of the sessions featured "animators," whose role was to help ordinary people to express their views. The hearings came in well over budget, at a cost of $6.5 million, even though the roughly 280 participating commissioners were paid only for their expenses. (This figure was tabled by Quebec treasury board president Pauline Marois in a March 1995 pre-budget document, which also estimated the total cost of the coming referendum at $70 million.)[46] Such an unexpectedly exorbitant price tag was a gift to Parizeau's critics in the National Assembly, who again accused him of squandering public money on his partisan obsessions. Most of the hearings were broadcast on Quebec cable TV, but they proved to be a "ratings bust," in the words of one sardonic observer, "because they couldn't possibly compete with the live coverage of the O.J. Simpson trial."[47]

The commissions heard much of what they expected to hear—endorsements of Quebec sovereignty, advice on the referendum question (including 200 alternative wordings), and input into the drafting of a new constitution. And despite the boycott by Daniel Johnson and other federalists, Quebecers unsympathetic to separation showed up to express their views. One pointed example was the appearance of Hull mayor Yves Ducharme at the Outaouais commission to warn that the separation of Quebec could produce an economic "disaster" for his city. "We need guarantees, not just words," Ducharme said. "We need clear, detailed answers."[48]

In general, however, the hearings did not go as anyone had expected. Quebecers felt no obligation to keep to the premier's agenda, voicing instead their varied and idiosyncratic concerns about life in the province. People showed up to play patriotic folk songs on their guitars, to complain about their pension benefits, to lobby for drug rehabilitation, to complain about video poker machines, abortion, and school board funding, to discuss daycare, poverty, and milk production, to advocate for a pacifist and arms-free Quebec, and to grouse about the cost of the hearings themselves. In one renowned incident, a woman from the Lanaudière region of Quebec attended a hearing to complain about having to pay long-distance charges to call her friends in a neighbouring village. Such a cacophony amounted to the law of unintended consequences at work. "The commissions produced a 'boomerang' effect that magnified the cleavages in Quebec society," an academic study later noted. "Rather than galvanize support for sovereignty, as the PQ had hoped, the commissions alienated minority groups, splintered francophone Quebecers, and failed to structure any consensus on Quebec's future as a sovereign nation."[49]

Worse yet for Jacques Parizeau, support for sovereignty did not budge. The anticipated breakthrough did not materialize. In late January, a Créatec/CROP/SOM survey of 10,000 Quebec voters (described as the largest ever conducted in Canada) revealed that 60 per cent would vote No on the question "Do you want Quebec to separate from Canada and become an independent country?"[50] The same poll also found that 62 per cent of Quebecers preferred a clear and direct question on Quebec separation, compared with only 25 per cent who said that they preferred Parizeau's question referencing the PQ's draft bill.[51] One month later, in late February, when the sovereignty hearings were in full swing, a CROP/Environics poll found that the historic 60–40 split in favour of federalism was holding fast.[52] A Léger and Léger poll taken at the same time showed that roughly 70 per cent of the undecided voters in

Quebec—the butterflies—were paying little or no attention to the commissions.[53] Some commissioners noticed that sovereignists attending the hearings had grown increasingly disconsolate. "Why a hasty referendum, Mr. Parizeau?" asked retired businessman André Pépin at a session of the Montérégie commission in Vaudreuil. "Why not give your team time to prove itself? Let the next election serve as the referendum, and Quebec's adversaries will be confounded by a crushing majority."[54]

As if all of this were not disheartening enough for Jacques Parizeau, the premier faced mounting criticism from within Quebec that his obsession with sovereignty was impairing his ability to govern. "The Parti Québécois declared itself ready to take power, and the voters trusted it," wrote Jean-Jacques Samson in *Le Soleil*. "Yet the achievements of the first six months are few and far between. The mandate from the Quebec population was to govern, not to devote every bit of energy to the promotion of sovereignty."[55] The premier took yet another hit when Quebecers reacted with equanimity to Paul Martin's hell-or-high-water budget in February, which sought to cut federal spending by almost $14-billion over two years. All of a sudden, one of the sovereignists' most potent economic arguments—that Quebec should detach itself from an insolvent Canada—looked untenable, if not fanciful. Paired with new analyses from the likes of veteran economist Marcel Côté, who warned his fellow Quebecers that sovereignty would usher in an "unprecedented convergence of negative economic factors" (currency devaluation, rising interest rates, capital flight, layoffs, the collapse of the construction industry), little remained of the premier's easy assertion that Quebecers would be economically better off after a Yes vote.[56]

All of this was music to the ears of the No side, of course. The sovereignty hearings "appear to be going nowhere," observed an elated Jean Chrétien.[57] There was no getting around it, admitted Montreal commission chair Marcel Masse. The public "is not prepared to approve the draft law in its present state."[58]

A battered Jacques Parizeau was forced to acknowledge the obvious. On March 26, he told the youth wing of the PQ that "Quebecers aren't ready right now to vote in favour of sovereignty."[59] Ten days later he announced that he was postponing the referendum. "Given what's at stake and Quebecers' thirst for information," he conceded, "it would be hasty to hold a referendum this spring."[60] Speaking before the sovereignty commission in Beauport, Parizeau's deputy premier, Bernard Landry, lauded the decision. "I do not want to be the second in command of the Light Brigade which was exterminated in the Crimea in twenty minutes because of the irresponsibility of its commanders," he said. "Our troops do not want to be sent to the slaughter-house."[61]

~

No longer content to merely stand back, mind their manners, and let the separatists dig themselves into holes of their own making, emboldened federalists now demanded that Jacques Parizeau keep his promise to Quebecers and get on with his referendum vote. "Every day that that decision is not taken," said Daniel Johnson, "other decisions on social, economic, budgetary and fiscal matters, as well as our relationship with the rest of Canada, are left in abeyance. For a government that said they were really going to move and shake, all we've had are delays and delays, commissions and committees. They're all talk and no action."[62] Jean Chrétien was equally bullish. "For me, it's quite evident that the people want to settle the matter, and I don't think they will gain anything waiting until the fall. There will be advantages for Quebecers if we settle this."[63] Asked when he thought the referendum should be held, Chrétien was unambiguous. "*Au plus sacrant,*" he replied. ("As soon as bloody possible.")[64]

Though Canadian federalists had no way of knowing it, the apparent disintegration of Jacques Parizeau's *projet de souveraineté* in the spring of 1995 marked the high-water point of the No campaign, such as it was. And notwithstanding the acknowledged danger of provoking a backlash among Quebecers, the federalists' barbs smacked increasingly of condescension and hubris. Even the normally cautious Daniel Johnson took to mocking the beleaguered premier. "We've come a long way from the exemplary ethic they claimed they wanted to bring to government," Johnson told a Montreal fundraiser in early March. "It's got to the point where Jacques Parizeau probably wants to distribute a card on which the word 'Yes' is written, and he'll say: 'Just write the question down beside it.'"[65]

Many Canadian pundits followed suit, haughtily pronouncing Parizeau's referendum gambit DOA. "Separatism is dead," wrote University of Toronto historian Michael Bliss. "Really, is there more than about a 2 per cent chance that Quebec will not be part of Canada in the year 2000?"[66] *Toronto Star* columnist Richard Gwyn agreed. Sovereignty, said Gwyn, had gone the same way as Monty Python's parrot.[67]

"Is there still someone who wants to hold a referendum on sovereignty in 1995?" asked Jacques Parizeau dejectedly en route to a meeting with his three closest advisors.

"It would be an exaggeration to say that those who wanted a referendum in 1995 were in the room with the premier," said one of those present, PQ strategist Jean-François Lisée. "It would be an exaggeration, but just barely."[68]

CHAPTER SEVEN

Les Virages

Lucien Bouchard had never been the sort of man to sit on his hands and wait for others to act. Even as Jacques Parizeau was scrambling to salvage what remained of his sovereignty plan, the Bloc leader—as he had done so many times before—was charting his own course.

Quebec sovereignists, Premier Parizeau among them, had always said that there were many paths to sovereignty. So no one was overly surprised when some leading Quebec nationalists began to voice their own constructive criticisms of the premier's referendum strategy. In late February, for example, Université Laval political scientist Guy Laforest told *Le Devoir* he thought the premier would be better off delaying his referendum beyond 1995 than suffering the ignominy of a federalist victory. "In order for his project to have any chances of winning," said Laforest, "Mr. Parizeau had to meet three conditions: a flawless government, a vast non-partisan coalition and an exhilarating process. Nearly six months after the election of a Péquiste government, none of the three conditions have been met."[1] Laforest's intention was not to undermine Jacques Parizeau but to light a fire under him.[2] Like many sovereignist intellectuals in Quebec, in fact—a group the premier himself called "the persistent pens"—Laforest had taken up a front-line position defending Quebec's right to self-determination against some of Canada's constitutional heavyweights.[3] His credibility as a principled sovereignist was above reproach. When he spoke, people listened.

But as it happened, the intended object of Professor Laforest's remarks, Premier Parizeau, was on vacation in Mexico, incommunicado, and it was Lucien Bouchard, newly returned to active political duty, whose imagination he fired. Asked what he thought of Laforest's comments, the Bloc leader said that he thought postponing the referendum would be unwise. "I think we have to hold it," he said. "It makes no sense to wait even longer for Quebecers to decide."[4] Then, in the next breath, Bouchard casually floated an idea he knew was anathema to Jacques Parizeau and many other hard-line separatists. "The [referendum] question should make some reference to an economic union," he suggested. "Perhaps the question wouldn't lead to sovereignty the night of the referendum vote but would lead there automatically if there is an economic association with the rest of Canada."[5]

Bouchard's remarks rocked Quebec, as he undoubtedly knew they would. "Dust off the hyphen," exclaimed Montreal columnist Don Macpherson. Talk of René Lévesque's sovereignty-association was back in the air.[6]

With Jacques Parizeau away, it fell to PQ deputy premier Bernard Landry to react to Bouchard's proposal. And react he did, though not as anyone expected. The idea of an economic union was already implied in the PQ's draft bill, said an enthusiastic Landry. "If it has to be made explicit, why not?"[7]

The deputy premier could have cleaved to his boss's referendum plan and defended his government's draft bill as written. Indeed, under normal circumstances, it was virtually unthinkable that he would do anything else, given the premier's temporary absence. But this was a critical moment for the "people and the nation" of Quebec, as Landry liked to say. If the achievement of a Yes vote meant tweaking the referendum question a little, then so be it. Landry was a hardened veteran of separatist politics who had cut his teeth in René Lévesque's first cabinet. He could sense which way the wind was blowing. It was spilling out of Jacques Parizeau's sails and filling Lucien Bouchard's.

~

Just moments before he escorted by-election winner Lucienne Robillard into the House of Commons on February 22, Jean Chrétien surprised her by naming her to two cabinet portfolios: minister of labour and minister responsible for the federal campaign in the Quebec referendum. Announcing her appointment, the prime minister noted that it was the same job Pierre Trudeau had given him before the 1980 referendum. "I think he can teach me," said Robillard of Chrétien. "And he won in 1980, so I hope I can do exactly the same thing."[8]

The forty-nine-year-old Robillard, a social worker by training, had been the MNA for the riding of Chambly until narrowly losing her seat to a PQ candidate in the 1994 provincial election. Bringing her into the federal cabinet was intended as an "olive branch" to the provincial Liberals. "She had been a good provincial cabinet minister," Eddie Goldenberg later recalled, "with a reputation of being a solid performer who could be trusted not to make mistakes."[9] Robillard could also be tough. "I tell you, we'll have a big fight," she asserted in a mid-February speech. "All the people who believe in Canada will be together."[10] But was she tough enough to withstand the onslaught that awaited her in the House of Commons? "This is the same woman who sat next to [Daniel] Johnson when they said the status quo was unacceptable," sniped the Bloc's Gilles Duceppe. "Now she'll defend the status quo with the architect of 1982. She will have to explain where her rumba-dancing on the constitution is leading her."[11]

The witty but incisive Duceppe had struck at the heart of the feds' own looming referendum dilemma. Jacques Parizeau's stalled sovereignty initiative was a boon to the Chrétien Liberals—but only superficially, since it relieved them of having to formulate an inspired, creative, workable alternative to the sovereignists' grand plans. The prime minister's tough talk on Parizeau's draft bill was adroit, to be sure—unconstitutional and gutless, he called it—but tough talk alone would not cement Quebecers' loyalty to Canada. Skewering Parizeau might be a clever *tactic*, but what was the overarching *strategy*?

For months, the feds' own answer to this question was that they were defending not the status quo but flexible federalism. "Our federalism is flexible," Jean Chrétien would say. "We must be practical and tackle one problem at a time, in the best interests of all Canadians."[12] Since their election victory in 1993, Liberal ministers liked to boast, they had signed fifty-four agreements with the provinces, nine of them with Quebec. "We solve problems as they arise," said Marcel Massé of his government's record. "We just believe it's better to solve the problems in a pragmatic way, [rather] than in a constitutional way."[13] How, exactly, this conception of federalism marked a departure from the status quo the Liberals were reluctant to say. Their party had, after all, been "solving problems" with the provinces since Laurier's time and arguably earlier. What they did say was that "flexible federalism" was not synonymous with "renewed federalism," the phrase Pierre Trudeau had used during the 1980 referendum campaign to shore up the No vote, and one which the sovereignists still held against Jean Chrétien.

Beyond that, as extraordinary as it seems in retrospect, the feds' overarching strategy was to act as if the sovereignist threat was no threat at all. "The sense in Ottawa was that we should not formally organize contingency plans," Justice Minister Allan Rock later observed. "I don't recall there having been an express instruction from the Prime Minister's Office or anywhere else. But I think it was understood that we were not going to be engaging in contingency planning because to do so would signal weakness."[14] Seen in the light of this ostrich-like reflex, Jean Chrétien's appointment of Lucienne Robillard was intended to send a blunt message to the Yes camp. The prime minister was so confident that Quebecers would vote No to sovereignty, he was signalling, that he could put a rookie in charge of the national unity file and devote his own energies to the country's more pressing problems. Asked what he thought about Lucien Bouchard's and Bernard Landry's idea of changing the referendum question to include some kind of association with Canada, Chrétien was cocky and dismissive. "The PQ at this moment is in a complete mess," he replied, "and they will probably withdraw their question."[15]

The vacationing Jacques Parizeau, on the other hand, understood immediately what Bouchard's musings had portended—and so did his anxious aides.[16] No sooner had the premier returned home than he was mired in requests from eager sovereignists to build some kind of union with Canada into his referendum plan. A journalist asked him his opinion of sovereignty-association. "I am not exactly a fan of that," Parizeau replied drily.[17]

Yet as even his critics noted, the premier was learning how to adapt. The essence of his draft bill remained Section One: *Quebec is a sovereign country*. Beyond that, he conceded, anything might be possible. "If the rest of Canada suddenly made interesting proposals after sovereignty," he observed, "I wouldn't say I wouldn't look at them."[18]

~

On April 5, when Jacques Parizeau announced the postponement of the referendum, Lucien Bouchard saw an opening. Just two days later, he was scheduled to address the first "national" convention of the Bloc Québécois in four years, which meant a live audience of roughly 1,400 party faithful in Montreal and massive media exposure throughout Quebec. The time would never be better, reasoned the Bloc leader, to breathe new life into the *péquistes'* faltering sovereignty campaign. Without consulting either the premier or his own party delegates, Bouchard and his closest aides drafted a twenty-page speech centring on the theme of *un virage*—a sharp turn. It would, in the words of Quebec sovereignist Daniel Turp, mark "a turning point in the history of contemporary Quebec and Canada."[19]

Bouchard's appearance at the Bloc convention the evening of April 7 was choreographed to take full advantage of both his natural charisma and the aura that had built up around him after his near-fatal illness. Leaning on the cane that had for many Canadians come to symbolize his courage and determination, Bouchard moved slowly through the crowd, stopping frequently to greet delegates and accept their well-wishes. Many had not seen him in person since his hospitalization and met him with moist eyes. By Bouchard's side—indeed, holding his hand as he approached the stage—was his wife, Audrey Best, whose loyalty and courage throughout her husband's ordeal had also touched the hearts of Quebecers. As he took the podium, the cheering of the crowd was thunderous. Fit and focused in his tailored black suit and blue power tie, Bouchard conveyed a powerful message: this was a moment of truth, for him and for the party he personified.

Bouchard knew that his first task was to inspire. He opened his speech with invocations of Québécois pride and exhortations for the people to take a "leap of faith" on sovereignty. "My grandparents, Joseph and Lydia Bouchard, didn't ask for guarantees," Bouchard told the crowd. "And René Lévesque didn't ask for guarantees of success before forming the Parti Québécois and setting Quebec on the road to its future."[20] Thanks to the PQ's sovereignty commissions, he continued, Quebecers had been spared a "premature" referendum. The people were "ready to say Yes to a unifying project," but with a crucial caveat. "The sovereignty project must quickly embrace a change of direction [*virage*] that will draw Quebecers closer to one another and to the project itself, and will open up a credible future path for new Quebec–Canada relations."[21] What was needed, said Bouchard, was "a new economic partnership between a sovereign Quebec and Canada" and a joint European Union–styled parliament to govern it. And if Quebec voters could not be persuaded to support such a partnership, the referendum should be postponed, for years if necessary.[22]

Less than six metres away, seated in the audience for Bouchard's epochal speech, was Jacques Parizeau, cameras trained on his every gesture. He had little choice but to join the crowd and applaud his sovereignist ally. But beneath his frozen grin, he was unnerved by what he had heard. In one stroke, Bouchard had gutted the PQ's *projet de souveraineté*, supplanting it with his own blueprint for sovereignty-association. Parizeau knew full well what the word *virage* implied—a two-referendum scenario *à la* René Lévesque, in which Quebecers would first vote on sovereignty and later on a partnership deal with Canada.[23] It was exactly the sort of scenario that the premier had spent the last decade working to avoid. It was 1980 all over again.

Moreover, there was something of the personal in Bouchard's challenge to Parizeau. The leader of the Bloc Québécois was telling the leader of the Parti Québécois to "back off," as one observer put it, which was tantamount to hijacking the referendum debate.[24] Lest anyone miss his meaning, Bouchard reinforced it over the next few days in bluntly worded public statements. Jacques Parizeau's views and his own were distinct, he said, and the premier's were plainly in retreat. "Obviously the population doesn't like, doesn't accept, the full scope of the [PQ] project as it is," Bouchard observed. "I think we lost ground in the last month because we had to wait for the results of the consultation and the silence was very costly for us." Pressed about his idea of a joint Canada–Quebec parliament, he acknowledged that "the Parti Québécois never agreed with that." Asked whether Parizeau could count on his unconditional support, Bouchard refused to dissemble. "I have to wait before giving any unconditional agreement," he replied. "I will not sign any blank cheque to anyone. That wouldn't be responsible."[25]

Jacques Parizeau's private reaction to Bouchard's effrontery was reportedly "defiant."[26] His public response was to assert his own authority—which, of course, reinforced the impression that he thought Bouchard had deliberately undermined him. "There is one matter on which there must be no confusion," said Parizeau. "I am the premier of Quebec."[27] In response to Bouchard's suggestion that the referendum should be delayed indefinitely, the premier stood his ground. "I insist on saying one thing here," he said. "The referendum on sovereignty will take place in 1995. It always has been a formal commitment."[28]

Undeterred, Bouchard volleyed back, threatening to boycott a losing sovereignty campaign. "If, in the fall, nothing has changed and we realize that we are still at 44 or 43 per cent," asked the Bloc leader, "do we hold a referendum we know we will lose? If there is one thing I do not wish, it is to assist or participate—we will see—in a referendum campaign that will lead us to sure defeat."[29]

Parizeau retorted that he thought Bouchard's idea of a European-styled union was pure wishful thinking.[30] "You will understand my skepticism as to the possibilities [that] English Canada will ever accept things of that kind," said the premier, "when even a toothless definition of a distinct society was unacceptable."[31] Polls continued to show that Parizeau was dead right about this.[32]

The bickering continued for three long days—all of it in public. "If we call it a turn each time someone has an interesting idea," quipped the premier, "we'll end up with stiff necks."[33] Within Quebec, some observers downplayed the schism, arguing that disagreement was simply disagreement and that Bouchard and Parizeau could easily rise above their differences for the referendum campaign. Others maintained, in contrast, that the feud was ferocious, bringing to light divisions that had always been present in the separatist movement. Almost everyone agreed that, as the *Globe and Mail* put it, "both leaders, men of tremendous egos, had become trapped in a game of one-upmanship."[34]

Parizeau, who had the most to lose, adopted a diversion strategy. "They tell me there's a spat in the sovereignist camp," the premier observed. "I say yes, perhaps there is a spat in the sovereignist camp on a certain number of ideas and objectives, things like that. But how come there's no spat among my [federalist] adversaries? It's the absence of a spat that comes from nothing. They don't know what to propose."[35] The premier knew that his feud with Bouchard was a gift to the No side and tried to forestall the inevitable. But once again, the canny Daniel Johnson took full advantage. How could the premier make any claim to credibility when it came to achieving "stable relations with our neighbors," asked Johnson, when he "is unable to get along with his main ally, Lucien Bouchard?"[36]

A public spat between the two leading lights of the Quebec sovereignty movement could not be permitted to go on forever. Not surprisingly, it was Jacques Parizeau, isolated and under siege, who was forced to sue for peace. There were whispers that several ranking PQ cabinet ministers—including deputy premier Bernard Landry—had been part of the *Bouchardiste* "putsch" against Parizeau.[37] Mario Dumont came out in support of Bouchard's idea of an EU-styled partnership, saying that it represented an opportunity to broaden the "rainbow coalition."[38] So did a group of Quebec academics that included Guy Laforest.[39] At a reportedly chilly meeting of Parizeau,

Bouchard, and their top advisors on April 10, there was a consensus that the spat had hurt the sovereignist cause and that damage control was in order. A chastened Parizeau told the National Assembly the next day that despite appearances the schism was not serious. An important debate had merely been opened. "There are those who currently believe that a change of direction must be taken in certain things," he acknowledged. "Others believe, on the contrary, there is no reason to change direction. This is going to be discussed."⁴⁰

What was needed, Parizeau knew, was an honourable means of mending sovereignist fences. His timing was fortuitous. In a final effort to salvage the work of the PQ sovereignty commissions, the premier had in March announced the formation of a national sovereignty commission comprising the heads of the eighteen regional commissions and members of the PQ, Bloc Québécois and ADQ. This "super-commission" was scheduled to table its report on April 19, just days away. Parizeau knew a fig leaf when he saw one. He began laying the ground for his own *virage*. "We will wait for the commissions," the premier told the National Assembly during one of his many animated debates with Daniel Johnson. "Until April 19, we will continue to listen to Quebecers, and then we will hear from the national commission, which is the result of the great effort at democratic reflection that took place in Quebec."⁴¹ If the report of the super-commission recommended sovereignty-association, Parizeau was signalling, he would move with the people.⁴²

The 102-page *Report of the National Commission on the Future of Quebec* was tabled as scheduled in a formal ceremony in the Salon Rouge of the National Assembly—yet another effort by Premier Parizeau to attach pomp and circumstance to the sovereignist paper trail. The premier attended, of course, along with his wife, Lisette Lapointe. Representing the Bloc Québécois were Gilles Duceppe and Michel Gauthier. Lucien Bouchard was not present. He remained at home in Montreal, fuelling speculation that his differences with Parizeau remained unresolved. The text of the report, which Parizeau and his aides had read in advance, surprised no one. "Sovereignty is the only option likely to satisfy the collective aspirations of Quebecers," it stated. "Once it is achieved, sovereignty will signal for Quebec a new beginning in a partnership with Canada that does not eventually exclude some form of political union."[43]

Parizeau gave a short speech at the tabling ceremony, choosing his scripted words fastidiously and taking no questions afterwards. "The challenge to the government is to integrate the recommendations of the commission, the recommendations of Quebecers into its plans," said the premier. "At first glance it seems to me that this approach offers the grounds of common agreement for several forces in the camp for change. For my part, I find my convictions and my struggle. It seems to also have an echo of the proposals made recently by Lucien Bouchard."[44] Speaking directly to the commissioners arrayed behind him, including super-commission chair Monique Vézina, Parizeau dipped his toe in the sovereignty-association pool for the first time. "You are asking us to clearly indicate that Quebec's accession to sovereignty does not exclude forms of political union that would be mutually advantageous to Quebec and Canada," he said. "I say to you frankly that the national commission report gives us a strong hand in establishing the gradual progression between the unavoidable economic association, the desirable political association, and the association that is conceivable."[45] Later the same day, Parizeau announced that he would be amending his draft bill on sovereignty and launching a new round of consultations with his caucus and riding associations. There was no time to lose.

On April 22, Parizeau and Lucien Bouchard held a joint press conference to announce the end of their feud. "There was a spat and how was the spat solved?" asked the premier. "By the voice of democracy— that is, the voice of the national commission. Mr. Bouchard and I will conduct the referendum campaign hand in hand."[46] Having plainly usurped Parizeau, Bouchard now endeavoured to be gracious. "This was not a contest between people," he said. "It was not a test of wills. It was just a strong contribution—a tough contribution I admit it—to how the project would be defined. But Mr. Parizeau is clearly in charge. I never, never, never contested Mr. Parizeau's leadership."[47]

Two days later, on April 24, Jacques Parizeau announced that a formal offer of political union with Canada would be made before the referendum on sovereignty. "Quebec must draw its own [sovereignty] project and should also suggest in good faith various possibilities of cooperation with Canada," he said.[48] Pressed by Daniel Johnson in the National Assembly to move beyond "clowning and buffoonery" and explain his "zigzag tactics," Parizeau did his best to paint his retreat from *séparatisme* as forward-looking and well-suited to the times. Like Canada and the United States, he explained—sovereign countries with a complex network of economic linkages—Canada and a sovereign Quebec would continue to be bound by NAFTA and the GATT. "The fundamental economic association of Canada and Quebec will remain indestructible," said Parizeau.[49]

It was a well-rehearsed argument, but not one that Quebecers had ever expected from a stalwart separatist like Jacques Parizeau. The premier himself understood this. "I know I'm not the most credible of individuals," Parizeau conceded. "I tried for years to set up a system where the basic elements of economic association could not be changed. Now people tell me, go one step further, offer other forms of association that are not necessarily inevitable. All right, I'm game, I'll try. But I need the help of all the others in the sovereignty family."[50]

～

Quebecers' responses to Bouchard's *virage* and Parizeau's *volte-face* varied. Some expressed sympathy for the premier's dilemma. Others applauded the sovereignists' dogged determination to achieve "*un rapport rassembleur*" ("a unifying relationship").[51] There was general agreement that the super-commission had given Parizeau a "graceful way out of the rift with Bloc Québécois Leader Lucien Bouchard," as one observer put it.[52] More than this, there was an acknowledgement within Quebec that the spat, the ensuing debate, and the eventual consensus in favour of a new partnership with Canada were part and parcel of a national conversation Quebecers had been conducting since the Quiet Revolution. As the sardonic but astute professor Daniel Latouche noted, this was an aspect of Quebec politics about which English Canadians sometimes seemed wilfully obstinate. "Poor Lucien," wrote Latouche in the wake of the sovereignists' reconciliation. "Now he knows that it's actually easier to convince Jacques Parizeau than almost anybody west of the Ottawa River."[53]

Latouche was exactly right. English Canadians almost to a person—their credulity already strained by what they perceived as separatist scheming on the draft bill and the sovereignty commissions—saw the old, familiar strains of opportunism and megalomania in Bouchard's triumph over Parizeau. The Bloc leader showed "breathtaking arrogance," fumed Montreal *Gazette* columnist William Johnson.[54] "Bouchard can't stand anyone else being in charge," said *Toronto Star* columnist Rosemary Spears.[55] "The knife wounds in Jacques Parizeau's back look familiar," wrote Jeffrey Simpson, alluding to Bouchard's betrayal of Brian Mulroney five years earlier.[56] An irascible Andrew Coyne announced the "slow death" of separatism in the face of Quebecers' deep and irreconcilable divisions.[57] Did Jacques Parizeau actually believe that Canadians would trade the current federal arrangement, in which Quebec had 25 per cent representation in parliament, for some new partnership in which it would have 50 per cent?[58] "The [super-commission] report is dishonest to the core," answered the *Toronto Star*. "This is a profoundly cynical document, drawn up by propagandists who are prepared to promise anything to get people to vote for separation."[59] The consensus among Canadians living outside Quebec was that "silly season" had opened in the province.[60]

Yet the events of April 1995—the wholesale recasting of the *projet de souveraineté* in the direction of a new partnership with Canada—were ominous for Canadian federalists. "It's a whole new ball game," the *Toronto Star* correctly noted.[61] Even before the release of the super-commission report, an Environics survey showed that 51 per cent of Quebecers would support sovereignty if it came bundled with an association with Canada. A Léger and Léger poll taken immediately after Bouchard's *virage* speech put the number at 53.1 per cent—fully 9 per cent higher than the number of Quebecers who said they would vote Yes for sovereignty alone.[62] The tide had turned, boasted an increasingly confident Lucien Bouchard. The polls were "extremely positive," he observed. "They give us a majority and we know we're going to win—we know that now. We're working on a winning formula."[63] Pollster Jean-Marc Léger agreed. "If federalists don't put forward soon any new proposals or alternatives," he warned, "the PQ has, as of now, equal chances to win or to lose the referendum."[64]

The immediate, visceral reaction of the federalist No camp was to attack sovereignist conceit and insist that the issue was Quebec separation, plain and simple. "We have to keep repeating the reasons to vote No," said Michel Bélanger, head of the No campaign.[65] Daniel Johnson agreed. "We can't unilaterally decree a marriage while drawing up the divorce papers," he said drily. A testy Jean Chrétien was asked his opinion of the super-commission report while inspecting peacekeeping troops headed for war-torn Bosnia. "If you want to separate, do it," snapped the prime minister. "But don't try to have the best of both worlds at the same time. Why get out to get back in? It's a waste of time."[66] A week later, speaking from prepared notes at a Liberal fundraiser in Montreal, Chrétien accused the PQ government of cynically trying to mislead Quebecers. "This way of governing shows—and I measure my words very carefully—a contempt for democracy," he said.[67] English-Canadian pundits again applauded the federalists' tough line. "No divorce with bedroom privileges," they insisted.[68]

Seen in retrospect, late April 1995 marked a fork in the road for Jean Chrétien, Daniel Johnson, and their federalist allies. It was their last opportunity to respond forcefully to the sovereignists' program without seeming opportunistic or desperate themselves. They could have reacted to the retrenchment of the Yes camp by offering Quebecers something substantive—either by way of constitutional reforms or, more plausibly, by articulating a defence of Canada that challenged the cliché that the country was a "dead end." Reform leader Preston Manning demanded that, at the very least, Jean Chrétien explain his position on sovereignty-association and commit himself to a Canada-wide "clear-the-air" referendum if the Yes side won in Quebec.[69] Other increasingly anxious federalists made similar appeals.

But the leaders of the No side would have none of it. There would be no change in strategy. "The only thing that you have to tell the Quebecers at this time," Jean Chrétien told reporters, "is that the project that is being proposed is the separation of Quebec from Canada. And everybody knows Quebecers don't want to quit Canada."[70]

~

On May 19, 1995, Jacques Parizeau, Lucien Bouchard, and Mario Dumont met in a Montreal hotel to begin negotiations on a joint "action plan" for a fall referendum. Less than a month later, on June 12, the three reunited for a public ceremony at the Château Frontenac in Quebec City. There they signed off on a seven-page "Tripartite Agreement" that would form the basis of a united Yes campaign. "We have reached agreement on a common project to be submitted in the referendum," read the preamble of the accord, "a project that responds in a modern, decisive and open way to the long quest of the people of Québec to become masters of their destiny." Photographs of the three leaders smiling and linking arms made the nation's front pages. They christened their new alliance the *camp du changement* (camp of change).

The tripartite accord envisaged both Quebec sovereignty—defined as full control of taxes, laws, and treaties—and a negotiated "partnership" with Canada. After a Yes vote in a fall referendum, according to the document, the National Assembly would have one year to negotiate a new economic and political deal with Canada. If these negotiations were successful, Quebec sovereignty would be declared and the new treaty with Canada ratified. "If the negotiations prove to be fruitless," on the other hand, "the National Assembly will be empowered to declare the sovereignty of Québec without further delay." The accord provided for the creation of a "Partnership Council" composed of an equal number of ministers from each country. The decisions of this council would require unanimity, giving both countries a veto. A "Parliamentary Assembly" with proportional representation from each country would serve as a chamber of sober second thought. A "Tribunal" would adjudicate disputes, and a "Secretariat" would serve as the partnership's permanent bureaucracy. Areas of common interest for the new partnership would include trade policy, transportation, defence, monetary policy, environmental protection, and postal services.

The June 12 accord was a masterful mélange of the ideas and prerogatives of all three sovereignist leaders. Mario Dumont got a blueprint for sovereignty-association that conformed to the ADQ platform in almost every important respect. The key exception was the insistence that Canada and Quebec be equal partners, fifty-fifty, in any new union—the principle on which Lucien Bouchard was prepared to stake his career. The big winner, however, was Jacques Parizeau. By the terms of the accord, Quebec would become sovereign within a year of a Yes victory, with or without a new deal with Canada. This was the most ingenious compromise embodied in the accord. Lucien Bouchard believed that Canada would have no choice but to play ball after a Yes vote and quickly negotiate a new deal with Quebec. The threat to Canada's bond rating alone would force it to the bargaining table. Parizeau was far less sanguine. To him—and to many Canadians watching from the sidelines—the idea that Confederation could be renegotiated from the ground up in twelve months was fanciful.

At the signing ceremony, Premier Parizeau stated that the tripartite agreement had "historical importance."[71] He was correct about this. But what made this historic compromise between Parizeau-styled separatism and Bouchard-styled sovereignty-association possible—what had changed since René Lévesque's day—was the rules governing international trade under globalization. The text of the accord revealed unmistakably that behind Quebec's velvet-gloved offer to negotiate a new deal with Canada lay the iron fist of NAFTA and the GATT. "The new rules and the reality of international trade will allow a sovereign Québec, even without a formal Partnership with Canada, continued access to external markets, including the Canadian economic space," it stated. "Moreover, a sovereign Quebec could, on its own initiative, keep the Canadian dollar as its currency." Quebec no longer needed Canada's blessing to become a sovereign state because Canada could no longer leverage Quebec's economy.

Little wonder that Jacques Parizeau was happy with the agreement.

"Sovereignty will be achieved," he said.[72] Years later, Parizeau recollected—entirely accurately—that although the partnership idea had been "forced" on him at the Bloc Québécois convention, it had not come at the expense of his bedrock convictions. He had held the line. "[A] refusal by Canada to negotiate would not stop Quebec from moving forward," he recalled proudly.[73]

For Quebecers, perhaps the most salient clause in the tripartite accord concerned the proposed partnership negotiations with Canada. Hoping to attract not only the undecided butterflies but also disgruntled federalists to their sovereignty project, the three party leaders promised to bring full transparency to the negotiating process. At the signing ceremony, Lucien Bouchard was emphatic on the point. "It is a sacred commitment of sovereignists that the offer will be made to Canada," he said.[74] Jacques Parizeau felt so strongly about the need for openness that he proposed naming provincial Liberals to the negotiating committee.[75]

Surprisingly perhaps, the only stick in the sovereignist mud was Mario Dumont. He rightly perceived that the tripartite accord was an agreement of convenience that might undermine his fledgling ADQ in the long run. But he signed off on it anyway, reasoning that it would be better to be a player in the referendum campaign than to watch it from the spectators' gallery. Asked how he felt about sharing podiums with Parizeau and Bouchard through a long campaign, Dumont was unenthusiastic. "They won't be the most exciting moments of my life," he mused.[76]

Quebec pundits could see that the separatist accord marked a watershed. "What is important in this deal," wrote Gilles Lesage in *Le Devoir*, "is that the sovereignist side has managed to squeeze out of the dead end where it was stuck by enlarging its base of support, and reassuring soft nationalists that things won't move too quickly after a Yes vote."[77] *Le Soleil* editorial writer Jean-Jacques Samson took a slightly more jaded view. The accord would "significantly complicate life for the federalist forces," he wrote. "The new institutions proposed and the power-sharing that is envisaged reflect the aspirations of a large number of Quebecers, who will see this model as a political and constitutional paradise. Many of them won't be overly concerned with its feasibility."[78] *La Presse* columnists dismissed the new *projet de souveraineté* as pure opportunism. "This 'offer' is not serious," wrote Lysiane Gagnon. "Worse, it is without honor."[79] Editorial writer Pierre Gravel agreed. "It's an insult to the intelligence of voters who define themselves as undecided to pretend they will be swayed by this vulgar trickery designed to eke out a Yes by promising to limit its consequences," he wrote. "It's also profoundly contemptuous to sovereignists themselves."[80]

Ordinary Quebecers seemed more impressed than the pundits. In the wake of the accord, pollster Jean-Marc Léger made the prescient announcement that popular support for sovereignty had jumped from 44 per cent to 47. Given the shrinking number of undecideds, he surmised, the referendum was now a virtual dead heat. "If this referendum campaign unfolds as the 1980 campaign did, 47 per cent of Quebecers will vote Yes," said Léger. "It wouldn't take much to change the opinion of 6 per cent of Quebecers and find ourselves with a Quebec voting for sovereignty."[81]

~

A chorus of derision could be heard wafting across the Ottawa River.

Jean Chrétien's response was to disparage the new polls along with the tripartite accord itself. "It's a mirage," he insisted. "It is still a proposition for separation, but they don't have the guts to say they are separatists." Chrétien ridiculed the sovereignists' proposal for a new union with Canada in which Quebecers would retain the privileges of Canadian citizenship. "They want to have the same passport, but who will pass the legislation on citizenship for Canada, if everybody has the right to veto the other?" he asked. "It is not very realistic. I don't know how you could manage to have an army if everybody has a veto right."[82]

Reform Party constitutional critic Stephen Harper, until now content to attack Jean Chrétien and his top ministers, took direct aim at the sovereignists. "It continues their same agenda," said Harper of the tripartite accord, "to trick Quebecers into voting for sovereignty by telling them that they are really voting for a new economic and political association. If Quebecers vote Yes they will be voting for separation. And they will put into place a set of forces that will inevitably lead to the breakup of the country in a way that is negative and is not anything like the pact that these three clowns are signing."[83] Tory leader Jean Charest, by now a prominent and popular spokesperson for the No camp, dismissed the accord as a "non-starter."[84]

Former prime minister Joe Clark, the main architect of the 1992 Charlottetown Accord, knew better. Indeed, Clark emerged as the leading federalist Cassandra in June 1995, a lone voice cautioning Canadians not to discount the appeal among Quebecers of the sovereignists' partnership plan. "We can't take a federalist victory for granted," said Clark. "There is going to be a fight. To me, there is no doubt that separation could happen."[85] Some Canadians responded to Clark's entreaties with contempt. He held merely a "community of communities" view of Canada, sniffed a *Toronto Star* editorial, and thus had "stumbled squarely into the separatist trap." Clark would do far better to keep his opinions to himself and support Jean Chrétien's strategy of ignoring the separatists, said the *Star*. "No one, least of all a former prime minister, should be suckered by these separatist theatrics."[86] Toronto business writer Jonathan Ferguson speculated that if Clark's comments had been faxed out to the world's trading desks, they might well have torpedoed the Canadian dollar and scared away jittery investors. "Joe Clark should just put a sock in it," Ferguson concluded.[87]

Across Canada, English-language editorialists adopted the same acid tone in the wake of the sovereignists' June 12 accord. The deal, they said, smacked of separatist desperation, or cynicism, or delusion, or a combination of all three. "If [partnership] negotiations went well, Quebec would separate," fulminated the Montreal *Gazette*. "If negotiations didn't go well, Quebec would separate. Little wonder the leaders were smiling. It must have been hard to keep a straight face."[88] *Gazette* editor-in-chief Joan Fraser claimed to be saddened by the "spectacle" of Jacques Parizeau turning himself into a "moral pretzel" and cynically agreeing to a plan of negotiations with Canada that he knew would fail.[89]

The *Ottawa Citizen* accused the Quebec premier of patching together a coalition of "wishy-washy sovereignists and hard-line separatists" who were bound together by nothing but "a lie."[90] The *Globe and Mail* called the partnership scheme cynical and condescending towards Quebec voters. "The separatists can dress up the question," said the *Globe*. "They can package it, qualify it, cloak it in nuance, euphemism and subtlety. They can do all of that, but at root, this is about independence, not about association."[91]

Obstreperous though they plainly were, Jacques Parizeau's anglo critics grudgingly conceded him one crucial point. In the words of a Montreal *Gazette* headline, "Despite Flip-flops, Parizeau Will Probably Live Up to Deal."[92]

~

On June 21, a little more than a week after signing the tripartite accord, Lucien Bouchard casually launched the sovereignist referendum campaign—three days before Jacques Parizeau was scheduled to make it official. "Starting today or tomorrow," said Bouchard, the referendum would be the "only preoccupation" of the Bloc Québécois caucus. "Mr. Chrétien will be preoccupied by that 100 per cent as well. We mustn't pretend that in the next two or three months there will be any other concerns."[93] The prime minister was unimpressed, and he did not appear to be pretending. "I hope," he told the House of Commons, "that if they commit themselves only to the referendum and they no longer want to do their work as MPs that they'll return their salaries."[94]

Bouchard had again stolen Jacques Parizeau's thunder, but the premier did not seem to mind. He now had his eyes on the prize—a majority vote for a sovereign Quebec. "At the end of July," said Parizeau, "we're all going to hit the ground, start doing tours and meeting the greatest number of people." He advised his *péquiste* colleagues to take their vacations "as rapidly as possible."[95]

As Canadians headed into the summer season of baseball tournaments and backyard barbecues, the referendum battle lines were coming into view. The sovereignists would campaign on their new partnership accord, and the federalists would stonewall them with accusations of mischief and skulduggery.

Many ordinary citizens drew the obvious conclusion: this was a debate they could afford to put on the back burner while they were off enjoying their summer holidays. The squabbling had been going on for eight months, after all, and still there was no referendum question and no date.

CHAPTER EIGHT

Declaring Sovereignty

The short Canadian summer of 1995 came and went. Canadians and Quebecers alike enjoyed a pleasant but wet holiday season, taking more pleasure in their lush gardens than their soggy street festivals. From May to September, Canadian news junkies were swept up in a national drama of almost unprecedented intrigue and pathos. It was not the story of the Quebec referendum campaign but the sensational trial of serial rapist and murderer Paul Bernardo and the even more salacious revelations of the role his ex-wife, Karla Homolka, had played in his crimes.

A national poll taken in the middle of the summer revealed that, in fact, Canadians had lost interest in the referendum debate. Only 22 per cent of voters thought national unity was among the most important issues facing the country, down from 35 per cent in March. Everyone drew the obvious conclusion: the net effect of the referendum campaign to date was to turn people off.[1] "Rarely have we so clearly seen the desire of citizens to get it over with," observed Claude Masson, associate publisher of *La Presse*. "The debate doesn't reach the soul nor the minds of Quebecers. It's as though politicians are speaking in a desert."[2] The word on the streets and in the cafés was that Quebecers were not even discussing the referendum. "I can't wait for it to be over," said twenty-nine-year-old Montrealer Guylaine Chabot. "Instead of influencing us, it is sickening us. I'm fed up with this. My friends and I never discuss it. It is secondary."[3] The alienation felt by some young Quebecers found expression in the popular book *Quebec Is Killing Me*, written by twenty-year-old McGill law student Hélène Jutras. "There are no jobs, there is no money, and the deficit is not going down," wrote Jutras. "I don't believe in independence anymore, and I would hope sincerely we stop talking about it."[4]

At the end of August, a group of four sovereignist academics with considerable polling experience—Jean-Herman Guay, Pierre Drouilly, Pierre-Alain Cotnoir, and Pierre Noreau—published an open letter counselling Jacques Parizeau to postpone his referendum. The Yes side had been far too optimistic in its reading of the survey data, the four had concluded, and was not within striking distance of a winning vote. In particular, polls extrapolating a fifty-fifty split among undecided voters were far too rosy, since nationalists had typically received only one-third and sometimes only one-quarter of the undecideds in the past. "Victory is much too improbable," lamented the academics.[5] The open letter was contentious in Quebec but extremely well received in English Canada, where its authors were dubbed "the Four Pollsters of the Apocalypse."[6]

That was not the only good news for the federalist No side. Polls showed that Jean Chrétien's approval ratings among Quebecers had risen markedly since he had become prime minister. In 1993, on the eve of the federal election, 16 per cent of Quebecers ranked Chrétien as the leader they most trusted. By July 1995, the number had risen to 43 per cent.[7] The prime minister knew that this figure was volatile and could just as easily deflate in the heat of the referendum campaign. But for now, he claimed to be right where he wanted to be. "I'm not losing any sleep," Chrétien said heading into Labour Day weekend. "I'm extremely confident."[8]

~

Back at No headquarters in Montreal, it was a different story. Acting on his own initiative, Daniel Johnson had in late August opened the Pandora's box of constitutional reform, something Jean Chrétien had said the federal government would not do. A schism in the No ranks opened, albeit tentatively and beneath many Quebecers' notice. But it handed the sovereignists a powerful weapon in their battle with the federalists: the accusation that Chrétien had pulled the leadership of the No campaign out from under Johnson.

The first fissure in the federalist ranks appeared in early August, when the youth wing of the Parti libéral du Québec requested that Daniel Johnson present Quebecers with a concrete alternative to sovereignty. "There is a reality that exists in Canada, you don't have to be afraid to say it," said PLQ youth president Claude-Éric Gagné. "There are provinces that, like Quebec, are calling for decentralization. Canada has to decentralize. What we are asking for is to provide details of that reality. That is the future of Canada. That is the future of Quebec."[9]

Johnson's first instinct was to circle the wagons and bring the young renegades to heel. "This is a referendum," he scolded them, "not an election, and this is not a multiple choice question. It's either Yes or No on separation."[10]

But on August 13, in a speech to 600 young Liberals, Johnson spoke expansively about the kinds of changes that would be possible after a No vote on sovereignty. To bring Quebec fully into the Canadian Constitution would require, at a minimum, distinct-society status and a restoration of Quebec's historic veto. These were the principles that Liberals had brought to Meech Lake, and they would assert them anew under Johnson's leadership. "A No is a No to a precise project that's on the table today," he said. "It's not a No to our distinct identity, to our history, to our national aspirations or our demands. Our No keeps open all the options that will allow the federation to evolve."[11]

The speech was front-page news in Quebec. "Johnson Commits Himself to Claiming the Right of Veto and Distinct Society," announced *Le Devoir*.[12] The young Liberals took credit for lighting a fire under their leader, while his sovereignist adversaries congratulated him for sharpening the debate.[13] Outside francophone Quebec, however, Canadians' response to Johnson's speech was cool. The Liberal leader should "learn the virtue of silence," they agreed, and not let a young pretender like Gagné, representing only 10 per cent of the Liberal party, force his hand.[14] "I think all of the special status issues are off the table as far as the rest of Canada is concerned," Reformer Stephen Harper again warned. "I don't care if you call it distinct society or sovereignty association. There isn't the stomach or support in the rest of the country for that kind of thing."[15]

Johnson's constitutional musings caught Jean Chrétien unawares. His initial reaction was to downplay any perceived breach in No-side solidarity. "At the moment, the problem is the referendum and the referendum is on the separation of Quebec," said the prime minister. "There is absolutely no contradiction. A political party always has a position to develop and [Johnson] talked about the constitutional principles of his party. That's normal."[16] Ten days later, however, facing enormous public pressure to follow Johnson's lead and put something concrete before Quebecers, Chrétien felt compelled to state that the position of his government had not changed. He had no intention of reopening the Constitution. "What we have to offer," said Chrétien, "is not very complicated. We are offering the best country in the world, Canada. That's what we're offering."[17] This blunt statement, too, made the headlines in Quebec. A *Le Soleil* headline said it all: "*Chrétien ferme la porte à Johnson*" ("Chrétien Slams the Door on Johnson").[18]

Again Lucien Bouchard saw an opening and took full advantage. Speaking extemporaneously to a hometown crowd of 1,200 at Alma, Quebec, where he was joined onstage for the first time by Jacques Parizeau and Mario Dumont, the Bloc leader gave a raucous address. "What gall!" said Bouchard. "[Johnson] got his marching orders today from his masters in Ottawa. They all said to him today, 'It's not you who speaks for the No side. You're not allowed to have ideas and initiatives for Quebec. You, Daniel Johnson, should lie down and shut up.'" The enthusiastic crowd urged Bouchard on. Unless Quebecers voted for sovereignty, he railed, they would become "a laughable minority" at the mercy of the federal government and the other provinces. "If the No wins, Ottawa will have a big party and English Canada will be rubbing its hands. They'll say we were right in saying Quebecers wouldn't go all the way. It will be Jean Chrétien who was right."[19]

An irate Daniel Johnson immediately took Bouchard to task, calling him arrogant and autocratic. "Who does he take himself for exactly?" asked Johnson. "Some sort of archbishop to distribute certificates of being good Quebecers or not on the basis of whether you agree with him that we should vote Yes or No? We are 6 million. To my knowledge we are all Quebecers."[20]

Johnson was "clearly embarrassed" by the feds' chilly response to his proposals, as *Journal de Montréal* columnist Michel C. Auger observed poignantly.[21] But it was equally obvious that he believed he had to do something, anything, to avoid being cast in Quebec as the defender of the status quo. Chrétien's unyielding refrain—*Quebecers are not interested in separation, and Canadians are not interested in discussing the Constitution*—had boxed him in.

Embarrassed though Johnson may have been, a Léger and Léger poll published in late August vindicated his political instincts. The survey showed that 63.9 per cent of Quebecers wanted the No side to put a new offer on the table, and only 22.6 per cent did not.[22]

~

Jacques Parizeau's summer had not been as balmy as he might have liked, either. In mid-July, for the second time since taking office, the premier's own words embroiled him in a furor of potentially calamitous proportions. (The first was his remark to the *Los Angeles Times* about Ontarians putting their feet to the Quebec flag.)

Chantal Hébert, Ottawa bureau chief of *La Presse*, broke the story on July 11, citing diplomatic "meeting notes" leaked to her by Michel Duval at Foreign Affairs Canada. The notes were based on information provided by the Dutch ambassador to Canada, Jan Fietelaars. On June 13—the day after he had signed the tripartite accord—Premier Parizeau had attended a private reception for fifteen European ambassadors at the German embassy in Ottawa. He was accompanied by Jean-François Lisée and his head of protocol, Jacques Joli-Coeur. When the conversation turned to the Quebec referendum, Parizeau told the diplomats that what counted most was to get a majority Yes vote from

Quebecers. After that, he said, "they would be like lobsters thrown in boiling water."[23] The implication of Parizeau's turn of phrase was obvious. There would be no exit from a Yes vote. Quebecers would be trapped.[24]

Once Hébert's story broke, the European diplomats scrambled to put out a unified denial. Because the EU had a Spanish president, the embassy of Spain issued the official statement. "The meeting was of a strictly private nature," read the demarche. "For that reason, [Spanish Ambassador José Luis Pardos] declines to comment on the article published in *La Presse* but he insists that Mr. Parizeau did not make the remarks attributed to him." Dutch ambassador Fietelaars back-pedalled. "There is not a word in [the *La Presse* story] that is in conformity with the truth," he said.[25] Sovereignists expressed outrage. Bernard Landry attacked the federal government for leaking "a false report to diminish [Parizeau's] honour and credibility in a very vicious way."[26] Foreign Affairs must investigate the leak, Landry demanded, and issue an apology to the premier of Quebec.

The redoubtable Chantal Hébert was unmoved. "The story speaks for itself, and it was written following all the rules of journalism," she said.[27]

Before long, it came to light that the premier's office had asked *La Presse* to hold the lobster story for seventy-two hours, a request the newspaper had granted. Among the efforts made by the PQ to get to the bottom of the matter in that three-day period was a telephone call from Bernard Landry to Ambassador Fietelaars. Jean-François Lisée later recalled the disheartening outcome of these investigations. "Our first reaction was: it's an invention," he said. "But in good faith, we wanted to check it out. We consulted the others who had been present, people from the European embassies. It was then that we realized that Parizeau probably said it."[28]

The premier himself, vacationing in France in mid-July, offered no comment on the story. Jean Chrétien declined to comment as well, but PMO spokesperson Leslie Swartman suggested that Parizeau's alleged lobster remark "confirms what we've been saying all along, that the referendum is a vote on the separation of Quebec from Canada, and it is a point of no return."[29] Daniel Johnson was less reserved. "With the arro-gance of someone who congratulates themselves prematurely at tricking Quebecers, Parizeau persists in his contempt for all of those who don't think like him," said Johnson. "The first two lobsters that he caught were Lucien Bouchard and Mario Dumont."[30] On open-line radio shows, the lobster simile served as a proxy for the entire referendum debate, fed-eralists heaping scorn on Parizeau for being sneaky and unscrupulous, separatists attacking the mischief-making of the federal government. One caller to a Montreal radio show suggested that Parizeau's lips had undoubtedly been loosened by alcohol. Another remonstrated. "I just want to tell you to lay off Parizeau on his drinking," she said. "He doesn't drink. You're just an idiot."[31]

Parizeau's faux pas ignited the national press corps. The premier had said repeatedly that "a vote for the 'new entente' will mean a vote for sovereignty," wrote Lysiane Gagnon at *La Presse*, "and too bad for the lobsters who voted in favor of 'renewed federalism.'"[32] The remark might turn out to be Parizeau's "Big Mistake," said Joan Fraser at the Montreal *Gazette*, "the error so glaringly stupid that you never recover from it." There was no point in denying that the premier had made the wisecrack, she added. "It is the kind of thing that one can perfectly envisage Mr. Parizeau saying. He is in his element with small groups of intelligent people. That is when he is at his wittiest, when he gets off his best one-liners and when he most enjoys explaining how devilishly clever his strategy is."[33] A lobster never gets out of boiling water alive, said a *Globe and Mail* editorial, and Quebecers knew it. "Thanks to the imaginative Mr. Parizeau, [they] understand the government's menu a little better today."[34] Barry Nelson of the *Calgary Herald* coined the nickname "Lobster Jack" for the premier.[35] Political cartoonists from coast to coast evinced an unanticipated mastery of crustacean anatomy.

Jean Chrétien would not exploit the lobster comment for political advantage—no doubt reckoning that Parizeau was having no trouble finding his own way into hot water.[36] But the prime minister could not stop some of his old friends from savouring the moment. Just days after the *La Presse* story broke, a group of Quebec federalists connected with the magazine *Cité Libre* founded the Ordre national du homard (National Order of the Lobster). The inaugural meeting was held at La Maison Egg Roll on Montreal's Notre-Dame Street—the site of Pierre Trudeau's famed attack on the Charlottetown Accord in 1992—and co-hosted by Liberals Roger Rolland and Jacques Hébert. "The idea is to make Quebecers relax and laugh a bit," said Hébert. "We can use a few laughs amid this lugubrious campaign."[37] Across Canada, federalists took to wearing lobster lapel pins. An Ottawa restaurant featured a dish called Lobster Parizeau. When a high-ranking Quebec official left his post in Ottawa, he was given a lobster as a farewell present.[38]

Whether or not lobsters factored into the equation, a late-summer SOM poll had revealed that Lucien Bouchard was now twice as popular among Quebec voters as Jacques Parizeau. The same poll showed that Jean Chrétien's popularity among Quebecers had surpassed Daniel Johnson's.[39]

Bouchard took note. In a series of fiery speeches, he escalated his attacks on the prime minister. "[Jean Chrétien] is dreaming every night to increase the power of Ottawa and encroach more on Quebec jurisdiction," the Bloc leader charged, "and obviously after a No [vote] that will be the first thing that Mr. Chrétien will do."[40] With the House of Commons reconvening on September 18, said Bouchard, parliament would become a key battleground in the sovereignty debate. "It will be the issue of the hour, probably the most fundamental debate ever held in a Canadian parliament. It's not about attacking a government or a personality. It's about discussing the future of Quebec and of the rest of Canada, and I have no doubt that people will be very interested. I don't know too many people who are not interested in the future of their children."[41]

~

The future of Quebec and the rest of Canada arrived over Labour Day weekend, when the PQ government announced that it was ready to unveil its revised bill on sovereignty. The ceremony would take place on Wednesday, September 6, before a live audience of 1,000 at Quebec's Grand Théâtre and across the province by television. Members of the eighteen sovereignty commissions would be in attendance. So would the six distinguished Quebecers—Jean-François Lisée, singer Gilles Vigneault, writer Marie Laberge, sociologist Fernand Dumont, and constitutional experts Andrée Lajoie and Henri Brun—tasked by Premier Parizeau to co-author a preamble to the bill, a declaration of independence worthy of a new nation.

The scene outside the theatre on September 6 belied the pollsters' claims that the sovereignty debate had left Quebecers cold. As sovereignists streamed into the venue, they were confronted on the street by an estimated 100 federalist protesters—identified in the press as mostly "elderly people" waving Canadian flags.[42]

"Will independence give me a job?" shouted Jean-Claude Lemoine, an unemployed federalist in his fifties. "Will our young people have work when they graduate?"

"Well there, you're in Canada and you're out of work," responded sovereignist Claude Peron. "When we get control of job training, we'll know what to do with it."

"Lucien Bouchard is an opportunist," replied Lemoine.

"Now you're spitting on Quebecers," said Peron.[43]

Inside the theatre, the unveiling ceremony was stage-managed for maximum emotional impact. As the house lights dimmed, Jacques Parizeau alone took the stage, making his introductory remarks under a single spotlight. Lucien Bouchard and Mario Dumont were absent, reportedly because they did not share the premier's love of "high mass," as Dumont himself put it. Thus it was Parizeau's and the Parti Québécois's moment to shine, and the premier could not have been happier. "The sweeping principles which will guide the Quebec of tomorrow," Parizeau told his rapt audience, "the values and the duties that we will want to adopt for lives in society, no one can invent them except Quebecers themselves. And that is why we are here today."[44]

After Parizeau's short speech, two of the authors of the 1,500-word declaration of sovereignty—Gilles Vigneault and Marie Laberge—stood behind separate podiums, each under a single spotlight, and read it aloud. A montage of powerful images of Quebec flowed on a giant screen between them. It was a dramatic and moving performance, climaxing with Vigneault and Laberge announcing in unison, with a soaring, backlit *fleur-de-lis* flag fluttering on the screen, "We, the people of Québec, through our National Assembly, proclaim: Québec is a sovereign country."

As the television cameras panned to the applauding Parizeau, it was evident that he was as overcome with raw emotion as he ever got. This was one of the only moments in the entire 1995 referendum campaign when Quebecers got to see Jacques Parizeau within arm's reach of his sovereignist dream, unencumbered by disappointing polls or distasteful political compromises, so close that he could practically touch it.

The text of the preamble opened with a poetic homage to the history and the people of Quebec, borrowing heavily from familiar nationalist themes. "The time has come at last to harvest what has been sown for us by four hundred years of men and women and courage, rooted in the soil and now returned to it," stated the document. Quebec's political grievances, from the promise of the Quiet Revolution, through the betrayal of 1982, to the failure of Meech and Charlottetown, were précised. "Canada, far from taking pride in and proclaiming to the world the alliance between its two founding peoples, has instead consistently trivialized it and decreed the spurious principle of equality between the provinces." Sovereignty was the only remaining option, stated the preamble—an inclusive, outward-looking, and humane sovereignty many *péquistes* had been working towards since the Sixties. A sovereign Quebec would respect the rights of First Nations, Anglo-Quebecers, and immigrants, and "acknowledge our moral duties of respect, of tolerance, of solidarity towards one another." It would eschew "authoritarianism and violence," and guarantee "the civil and political rights of individuals." It would enshrine "the equitable sharing of wealth" as its governing social principle.

The unveiling of Bill 1, as the *Act Respecting the Future of Quebec* was now known, followed. Much of it borrowed from the PQ's earlier (December 1994) draft bill, including sections providing for a new Quebec constitution, protections for non-francophones, consideration for transitioning federal civil servants, the establishment of Quebec's own judicial apparatus, and the continuity of Canadian law in the interim. As before, Quebec citizenship would be automatic for any Canadian living in the province on the day sovereignty was declared. The currency of Quebec would be the Canadian dollar. Quebec would secede with its existing borders intact and inviolable.

Gone from the new bill, however, was the powerful opening proclamation of the original, *Quebec is a sovereign country*. In its place appeared a new Section One, two clumsily worded sentences embodying the compromises that had since been imposed on Jacques Parizeau: "The National Assembly is authorized, within the scope of this Act, to proclaim the sovereignty of Québec. The Government is bound to propose to the Government of Canada the conclusion of a treaty of economic and political partnership on the basis of the tripartite agreement of June 12, 1995 reproduced in the schedule." The penultimate clause of the new bill explained how it would come into force:

> The negotiations relating to the conclusion of the partnership treaty must not extend beyond October 30, 1996, unless the National Assembly decides otherwise. The proclamation of sovereignty may be made as soon as the partnership treaty has been approved by the National Assembly or as soon as the latter, after requesting the opinion of the orientation and supervision committee, has concluded that the negotiations have proved fruitless.

Taken together, the preamble and Bill 1 were bulky and complex. Yet their essence was easily comprehended. Sovereignists—men and women committed to the political autonomy of Quebec—were asking Quebecers for the authority to negotiate a new deal with Canada and to declare independence unilaterally whether or not the negotiations succeeded. As Denis Lessard of *La Presse* noted bluntly, "A Yes in the referendum is clearly a vote for Quebec sovereignty."[45]

Still utterly confident of victory, Jean Chrétien offered no official response to the PQ declaration. Quebec Liberal MP Patrick Gagnon observed that it was not only bad history but written as if the authors "had a score to settle."[46] Daniel Johnson called the PQ's unveiling ceremony political grandstanding and the preamble a misrepresentation of history. "It's a miserable failure to the extent that it rests totally on a biased view," said Johnson. "It's a very feeble attempt on the part of the government to have history support Quebec's separation. History does not support that view."[47] Johnson took a page from the angryphones' playbook, charging that the PQ declaration embodied the aspirations of old-stock Quebecers and no one else. "It claims that Quebecers who vote No have no pride in who they are, in their identity, in their contribution to building Quebec and Canada," said Johnson. "I reject this view of history. We can vote No and be proud."[48]

Outside of separatist circles, Quebecers' responses were muted, even pensive. *Le Devoir* announced "*Une Déclaration de souveraineté toute en lyrisme*" ("A Declaration of Sovereignty Full of Lyricism") and suggested in an editorial penned by Lise Bissonnette that the preamble evoked "perilous and captivating" possibilities.[49] At the *Journal de Montréal*, in contrast, Jean-V. Dufresne lamented that the preamble set a "not very promising" tone for the country of Quebec. "It's as if the people of Quebec want to dream of independence for the sole pleasure of avenging history," he wrote.[50] Under the headline "*La complainte des dinosaures*" ("The Lament of Dinosaurs"), Alain Dubuc at *La Presse* wrote that the *péquistes* had again demonstrated that they were "cut off from Quebecers and their reality."[51] Lysiane Gagnon at *La Presse* suggested that the document seemed to have been written by "docile students" repeating by rote "the most hackneyed clichés of PQ propaganda." The preamble's evocation of "our collective heart" she called "bizarre," given modern Quebec's diversity. So, too, was the PQ's goal of establishing some new political and economic union with Canadians who had ostensibly treated Quebecers so cruelly.[52]

Elsewhere in Canada, disbelief and frustration continued to mount. Jeffrey Simpson remarked in a scathing *Globe and Mail* column that Thomas Jefferson's immortality as the author of the

American Declaration of Independence was in no way threatened by the Quebec declaration. Calling the preamble a "verbal swamp," Simpson suggested that the "spectacle" at Le Grand Théâtre may have played well to the separatist "rent-a-crowd," but even Lucien Bouchard and Mario Dumont knew that "there were better ways to spend part of an afternoon."[53] The *Toronto Star* called the ceremony "cheap political theatre" based on "the lie that Canada has 'sold out' Quebec since Confederation."[54] A *Vancouver Sun* editorial called the preamble "half-poetical, half-paranoiac," and accused Parizeau of a "classic bait-and-switch."[55] University of Toronto historian Michael Bliss claimed to be astonished by the "self-serving, blinkered view of Canada's evolution propounded by the separatist text." Go to Quebec and look around, he implored Canadians. "What a silly travesty. You don't have to know anything about history to see that the original French settlers of the valley of the St. Lawrence have preserved their identity, multiplied, and prospered as part of Canada."[56]

～

Quebecers took note of this chorus of derision, of course. "The English media are attacking Parizeau," *Le Soleil* observed bluntly.[57] The premier himself had never shied away from the role of *provocateur* and might well have savoured the firestorm his declaration of independence had sparked in the country he was planning to leave. But he had little time to dwell upon the matter. On September 7, the day after he unveiled Bill 1, Parizeau announced the long-awaited question over which Quebec's second sovereignty referendum in fifteen years would be fought. "Do you agree that Quebec should become sovereign, after having made a formal offer to Canada for a new economic and political partnership, within the scope of the bill respecting the future of Quebec and of the agreement signed on June 12, 1995?" Four days later, the premier tabled the question formally in the National Assembly.

It was an inelegant and convoluted question. As Quebecers well knew, the premier himself would have preferred something more direct. "The question was not as clear as I would have liked it because it alluded to a bill and to an agreement," he later acknowledged.[58] Daniel Johnson happily accused Parizeau of falling into his own trap of words. "It is only through confusion and obfuscation that the Parti Québécois believe they can trick Quebecers into voting Yes," Johnson remarked after reading the text of the referendum question. "The fog-maker is at work."[59] Pressed by Johnson in the National Assembly to explain to Quebecers how he had travelled so far from his separatist moorings, Parizeau again alluded to the catalyzing influence of the sovereignty commissions. "I've evolved," said the premier. "I listened to the people of Quebec, and indeed, that's what they suggested." Quebec voters were fully capable of reading the preamble, the statute, and the text of the tripartite accord, and of making an informed decision on their collective future, said Parizeau. "Quebecers will have their country."[60] The date of the referendum would almost certainly be October 30, 1995, given Quebec's strict rules on the timing of writs.[61]

The motion to table Bill 1 in the National Assembly passed easily, putting in motion a stirring debate on Quebec history and culture that lasted for several days. Jacques Parizeau used his virtually unlimited floor time in the legislature on September 11 to present a familiar history lesson to Quebecers, starting with the Plains of Abraham and culminating in "the coup of 1982."[62] Federalists led by Pierre Trudeau had betrayed an idea of Canada that had held sway since the eighteenth century, charged the premier, namely that Quebec was "a nation within a nation."[63] And despite the best efforts of "many Canadians of good will"—Brian Mulroney, Lucien Bouchard, Robert Bourassa, Marcel Masse, Monique Vézina, David Peterson, Grant Devine, even Paul Martin—a majority of their compatriots had rejected the minimal accommodations of the Meech Lake Accord and handed power to the *Trudeauiste* Jean Chrétien.[64] "On the night of his [1993] election, when Chrétien gave another destroyer of Meech, Clyde Wells, a hug on camera," said Parizeau, "he handed Quebecers the symbolic image that marked the end of the federalist dream of Quebec."[65] Bill 1 and the referendum vote, concluded the premier, would allow Quebecers "of all origins and all walks of life" to finally achieve "their goals of equality and recognition."[66]

Daniel Johnson answered the premier with a long, meticulously crafted speech in the National Assembly on September 12. It was immediately clear that Johnson was now taking the sovereignist threat extremely seriously. "This debate is of unprecedented importance," he said. In contrast with other referenda and other elections, the vote on October 30 envisaged "the end of the Canadian experience, ending Canada as we know it. That would be telling our neighbors 'Rebuild what we have destroyed.' This is the historical significance of this vote. Its effects are unprecedented."[67] Jacques Parizeau's putative history lesson of the previous day, said Johnson, was little more than "a long tirade of bullying." Quebecers were not an "endangered species," and they did not travel in "canoes and snowshoes." On the contrary, Johnson asserted, contemporary Quebecers could boast unprecedented "vitality and influence." They had progressed over the previous twenty-five years to become world leaders in fields as diverse as biotechnology and transportation, the performing arts and sport.[68] Johnson's voice cracked with emotion when he recalled how his father's dream of a French Quebec had been realized in the thirty-five years since his death.[69]

In the second half of his hour-long speech, Johnson addressed Quebecers' well-documented fears of economic dislocation, estimating the odds of Canadians agreeing to a new partnership with Quebec at roughly one in a thousand. But his overriding concern was that a Yes vote in the referendum would be *irréversible*—a word he used eight times.[70] Jacques Parizeau's referendum question was not like the one René Lévesque had put forward in 1980, Johnson warned. It would not open the door to negotiations with Canada. Rather, the PQ's scheme allowed the government of Quebec to issue a "unilateral declaration of independence" and to do so "almost instantly" after a Yes vote.[71] There would be no turning back, irrespective of how accommodating Canadians might prove to be. Quebecers had many excellent reasons to vote No, Johnson asserted, but the best of them was also the best known. There was no better place for Quebecers to realize their national dreams than within the Canadian federation that they had helped build over centuries. They did not have to sever themselves, nor their "children and grandchildren," from their past. "Quebec is, today and forever, a distinct society," Johnson concluded, "free and capable of fulfilling its destiny."[72]

Jean Chrétien waited several days before responding publicly to Jacques Parizeau's referendum question. Although he thought it dishonest and misleading, the prime minister said he relished the opportunity to finally put the sovereignist threat to rest. "There is a need for a vote," said Chrétien, "and it's very clear in my mind that it will be the last one and, of course, Canada will win." Asked during a talk at the University of Toronto why he thought the October referendum would settle the matter once and for all, Chrétien offered a blunt, unscripted reply. "Because the people are fed up," he said. "I've been in Quebec this summer talking to people. They don't want to hear about it. They want to have a good economy, they want to have a good job, they want to have good social programs, they want to live a happy life. And it's what Canada is offering to them." The prime minister refused to speculate on what might happen after a Yes vote, calling the matter "hypothetical." Instead, he followed Daniel Johnson's example and stayed resolutely on message, repeating four times in ten minutes that a Yes vote meant "a one-way ticket to separation." Jacques Parizeau and Lucien Bouchard were "hiding the truth" and would be "clobbered" if they asked an honest question, said Chrétien. "Why don't these guys want to tell the truth? I have no problem with the truth. I'm a Canadian. It's the best country in the world, and you all know that Canada will win."[73]

~

As Quebecers took stock of Bill 1 and the text of the referendum question—as generalizations about sovereignty gave way to specifics, that is—public debate in the province sharpened. The plausibility of the PQ's proposed partnership with Canada was widely disputed, since, as Jean-V. Dufresne of the *Journal de Montréal* observed, Canadians were unlikely to accept such a "humiliating surrender."[74] Three leading francophone editorialists—Alain Dubuc, Jean-Jacques Samson, and Lise Bissonnette—called upon the premier to commit himself to a second referendum in the event of a Yes victory, to allow Quebecers to ratify the terms of any new deal with Canada. Their appeals were buttressed by an August SOM poll showing that three-quarters of Quebecers wanted the details of the separatists' proposed union with Canada published before the referendum vote.[75]

Another criticism of the referendum question was that, in referencing two extraneous documents, it obliged Quebecers not merely to vote on sovereignty but to make a study of it. Federalist political scientist Stéphane Dion, for example, accused the PQ of undermining its own grand strategy since Quebecers who lacked the time or inclination to read Bill 1 might think the government was hiding something. "If it's too complicated people will say No," said Dion flatly.[76] Sovereignist Pierre Drouilly, one of the "Four Pollsters of the Apocalypse," asserted bluntly that the referendum question was so complicated as to make it irrelevant. What would really matter, he suggested, was how the debate was framed in the weeks leading up to the vote. Southam News columnist Anne McIlroy called the referendum question all the more cynical for taking aim at the butterflies. "As they head back to their ridings this weekend to begin the referendum campaign," wrote McIlroy, "Parti Québécois politicians know who they are after: The low income, poorly educated and unpoliticized Quebecers who make up a good portion of the undecided voters."[77] Literacy advocates wondered how the estimated 28 per cent of the Quebec population that was illiterate would navigate the referendum process.[78]

Not all public commentary on Parizeau's referendum question was critical. Some observers, including the highly esteemed Université Laval political scientist Louis Balthazar, argued that the question spoke directly to Quebecers' complex political desires. There was no point in asking Quebec voters if they wished to separate from Canada, wrote Balthazar. It was clear that they did not. They were, however, "attached enough to their Quebec identity that they are ready to reconsider the Canadian union." Sovereignty combined with partnership was not merely a "winning combination," concluded Balthazar, but "the only sensible question to ask Quebecers."[79]

Yet however much the PQ's "winning combination" may have

resonated among Quebec's intelligentsia, a Créatec poll conducted in mid-September suggested that many ordinary Quebecers were indeed confused by Bill 1. Among those intending to vote Yes, for example, 49 per cent believed that sovereignty would be declared only after a partnership deal had been struck with Canada. The same survey showed that 28 per cent of committed Yes voters also thought a sovereign Quebec would still be a Canadian province—a statistic that would be cited routinely by federalists for the remainder of the campaign.[80]

Quebec's anxious allophones found little inspiration in either Bill 1 or the phrasing of the referendum question. "I don't see myself reflected in this declaration of independence," said Keder Hyppolite, the Haitian-born director of the Service d'aide aux néo-québécois et immigrants. "It's a text that offers an old-fashioned vision, in old-fashioned poetic language, but it doesn't square with today's reality of a cosmopolitan Montreal."[81] Spokespersons for various Jewish, Arab, and European-based organizations in Quebec registered similar objections. "It puts too much emphasis on the Québécois fact, and on Quebec culture," observed Nick Pierni, the Quebec head of the National Congress of Italian Canadians.[82] In typical fashion, Montreal novelist Mordecai Richler penned a scathing critique of Quebec sovereignists for the *Financial Post,* mocking their faux humiliations and predicting "political bedlam" in Canada if they prevailed.[83]

Outside Quebec, the consensus among politicians willing to speak on the record was that Jacques Parizeau was dreaming if he thought he could declare independence and then cut a new deal with Canada. "The vote they're talking about here is final," said Reformer Stephen Harper, whose position was now indistinguishable from Jean Chrétien's. "This is not 1980. This is not negotiation for a mandate to do something. This is not even negotiating. This is [a notification] that Mr. Parizeau will declare sovereignty. It's final."[84] The premiers concurred. "If you are a province of Canada," said Newfoundland premier Clyde Wells, "you have the right to be a full participant in the political and economic partnership with Canada. If you're a foreign nation, you have no such right."[85] B.C. premier Mike Harcourt called the referendum question "dishonest."[86] New Brunswick premier Frank McKenna called it "confusing" but expressed confidence that "Quebecers will see through the duplicity."[87] "No matter how the PQ tries to disguise it in this question," added Saskatchewan premier Roy Romanow, "Quebecers should know what they are deciding is whether to become an independent country. Period."[88]

The same exasperation was audible throughout English Canada. Jacques Parizeau had promised "a clear question," charged the Montreal *Gazette*. "But instead, he has delivered a plan crafted to confuse and trick voters as much as possible into voting Yes, even if they do not support independence. It smacks of dishonesty."[89] A *Globe and Mail* editorial observed caustically that the sovereignist leaders had set for themselves a daunting challenge. "They have only 60 days or so to convince a skeptical people that their lot is so unhappy, their achievement so empty, their history so trivial, their faith so unfounded and their future so hopeless that the only answer is to leave one of the world's most successful federations."[90] Columnist Jeffrey Simpson wondered how Premier Parizeau could imagine negotiating the simultaneous disintegration and reintegration of Canada and Quebec. "It is even harder to imagine—indeed it is inconceivable—that the rest of Canada could negotiate anything," added Simpson, "since something called 'the rest of Canada' does not exist, in fact or in law."[91] The *Toronto Star* called the referendum question "cowardly and manipulative."[92] Columnist Richard Gwyn likened Parizeau's "fanciful and airy" offer to the hucksterism of a TV shopping channel.[93]

For their part, ordinary Canadian anglos showed little enthusiasm for appeasing Quebec sovereignists. A mid-September CROP poll showed that a majority of Canadians outside Quebec would be open to minor constitutional change after a No win in the referendum, but only 19 per cent would agree to major changes. The same poll showed that 65 per cent of Canadians opposed special powers for Quebec.[94] As for the specifics of Parizeau's sovereignty proposal, 71 per cent of non-Quebecers opposed an economic partnership with a sovereign Quebec, 80 per cent opposed Quebec's use of the Canadian dollar, and 75 per cent opposed Quebecers retaining Canadian citizenship and Canadian passports.[95] In late September, the city council for Surrey, British Columbia, voted to sell off its Quebec bonds, worth $30-million (prompting Lucien Bouchard to warn, "If they dare do that now, imagine what they will dare do after a No").[96] A Calgary group calling itself Canadian Advocates for Reason and Equality (CARE) drafted a petition telling Quebecers that a Yes vote would mean the loss of Canadian citizenship, passports, Bank of Canada privileges, and access to trade deals.[97] A "Go Quebec Go" bumper sticker appeared, courtesy of controversial Victoria lawyer Doug Christie. Comedian Rick Mercer decapitated a Jacques Parizeau lawn ornament in his one-man show at the National Arts Centre, causing his audiences to "roar" with joy.[98]

~

On September 8, just as Quebecers were beginning to digest the wording of Bill 1 and the referendum question, Quebec Superior Court justice Robert Lesage ruled on the legality of the PQ's referendum process.

The occasion for the decision was a legal challenge from Quebec lawyer Guy Bertrand, who had earlier in the year identified Jacques Parizeau's referendum strategy as "suicidal." Calling the June 1995 tripartite agreement "yet another swindle to guarantee a referendum victory," Bertrand decided that he "could not stand by and watch a *coup d'état* being staged."[99] In August, he sought an injunction against the government of Quebec to stop the referendum, arguing that his Charter rights as a Canadian citizen would be violated if the PQ government was free to declare independence unilaterally after a Yes vote. The official position of the PQ government was that the court had no jurisdiction in matters pertaining to the sovereign powers of the National Assembly. When Justice Lesage rejected a government motion to this effect and agreed to hear Bertrand's case, lawyers for the government simply withdrew from the proceedings.

Lesage's forty-four-page decision was a mixed bag, allowing both sides to claim victory. The government's sovereignty bill did indeed constitute a threat to Bertrand's constitutional rights, Lesage wrote, which meant that a unilateral declaration of independence would be illegal and unconstitutional.[100] But Lesage drew the line at granting Bertrand's injunction. "It must be understood that the population wants to express itself," he wrote in his decision. "Issuing an injunction against the holding of the referendum risks creating a more serious wrong than the one that we want to prevent."[101] Lesage's ruling was plainly good for Jacques Parizeau, since it meant that he would not have to defy a court order to hold his referendum.[102] For his part, Bertrand allowed that Lesage had "acted wisely," in the sense that he had laid the ground for a legal and democratic negotiation with the rest of Canada after a Yes victory, but he worried that His Lordship had "underestimated the deceit of which the separatist élite is capable."[103]

Relief was a dominant theme in French-language commentary in the wake of the Bertrand ruling. *Le Devoir*'s Gilles Lesage observed that the court's decision not to grant Bertrand's injunction showed "common sense."[104] Alain Dubuc at *La Presse* thought Judge Lesage had overstated the threat to Quebecers' rights, since even after a Yes vote "Quebec would remain in a state of law, with a charter that would protect rights like that of Canada."[105] Michel C. Auger of *Le Journal de Montréal* worried that Lesage's ruling might offend Quebecers "who believe, correctly, they have no lessons to learn in this regard."[106] All agreed that the prospect of a federally appointed judge in Quebec pronouncing the referendum illegal was a political hornet's nest that Quebecers could do without.

Angryphones like William Johnson at the Montreal *Gazette* were, of course, delighted with the Bertrand decision. They had been proclaiming the illegality of Jacques Parizeau's secession plan from the day he had introduced his draft bill on sovereignty. "[The] threat to secede is based wholly on incantation, mystification, bluff and intimidation," wrote Johnson. "It has no basis in the constitution of this country, and we are not a banana republic that can flout its constitution."[107] Andrew Coyne made the same case in several angry op-ed pieces for the *Globe and Mail.* The sovereignty of Quebec could be achieved legally, wrote Coyne, "only by an act of Parliament and the several provincial legislatures. The Premier of Quebec has formally announced his intention to violate the Constitution. The Republic of Quebec will be founded on lawlessness."[108]

Seen in retrospect, the Bertrand decision was an important milestone in the referendum campaign, but not the one that legalists like William Johnson and Andrew Coyne might have liked. Rather, in one fell swoop and with impeccable timing, Justice Lesage conferred upon Jacques Parizeau's referendum process a legal legitimacy that put it beyond the reach of the PQ's constitutionally minded critics, at least for the remainder of the 1995 campaign. As Osgoode Hall professor Patrick J. Monahan had been warning Canadians for months, the fact that a unilateral declaration of independence (UDI) from Quebec was illegal and unconstitutional meant relatively little. In the event of a Yes vote and the likely failure of negotiations with the rest of Canada, the PQ government intended to proceed with a law declaring Quebec a sovereign state. "If Canada simply acquiesced and did nothing to assert its rights, then the Quebec UDI would ultimately become legally effective," Monahan concluded. "Quebec would have successfully sidestepped the existing Canadian constitutional rules and established a new constitutional order based on a revolutionary break with the past."[109]

What mattered, in other words, was not so much the textbook question of legality but the position of the federal government. How far would Ottawa be willing to go in challenging Jacques Parizeau's declaration of independence after a Yes vote? Only Jean Chrétien knew the answer to this question, and he was not saying a word. It was, he insisted, purely hypothetical.

～

Canadians outside Quebec had made no secret of their low opinion of Bill 1. If anything, the Bertrand decision only lowered it further. Indeed, English Canadians' hostility towards the PQ's proposed referendum process was so visceral—and so monolithic—that when they stood back to take stock of national unity on the eve of the campaign, many realized that they had played directly into Jacques Parizeau's hands.

The possibility that antipathy towards the sovereignists might be misconstrued as antipathy towards Quebec seemed to strike everyone at once. Caution once again became the federalist watchword. Speaking at a $350-a-plate Liberal fundraiser in Vancouver, Jean Chrétien politely urged Canadians to keep to the high road. "I have a lot of scars to show for [the referendum]," he said. "It's easy to get mad, but you didn't do that. You have just told Quebecers, by the way you have handled the situation up to now, that you want Quebec to remain in Canada."[110] The premiers of Atlantic Canada quietly agreed among themselves to maintain a stoic silence for the rest of the referendum campaign.[111] Canadian business leaders followed suit. "We're very sensitive to what we say," observed Thomas d'Aquino, head of the Business Council on National Issues (BCNI). "We have to be constructive, helpful."[112] Even the Montreal Canadiens hockey team adopted a policy of strict neutrality to "avoid giving any offence."[113]

It was all too much for *Calgary Herald* columnist William Gold. "Is it really the duty of a Canadian public commentator to put a sock in it while three guys from Quebec work to break apart that self-same Canada?" asked Gold. "Seems like it. Ever since the re-election of the Parti Québécois under Jacques Parizeau, and especially since he made common cause with the Bloc Québécois' Lucien Bouchard, English Canadian commentators have heard one clear message. DON'T SAY WHAT YOU THINK! *Shhh.* And *shhh* again. Don't say what you think, or you'll make them mad."[114]

CHAPTER NINE

Down to Business

In accordance with Quebec's *Referendum Act,* the debate in the National Assembly on Jacques Parizeau's referendum question was capped at thirty-five hours. All members of the legislature were given the opportunity to speak, and speak they did.

According to the official *Journal des débats de l'Assemblée nationale* (*Hansard*), more than 335,000 words were spoken by Quebec MNAs over seven days of formal debate. Jacques Parizeau and his closest aides had hoped that this conversation—broadcast daily into the living rooms of Quebecers—would pique voters' interest in the referendum process and, of course, draw them to the Yes side. But once again, in a manner reminiscent of the ill-fated sovereignty hearings, the puck did not bounce their way. Revelations from the office of the minister in charge of restructuring, Richard Le Hir, proved devastating to PQ momentum. By the time the marathon session ended on September 20, the premier found himself once again on the ropes, his numbers slipping, his adversaries gloating, and his own MNAs grumbling that the entire exercise had been a waste of precious time.

The great debate in the National Assembly had begun promisingly enough, with Jacques Parizeau's provocative speech about Quebec history on September 11 and Daniel Johnson's measured rebuttal the following day. But on Wednesday, September 13, the Quebec press revealed that a committee of government bureaucrats had been working for months on a draft treaty for presentation to Canada after a Yes vote. In truth, this was not much of a scoop. "It's only normal that we prepare our negotiating position," said Intergovernmental Affairs minister Louise Beaudoin nonchalantly, adding that the cabinet had not yet seen the work of the committee.[1] Even so, Daniel Johnson gambled that Jacques Parizeau was vulnerable on the question of transparency, and accused him of "hiding documents that were paid for by public funds."[2] The charge was serious, prompting the Speaker of the legislature to scold Johnson for his unparliamentary conduct. Parizeau himself was unfazed, acknowledging that many government officials were indeed working on "the negotiations that I hope Canada will accept once Quebecers have said yes in the referendum."[3] The leader of the opposition should keep to the real debate, Parizeau added, so as to avoid "swimming in complete confusion."[4]

Johnson did not relent. He quoted the premier's own words back to him. It was Parizeau himself who had referred to "*d'autres études*" (other studies) that were "paid for by public funds" and concerned "the future of Quebec."[5] Again Johnson accused the premier of hiding documents, betraying the confidence of Quebec voters, and showing contempt for the truth. And again the Speaker censured him.

There the matter might have rested if Jacques Parizeau had kept to his own game plan, defending Bill 1 and extolling the virtues of a Yes vote. Instead, the premier made a fateful choice. He took Johnson's bait. "Studies?" he replied. "This gives me the opportunity to say a few words about these studies."[6]

From that moment, Jacques Parizeau lost control of the debate, never to regain it. For the remainder of the session—four agonizingly long days—he and his ministers were pummelled by Daniel Johnson and the Liberals for their artful handling of at least sixteen reports produced by the Institut national de la recherche scientifique (National Institute of Scientific Research, or INRS). At the centre of the storm was a commissioned study by Quebec economist and one-time advisor to Lucien Bouchard, George Mathews. Johnson accused Parizeau of first trying to persuade Mathews to amend his conclusions about the negative impact of a Yes vote and then, when Mathews refused, of trying to bury his study. "Does the Prime Minister intend to limit his attempts to censor information, to censor documents Quebecers paid for?" Johnson demanded.[7] Parizeau appeared to be blindsided by the question, offering precisely the sort of contradictory reply that made it look as if he was concealing something. "The document does not exist," said the premier. "No. The Institut national de la recherche scientifique has blocked the study. Not the government."[8] Parizeau then said that he would call upon his minister of restructuring, Richard Le Hir, to clarify the situation. This was a yet another gift to Daniel Johnson, who reminded the legislature that Mathews was already on record as saying that Le Hir had lied about his study. (When asked by the Speaker to withdraw the word *lie*, Johnson replied that he would do so if the word had come out of his own mouth, but since it had come from Mathews's, he would not. "It's as simple as that.")[9]

By Thursday, September 14, accusations from the opposition Liberals that government ministers were lying, hiding documents, and misleading the legislature had reduced the tone of the discussion to an "outbreak of schoolyard belligerence," as one observer put it.[10] Epithets were hurled from all corners of the legislature. In the midst of the row over the Mathews document, Mario Dumont interrupted the proceedings to register a point of order. "I do not know, Mr. Speaker, if the microphones have captured the exchange," he said, "but I do not appreciate the official opposition calling me 'a little asshole.'"[11] This would not be the last interruption of its kind.

When he finally entered the raucous debate over the INRS studies he was accused of burying, Richard Le Hir, acknowledged by many Quebecers to lack the rhetorical skills required of successful politicians, tried to play it straight. "I have nothing to hide," he told the National Assembly, "and all studies will be made public within fifteen days. So, the opposition will be able to appreciate that there is nothing hidden."[12] The Liberals responded by accusing Le Hir not merely of shelving reports whose conclusions he did not like but of cynically awarding lucrative research contracts to the friends of senior bureaucrats in his own ministry. Le Hir claimed to be offended by this "smear"—a word he later had to retract from the official record.[13] He dared his Liberal opponents to level such accusations outside the legislature where they would not be protected by parliamentary privilege.

Over the last two days of the debate, Daniel Johnson himself led the charge against Le Hir in the legislature, accusing him of commissioning studies that deliberately hid the "transition costs" of sovereignty, including "economic uncertainty, lower employment and lower investment."[14] Le Hir found himself out-manoeuvred, his repeated promises to publish his studies ignored, his opponents openly mocking him. Johnson's attack on the government climaxed on September 20 with a bombshell question for Jacques Parizeau from which many commentators thought the Yes camp might never recover. "In light of these facts," demanded Johnson, "would the Prime Minister tell us, first, that he intends to stop these maneuvers aimed at hiding information from our citizens, second, that he intends to publish all of these studies and, finally, in light of the behavior, the decisions and the answers of his minister of restructuring, that he ask him to resign because he lied to the public and the House?"[15] Reprimanded once more by the Speaker to withdraw the word *lie* from the public record, Johnson allowed the phrase "mislead the House and deceive the people" to be used in its place.[16] But the damage was done. As Jacques Parizeau acknowledged from his seat in the legislature, Johnson's performance had been a tour de force. "I guess with that he'll have the front pages of the newspapers tomorrow morning," conceded the premier.[17]

Thus ended the formal debate on Bill 1 and with it, the last session of the Quebec National Assembly before the October 30 referendum vote. In the words of *Globe and Mail* correspondent Rhéal Séguin, it had been "a week of calamity" for the sovereignists.[18] The Liberals had knocked the government so far off message that it never came close to rolling out its Yes campaign as planned. "We stuck to our game plan from beginning to end," bragged Liberal MNA John Ciaccia, "and we wiped them out."[19] Jacques Parizeau admitted that frustrated members of his caucus had "let some steam out" during their private meeting on September 20.[20] "We lost a week," said one disgruntled PQ MNA. "It's clear support for the Yes isn't any stronger today than it was a week ago. We don't have the momentum."[21] Polls showed support for the Yes side softening, prompting some sovereignists to whisper that it was still not too late to call the referendum off.[22] "Unless there's a plan B that they haven't told us about," said one *péquiste* organizer, "our best hope at this point is for a miracle."[23]

Seen from Premier Parizeau's perspective, only one aspect of the marathon session had gone according to plan. The motion to approve the final text of his referendum question passed the National Assembly easily, seventy-seven votes to forty-four.

—

As well as setting out the formal timetable for referenda, Quebec's 1978 *Referendum Act* mandates the creation of "national committees" to represent the opposing positions, the Yes and No sides, in any referendum contest. The rationale is to allow party divisions to be "set aside temporarily," and to clearly and transparently assign responsibility for campaign spending.[24] The *Act* also specifies that Quebecers may vote on either a bill or a question. Although Jacques Parizeau's referendum question made explicit reference to two documents, Quebecers were asked in this instance to vote on the question itself and not on Bill 1.

During the campaign, which would begin officially on October 1, only the Yes and No committees were legally authorized to spend money, and they were limited to exactly $5,086,980 each (a figure calculated as one dollar per elector). Half of this amount—$2,543,490—was granted to each side as a government "subsidy." The bulk of the remainder, just over $2.5-million each, came directly from political parties. During the "pre-referendum period" proscribed by the *Referendum Act,* MNAs were required to register with Quebec's chief electoral officer for one or the other side. As expected, seventy-seven MNAs signed up for the Yes side, including all members of the PQ caucus, Mario Dumont of the ADQ, and Jean Fillion, a one-time PQ MNA sitting as an independent.

The forty-seven members of the Liberal caucus registered for the No side. Jacques Parizeau and Daniel Johnson were designated the official chairpersons of their respective committees.

The intent of the *Referendum Act* is to level the playing field, to keep the game fair, and, above all, to ensure that a referendum victory cannot be bought. These are, without question, the most noble of motives in any parliamentary democracy. But because the law deals only with the timing of formal campaigns—defined as the twenty-nine-to-thirty-five-day period before a referendum vote—there was virtually unlimited scope in 1995 for the two sides to organize, strategize, and fund-raise well before the official campaign began. Practically from the moment the Parti Québécois took power in late 1994, each camp began fashioning its strategies and organizing its troops—from the key strategists and big donors at the top to the numerous grassroots organizers at the local level. And from the start, officials from both sides surveilled their adversaries warily, routinely accusing them of dirty tricks and abuses of power, particularly when it came to fundraising and advertising spending. For most of 1995 and indeed beyond, the fastidiously neutral chief electoral officer of Quebec, Pierre-Ferdinand Côté, and the three members of the quasi-judicial Conseil du référendum would be called upon to officiate the various charges and counter-charges levelled by each side against the other.[25]

Yes-side fundraising and spending were coordinated by the Conseil pour la souveraineté du Québec (Council for Quebec Sovereignty), which had been launched in April 1995 with $150,000 in seed money from the Parti Québécois. Headed by former PQ finance minister Yves Duhaime, the Conseil skirted Quebec's strict laws on political donations by collecting money from corporations and unions "in secret."[26] The first of the Conseil's many advertising blitzes was a $225,000 spring billboard campaign centring on the theme "We have the right to be different."[27] After the signing of the June 1995 tripartite agreement, the Conseil sent postcards to Quebec households featuring a picture of the three sovereignist leaders and toll-free numbers Quebecers could call for information about the initiative. In August, it followed with a TV ad campaign reportedly costing $2 million, prompting federal inter-governmental affairs minister Marcel Massé to charge that, in fact, the Conseil had already spent in excess of $11 million—twice the advertising spending allowed by the *Referendum Act*. Asked to comment on Massé's accusation, Duhaime replied unapologetically that the Conseil was simply following the example set by the feds' own Canadian Unity Council. Anticipating that the "orgy" of federal ad spending during the 1980 referendum campaign would be repeated in 1995, Duhaime had no intention of being caught flat-footed.[28]

From the moment he took power, Jacques Parizeau was accused by Canadian federalists of using the vast resources available to provincial governments to promote his own partisan agenda—most notably in the case of his public sovereignty hearings. There was truth in this charge, at least in the sense that Daniel Johnson had far fewer resources with which to run his No campaign. What Johnson did have, however, was virtually unlimited access to the research, communications, and human resources of the federal Liberal government. Starting in late 1994, Jean Chrétien's top advisors—Eddie Goldenberg, Jean Pelletier, Patrick Parisot, John Rae, and Eric Maldoff—began meeting regularly in Montreal with Johnson's top people—Michel Bélanger, Pierre Anctil, John Parisella, and Lisa Frulla. Federal Tory organizers Pierre-Claude Nolin and Jean Bazin also joined the group, acting as Jean Charest's envoys. Together, they made up "a coalition of federalist forces in Quebec that would co-operate in coordinating strategy for the referendum," as Goldenberg later recalled.[29] But far more importantly from Daniel Johnson's point of view, they put the resources of the federal government at the disposal of the provincial No committee.

To Jean Chrétien's great disappointment, the federal and provincial members of this No coalition never gelled. "The No team," said Chrétien, "wasn't using the federal Liberals well, if at all. When I went to shake hands with the volunteers at the No headquarters in Montreal, I was surprised to find how few I knew. The place was full of provincial Liberals and federal Tories."[30] Jean Pelletier, Chrétien's chief of staff, later recalled the thorny politics of the coalition. "Within the

Johnson team," he observed, "there was always the old team of [Robert] Bourassa, which hated Jean Chrétien." No one was surprised, therefore, when Johnson's advisors "put Chrétien and all the federal ministers in a closet and closed the door."[31] Pelletier later remembered wasting plenty of time in meetings with Johnson's people. "I went to Montreal three times a week," he said. "They were polite and courteous, but we knew nothing. It was a dialogue of the deaf."[32]

In early 1995, the feds created their own referendum committee. Headed by career diplomat Howard Balloch, now serving as cabinet deputy secretary for Operation Unity, the committee worked out of the Privy Council Office in Ottawa and reported to Marcel Massé. Working quietly behind the scenes, Balloch's organization was known to insiders only as the Unity Group. With a budget of $6 million and upwards of seventy employees—twenty-two functioning as a sub-group to monitor media related to the referendum—the group conducted polls and supplied daily briefings for officials in the PMO and Lucienne Robillard's office. In February 1995, Bloc Québécois whip Gilles Duceppe accused Massé of managing the group in secret. "There was no announcement," said Duceppe. "They should tell us the budget, and who works there, and what they are doing and under whose orders."[33] Massé responded with typical casualness. "There is really no secret about it," he said. "We have a group of forty people to give us a better analysis, that's all. One must remember the Bloc uses a good part of its research budget to analyze the question of sovereignty and share the conclusions with their brothers in the PQ."[34]

One of the first initiatives of the Unity Group was to distribute a four-page memo asking Canadian business and bank executives to promote federalism during the referendum campaign. "Speak on behalf of the company's best interests," the memo coached its intended audience. "Focus on the message that the same things that are good for the company are also good for the country. This includes issues such as a stable economy and politics, good government, fiscal responsibility, and No to separation for economic reasons." Executives of Quebec companies were specifically encouraged to "get involved locally—the goal being a low-key, local impact."[35]

The Canadian Unity Council (Conseil pour l'unité canadienne, or CUC)—the group mentioned en passant by Yves Duhaime—had been in existence since 1964 and functioned ostensibly as a non-partisan vehicle for the promotion of Canadian federalism. Although it had deep connections to corporate Canada and to leading figures in both the federal Liberal and Tory parties, the CUC enjoyed non-profit status and operated, nominally, at arm's length from government. Quebec sovereignists complained during the referendum campaign that big corporations like Alcan, Procter and Gamble, Dow Chemical, and Maclean-Hunter had no business lowering their tax liability by making charitable contributions to the CUC. But beyond that, they could say little.

On September 7, 1995, however, executives of the CUC quietly registered a new lobby group, Option Canada, in Montreal, headed by one-time Paul Martin advisor Claude Dauphin. There was never any question: the raison d'être of this new unit was to directly influence the outcome of the referendum vote. Over the course of its eight-week lifespan, Option Canada would spend roughly $11 million on research, polling, and advertising for the No campaign—activities that violated the spirit if not the letter of the *Referendum Act* and would later ignite an acrimonious dispute in Quebec over federal spending irregularities.

～

Since the *Referendum Act* prohibited advertising during the first week of the official campaign, October 1 to 6, both sides blitzed the province in late September.[36] The No camp was the first out of the gate, brazenly planting a No poster in front of Premier Parizeau's official residence. Billboards for the No side featured the headline *La Sépa NON ration?* set against a bold blue and red background, accompanied by the slogan "The real question is: Do you want separation?" The same motif was featured in full-page ads in the Montreal *Gazette* and *La Presse* the week of 17 September and thereafter in other print media. A week later, Yes-side billboards and posters appeared all over the province, heralding "*Oui au changement*" (Yes to change) or the even more imaginative "*Ouibec.*" Over the last week of September alone, the Yes committee reportedly spent $100,000 on ads, including a full-page ad in *La Presse* costing $17,000.

Everyone acknowledged that in the battle of the print ads, the sloganeering of the No side was no match for the inspired pop art of the Yes. The *Oui* posters were "striking, clever and fun," *Globe and Mail* reporter André Picard observed, "a marked contrast to the drab, intellectual image the public has of the sovereignists."[37] Simple but evocative, Yes-side designs featured the word *Oui* with the letter O modified by symbols that included the loonie, a daisy, a globe, and a peace sign. Even Joan Fraser at the Montreal *Gazette* conceded that this imagery was inspired. "The heck with expert opinion," she wrote. "Diehard federalist though I am, I like the signs. Maybe the peace one is a tad passé, what with the end of the Cold War and all, but the daisy gives me a lift every time I see it."[38] Like the television ads that showed Lucien Bouchard in soft focus amid informal surroundings, the hippie-styled poster campaign was aimed specifically at female voters, still the majority of the elusive butterflies.[39]

In early October, the French-language CBC network, Radio-Canada, caused a furor among Quebec sovereignists by refusing to air a television ad produced for the Yes side. The spot showed canned clips of Daniel Johnson, Jean Chrétien, Lucienne Robillard, and Preston Manning saying the word "No" as a voice-over intoned, "We'd like a stronger Quebec" and "We'd like a French Quebec." In defence of the decision not to air the ad, a Radio-Canada spokesperson called it "misleading and deceptive," and in violation of CBC's advertising code of ethics.[40] Private TV stations voiced no such reservations and ran the ad. Lucien Bouchard accused Radio-Canada of bending to pressure from the Prime Minister's Office. "Radio-Canada has just put all its weight behind the No forces in an extraordinary way," he said.[41] The irony could not have been lost on the Bloc leader, since Jean Chrétien, like Pierre Trudeau before him, viewed the network as a nest of separatists. Daniel Johnson claimed to be personally insulted by the ad. "I was never asked whether I am in favor or not of a French Quebec," he insisted. "The answer is yes, if I'm asked. The answer is yes, I'm in favor of employment in Quebec. The answer is yes, I'm in favor of lower taxes. So having me on television say no to those questions is a total misrepresentation of reality. It's a fraud in any language."[42]

～

On Monday, September 18, while Jacques Parizeau and Daniel Johnson were jousting in the National Assembly over Richard Le Hir's studies, a new session of parliament opened in Ottawa. All agreed that, with forty-one days to go before the referendum vote, the session would be historic. "I can make a commitment," Lucien Bouchard told the press. "It will not be boring."[43] Jean Chrétien agreed. "It will be fun!" he said.[44] "I expect we'll see a great personal battle between Mr. Chrétien and Mr. Bouchard, like two gladiators," added Stephen Harper.[45]

For the prime minister, the debate in the House turned out to be animated and intense, but not much fun. Chrétien had always said that the onus was on the separatists to explain to Quebecers what they had to gain by leaving the best country in the world. He wanted to use the parliamentary debate to go after Lucien Bouchard. Instead, for three days, he was interrogated by Bloc and Reform MPs about how the federal government intended to respond to a Yes vote.

The conversation in the House took this unexpected turn because on September 12, Lucienne Robillard had casually thrown a comment out to the Ottawa press corps that proved to be a serious misstep. "We always said the Quebecers have the right to express themselves about the future of Quebec in Canada," Robillard said. "We are in a democratic country. We'll respect the vote."[46] The minister undoubtedly meant her remark as an anodyne statement of the government's democratic bona fides. What she quickly discovered, however, was that it opened up a virtually bottomless can of worms. Her boss quickly set her straight. Asked point-blank whether his minister had misspoken, Jean Chrétien replied, "You know, there is a vote and of course we receive the result of the vote. But you're asking me a hypothetical question. I'm here standing in front of you telling you that I believe we will win."[47]

Chrétien had in late 1994 called Jacques Parizeau's draft bill "completely illegal and non-constitutional"—a position that had since been reinforced by the Bertrand decision—but beyond this he had studiously avoided saying anything about how the government might respond to a Yes vote. In public, he called the matter hypothetical. But in private, Jean Chrétien knew that the day might come when he would have to defend the prerogative of the Government of Canada not to recognize the legitimacy of a Yes vote in Quebec. As some of Canada's leading constitutional minds had already concluded, "it seems inconceivable that Canada would simply acquiesce in a Quebec UDI."[48] Chrétien's sovereignist adversaries had tried for months to draw him out on the issue but to no avail. Now it looked as though his own minister had forced his hand. As *Le Devoir*'s front-page headline for September 13 shouted, "To recognize or Not to Recognize? Jean Chrétien Still Refuses to Consider the Consequences of a Majority YES, but Lucienne Robillard has Opened a Breach."[49]

The stage was thus set for a parliamentary debate of real substance, but only if the Bloc Québécois could leverage Lucienne Robillard's comments against the prime minister. Lucien Bouchard knew that the stakes were high. When he took his seat in the House at the opening of the session, he took direct aim at Chrétien, starting with his treatment of Robillard.

"What was so wrong about the minister's statement," demanded Bouchard, "which reflected the most elementary principles of democracy, that would justify the humiliating retraction he inflicted on her?"[50]

Chrétien offered his standard reply. "As far as I am concerned," said the prime minister, "the country has other problems to deal with as well, and I will not spend my time answering hypothetical questions from the Leader of the Opposition."[51]

Bouchard then asked whether the prime minister would also be reprimanding Daniel Johnson for recognizing Quebecers' right to decide their own future.

"I have always said they had the right to have a referendum in Quebec," Chrétien replied. "Quebecers can be consulted and can explain their point of view."[52]

Bouchard understood immediately that Chrétien's use of the word *consulted* implied that he saw the referendum as non-binding.

"I think we should consider this from the legal point of view," asserted the Bloc leader, "and I may remind the Prime Minister that the National Assembly and the Quebec Government based their referendum strategy on the right of peoples to determine their own future in a peaceful and democratic manner. I want to ask the Prime Minister whether he recognizes the right of Quebecers to do so."[53]

Chrétien again tried to divert the conversation, but Bloc MPs would have none of it. House leader Michel Gauthier demanded that the prime minister "tell us clearly whether or not he will respect the choice expressed by Quebecers in the upcoming referendum."[54]

"I would like the opposition to tell the government that they will respect a No vote," Chrétien replied. "We won the referendum in 1980 but they did not respect the wishes of Quebecers."[55]

Preston Manning then entered the fray, stoking the already raucous debate. The Reform leader demanded that Jean Chrétien clearly delineate the government's position for the benefit of all Canadians.

"Will the Prime Minister make clear," Manning demanded, "that a Yes vote means Quebec is on its way out, that a No vote means Quebec is in the federation for the long haul, and that 50 per cent plus one is the dividing line between those two positions?"[56]

"Shame, shame!" cried Liberal backbenchers.

Chrétien tried to turn the tables on Manning.

"I have been asking [the *Bloquistes*] for a long time in this House of Commons to give us a real question, an honest, clear question on separation," said the prime minister. "They have clouded the issue talking about divorce and remarriage at the same time. They want me on behalf of all Canadians to say that with a clouded question like that with one vote I will help them to destroy Canada. You might, I will not, Mr. Manning."[57]

Liberal MPs leapt to their feet to give their leader a standing ovation.

Lucien Bouchard resumed his attack on Jean Chrétien the next day, September 19.

"The fog thickened yesterday around the Prime Minister's real intentions, following statements he made in this House," said Bouchard.

"Will he, as the Reform Party did yesterday, respect Canada's democratic traditions and recognize a Yes or a No to the Quebec referendum question as equally valid?"[58]

"Today, we have a confusing and ambiguous question," Chrétien replied, "and I am asked whether we would recognize a vote with a majority of one. As Mr. Johnson put it so well yesterday, we are not about to separate from Canada on the basis of a judicial recount."[59] (Johnson had said that he thought it "a little bizarre" to break up a country on the basis of a judicial recount, prompting Quebec sovereignists to accuse him of caving in before Jean Chrétien.)[60]

Preston Manning again demanded that the prime minister state his position.

"Will the Prime Minister now make it perfectly clear to Quebecers that a Yes vote means separation and not just a new round of bargaining with the federal government?" he asked.[61]

At this point, Jean Chrétien made a calculated gamble. He divulged for the first time that he might not honour a close Yes vote.

"I will not break up the country with one vote," said the prime minister. "It is not real democracy. Real democracy is to convince the people they can express themselves clearly, which is what we are doing."[62]

~

Chrétien's statement was a show-stopper, as all Canadians well knew, and it enlivened the referendum debate across the country as nothing had in months. "PM Won't Pledge to Honour Yes Vote" blasted the headlines, "*Chrétien met en doute la reconnaissance d'un OUI serré*" ("Chrétien Uncertain about Recognizing a Close Yes").[63] In Quebec, some francophone pundits were outraged by Chrétien's statement, as he undoubtedly knew they would be. "A true democrat cannot suggest such a highjacking of democracy any more than he can accept the results at the ballot box only if they suit him," fumed Michel C. Auger at the *Journal de Montréal.*[64] Yet polls had consistently shown that a majority of Quebecers themselves shared Chrétien's perspective. A summer 1994 survey, for example, revealed that 71 per cent of Quebec voters believed a majority of at least 60 per cent should be required to take the province out of Canada.[65] "Why should Mr. Chrétien be forced to accept a Yes," queried a female caller to a Radio Canada television show, "while Mr. Bouchard said very clearly last week that he won't accept a No vote?"[66]

Some Canadian anglos were delighted to hear that the prime minister had finally drawn a line in the sand, but most perceived that Chrétien had been knocked off his game. "Chrétien must stick by his original, correct strategy," counselled an *Ottawa Citizen* editorial. "The issue on October 30 is clear—separation, Yes or No. Jean Chrétien allowed himself to be diverted this week from a winning, principled strategy for the Quebec referendum."[67] The prime minister should never have fallen into Preston Manning's trap, wrote Lysiane Gagnon. "He made his first big blunder of the campaign."[68]

In truth, the big loser was the man who had laid the trap. "I think Mr. Manning's behavior is disgusting," said Jean Charest flatly. "He's letting his own country down."[69] Columnist William Johnson called Manning's position madness. "To change the constitution of his Reform Party requires a two-thirds vote at a convention," Johnson fumed. "But to break up a country requires only a 50-per-cent vote in a plebiscite in one part of the country, regardless of the question asked or what rules are enforced? Manning has wandered into the wrong country."[70] Westerners, for whom Manning claimed to speak, expressed similar sentiments. "Is [Manning] so bedazzled by the prospect of scoring political points that he can't see that he's playing right into separatist hands?" asked Paul Minvielle on the editorial page of the *Victoria Times-Colonist*.[71] Norm Ovenden at the *Edmonton Journal* wondered whether Manning wanted so badly to be prime minister that "he'd settle for second best as head of a much smaller country."[72]

The leaders of the Yes side were delighted by such acrimony in the federalist ranks, of course. "I would say it is probably a courageous stand that Reform is taking now," said Lucien Bouchard. "The Liberal Party is now trying to drag the Reform Party into a denial of democracy. For me, it is sad."[73]

With such expressions of sympathy coming from the leader of the Bloc Québécois, Manning knew he was in trouble. After Question Period on September 19, he sought a private meeting with Jean Chrétien, presumably in search of some common federalist ground. "I did not break his legs or his arms," the prime minister later joked about their tête-à-tête. "We had a very civilized discussion."[74] Manning's conciliatory tone after this meeting was immediately apparent. "There is not a federalist in the House who does not want to defeat the Bloc and its separatist allies in the referendum and bury this secession issue six feet deep," he told parliament.[75] Lucien Bouchard drew the obvious conclusion, accusing Chrétien of bringing the Reform leader to heel. "I see that the arm-twisting was fruitful since Mr. Manning didn't dare repeat what he had said before," said the Bloc leader. "The Reform Party has made the news for two days because, indeed, there was an element of extraordinary novelty—it was the only party in English Canada that had the courage to stand up in the House to tell this government it is antidemocratic."[76] CTV's Craig Oliver asked Manning if he was angling to be the prime minister of a Canada without Quebec. "I'd rather be a backbencher in the parliament of a united Canada," Manning replied, "than to be the first minister in a broken Canada."[77]

Preston Manning and Stephen Harper would continue for the remainder of the fall parliamentary session to promote their program of radical decentralization accompanied by, if necessary, a Canada-wide referendum after a Yes vote in Quebec. But they abandoned their pose as *agents provocateurs* and with it any hope that they could significantly influence the October 30 referendum vote. Both Manning and Harper would head to Montreal in mid-October to give speeches and interviews. "At a minimum," Manning later said, "we hoped to show that there was support for 'changing federalism' in the part of the country we truly represented—the West—and to invite Quebecers to vote No." But the truth was that for the remainder of the referendum campaign, as Manning himself lamented, "Reform's influence in Quebec was marginal."[78]

Lucien Bouchard and his Bloc Québécois comrades discovered that they, too, had got about as much as they could out of the prime minister. After Chrétien said that he might not honour a narrow Yes vote, Bloc MPs did everything in their power to keep his feet to the fire. "We knew for some time that, given a choice between Canada and Quebec, he chose Canada," asserted Lucien Bouchard, "but are we now to understand that, if forced to choose between democracy and federalism, he will choose federalism?"[79] "Can the Prime Minister tell me this?" added Michel Gauthier. "Just how far will he go in trying to subvert democracy? How far exactly?"[80] But Jean Chrétien stood his ground and shut them down. "As far as I am concerned," he told the House, "I have clearly stated that the Prime Minister of Canada cannot agree to independence from Canada as the result of a simple majority vote plus one on an ambiguous question. Come on!"[81]

The referendum would be debated in the House of Commons right up to voting day, but by late September the conversation was already cliché-drenched and moving in circles. In early October, the debate shifted decidedly away from the politics of Quebec sovereignty and towards the economic implications—trade, the debt, shared-cost social programs. Finance minister Paul Martin supplanted Jean Chrétien as the leading voice for the government. But as Lucien Bouchard well knew, interminable chatter about debt-sharing was not going to win Quebecers to the Yes side. By October 1, half of the Bloc caucus was routinely absent from the House of Commons—including, increasingly, Bouchard himself. The implication was obvious. As the Bloc leader himself admitted, "I guess we will be more and more attracted by the campaign itself since it has officially begun in Quebec now."[82]

Jean Chrétien was triumphant. "We don't need to change our strategy," said the prime minister. "Mr. Bouchard's strategy was to destroy us in the House of Commons. He had given himself three weeks and he quit first."[83]

~

Daniel Johnson, Jean Charest, Lucienne Robillard, and other prominent Quebec federalists kicked off the No campaign unofficially with a rally in Montreal on September 24. The mood was buoyant. Plainly atoning for her earlier gaffe, an upbeat Robillard demanded that Lucien Bouchard honour a No vote. "It's obvious that the No side is going to win a definitive victory on Oct. 30," she said, "such a victory, Mr. Bouchard, that you cannot hold another referendum. When the Quebec population says no, it's no, Mr. Bouchard."[84] Jean Charest followed suit, lampooning the Bloc leader's "chameleon" past and predicting that he would once again change his colours after a No vote. "He will begin saying, starting October 31, that he is obliged to stay, that he doesn't like politics, but if you insist that he stays, he will stay and give Canada a last chance," joked Charest.[85] Daniel Johnson told the crowd of 1,000 that Mario Dumont had lost the support of half of his own riding association when he signed on with Parizeau and Bouchard. Dumont would be welcome to join the No team, he added.[86]

Energized by the confidence of the No leaders and the enthusiasm of the partisan crowd, Claude Garcia, president of the Standard Life Assurance Company and a prominent Quebec federalist, then took the stage. "Please keep working," Garcia told the crowd. "You must not just win October 30, you have to crush them."[87]

There was no mistaking Garcia's intent. He was stern, clear-eyed, resolute. He meant what he said. Sovereignists would later recall Garcia's unforgiving use of the word *crush* (*"il faut écraser"*) as a turning point in the campaign. "It looked like we'd hit rock bottom," said PQ strategist Jean Royer. "From the moment of Mr. Garcia's famous declaration, I felt a reverse trend taking hold."[88] Jean-François Lisée agreed, later recalling that the remark seemed to reflect "the mood of the Chrétien team (and that of the provincial Liberals)."[89] It was true that the Garcia sound-bite—in high rotation on Quebec television—hearkened back to the take-no-prisoners bravado of Trudeau-era federalists. As more than one observer noted, the fear of being crushed was the beating heart of Quebec nationalism. Daniel Johnson understood immediately that Garcia's words were a potential disaster for the No campaign. Speaking the next day in the Montreal riding of Viger, the Liberal leader distanced himself from such talk. "On the day following the referendum," said

Johnson, "no one should feel crushed. People should feel they either won or lost. But life goes on and that's very important."[90]

Jacques Parizeau's first instinct was to play the statesman and to again urge both sides to ratchet down the rhetoric. "In terms of decibels, it's going up a bit," said Parizeau, adding that federalists were using "really abusive terms."[91] But to the foot soldiers in the Yes camp, Garcia's remark was a gift, and they had no intention of squandering it. The Conseil de la souveraineté quickly launched ads in Quebec newspapers asking Quebecers if they wanted to be crushed. Television and radio spots replayed Garcia's speech with a voice-over warning, "A No in the referendum is to agree to be crushed."[92]

A contrite Garcia issued an open letter to Standard Life employees on September 28. "It's clear my comments offended many people," it read. "I apologize sincerely."[93] The matter did not end there, however. A spokesperson for Quebec Treasury Board president Pauline Marois announced the next day that the Quebec government intended to review its $11.5-million insurance contract with Standard Life. Jacques Parizeau was asked whether this review was politically motivated. "I'm not trying to make a vendetta with respect to Standard Life," the premier replied. "All I say is that political statements of the rabid variety attract attention and therefore we have a responsibility to look at the way the rules have been applied or not applied."[94]

~

The Garcia furor notwithstanding, Daniel Johnson and Jean Chrétien had good reason to be confident heading into October. Both men had acquitted themselves well in formal debate with their sovereignist adversaries, and Quebecers had noticed. A September 30 CROP poll gave the No side a comfortable 55–45 lead among committed voters. Only 11 per cent of Quebecers remained undecided. The Canadian dollar—that indicator of investor confidence in Canada—had risen 2.5 per cent since Jacques Parizeau had rolled out Bill 1 and his referendum question.[95] Prime Minister Chrétien had always said that he had no mandate to negotiate the secession of Quebec, and now he was on record as saying that he might not even honour a Yes vote. And yet even Quebecers, it seemed, were impressed by his principled stand. A CBC/ Southam News poll published on October 1 showed that 81 per cent of Canadians outside Quebec would want Chrétien to keep his job even after a Yes vote—and an astonishing 62 per cent of Quebecers agreed.[96]

None of this was great news for the sovereignists, of course. "I'm not saying the campaign is going marvelously well," Lucien Bouchard conceded in late September. "I say that we are in a tight spot, that we have to brace ourselves for a tough fight."[97]

As the referendum campaign lurched towards its dénouement, the national consensus was that the contest remained the federalists' to lose. Yet from the ranks of ordinary Canadians, and from young people in particular, the nascent stirrings of doubt and disbelief could be discerned. On September 25, deputy prime minister Sheila Copps cheerily told an audience of 700 Etobicoke high school students that the future of their country was secure because Quebecers would vote No.

"So if they vote to leave," asked one of the students, "you guys will be totally unprepared to handle it?"[98]

CHAPTER TEN

L'Effet Lucien

On October 1, Premier Parizeau issued the referendum writ as expected, cementing October 30 as the date of the vote. There would be no turning back.

Instead of charging out of the starting gate, however, the premier seemed hobbled by ennui. Just as his dream of a sovereign Quebec was coming into view, he appeared somehow to have lost the resolve to see it through. "At my age I don't even say come and change things with me," Parizeau mused during a chat with a student journalist. "I say change them. It will soon be over for me. I'm opening the door. Go ahead. Take your place."[1]

It was known that Parizeau had been suffering from the flu, and also that he was expending a good deal of energy behind the scenes to ease tensions between the PQ and the Bloc Québécois. His polling numbers had flatlined, and the thrashing he had taken from Daniel Johnson in the National Assembly had hurt his own morale and his party's. In late September, Parizeau and his senior ministers had unveiled an eighty-four-page document called *Le Cœur à l'ouvrage* (*Our Hearts in Our Work*), a magnum opus six months in the making that articulated the government's answer to the question *Sovereignty for what?* The study laid out in detail the myriad ways in which independence would improve the daily lives of Quebecers, particularly in job creation, health care, social programming, and education. Yet even this exercise failed to give the Yes campaign any noticeable lift. Quebec media gave *Le Cœur à l'ouvrage* almost no coverage. Ordinary citizens, who had the previous winter cried out for just such a social blueprint, seemed to have lost interest.[2] Given that they were now obliged to read the texts of the tripartite agreement and Bill 1 before casting their referendum votes, this was perhaps unsurprising.

The premier gave a televised address the evening of October 1 to launch the official campaign. "In five, ten or twenty years," he told Quebecers, "we must be able to say to our children and grandchildren, 'On Oct. 30, 1995, the hour of choice, I was there. I thought about it and took the right decision for our future.' No one can predict the future but it is possible that October 30 will be our last collective rendezvous. After that, as a province like the others, we will become perhaps individuals like the others. In the end, it is possible that history will say Chrétien was right: Our only difference will be to speak English with an accent."[3]

The speech was hardly the barn-burner sovereignists had hoped for. "I don't think it could have gone any worse," said one *péquiste* insider of the campaign kick-off, "although we aren't hitting the panic button yet."[4] Parizeau was "too much on the defensive," said Henri Massé, secretary-general of the Quebec Federation of Labour and a leading Yes supporter.[5] Though he was careful never to criticize the premier directly, ADQ leader Mario Dumont told reporters travelling with the Yes campaign that he was fed up with "the defeatist mind-set" of some sovereignists. He added that he had no intention of "acting like a loser" himself.[6]

～

With the referendum debate shifting towards economic issues and at least one federalist business leader from Quebec, Claude Garcia, pilloried for his impolitic remarks, Jacques Parizeau saw an opportunity. He perceived that the outspoken federalists in Quebec's corporate elite—men (and some women) who were closely identified with the Liberal party[7]—were vulnerable to charges that they were indifferent to the concerns of ordinary Quebecers. The premier needed to spark his flagging Yes campaign, and he now had the province's richest capitalists in his sights. He rolled the dice. He decided to impugn not merely their great wealth and influence—always fair game politically—but also their patriotism. And he knew that if his critique was going to have any impact on the referendum vote, particularly on the economically insecure but politically distracted butterflies, he would have to hit them hard.

On one level, Quebec's federalist business leaders had made sitting ducks of themselves. In mid-February 1995, they had joined forces to launch a new lobby group, the Quebec Business Council for Canada. Its charter members included Claude Garcia; Laurent Beaudoin, chief executive of Bombardier; Marcel Dutil, chief executive of Canam Manac; Paul Gobeil, vice-chair of Metro-Richelieu; Guy Saint-Pierre, chief executive of SNC-Lavalin Group; Raymond Cyr, chair of Bell Canada; and Gilles Ouimet, president of Pratt & Whitney. Chief spokesperson for the council was Pierre Côté, chair of Celanese Canada and a veteran of the 1980 referendum campaign. "We are going to ask the Quebec government some very fundamental questions over the coming weeks," Côté had announced in February 1995. "We're going to demand a business plan from the *indépendantistes*. They'll have to prove to the citizens of Quebec, their shareholders, that their plan is profitable."[8]

On another level, however, these captains of industry were untouchable. Like highly successful Québécois artists and athletes, they had benefited from a powerful populist mystique that framed their achievements as the pride of all Quebecers. The premier had always been careful not to antagonize small business owners and entrepreneurs, a core sovereignist constituency. But it was also well known in Quebec that Parizeau, the laissez-faire economist and former finance minister, had gone to great lengths to mollify big business while in opposition, assuring corporate executives that their interests would not be undermined by a Parti Québécois government. The Quebec premier was no Marxist. Using class conflict to leverage the sovereignist vote was not merely risky. It could be his undoing.

Parizeau's first tentative volley at the Quebec business elite came in late September 1995, when the PQ was trying to persuade Quebec voters that they would be spared the pain of Paul Martin's budget cuts if they supported sovereignty. "The federal government is looking at the possibility of reducing social benefits to lower its deficit," the premier said in a radio interview. "But it will not touch companies. Why do you think companies are for federalism and against Quebec sovereignty? Well, I, for one, will have no part of it."[9]

Then on October 3, alluding to a document leaked from within the feds' Unity Group, Lucien Bouchard accused Jean Chrétien in the House of Commons of clandestinely using federal industry grants to induce Quebec corporations to support the No vote. Under the sub-heading "Levers," the document listed "future procurement and indus-trial benefits" that would be available to Quebec firms within a united Canada. Bouchard called the feds' strategy "blackmail," pure and sim-ple.[10] "This is obviously a strategic document to get people from the business community aboard the No campaign," he charged.[11] Nonsense, said Jean Chrétien. "The purpose is not to blackmail anyone at all, in fact quite the opposite. It is so we can tell people that they can get ahead in Canada and that many industries in Quebec need the cen-tral government, to access its funding programs as well as to find mar-kets abroad."[12] Asked whether he thought Quebec business people had actually submitted to Ottawa's blackmail, Lucien Bouchard was careful not to overstate his case. "I don't think so," he said, "but what I do say is, here is an instrument available to the government to do that kind of arm twisting."[13] Jacques Parizeau's initial reaction was less diplomatic. He expressed regret that Quebec's "colonial" business elite could be "bought off" by the federal government.[14]

Speaking to Montreal's board of trade just hours after Bouchard's exchange with Chrétien, Bombardier CEO Laurent Beaudoin chastised the sovereignist leaders. "Some people were displeased that I expressed publicly my support for the No campaign," Beaudoin said. "It is as if only politicians, artists, intellectuals and union leaders have a right to express an opinion on the separation of Quebec from Canada. Ironically, the secessionists who like to hold up Quebec companies as models of what could be achieved by Quebec firms in an independent Quebec, ignore that Quebec companies have made their mark within a united Canada."[15] Beaudoin would later suggest that Bombardier might have to close the snowmobile plant in Valcourt if a sovereign Quebec failed to acquire access to NAFTA and the U.S. market.[16] Power Corporation's Paul Desmarais made similar statements, warning that the sovereignty option in the referendum would undermine the Quebec economy.

The premier was under enormous pressure to return fire. Henri Massé of the QFL, for example, called for a "counter-offensive" from the PQ government against Quebec business leaders who were aggressively trying to convince their workers to vote No.[17]

Yet Parizeau gave every impression that he did not have to be prodded. He was fed up with the not-so-secret collusion of Quebec's corporate elite and the anti-sovereignist Liberals. "All of a sudden, we are witnessing the eruption of a certain number of big businessmen," Parizeau told a Montmagny crowd on October 4, "and now we learn in the newspapers this morning that it was planned, programmed. These companies like Bombardier will receive or have already received substantial subsidies in order to have them say exactly what they are saying now. It's quite a shock."[18] Business leaders like Desmarais and Beaudoin were sending Quebecers a message, the premier thundered. "Don't move. You are never as beautiful as when you are on your knees. And if you even think of getting up from the ground, we'll leave."[19] The next day, Parizeau gave an even more rough-hewn speech in Matane. "Those who watch billionaires spit on us," he said, "those who are at their service and in their hands, have developed an inferiority complex. My friends, we have to get out [of Canada] with a bit of pride. It's not true that we're going to let them boot us in the ass constantly like this and make fools of us."[20] On October 6, the premier told the PQ national council, "The No camp has transformed itself before our eyes. It's become the club of billionaires, the club of privilege, arrogant and menacing."[21]

For many Quebecers, the spectacle of Jacques Parizeau scapegoating business leaders was disconcerting. His penchant for witty one-liners notwithstanding, they knew the premier as a man of states-manlike bearing, someone who understood that after the referendum all Quebecers would have to live together. Now, however, apparently des-perate to turn the Yes campaign around, he was prepared to drive deep wedges into Quebec society. For the first time since Parizeau became premier, Quebecers openly debated whether he would be fit to govern after the referendum vote.[22] "It's deplorable, to say the least," observed Daniel Johnson, "that the premier of Quebec and some of his ministers will use back-street language with people who don't happen to agree with them. That's what I think is unworthy of the premier."[23] Some pundits, including political scientist Guy Laforest, defended Parizeau's critique of the "unparalleled corporate, political and media power" of Quebec's business elite.[24] But even Lucien Bouchard acknowledged that Parizeau's polarizing rhetoric was hurting the sovereignist cause. "There are a lot of sovereignist businesspeople out there, more than we think," said the Bloc leader. "I'd like to hear some sovereignist businesspeople speak out about their vision of Quebec's future."[25]

For many Canadians outside Quebec, Parizeau's attack on franco-phone business leaders was a new low even for him. "Quebecers are being 'spat on,'" fumed a *Toronto Star* editorial. "They're being 'kicked in the ass.' They've been forced down 'on their knees.' It's the oldest sep-aratist trick in the book, and Quebecers will reject it. The separatists—sinking in their bid to sell Quebecers on the fanciful notion that they'd fare better in an independent country—have now set themselves on a reckless course. They hope to stir fears with the big lie."[26]

~

For several weeks, some of Jacques Parizeau's restless *péquiste* comrades had been wondering aloud whether Lucien Bouchard might be put to better use in the Yes campaign. Within the Parti Québécois caucus, the idea was called "Plan B."[27] On October 6, at a Montreal meeting of the PQ's sixteen regional presidents and 125 riding reps, Parizeau was beseeched repeatedly to invite the Bloc leader to play a more promin-ent role.[28] From the vantage point of ordinary Quebecers, these manoeuvres may have looked like a mutiny. But, in fact, acting on Parizeau's own instructions, Jean-François Lisée and Jean Royer had for weeks been conducting focus groups and surveys to determine how best to bring Bouchard into the Quebec ground campaign. Polls showed that the Bloc leader was not only more popular than the premier but more highly trusted. They also affirmed that undecided Quebec voters were more likely to vote Yes if sovereignty was bundled with the kind of partnership agreement Bouchard had been advocating. Making the Bloc leader the public face of the *camp du changement* made good sense, especially now that the debate in the House of Commons appeared to have run its course.

Premier Parizeau did not have to be sold on the idea. He knew which way the wind was blowing. But he also knew that the optics of promoting Bouchard in the home stretch of the referendum race would have to be managed carefully. "Adopting a new strategy in the middle of a political campaign is a highly risky and delicate operation that is rarely successful," federalist strategist Eddie Goldenberg later observed. "When it happens, it is seen as a sign of desperation and panic."[29] Parizeau knew that Goldenberg's boss, Jean Chrétien, would assail any sudden change in Yes-side strategy as yet another sovereignist trick. What was needed to promote Bouchard into a new leadership role, therefore, was not merely a plausible rationale but one that would provide political cover for the premier himself.

There was never much doubt about where the most suitable pretext lay. The tenet that a sovereign Quebec would be "bound" to negotiate a new partnership with Canada after a Yes vote had been written explicitly into both Bill 1 and the tripartite agreement. And despite his public admission that he was "not the most credible" proponent of this pledge, Jacques Parizeau had worked hard to reassure Quebecers that he would negotiate with Canada in the best of faith after a referendum victory. Convincing the undecideds to vote Yes meant bolstering their confidence in the partnership idea, and selling that idea was Lucien Bouchard's forte. All that was needed to put the Bloc leader firmly in the driver's seat was a mandate to negotiate with Canada when the time came.

The premier acted quickly. On October 6, he announced the appointment of a committee to monitor future negotiations between Quebec and Canada (the "surveillance committee").[30] The most distinguished of the five VIPs hand-picked by the premier to serve on the committee was seventy-eight-year-old Arthur Tremblay, Quebec's first deputy minister of education and a former Progressive Conservative senator and constitutional advisor to Brian Mulroney. A life-long federalist, Tremblay had rocked Quebec in late September with the announcement that he would vote Yes in the referendum. The other members of the surveillance committee were Serge Racine, president of furniture company Shermag; Denise Verrault, president of Verrault Navigation; Jean Allaire, one-time Liberal and founder of the ADQ; and Jacynthe Simard, head of Quebec's Union des municipalités régionales de comté. "I think it shows how seriously we look at these negotiations," said Parizeau of the new committee. "We intend these negotiations to be serious negotiations, negotiations in good faith."[31] Denise Verrault, a committed federalist, was asked about her role on the committee. "I was asked to do a job should it be a Yes in the referendum, and this is what I will do should it be a Yes," she replied. "This is not a political committee."[32]

The stage was thus set for the most important announcement of the Yes campaign, the naming of the *négociateur en chef* (chief negotiator). On Saturday, October 7, before a crowd of 1,500 at Université de Montréal, Parizeau himself stoked the youthful crowd into frenzied anticipation. "The chief negotiator must be a person who inspires deep confidence, not only in the majority of Quebecers who have voted Yes, but also in a great number of Quebecers who will have voted No. It will take someone who is a good negotiator, who knows English Canada, and who is a sovereignist. Lucien Bouchard!"[33]

Jean-François Lisée later recalled the effect Parizeau's rising voice had on the crowd. "It was as if an electric charge of 100,000 volts had gone through the seats," he said. "The audience bolted from their seats to applaud. It was a magic moment."[34] As Bouchard took the podium, he embraced Parizeau and beamed at the exuberant crowd. He plunged directly into his new role, taking direct aim at the prime minister. "Jean Chrétien has found himself in the way of Quebec every time Quebec wanted to move towards its future," said Bouchard. "Chrétien is never as miserable as when he sees Quebec stand up!"[35] Sovereignists were delighted. "Parizeau represents sovereignty," observed Gérald Larose, president of the Confédération des syndicats nationaux and a PQ activist. "Bouchard represents the partnership. This completes our strategy."[36] An unnamed PQ cabinet minister praised the premier for having the courage to step aside. "Mr. Parizeau has always said that he would put the interests of Quebec ahead of his party's interests. And that's what he has done."[37]

The premier himself was upbeat about the new arrangement. "We named as negotiator the man everyone agrees is the most popular in Quebec," he told reporters after the Montreal rally. "It's part of the unfolding of the operation. We don't need to increase the visibility of Lucien Bouchard. He already has a very great visibility."[38] For his part, Bouchard was gracious. "I'm not taking his place," the Bloc leader said of the premier. "Mr. Parizeau is in charge of the campaign. He is the leader of the Yes camp. He has simply given me a mandate as chief negotiator."[39]

Prime Minister Chrétien was unimpressed. The separatists could change bus drivers as often as they liked, he joked, but "the bus is going to separation anyway."[40] Daniel Johnson agreed, dismissing Bouchard's appointment as meaningless. "We're not running a beauty contest," he told a rally in Sept-Îles. "They're trying to make us believe that the Yes has already won and that they are getting ready to negotiate from a position of strength."[41] In private, Johnson was astonished at Bouchard's gall. "To put the squeeze on the premier of Quebec, while it was his project in the first place, took a lot of nerve!" he later recalled. "It was pretty unprecedented and, therefore, unforeseeable."[42]

What Bouchard's new job meant for Quebec and Canada was the subject of considerable conjecture. *La Presse* editorial writer Claude Masson observed astutely that the premature naming of the Bloc leader as chief negotiator put any actual negotiation in jeopardy. "Mr. Bouchard has now been compromised," wrote Masson. "He cannot spend his days savaging the federal government, attacking the provincial premiers and making fun of English Canada and then, after a Yes vote on Oct. 30, hold out a welcoming hand like a Good Samaritan. No sane negotiator for English Canada would believe he is acting in good faith."[43] Don Macpherson of the Montreal *Gazette* agreed but commended Parizeau for putting principle ahead of ego. "Even at age 65, Jacques Parizeau shows a remarkable ability to surprise us," he wrote.[44] A *Gazette* editorial asserted less magnanimously that Bouchard would bring "charisma, passion and disarming dishonesty" to the sovereignist campaign. "Unable to sell sovereignty on its merits, the Yes camp is now trying to make people think that the referendum is about giving Mr. Bouchard a mandate to negotiate a new deal with the rest of Canada. Nothing could be further from the truth. On Oct. 30, Quebecers will be voting on whether to give the Parizeau government a mandate to declare unilaterally Quebec independence."[45]

Outside Quebec, Bouchard's apparent usurpation of Parizeau was denounced in no uncertain terms. "Jacques Parizeau could not have chosen a more improbable 'negotiator' for a possible union with Canada than Lucien Bouchard," blasted the *Toronto Star*. "The Bloc Québécois leader may be a hero to separatists, but to the rest of the country he is a turncoat: a former Liberal who became a Mulroney Tory; a strong nationalist who turned federalist only to abandon Canada; a leader of Her Majesty's Loyal Opposition whose declared goal is to dismember the country."[46] Southam columnist Ken MacQueen spoke for the many exasperated Canadians who saw Parizeau's promotion of Bouchard as little more than a confidence trick. "Here at the Canadian Institute for Provincial Humiliation (Motto: 'We spit in your soup. We constantly kick your asses. On your knees, on your knees, on your knees, you're too small, you are incapable.') we are frankly worried that Jacques Parizeau won't go the distance. A scientific analysis of his recent utterances caused our ultra-sensitive Meter of Shame to blow a gasket."[47]

～

On Sunday, October 8, Lucien Bouchard joined Mario Dumont and other leading sovereignists on the Yes campaign tour. Jacques Parizeau stayed home. The passing of the baton was complete, and it had taken but twenty-four hours.

Bouchard's resuscitation of the flagging Yes campaign was immediate, exceeding even the most optimistic *péquiste* prognostications. Over the course of the weekend, ordinary citizens from across the province greeted Bouchard with the same adulation he had met in Montreal. Crowds chanted "Lucien, Lucien." (When Parizeau had headed a rally, they had cheered "*Oui, Oui, Oui!*") The Quebec press described this transformation as "Lucien-mania" and reported that he was now getting "rock-star" treatment.[48] And with Bouchard's every public appearance, the size and the enthusiasm of the crowds increased. "You feel it from him that he's a man who speaks with heart," retired plumber Raymond Lefebvre observed at a rally in the Plateau Mont-Royal district. "Parizeau is more like a technocrat, and we need people like him. But Lucien, he can talk to people in a way they understand. He carries people along with the strength of his conviction and with his big heart."[49] Construction worker Roger Langlois agreed. "People aren't sure about Parizeau," he observed. "But Lucien talks like one of us. With him we'll have a chance to build a country."[50] Some ordinary Quebecers spoke of Bouchard's near-death experience as having shored up his almost messianic popularity. Pundits spoke of *l'effet Lucien* (the Lucien effect).[51]

Globe and Mail columnist Jeffrey Simpson set out on the campaign trail in Quebec to see *l'effet Lucien* for himself. He reported that Bouchard's entry into the campaign had changed everything. "Here we are," Simpson wrote from Sorel on October 12, "at a beans-and-buns breakfast in a working-class town, in a hall already packed with cigarette smoke, and when Mr. Bouchard arrives, what a contrast his reception offers to that given the previous day by Yes supporters to Mr. Parizeau. With a brilliant command of French and a sure sense of pace, Mr. Bouchard touches his audience, as if reaching into every listener to locate the touchstone of pride."[52]

Out on the hustings, Bouchard's message for Quebecers was simple and direct. *Canadians would have no choice but to negotiate with Quebec after a Yes vote.* "They know they will not be able to resist the political pressure that will be brought to bear on them the day Quebec speaks as a people," he said. "With the onus that sovereignty will give us, English Canada has no choice." Bouchard explained that a partnership deal was not a dilution of the main goal, sovereignty, but its culmination. Only as equals could Quebec and Canada reimagine their future. "Mr. Parizeau has no right to negotiate anything but sovereignty," said Bouchard on Radio-Canada. "Anything less would be illegal and unimaginable. If we can put that into Quebecers' heads, that we're capable, that we're not small and that we have collective authority, and that if we speak as people, we can win this referendum."[53] In subsequent interviews, Bouchard speculated that, however grudgingly, the other provinces would have to follow Ontario's lead in negotiating a new relationship with a sovereign Quebec. "I think the rest of Canada would be very much interested to stick to Ontario, because Ontario will be the backbone of the rest of Canada," he said.[54]

Bouchard's appeal to Quebecers' "humiliation" had long been understood by his critics as garden-variety demagoguery. Now, however, with little more than two weeks left to inspire Quebecers to vote Yes, the Bloc leader tempered his famous passion with the cool detachment of a statesman, *à la* Parizeau. "We aren't interested in separating because we don't like the Rockies," he reassured Quebecers. "We've seen them. They are magnificent. A wonder of the world. The debate is whether Quebec accepts to be folded into Canada and renounce its identity."[55] To the suggestion that English Canadians would react with hostility to Quebec's partnership demand, Bouchard responded with equanimity. The negotiations would be conducted in an atmosphere of "extraordinary calm [and] serenity," he said.[56] Even more astonishingly, given his blistering personal attacks on Jean Chrétien, Bouchard adopted an almost brotherly tone vis-à-vis Daniel Johnson. "There's no doubt in my mind that Mr. Johnson is a genuine Quebecer," said Bouchard. "When the chips are down, he will be there with us to promote Quebec's interests."[57]

Riding a populist wave in Quebec, Bouchard moved decisively to distance himself from some of the débacles that had undermined Jacques Parizeau. On October 10, Bouchard dismissed the PQ's contentious sovereignty studies. "I don't want to hear anything about the Le Hir studies," he said. "Those are not my studies. Those are Mr. Le Hir's. That's past for me. That's the past campaign."[58] Two days later, Bouchard gave a warm speech to 500 Quebec business people in Sainte-Foy in an effort to mitigate the damage caused by Parizeau's verbal assault on big business. "Few groups have been exempted from the at-times-excessive rhetoric," he acknowledged. "Sometimes the people who pronounced words regretted them rapidly, if not later. But what we need to hope for above all, in the business community especially and in the Quebec community over-all, is that our differences of opinion never affect the solidarity that must prevail after the referendum."[59]

With new energy sizzling through the Yes campaign, Bouchard happily reported to his audiences that the federalists knew they were in trouble. "Imagine, the people who wanted to scare people are ending up panicking themselves," he asserted on October 11. "Why have the No side erased their triumphant and arrogant smiles from their faces? Why are they afraid? It's because the people on the No side are afraid of the day—the day is marked on the calendar, it's Oct. 30—that Quebecers will affirm themselves as a people and [Quebec] will present itself at the negotiating table, where Mr. Parizeau has sent me."[60] When Liberal senator Jacques Hébert casually mentioned to a journalist that Pierre Trudeau might join the referendum conversation, Bouchard responded with the same lively bravado. "He will be quite welcome in the debate, but I think it's a sign of panic," said the Bloc leader. "They are going back to their scare-mongering tactics and now they are trying to pull out the last spectre—Mr. Trudeau."[61]

Bouchard may have believed that Ontario was the key to a partnership deal, but this did not prevent him from lampooning Mike Harris, who had been elected premier of the province in June 1995. In a speech that ex-premiers Bob Rae and David Peterson had helped him write, Harris spoke about the Quebec referendum at Toronto's Canadian Club on October 12. "Let me be very clear," said Harris. "If Quebec separates, one thing is certain: Quebecers would no longer have access to the Canadian advantage, they would no longer be a part of Canada."[62] Bouchard was asked about Harris's remarks. "Who has an interest in putting up a fence between the two provinces?" he replied. "It's ludicrous. The truckers of Ontario will mass around Queen's Park to summon Mr. Harris to tear down those tariff barriers."[63] Several days later, Harris defended his government's 22 per cent welfare cut by telling Ontarians that he had once had to scrimp on food purchases and they could, too. Bouchard took full advantage. Impersonating Harris to riotous effect, he told a rally of Quebec college students that the Ontario premier was completely out of touch. "They can buy every month, two boxes of cornflakes—no sugar—two kilos of hamburger steak, ten bananas," said Bouchard. "I'm not making this up! It's written in the newspaper! He's come up with a menu for poor people!"[64]

Polls confirmed that within days of his elevation to chief negotiator Bouchard had breathed new life into the Yes vote. A Gallup/Radio-Quebec survey conducted between October 10 and 12 found the No vote leading by a margin of only 43–39, with 18 per cent undecided.[65] A Léger and Léger poll from the same period pegged the No vote at 50.8 and the Yes at 49.2 (though only by extrapolating the undecideds proportionately).[66] Just one week earlier, Léger had the Yes vote at 47.2 per cent. Sovereignists and federalists alike credited Bouchard with the two-point pop.[67]

Jean Chrétien—the man whom Bouchard had taken to calling the "apostle of infinite emptiness"[68]—could read the polls, of course. Perhaps recalling the sovereignist pollsters' caution that undecided Quebecers tended to vote No, the prime minister remained imperturbable. "Our [strategy] is working so we're not changing it," he said on October 14. "I was there in 1980. Do you remember the polls? So check them and look at the results and you will feel confident. Because last time it was much closer than this time and the result was 60–40."[69]

⁓

By the middle of October 1995, national unity was again the most press-ing of Canadians' political concerns and the Quebec contest the major preoccupation of the nation's political scribes. All seemed to agree on one thing: in such a close race, with such tightly scripted messaging, the leaders of both camps had to avoid gaffes at all costs. Even the slightest misstep could cost them the referendum, or so said the experts.[70]

In what turned out to be one of the most unexpected twists in the referendum campaign, however, the new *négociateur en chef* proved the experts wrong—not once but repeatedly. Soaring aloft on his 70 per cent trust rating among Quebecers, Bouchard was all but untouchable, even on verbal blunders that would have sent the likes of Claude Garcia or even Jacques Parizeau scurrying into full-blown damage control. This was the proof, if any were needed, that *l'effet Lucien* was real.

On Saturday, October 14, Bouchard spoke to a group of roughly 250 women at Ville d'Anjou. To underscore his message that Canadian federalism had prevented Quebec from setting its own social policy pri-orities, he invoked the spectre of population decline. "Do you think our demographics make sense?" asked Bouchard. "Do you think it makes sense that we have so few children in Quebec? We are one of the white races with the least children. It doesn't make sense."[71] Some audience members cheered Bouchard's statement, which explains perhaps why reporters covering the speech missed the phrase *races blanches* (white races). It was Tory leader Jean Charest, in fact, who picked up on it in a Toronto speech the next day. And from there it vaulted quickly onto the nation's front pages. "*Tempête autour des femmes*" ("Storm Around Women"), shouted *Le Devoir*.[72] "Was Bouchard Being Racist and Sexist, or Was He Just Stupid?" asked the *Ottawa Citizen*.[73]

Facing Lucien Bouchard in the House of Commons on Monday, October 16, with exactly two weeks left in the referendum race, Jean Chrétien went for the jugular. The leader of the opposition had made a "terrible blunder," said the prime minister, when he implied that "to be a good Quebecer, it is better to be white than coloured and it is certainly better to speak French than English."[74] An indignant Bouchard accused Chrétien of "distorting" his meaning. "Everybody knows there is a

problem with the birth rate in Quebec and that it concerns all governments," said Bouchard. "Everyone knows that in Quebec many couples,
and we all know people like that, would like to have children but cannot
afford to."[75] Chrétien countered by reading Bouchard's original *races
blanches* statement verbatim into the parliamentary record. "There are
Quebecers of every colour and every religion," he concluded solemnly.[76]

After Question Period, Bouchard fumed at Chrétien's opportunism.
"There is a demographic problem in Quebec," he told a press scrum. "I
quoted the technical term of demographers that among the population
of white races, the [Quebec fertility] rate is one of the lowest and I have
said this is unacceptable because we must preserve the choice of couples
to have children." Bouchard dismissed any suggestion that his remark
smacked of racism. "Me a racist?" he asked. "That's ridiculous. That's
a lie. I want an open society in Quebec. I want women to feel equal, to
have equality of opportunity."[77] Sought out by the press, demographers like Université de Montréal's Evelyne Lapierre-Adamcyk distanced
themselves from Bouchard's remark, insisting that the term *race* was
not part of their professional jargon. But Jacques Parizeau rose to his
ally's defence. "If you're asking whether the majority of the population
is rather white in the face, while other members of the same population
are of other colors, I will say yes indeed," said the premier. "I don't see
what's shocking unless you're nitpicking."[78]

As Parizeau well knew, there was more to some Quebecers' anxiety
about Bouchard's remark than mere nitpicking. Even the most innocu-
ous race talk fuelled the old fears that what sovereignists really desired
was "a French ethnic state" in North America. "If Mr. Bouchard is not
racist," charged Daniel Johnson, "he's clearly surrounded by people who
have a racist vocabulary, which he borrows from. [His statement was]
by far the most outlandish statement by an elected official in Canada
that I have heard in my life."[79] Daniel Johnson's wife, Suzanne Marcil,
echoed her husband. "I don't think anybody can ever tell women what
to do with their bodies," she said. "It's degrading, it's humiliating."[80]
Jamaican-Canadian Montrealer Ivyline Fleming was asked her opinion
of Bouchard's remarks. "If he wants more babies now, it's racist," she

replied. "That means to say he wants all the French people to go and have babies so the ethnic groups wouldn't exist any more."[81] A communiqué from the anti-racist organization SOS Racisme warned that Bouchard's words "could be perceived by fascist or white supremacist groups as legitimizing their actions."[82]

Leading sovereignists, particularly in the Bloc Québécois, had worked hard to promote a territorial and linguistic version of Quebec nationalism. Lucien Bouchard self-identified as an "old stock" Quebecer, but he openly celebrated Quebec's growing diversity and—in instances like his public reprimand of Bloc MP Philippe Paré the previous winter—he led by example.[83] Yet as Université Laval political scientist Louis Massicotte noted astutely, the old "*Québec aux Québécois*" brand of nationalism continued to appeal to some less-worldly separatists.[84] Seen in this light, Bouchard's invocation of a demographic crisis before an audience of women gave every appearance of a calculated gamble to attract the butterfly vote.

But Bouchard's defenders were many—and many of them were women. Françoise David, president of the Fédération des femmes du Québec, stood shoulder to shoulder with the Bloc leader at the height of the controversy on October 17. "Our primary interest here should be decent family policies," said David. "As a result, we want no part of this campaign of denigration of Lucien Bouchard."[85] Later the same day, Bloc MP Pierrette Venne told the House of Commons that Bouchard was working selflessly to improve the lives of all Quebecers. "The women of Quebec do not wish to be used as a red herring," said Venne. "Quebecers, both men and women, want the focus to be on true debate, not on blackening the character of a man of integrity, a man without a racist or sexist bone in his body."[86]

As for Bouchard himself, he knew that the tempest over his questionable choice of words had, at the very least, cost the Yes campaign valuable time. "I inappropriately used the words *race blanche* and I regret I used these words because it probably makes some people in Quebec feel they were excluded from the people of Quebec," he said. "I am not apologizing, I do not apologize."[87]

Bouchard was lucky in one respect. On October 12, Liberal senator Jacques Hébert was overheard calling Quebec journalist Josée Legault a *"vache séparatiste"* ("separatist cow").[88] Hébert apologized for the remark, but he knew that such a political slur, coming from a federal Liberal at the height of the referendum campaign, was likely to stick to the prime minister. Sure enough, on October 16, the same day that he was condemning Bouchard for his *races blanches* remark, Jean Chrétien was compelled to distance himself from his old friend in the House of Commons. "I was not present," he said of Hébert's comment. "I am told it was made in a private conversation. It was not said publicly, but if it was made, I deplore it."[89]

The prime minister was awakening to the new reality of the campaign. He had been forced to publicly censure an unelected Liberal senator while Bouchard himself "got away with an ethnocentric comment for which any other politician in Canada would have been clobbered."[90]

This double standard was about to get worse. On October 15, the day after his *races blanches* comment, Bouchard made two more public pronouncements that left his opponents' heads spinning. The first concerned the impact of a Yes vote on the Quebec economy—now the federalists' main campaign issue. "I'm sure there will be no economic hardship if we vote Yes," Bouchard casually told a press scrum. "If we vote Yes it means that democracy will have spoken, that there will be solidarity here, all of us will be united to work in the same camp."[91] Later that day, Bouchard spoke before 500 sovereignty supporters at Collège Ahuntsic in Montreal. "A Yes has magical meaning because with a wave of a wand it will change the whole situation," he told the students. "With the wave of a wand it will have the effect of provoking new solidarity, that is to say it will become a new rallying point for all Quebecers. The day after sovereignty there will be no more federalists, no more sovereignists. There will be only Quebecers."[92]

Jean Chrétien seemed genuinely nonplussed that the leading light in the Yes camp could make such facile statements with the future of Canada hanging in the balance. "We are heading for the 21st century," the prime minister inveighed in the House of Commons, "and

[Bouchard] says he has the answer, the magic wand. You wave the magic wand and poof, the studies commissioned by Le Hir vanish into thin air; another wave, and all the risks of separation disappear; another, and the concerns of everyone, from the Prime Minister of Canada to the leaders of other countries, are no more. And then suddenly, another wave and Mr. Parizeau, the leader of the No side, has vanished."[93] Chrétien was not alone. "The whole pitch to Quebecers of life after a Yes vote has a fairy-tale quality about it," wrote Jeffrey Simpson in the *Globe and Mail*.[94] The *Toronto Star* published yet another combative editorial. "Lucien Bouchard wants Quebecers to wave a 'magic wand' and, presto, everything will be better," said the *Star*. "He wants Quebec's white women to have more babies so that the 'white race' continues to hold its own against newcomers. And he promises there will be 'no economic hardship' if Quebec separates. What planet is this man on? Bouchard's credibility ought to be in tatters today after such absurd comments."[95]

～

Yet Bouchard's credibility was not in tatters. Polls showed that the Yes campaign had not been hurt by his questionable public statements. On the contrary, the sovereignists were now within the pollsters' margin of error of winning the referendum.[96] And the reason for this, as CROP spokesperson Alain Giguère noted, was not that Quebecers' fundamental political views had changed but that "Lucien Bouchard has reassured people who had been hesitant about voting Yes."[97]

Jacques Parizeau was delighted, of course. Now that the momentum was entirely on the sovereignists' side, he felt compelled to remind Quebecers that if the post-referendum negotiation with Canada was "going nowhere," they could simply opt for independence. "We're going to make Quebec sovereign," said the premier, "we agree on that. If there is a new partnership, bravo, perfect, and I believe there will be one. If there isn't, we declare sovereignty."[98]

An emboldened Lucien Bouchard made the same point on October 19. "I want it clearly understood that the question is on sovereignty and partnership after, but they aren't dependent," he said. "There's no hyphen between the two."[99] Never before had Bouchard publicly placed sovereignty before partnership, or spoken openly of what he was now calling a "double mandate."[100] As CTV's Lloyd Robertson observed, Bouchard's apparent shift towards Parizeau's more hard-line position marked "one of the most dramatic developments so far in Quebec's referendum campaign."[101]

By now, Jean Chrétien realized that he had grossly underestimated Lucien Bouchard's charismatic appeal. "Bouchard returned from Ottawa to Quebec like a prophet descending from the mountain to lead his people to the promised land," the prime minister later recalled. "It wasn't rational or even credible, but crowds came forward to be in his presence and ask him to bless the flag of Quebec. The miracle of his recovery, coupled with his demagogic oratory, lent him an aura that no logic or fact could penetrate."[102] Chrétien's advisor Eddie Goldenberg understood, as perhaps his boss did not, that Bouchard's appeal was not entirely ethereal. "As long as Parizeau had led the Yes forces, Quebecers understood his separatist objective and were ready to vote No in large numbers," Goldenberg observed. "Once Bouchard took over the leadership of the campaign, however, he was able to downplay the fundamental rupture of the country that separation would entail."[103]

Outside francophone Quebec, many Canadians were as bewildered by *l'effet Lucien* as their prime minister. Some wondered whether Quebecers had suddenly lost their capacity for rational thought. "Think about it," wrote Norman Webster of the Montreal *Gazette*. "Just three weeks ago, the Yes campaign was going nowhere. One solid year of separatist propaganda had made little impact. Then what happened? Parizeau stepped back and Bouchard stepped forward. That's all, that's it. No new information appeared, no new arguments; Bouchard himself said absolutely nothing new. Yet suddenly, we found ourselves witnessing a great new drama, the perfect TV story. The screens were filled with images of St. Lucien before adoring multitudes—exciting, stirring images. Voters bathed in clips of the Moses-Christ figure describing the promised land."[104]

As this simplistic, quasi-mystical reading of Bouchard's charisma reverberated throughout English Canada, thoughtful francophones like *La Presse* columnist Chantal Hébert—always a perspicacious interpreter of Quebec to the rest of Canada—contributed their own much-needed correctives.

"Is Lucien Bouchard the Pied Piper of Quebec politics?" asked Hébert. "In a classic case of fairy-tale coverage, that is the impression being left with many Canadians." It was true that ordinary people held Bouchard in high esteem, Hébert argued, but that was precisely because they had travelled the same tortuous path he had. "Like him, they admired Pierre Trudeau, voted for René Lévesque, were turned off by the patriation of the Constitution, took a chance with Brian Mulroney, supported the Meech Lake Accord and then, when it failed, started giving sovereignty a hard second look." To those Canadians who believed that Bouchard appealed to "the narrowest, meanest streak of Quebec nationalism," Hébert offered the reminder that Bouchard's recent converts were not hard-line separatists but "moderate nationalists, whose first instinct was to vote No because they had come to see many of the emotional attributes of sovereignty as outdated."

Daniel Johnson, Jean Chrétien, and the rest of Canada's federalist leaders had to face a cold, hard truth, said Hébert. They had created a vacuum, and Lucien Bouchard had simply stepped into it. "Months ago, the No camp decided to go for broke. It gambled that, when all was said and done, most Quebecers would prefer an unchanged Canada to a sovereign Quebec."[105]

CHAPTER ELEVEN

Federalist Setbacks

There was no *effet Daniel* during the referendum campaign. No one accused Daniel Johnson of being the Pied Piper of anything.

On the contrary, as Jacques Parizeau had predicted, Johnson's pragmatic, journeyman *Non* proved to be no rhetorical match for the soaring idealism of Lucien Bouchard's *Oui*. In the National Assembly, in his stump speeches, in campaign advertising, and in the official *Non* booklet distributed to all Quebec households in mid-October 1995, Johnson was bound to an unsentimental three-point script: separation was *le seul enjeu* (the only issue), the sovereignists' offer of partnership was *une illusion*, and *les conséquences économiques de la séparation* would be disastrous.[1] During the campaign, Johnson appeared to be genuinely ambivalent about Canada, which made him an easy target of the sovereignists. The official *Oui* booklet opened with a series of excerpts from Quebec's postwar premiers. Daniel Johnson Sr. was quoted as saying, "*J'aimerais être le premier président d'une République du Québec*" ("I would like to be the first president of a republic of Quebec"). Daniel Johnson Jr. was quoted as saying—in English—"I am a Canadian first and foremost."[2]

The implication was obvious. Johnson was not a true Quebecer.

~

What Johnson did have going for him was Quebecers' extremely well-documented fear that sovereignty would bring economic catastrophe. For months, economists had provided a steady stream of prognostications about what sovereignty would mean for the Quebec economy, and pollsters meticulously tracked their impact on Quebec voters. In the popular press alone, the number of articles on the economic fallout of a Yes vote numbered in the hundreds.

Sovereignists routinely accused federalists of fear-mongering when it came to the Quebec economy, and they had a point. "Quebec's divorce from Canada would be long, painful and more costly than most people can imagine," Business Council on National Issues president Thomas d'Aquino announced in early October. "In such an environment, partnership would be unthinkable."[3] Jason Kenney, president of the Canadian Taxpayers Federation, warned Quebecers that they stood to lose almost $11 billion—or $3,272 per person—with a Yes vote.[4] Economists from Edward Neufeld to Marcel Côté predicted massive increases in the provincial deficit after a Yes vote, from the current $5 billion to between $15 billion and $25 billion.[5]

But the main economic issue for recession-battered Quebecers was jobs, and Jacques Parizeau had known it even before becoming premier. The recession of the early 1990s had hammered the province. The provincial unemployment rate had spiked to 13.2 per cent in 1993.[6] By 1995, it had receded, but only to 11.5 per cent—two points higher than the national average. In an August 1995 SOM poll, 52 per cent of Quebecers chose "employment/economy" as the province's top political priority. Only 6 per cent chose sovereignty.[7] Taking full advantage of such numbers, Daniel Johnson had for months attacked Jacques Parizeau's sovereignty project as a diversion that Quebecers could ill afford. By October 1995, Johnson was predicting—on the basis of eleven studies written over the previous four years—that Quebec would lose 92,300 jobs after a Yes vote.[8]

Federal finance minister Paul Martin was even more outspoken on the economic folly of the sovereignist cause. Typical of Martin's approach was a September 1995 speech to a meeting of the Association des MBA du Québec (AMBAQ) in Montreal. "Let's not fool ourselves," said Martin. "Separation is separation. Purely and simply, it means the certain destruction of our economic and political union with Canada. What does that mean for Quebecers? Let there be no ambiguity about the consequences of breaking up. The use of the Canadian passport? Gone. Equalization payments? Gone. Federal transfers to Quebec? Gone."⁹ Martin's AMBAQ speech made headlines across Canada, prompting Lucien Bouchard to exert some leverage of his own. "It's obvious that one of the first steps of English Canada will be to run after Mr. Parizeau to ask him—to *beg* him—to sit down and discuss what should be [Quebec's] share of [the debt]," said Bouchard. "And it would not be possible for the rest of Canada to say no to everything to Quebec and at the same time ask [for] a huge cheque from the Quebec government to help them to pay back the debt. Everything will be linked."¹⁰

Daniel Johnson's and Paul Martin's tough talk on the Quebec economy had had the desired effect. The perception that the sovereignists were concealing their own bad news undoubtedly helped. Two-thirds of Quebec business leaders believed sovereignty would be accompanied by economic decline, which in turn made ordinary Quebecers extremely jittery.¹¹ But that was before *l'effet Lucien*. All of a sudden, in mid-October 1995, it became clear that the Yes vote was gaining ground with every reassurance from Bouchard that Quebecers could protect their niche in the North American economy. Blind-sided federalists saw no alternative but to inject even more doom into their doomsday scenarios for the Quebec economy—little realizing that Quebecers had had their fill of it.

The point of no return came on October 17. Speaking to a group of business people in Quebec City, Paul Martin posed the question "What would a Yes vote jeopardize?" His answer: "Ninety per cent of our exports would be threatened—close to one million jobs."¹²

A million jobs threatened. It was a bold claim, to say the least, but Martin denied that he was fear-mongering. "If stating the facts as they are scares people," he remarked after his speech, "then maybe people ought to pay attention to the facts."¹³ Such condescension from the federal minister of finance was too much for many Quebecers. Premier Parizeau, who was campaigning in Hull, mocked Martin's hyperbole. "Last week Mr. Johnson said we would loose 100,000 jobs," he observed.

"This week Mr. Martin says one million jobs are in jeopardy. If the trend holds, next week we will have to import unemployment!"[14] It was one of Parizeau's best one-liners of the campaign (he got it from the quick-witted Jean-François Lisée), and Quebecers applauded him for it. No one on the provincial No team had been consulted prior to Martin's million-jobs speech, but this was little consolation for Daniel Johnson, who was already portrayed by the sovereignists as taking his marching orders from Ottawa.

Polls would later confirm that Martin's remark had exactly the opposite effect on Quebecers than the one he intended. They began to tune out the economic arguments of the No side en masse.[15] "People are saying this is the final straw," CBC Radio personality Bernard St-Laurent reported after speaking with many ordinary Montrealers. "They're not going to listen to this scare crap any more."[16]

~

On October 17, ten days into Lucien Bouchard's tenure as *négociateur en chef*, two new polls were published. A SOM survey conducted for the Montreal *Gazette* and *Le Soleil* put the Yes vote at 42.9 per cent, the No vote at 43.4 per cent, and the undecideds at 13.6 per cent.[17] Even more dramatically, a *Toronto Star/La Presse* poll showed the Yes vote leading with 43.6 per cent, the No at 42.6 per cent, and 14 per cent of Quebecers undecided.[18] Bouchard was delighted. "I think we have the winning conditions in hand," he told a meeting of 300 Montreal lawyers. "We have never been so close to a great victory for Quebec. I think we're in the process of winning it."[19]

Jean Chrétien could see that the No campaign might be sputtering. The timing, at least, was fortuitous. On October 18, he was scheduled to speak before an audience of 800 at the Quebec Chamber of Commerce. Because this would be only his second major address in Quebec since the referendum campaign began, he resolved to hit Quebecers hard with the theme "Think it over before you vote."

How could Quebecers prepare for the twenty-first century? Chrétien asked. "By continuing to build a country which is undoubtedly one of the greatest successes of the twentieth century? Or, as the proponents of separation suggest, by starting all over again with the pieces of what we have destroyed?" It was not alarmist to point out the enormous economic risks of a No vote, the prime minister told his mainly business audience. "If you listen to [the sovereignists] they'll tell you that separation will be effected effortlessly, simply, easily, without any upheavals or difficulties, as if by magic, like casting a spell. Everything will go well and it won't cost a penny." They could not be more wrong. "Can Mr. Parizeau and his magician guarantee workers in the textile, agricultural, cultural and financial services sectors that there will be no negative consequences for them, for their families, for their communities? It's better to know now."

Chrétien then confronted Lucien Bouchard's mantra that English Canada would have no choice but to negotiate with a sovereign Quebec. "Who could this negotiator-in-chief talk to following a Yes vote?" asked the prime minister. Did Bouchard really believe that it would be the federal government representing the rest of Canada? "I absolutely have to lay to rest a myth that has been perpetuated for quite some time by the proponents of separation," said Chrétien. "They're depicting the rest of Canada as a monolithic bloc that speaks with a single voice. Nothing could be further from the truth. Canada with Quebec forms a country. No one knows what would be left without Quebec." There had never been any ambiguity about the prime minister's position on this issue. Quebecers needed to know that if they voted to break up Canada, there was no guarantee that they could negotiate anything with the fragments that remained.[20]

Chrétien closed his lengthy speech with an impassioned personal appeal to his fellow Québécois. "I am going to say No to separation," he said. "I will say it with pride. The pride of a Quebecer who believes in this country that we have built together. The pride of a Quebecer who believes that Quebec's essential place is in Canada. A Quebec which, by its language, its culture, and its institutions, forms a distinct society. And the pride that I feel being a Quebecer in no way contradicts something else that I am tremendously proud of, namely, of being Canadian."[21]

Just hours after his Chamber of Commerce speech, Chrétien revisited many of the same themes at a Liberal Party fundraiser. "We're not there yet," he told the party faithful. "We still have to fight."[22] Fighting meant hammering home the blunt message that a No vote in the referendum was a No to separation. Even though he was down in the polls, Chrétien was signalling, he was not prepared to discuss the Constitution in order to appease Lucien Bouchard.

Some Canadians applauded the prime minster for his continuing resolve.[23] But others could not believe that he would cling so stubbornly to the status quo with the referendum contest now in a virtual dead heat. "*Ottawa doit bouger*" ("Ottawa Must Move"), said *Le Soleil's* Jean-Jacques Samson flatly.[24] An incredulous Michel Gauthier, Bloc Québécois house leader, grilled Chrétien in the House of Commons. "In what should have been his most important speech in the referendum campaign, yesterday the Prime Minister simply gave Quebecers a warning by refusing to promise any sort of constitutional change to the present federal system," Gauthier charged.[25] The prime minister stood his ground. Canadians and Quebecers want an "end to talk of constitutional problems," he said, especially now that the "chief negotiator" had become the "chief separator."[26]

Smelling victory, the "chief separator" himself was only too happy to confront Jean Chrétien directly. "The more he talks," Bouchard joked, "the more the Yes side will increase!" The prime minister was plainly bluffing, said the Bloc leader, when he claimed that there might not be a constitutional entity called Canada with which a sovereign Quebec could negotiate a new partnership. On the contrary, Chrétien's only concern after a Yes victory would be to placate Canada's shaky allies and investors, which would mean acting decisively to stabilize the federal state. "It will not be an answer to say 'I'm going home to Shawinigan because I've not the mandate to do anything,'" said Bouchard. "The day after a Yes it will be absolutely imperative that the two prime ministers, Mr. Chrétien and Mr. Parizeau, publish something like a joint declaration to reassure all the financial markets."[27]

~

On Thursday, October 19, the slow-motion disintegration of the No campaign accelerated. Less than twenty-four hours after Chrétien's Chamber of Commerce speech, the Liberals' internal polling showed the sovereignists leading by a spectacular 54 per cent to 46 per cent. The No vote appeared to be in "freefall," the prime minister himself commented. "No one had a clue how to stop it."[28] The next day, an Angus Reid poll showed the Yes side leading by a more modest 51 per cent to 49, while a Léger and Léger poll showed the Yes side ahead 50.2 per cent to 49.8. Asked whether the No committee was panicking, Michel Bélanger put the best face he could on the unfolding disaster. "I don't think we are getting in any state like that," said Bélanger. "We always expected it would be a tough campaign."[29]

Chrétien's top advisor, Eddie Goldenberg, drove from Ottawa to Montreal that morning for an emergency meeting of the No team. There he found his provincial counterparts in full-blown crisis containment. After months of keeping Jean Chrétien at arm's length, they now wanted the prime minister to be "omnipresent" in Quebec for the remainder of the campaign.[30] Johnson's chief of staff, Pierre Anctil, urged Goldenberg to persuade the prime minister to give an emergency address on Radio-Canada under the provisions of the *Broadcasting Act*. But what Johnson's people most wanted from Chrétien was something concrete they could offer the undecided voters of Quebec—a commitment to reopen the Constitution, perhaps, or a timetable for devolving federal powers to the provinces. "For God's sake, you've got to give us something," Johnson aide John Parisella reportedly demanded.[31]

Out on the hustings, Daniel Johnson himself seemed to have lost his bearings. After a stump speech in Longueuil on October 21, he made his worst blunder of the campaign, telling reporters that it would be "desirable" for Prime Minister Chrétien to offer Quebecers constitutional reforms, including recognition of Quebec's distinct society and the restoration of Quebec's traditional veto. If the prime minister were to do this, said Johnson, it "would merely echo, from an important source, what we have been saying, what others are saying now. We're looking at change in Canada through a variety of very concrete ways and proposals."[32]

As it happened, on the Saturday afternoon that Daniel Johnson made this impromptu appeal for change, Jean Chrétien was at the UN in New York. He knew nothing about Johnson's Longueuil speech and, in fact, had been out of personal touch with his provincial counterparts for several days. When Canadian reporters asked him whether he intended to reopen the Constitution, Chrétien responded with his usual tough message. "We're not talking about the Constitution," he said. "We're talking about the separation of Quebec from Canada." Eddie Goldenberg later described the scrum as a trap, since the press knew what Johnson had said but the prime minister did not. Once Chrétien had fallen into it, the inevitable feeding frenzy followed. "*Chrétien dit non à Johnson*" ("Chrétien Says No to Johnson"), announced the front page of *La Presse*.[33] "No Side Splinters over Strategy," shouted the *Globe and Mail*.[34] Later that same Saturday afternoon, an anxious Daniel Johnson met up with Goldenberg at No headquarters in Montreal. "Eddie," he said, "I screwed up. I want to call and apologize to the prime minister."[35]

Alas, papering over the now public discord between the provincial and federal wings of the No campaign was not nearly as easy as issuing a private apology. For sixteen hours, working the phones between Montreal and New York, advisors to Jean Chrétien and Daniel Johnson hammered out the text of a "joint statement" designed to reassure Quebecers that they continued to speak with one voice. On October 22, with Chrétien still in New York, Johnson convened a news conference and read the joint communiqué aloud. "We state unequivocally that Quebec is a distinct society," it read. "We remind you that we have both supported the inclusion of this principle in the Canadian Constitution every time Quebec has demanded it. We supported it in the past, we support it today and we will support it in the future, in all circumstances."[36] The entire exercise had the air of a forced confession—not least because Jean Chrétien's opposition to the distinct-society clause in the Meech Lake Accord was notorious in Quebec.[37] As one unnamed federal strategist told journalist

Joan Bryden, "It sends the signal that we're panicking, that we're desperate, that we don't know what else to do."[38]

Given that it was loose talk with the press that had got him into hot water in the first place, Daniel Johnson would have done well not to take questions after reading the joint statement. But again he agreed to chat with journalists and again his extemporaneous comments took him well off script. Asked to provide some context for the joint communiqué, Johnson replied that his distinct-society remark "got out of control [and] Mr. Bouchard seized it." When a reporter reminded him that he and not Bouchard had put the prime minister in the hot seat, Johnson conceded that the fault was his. "If I did, I gave the wrong impression [and] I take the responsibility," he said. "We're not in a constitutional round. We're in a referendum battle to know whether we break the country and Quebec separates." As he left the scrum, Johnson grumbled that "the Yes side jumps on every single comma, opinion, word, expression and so forth."[39] It was not the noblest of sentiments coming from the man who had just weeks earlier driven Jacques Parizeau's *projet de souveraineté*, line by line, into the ground.

Lucien Bouchard could not have been happier with the unfolding melodrama in the No camp. Campaigning in Sept-Îles, he urged Daniel Johnson to cut his losses and join the Yes team. "Now that you know who you are dealing with, Mr. Johnson, now that your ally has shown his real face, don't you see that we will find ourselves together, you and your allies in the Quebec Liberal Party and us at the negotiating table when we face English Canada after a Yes vote?"[40] In Montreal, Bouchard told a group of college students that the prime minister's inflexibility would be his downfall. "All Mr. Chrétien can do at this point is make a few verbal pirouettes," he said. "But anything he can do now will push the undecideds toward us."[41] The Chrétien-Johnson schism had been so good for the Yes campaign that Jacques Parizeau and Lucien Bouchard had copies of the joint statement distributed to the national press without comment.

On October 22, the three sovereignist leaders—Parizeau, Bouchard, and Dumont—held their largest rally to date in Montreal. "*On veut notre pays!*" ("We want our country!") chanted the crowd of 5,000. When people looked back on the campaign, Lucien Bouchard told the audience, they might well conclude that Jean Chrétien's "No" to Daniel Johnson was "the most important contribution to clarifying the referendum debate." As usual when Bouchard took aim at the prime minister, his oratory took flight. "What did his No mean? This No is like a crude light projected on the sterility of a No vote. It is not only a No to Quebec sovereignty, it is a No to all change. It is a No to the notion of Quebec as a people. Mr. Chrétien wants a No so badly he's even ready to bulldoze Daniel Johnson out of the road."[42]

When Jacques Parizeau took the podium, he was happy to play the role of éminence grise and speak of Quebecers' rendezvous with destiny. "My friends," he told the crowd, "on October 30 we are going to be the founding people of Quebec. We are going to negotiate in good faith. We are going to extend our hand. But we'll do it as men and women certain of their country, certain of themselves, equal to equal, at last, for the first time in our history. [Canadians] deny that we are a people. We are a people. Never, never have we been so close."[43]

The next day, Newfoundland premier Clyde Wells, a man disdained in Quebec as a saboteur of the Meech Lake Accord, poured gasoline onto the sovereignist bonfire. "I'm not prepared ever to acknowledge that my quality of citizenship in this country is any less than the quality of a resident of another province by reason of language, culture, size of the province, economic power, color of my hair, ethnic origin or anything else," he said flatly.[44] Quebecers would later recall Wells's comment as one of the most insulting of the entire No campaign. Wells himself would concede only that it was badly timed.[45]

~

Jacques Parizeau's instincts were correct. Never had the sovereignists been so close to realizing their dream of a French state in North America. And never had Quebec federalists been so far from theirs, the dream they had inherited from Wilfrid Laurier, Louis St. Laurent, and Pierre Trudeau, that Quebecers could best achieve their national aspirations within a united, bilingual Canada. The disintegration of the No campaign in scant weeks had become a torment for Jean Chrétien, the more so for having been completely unanticipated. Gone was the cocky optimism of the previous spring, when he had demanded that Jacques Parizeau hold his vote *"au plus sacrant."* When he took the stage at the Verdun arena before 12,000 anxious Quebecers on October 24, and again when he broke down before his caucus colleagues the next morning, Chrétien knew that his "Don't worry, be happy" strategy was in tatters. It had given him little to fall back on, no plan B, nothing that his Quebec allies could build upon, as they had themselves reminded him so forcefully. With just five days remaining before the referendum vote, Chrétien would have to start over. He would throw himself into what remained of the campaign body and soul.

The afternoon of Wednesday, October 25, the prime minister taped an emergency address to the nation for broadcast across Canada that same evening. Crouching stiffly at his parliamentary desk, his face drawn and tired, the notes of his speech clenched between his hands, he gave every impression of a man in distress.

"For the first time in my mandate as prime minister," he began, "I have asked to speak directly to Canadians tonight. I do so because we are in an exceptional situation." Chrétien's message was for all Canadians but for Quebecers in particular, since their decision the following Monday would affect "the future of all Canada." Those who were "in all good faith" thinking of voting Yes as a means of changing Canada needed to listen carefully to the sovereignist leaders, said Chrétien. "They are very clear. The country they want is not a better Canada, it is a separate Quebec. Don't be fooled." In a plaintive voice, leaning forward into the eye of the camera, the prime minister asserted that Canada ought never to be taken for granted. "Once more, today it's up to each of us to restate our love for Canada. To say we don't want to lose it."

Midway through the twelve-minute speech, Chrétien restated his commitment to the reform of Canadian federalism. "I repeat tonight what I said yesterday in Verdun," he said. "We must recognize that Quebec's language, its culture and institutions make it a distinct society. And no constitutional change that affects the powers of Quebec should ever be made without the consent of Quebecers." The prime minister then appealed directly to undecided Quebec voters. "Do you really think that you and your family would have a better quality of life and a brighter future in a separate Quebec?" he asked. "Do you really think that the French language and culture in North America would be better protected in a separate Quebec? Do you really think you and your family will enjoy greater security in a separate Quebec? *Have you found one reason, one good reason, to destroy Canada?*"

Chrétien concluded his address with a personal appeal, stated soberly and without a hint of bravado. "In a few days, all the shouting will be over," said the prime minister. "You will be alone to make your decision. At that moment I urge you, my fellow Quebecers, to listen to your heart—and to your head. I am confident that Quebec and Canada will emerge strong and united."[46]

Before taping his speech, the prime minister had offered Lucien Bouchard equal time on the national airwaves. Some Canadians thought Chrétien daft, grumbling that "our Canadian niceness may be the death of us."[47] But this was no time, the prime minister reasoned, to hand the sovereignists an excuse to call the No side undemocratic.

Like Chrétien, Bouchard taped two speeches, one in each official language. But unlike the prime minister, who gave the same speech in both languages, Bouchard's addresses were different—dramatically so, in fact. When speaking in English, Bouchard kept to a comparatively tame script about the failure of constitutional reform and the need for Quebecers to break the impasse. "You will be upset on Monday night, especially if [you] have shown sympathy with Quebec," he told Canadians. "Yet Quebecers will make a decision, through a democratic process, the fairness of which does not afford any challenge." A Yes vote would mean that Quebec would become a sovereign country, but also that the government of Quebec would be bound to negotiate a new partnership with the Government of Canada. "Canada must also prepare itself for this negotiation," Bouchard said solemnly. "We have wasted too much money and time on sterile squabbles. Let us Quebecers recognize ourselves for what we are, a people, a vibrant country—proud, welcoming and confident."[48]

Much of Bouchard's French speech, in contrast, was taken up with excoriating Jean Chrétien. The reason the prime minister's "catastrophic remarks" were not credible, said Bouchard, was that the man himself was not credible. "This man, who turned his back on Quebecers each time they wanted to be recognized as a nation, this man has the bad manners to try, tonight, to make us believe that he foresees the recognition of Quebec's distinctiveness. How can he ask us to put ourselves at his mercy, by a second No? We won't be fools. The violated promises of 1980 and the odious blow in 1982 are too fresh in our memories. Mr. Chrétien, you won't serve us the same blow twice. We won't entrust you with Quebec's future."

To emphasize his point, Bouchard produced a prop—an oversized copy of the front page of the *Journal de Québec* for November 6, 1981, *la Nuit des Longs Couteaux*. It showed a photograph of Jean Chrétien and Pierre Trudeau laughing together beneath a headline that read "Lévesque Betrayed by His Allies."

Bouchard concluded his French speech with a powerful invocation of Quebecers' refusal to go on being humiliated. "It would be embarrassing to ask English Canada again to recognize us as a nation," he said. "All that is over. We are beyond pleas. But the day we grant ourselves nation status, we will grow to our real dimension. That day, I hope with all my heart for us, will be October 30. And then, the days that follow, we will have our first meeting of nations. Two nations that have never really met each other, who don't know each other well, will join together for the first time."[49]

The evening the speeches went to air, October 25, the sovereignists held a massive rally at the arena in Verdun where Jean Chrétien had spoken the night before. Ten thousand sovereignist faithful attended. The timing of the event allowed organizers to project Chrétien's televised address in real time, affording the crowd the opportunity to jeer him with shouts of "*vendu, vendu*" and stirring choruses of "Na Na Hey Hey Kiss Him Goodbye." The image of the *Journal de Québec* for November 6, 1981, was again deployed, this time on the arena's huge screens as a backdrop for Jacques Parizeau's speech. "Look at this front page," the premier told the crowd. "On one side, Jean Chrétien. Beside him, Pierre Trudeau. And they're laughing. Lévesque betrayed by his allies and they are laughing. Always remember this."[50]

When Lucien Bouchard took the podium, he, too, assailed the prime minister. "He wanted to deliver a speech *à la* Trudeau," said Bouchard of Chrétien's Verdun speech the night before, but he gave "only vague suggestions of change with no commitment, nothing concrete. Imagine when he promises something!" Again the Bloc leader asserted that the prime minister's No to Daniel Johnson was the "death knell" of Canadian federalism. "The answer is No, the answer has always been No to Quebec," he said. "There have been enough Nos for Quebec. From now on it will be a Yes. We have realized if we ever want to hear the beautiful word Yes, we'll have to pronounce it ourselves."[51]

~

A clutch of polls published on October 27 appeared to show that the federalists had arrested the "free fall" of the No vote.[52] The feds' internal polling was even more promising, showing "a definite upturn" in the number of voters intending to cast a No ballot.[53] If the undecideds were still inclined to tip backwards off the fence and vote No, the race was still the federalists' to lose.

Some No-camp strategists credited Jean Chrétien's emergency address with stabilizing the No vote. The broadcast had "focused the attention of Quebecers on the consequence of their vote like nothing else in the campaign," said Eddie Goldenberg.[54] Others believed, however, that the sovereignists' increasingly shrill personal attacks on the prime minister were their undoing. Lucien Bouchard's speech at Verdun was "not founded on a generous and constructive vision of the future," observed Jean Charest, "but on a settling of accounts with enemies, 'traitors,' whose worst sin lay in not thinking as [sovereignists] did."[55] This was certainly Jean Chrétien's view. "Even I was shocked by how low [Bouchard] stooped when he suddenly held up the front page of a nationalist newspaper from November 1981 showing Trudeau and me laughing at a joke during a break in the constitutional talks, and then dared to say that we had been laughing at Quebec. It was totally unfair, completely untrue, and absolutely the worst kind of demagoguery. It was the crudest stunt I had ever seen in Canadian politics."[56]

Fully recovered from the joint-statement imbroglio, Daniel Johnson had shared the stage with Jean Chrétien at Verdun and commended his recognition of Quebec as a distinct society. He did so again after Chrétien's emergency address. "The prime minister showed he's not only associated with change, but, in my view, promoting it," said Johnson. "That's a new vision of what can be accomplished that is in stark contrast to the bromides that we heard from Lucien Bouchard."[57]

The prime minister's emergency broadcast drew decidedly mixed responses from Canadians. An editorial in the *Victoria Times-Colonist* praised Chrétien for trying to puncture the "cocoon" of Quebecers who had been "seduced by a demagogue into a rapturous state of ignorance."[58] Dalton Camp, writing in the *Toronto Star*, called Chrétien's address "eloquent, sincere and appealing."[59] *Calgary Herald* columnist Don Braid, by contrast, lamented that Chrétien had spoken from his head and his wallet, but not his heart. "I watched Chrétien in English and then Lucien Bouchard in French," wrote Braid. "What a difference: Bouchard was magnificent—a leader propelled by a grand vision, however misguided and dangerous, for his people."[60]

In truth, as Jean Chrétien knew better than anyone, there remained outside of francophone Quebec a sea of simmering anger towards the sovereignists. "The big lie promulgated by Lucien Bouchard and those who can taste victory for the *Oui* side is breathtaking in its scope," fumed *Calgary Herald* columnist Catherine Ford.[61] Writing on the editorial page of the *Edmonton Journal*, Mark Lisac suggested that western Canadians had been "struck speechless" by Quebecers' irrationality, and in particular by Bouchard's stubborn refusal to accept "clear evidence that Canadians think Quebec is a distinct society."[62] Montreal *Gazette* columnist Jay Bryan offered a caustic pledge. "In keeping with the new spirit of good fellowship," he wrote, "this column pledges that during the entire remainder of the referendum campaign, we won't spit in the premier's soup, won't call him a pinstriped thug for intimidating political opponents into silence and will try hard to be more polite in pointing out that his promise of cost-free separation is a crude lie."[63] University of Windsor political scientist Heather MacIvor claimed not to understand Bouchard's appeal to Quebecers. "His speeches are full of lies," she observed. "But he is the most charismatic leader Quebec has seen in years."[64]

One of the few prominent Canadians to profess that he was "undismayed" by the possibility of Quebec's secession was newspaper mogul Conrad Black. As he told a University of Alberta audience on October 26, although he would "deeply regret" Quebec's departure from Canada, Black found the referendum campaign exhilarating and the prospect of Canada without Quebec potentially liberating. "No longer having to squander an inordinate amount of our national energy in unrequited passion with our parting compatriots, our choice would be enviable," said Black. "In particular, we could choose to flourish by merely jettisoning the Ozymandian wreckage of a failed bicultural state with the back-breaking and ultimately corrupt transfer-payment system and the mad binge of political correctness that have gone with it."[65]

Seen in retrospect, Conrad Black's unsentimental commentary highlighted an under-appreciated aspect of some Canadians' struggle with the sovereignty question. Many non-francophones did harbour a "passion" for Quebec, it was true. But they also harboured a passion for the Canada that Quebecers had helped make possible. A telling moment in Black's Alberta address came when he offered this hopeful prognosis for Canada in the aftermath of a Yes vote: "Without Quebec, a majority of Canadians would be electors of Ralph Klein and Michael Harris."[66] For many Canadians, the idea that a Yes vote might usher in the sort of downsized and deregulated Canada dreamt of by neo-con politicians merely added pathos to the unimaginable spectre of losing Quebec. Such a Canada would almost certainly jettison official bilingualism and multiculturalism (as per the Reform Party platform), followed by whatever remained of the liberal Just Society. Conrad Black was no "anti-French, anti-Kweebec noisemaker," to borrow Norman Webster's apt phrase.[67] But to the progressive My-Canada-includes-

Quebec crowd, Black's blueprint for a post-referendum Canada made Jacques Parizeau's *projet de société* look pretty good.

Conrad Black's claim to speak for a majority of Canadians outside Quebec also highlighted one of the great paradoxes of the No campaign. Jean Chrétien had maintained consistently that there was no Canada without Quebec, and so had most of Canada's constitutional experts. But polls showed conclusively that most ordinary Canadians did not share this view. In the final week of the referendum campaign, a Southam News/Angus Reid survey revealed that 82 per cent of respondents believed that the nine Canadian provinces outside Quebec "will stay together as a single country."[68]

Here was a Catch-22 if ever there was one. The more Canadians spoke and acted like a country that would continue without Quebec, the more they sounded like Lucien Bouchard and Jacques Parizeau.

~

In early October, just as the official referendum campaign was shifting into high gear, the Quebec Inuit, Crees, and Montagnais announced that they would hold their own referenda on Quebec sovereignty.[69]

The Crees were first out of the gate, on October 24, with the question "Do you consent, as a people, that the Government of Quebec separate the James Bay Crees and Cree traditional territory from Canada in the event of a Yes vote in the Quebec referendum?" Unsurprisingly, 96.3 per cent of Crees voted No.[70] At a Montreal press conference, Grand Chief Matthew Coon Come stated flatly that any attempt to include his people in a sovereign Quebec without their consent would be both unconstitutional and a violation of their human rights. "The message is clear," he said. "We won't go. This would be the kidnapping of the James Bay Crees. This would be the hijacking of a whole people and their lands. This we will not allow the separatists to do."[71] Erected behind Coon Come was a large map of Quebec. It demarcated the northern two-thirds of the province (territory ceded to Quebec by an act of the federal parliament in 1898 and again in 1912) as Cree and Inuit land. This land-mass included the enormous Hydro-Québec installations around James Bay, potent symbols of modern Quebec's economic might.[72] If Quebec were to leave Canada, Coon Come was signalling, the Cree and Inuit, with a combined population of fewer than 20,000 people, would leave Quebec and take much of the province with them.

To remind Canadians of their duty to first nations, the Crees ran a full-page ad in the *Globe and Mail* on October 26. "We the James Bay Cree have voted No to separation from Canada," it read. "We ask Canadians to uphold the Canadian Constitution, our treaty and fundamental human rights, and the rule of law. We ask Canadians to support our right to remain, with our traditional territory and its hydro-electric and other natural resources, in Canada."[73]

David Cliche, Parti Québécois spokesperson for native affairs, responded to the Cree by reiterating his government's position that the borders of Quebec were inviolable. "I agree that the Crees' rights shouldn't be jeopardized by a sovereign Quebec," said Cliche. "But I disagree with their position that they can remain attached to Canada after Quebec's secession."[74]

The Inuit and Montagnais referenda followed on October 26. Ninety-five per cent of the Inuit voted No to the question "Do you agree that Quebec should become sovereign?"[75] "The Inuit have stood up to be counted," said spokesperson Zebedee Nungak. "We've had the sovereignist leaders dismiss this exercise but that doesn't diminish our determination one little bit."[76] A near-unanimous 99 per cent of the Montagnais also said No to an affiliation with a sovereign Quebec. "The message is clear," said Montagnais leader Guy Bellefleur. "We will refuse the forcible inclusion of our people and traditional lands in an independent Quebec state."[77] Although the Mohawks of Quebec did not hold a referendum, Kahnawake chief Billy Two Rivers agreed with the other aboriginal leaders. If Quebecers could secede from Canada, he said, the Mohawk could secede from Quebec.[78]

At a meeting of roughly 100 aboriginal leaders in Ottawa on October 26, delegates called on the federal government to "break its silence" on the issue of Quebec sovereignty.[79] The Government of Canada had a duty to protect the rights of Quebec's aboriginal people, they asserted, which meant intervening decisively in any negotiations with the government of Quebec after a Yes vote. Ovide Mercredi, national chief for the Assembly of First Nations, left little doubt about his federalist inclination, calling Quebec sovereignists "defeatists" for refusing to work co-operatively for change with other Canadians. But it was Matthew Coon Come who received a standing ovation from conference delegates for his stern defence of aboriginal autonomy. "We are not in the federal camp," he said. "We are not in the provincial camp. We are in the Cree camp."[80]

Prime Minister Jean Chrétien proved unwilling in the last week of the Quebec referendum campaign to break his own silence on native leaders' demands. Conjecture about the feds having to "partition" Quebec after a Yes vote or even send in federal troops to secure aboriginal lands was already running rampant in Canada—fuelled by statements by experts like Osgoode Hall professors Patrick J. Monahan and Kent McNeil to the effect that aboriginals' consent would be imperative in any secession deal. Polls showed that 80 per cent of Canadians outside Quebec thought aboriginal people should not be forced to secede from Canada, and that the federal government had an obligation to defend their rights. But, as pollster Darrell Bricker noted, upwards of half of the Canadians who took this view did so as a "spiteful and vengeful" reaction to Quebec sovereignists.[81]

With their eyes focused on the non-aboriginal vote in Quebec, the leaders of the No camp, Jean Chrétien foremost among them, had little to gain from entering this particular minefield. But the federal minister of Indian affairs, Ron Irwin, was not a major player in the No campaign and had the prime minister's blessing to speak freely. Aboriginal people were not "cattle" to be shunted between countries, he told the chiefs' conference on October 27. Aboriginal people had the right to remain in Canada after a Yes vote, said Irwin, and to do so with their territories intact. If Canada's borders were divisible, then Quebec's were as well. The federal government had to "walk a very fine line in Quebec," Irwin conceded, but he added that the prime minister "feels the same way as I do."[82]

In point of fact, the prime minister had his own agenda where Quebec's aboriginal people were concerned. He was quietly hoping that on October 30 they would break their historic pattern of abstaining from voting in non-aboriginal referenda.

~

Until the prime minister of Canada made his emergency broadcast to the citizens of his country, on October 25, the outside world showed little interest in the Quebec referendum. But now, with the polls too close to call and Canadian federalists pulling out all the stops to salvage a win, everyone took notice. By the final weekend of the referendum race, roughly seventy foreign media crews had descended upon Montreal. Most expressed genuine bewilderment at what they found there. "If a rich, modern, peaceful country such as Canada can fly apart," said a typical story in the British *Independent*, "then what hope for the rest of us?"[83]

Every once in a while world leaders had offered Canadians well-intentioned words of wisdom on national unity. While attending an international conference in early October, for example, former prime minister Brian Mulroney persuaded former presidents George Bush Sr. and Mikhail Gorbachev to make brief statements in support of Canadian federalism. "I am a staunch believer in one Canada," said Bush. "I'm not trying to influence anything, but I would hate to see Canada divided."[84] Gorbachev agreed. "The lesson of the Soviet Union," he said, "and I think it's an important lesson, is that any breakup can produce very severe strains, very serious difficulties."[85] Jean Chrétien later recalled that many of the UN delegates he had encountered in New York told him privately that they were dismayed by the deeds of Quebec sovereignists. They thought it was a "mystery and a tragedy" that Canada should be on the verge of breaking up, he wrote. "And for what? To overthrow the shackles of oppression, injustice, or persecution? It was impossible to explain without drawing looks of disbelief and impatience."[86]

Yet world opinion mattered enormously to both sides in the referendum debate, since it is international recognition that confers legitimacy upon peoples and states. Jean Chrétien was beside himself, for example, when French president Jacques Chirac casually told American broadcaster Larry King on October 23 that France would have to think seriously about how to respond to a Yes victory in the Quebec referendum. Jacques Parizeau and his senior ministers had been courting French officials doggedly since taking power, hoping that France would spearhead international recognition of Quebec after a Yes vote. Chrétien knew that French recognition of Quebec could be disastrous for Canada—the start of an official-recognition snowball that might end with Quebec taking its own seat at the UN. Even some of Canada's most conservative jurists acknowledged reluctantly that the breach of the Canadian constitutional order envisaged by Jacques Parizeau might be "legal," since all successful revolutions bring "a new legal order" into existence even though they begin as illegal challenges to established authority.[87]

In the international-recognition sweepstakes, the big prize was the United States. Parizeau and his ministers had been working behind the scenes to prepare the ground for American recognition of Quebec after a Yes vote, much as they had in France. But here their prospects were not nearly so promising. President Bill Clinton had no desire to see Canada break up, nor did Secretary of State Warren Christopher. And as the sovereignists well knew, Clinton's man in Ottawa, U.S. ambassador James Blanchard, was colluding actively with Eddie Goldenberg and his team to thwart a sovereignist victory in the referendum.

On October 18, at Ambassador Blanchard's urging, Secretary of State Christopher responded to a reporter's question about the Quebec referendum in a manner designed to convey his administration's support for a united Canada. "I don't want to intrude on what is rightfully an internal issue in Canada," said the secretary of state. "But, at the same time, I want to emphasize how much we've benefited here in the United States from the opportunity to have the kind of relationship that we do have at the present time with a strong and united Canada."[88] Christopher went on to remark that the place of an independent Quebec within NAFTA and other such pacts was by no means assured. The next

day, Quebec's deputy premier Bernard Landry dispatched a formal diplomatic letter to the secretary of state, one that had been written by
Jean-François Lisée and approved by Jacques Parizeau. "Quebec is now
living a historic moment," the letter read. "Should American declara-
tions be publicly perceived as a factor in the decision that Quebecers are
to make, they would enter into our collective memory and the history
books."[89]

Landry later denied that he had threatened Christopher, but the
episode handed the No forces fresh ammunition when they most
needed it. "If we separate Monday," observed Daniel Johnson, "we're
going to have to renegotiate the North American Free Trade Agreement
with the Americans. And Bernard Landry, in a lack of judgment that is
unparalleled and unprecedented in Quebec, says to the Americans that
they should abstain and he threatens and intimidates them. Who does
he think he is?"[90]

On October 21, while he was in New York, Jean Chrétien spoke with
Bill Clinton at a private reception. The president asked how the referendum campaign was going.

"It's getting pretty tough," Chrétien replied.

"You know, Jean," Clinton said, "it would be a terrible tragedy for
the world if a country like Canada were to disappear. Do you think it
would help if I said something?"[91]

Four days later, Clinton responded to a planted question from a
Canadian reporter posted to Washington, D.C. "Mr. President, are you
concerned about the possible break-up of Canada and the impact it
could have on the North American economy and U.S.-Canadian trade
relations?" asked the journalist.

"Let me give you a careful answer," said the president. "When I was
in Canada last year, I said that I thought that Canada had served as a
model to the United States and to the entire world about how people
of different cultures could live together in harmony, respecting their
differences, but working together." Of course, the referendum vote was
an "internal issue" for Canadians to decide, said Clinton, and he would
not presume to interfere. "But Canada has been a great model for the

rest of the world and has been a great partner for the United States, and I hope that can continue."[92]

~

The frenetic intensity of the final week of the campaign gave way to at least one light moment. On October 26, Quebec radio personality Pierre Brossard placed a call to Buckingham Palace and proceeded to impersonate Jean Chrétien over a seventeen-minute conversation with Queen Elizabeth II.[93] The conversation began with small talk about the Queen's Halloween plans and then segued to the Quebec referendum. "The Canadian political situation is very critical," said Brossard in his best Chrétien accent. "Our latest polls are showing that the separatists are going to win the referendum of the independent [sic] of Quebec."

"Well, it sounds as though the referendum may go the wrong way," replied the Queen. "If I can help in any way, I will be very happy to do so."[94]

Quebec radio listeners may have thought the prank hilarious, but palace officials were not amused by Brossard's "carefully contrived confidence trick," as they put it. They reported the incident to the Canadian prime minister's office, prompting one humourless aide to announce, "We have absolutely no comment on this issue." As for Brossard, he apologized to the Queen.

With only a few days left in the campaign, the No forces appeared to have survived *l'effet Lucien*, the sovereignist surge in the polls, and an embarrassing schism in their own ranks. In the meantime, however, many ordinary citizens had run out of patience with the feds' top-down, father-knows-best approach. A *Calgary Herald* editorial captured the emerging *zeitgeist*: "Early in the debate, a confident federal government told Canadians outside Quebec to stay clear of the hustings. Leave everything to the professionals. That seemed reasonable and we complied. Now with the Yes side threatening to win the race, many fear we should have been more direct and forthright in our appeals for a united Canada." The *Herald* advised Canadians to take matters into their own hands. "March in a public demonstration. Telephone or write letters to politicians—better yet to people selected at random from the Montreal and Quebec City telephone directories. Call talk radio programs. Write letters to newspaper editors. Put Canadian and Quebec flags in your window. None of those gestures will sway the vote by themselves. But if we don't make them, we will have done nothing to save our nation in a time of crisis."[95]

Similar sentiments were expressed in every region of the country, sometimes in considerably less diplomatic language, sometimes accompanied by tears of frustration and worry. The experts had made a terrible botch of the campaign, and the future of Canada was hanging in the balance. It was time for ordinary Canadians to take a stand.

CHAPTER TWELVE

Amour à Montréal

On Monday, October 23, two days after his forty-first birthday, federal fisheries minister Brian Tobin arrived at his Ottawa office in a state of agitation. Sitting around a boardroom table with his top staffers—the same group that had masterminded his famed "Turbot War" against the Spanish the previous spring—Tobin was struck by the eerie disconnect between their mundane discussion of ministry business and the unspoken reality that Canada might be on the verge of breaking up. Ten minutes into the meeting, he dispersed the group and adjourned to his office with his deputy minister, Bill Rowat, and his executive assistant, Gary Anstey. "Gentlemen, this whole situation is surreal," Tobin told them. "Here we are facing at the very least a possible constitutional crisis in a week's time, and we're behaving as though everything were normal. And it's not."[1]

Tobin asked his aides if they knew of any scheduled federalist events they could join. His policy director, Francine Ducros, was in touch with Phil O'Brien at the Quebec Business Council for Canada and knew that he was planning a noon-hour rally at Place du Canada in Montreal for the following Friday, October 27. The council had drawn 3,500 Montrealers to its first downtown rally, on October 18, but O'Brien figured that with better planning the follow-up could be far more grand. When his colleague Pierre-Claude Nolin applied for a permit for the October 27 event, he estimated that the crowd would number between

10,000 and 15,000 people. Tobin saw immediately that O'Brien's unity rally had excellent growth potential. Place du Canada's 1.4 hectares of groomed lawns could easily accommodate a crowd of 30,000, and the adjacent Square Dorchester, just across Boulevard René-Lévesque, could hold thousands more. Tobin imagined that he and his associates could, even at this late date, make a significant contribution to the event—promoting it, organizing logistics, and perhaps even bringing in a prominent federalist speaker or two.

Tobin decided he would make a few calls, starting with Frank McKenna. The New Brunswick premier gave every impression that he had been waiting for his phone to ring. "If you're asking me if I can help out by bringing people to Montreal," McKenna told Tobin, "you can count on it. I'll be there. Tell me when and where, and I'll bring as many New Brunswickers as I can."[2]

Tobin's next call was to Lloyd Axworthy, the veteran Manitoba MP now serving as federal minister of human resources development Canada. Axworthy thought the idea of inviting people from all over Canada to Montreal was a good one, but raised the obvious question: how could it be accomplished over such vast distances, on such short notice, and on a weekday? "If we got an aircraft," Tobin asked Axworthy, "could you fill it up?" Of course, Axworthy replied.[3]

Tobin worked the phones all morning, calling in markers and appealing to his colleagues' patriotism. "I called senators, cabinet ministers, MPs, premiers, anyone I knew who shared my concerns and who would agree to take action," he later recalled. "My message was the same: we have to do something. There is a rally in Montreal on Friday. Let's gather as many Canadians as we can and have them deliver the two words that could make a difference: *we care*."[4]

In the afternoon, Tobin rang Hollis Harris, president of Air Canada. He told Harris that he "was speaking not as a minister of the Crown but as a private citizen"—an obfuscation that Tobin would later repeat when accused by the Yes camp of violating Quebec's strict referendum spending limits. "You want planes," Harris told Tobin, "I'll get you planes. We'll put them where you need them. Count on it."[5] Harris agreed to provide special charter flights to Montreal from Vancouver, Calgary, Edmonton, Regina, and Winnipeg. Tobin then called Kevin Jenkins, CEO of Canadian Airlines, and made the same pitch. Several hours later, Jenkins called him back with good news. Canadian would post special "unity rates" for flights to Montreal, some discounted by up to 90 per cent. For flights less than 800 kilometres, the fare would be $99. For longer flights, the fare would $199. Air Canada then agreed to match Canadian's discounted fares—purely for "commercial reasons," it claimed. To take advantage of these unity fares, Canadians had to fly to Montreal on Thursday, October 26, and return home on Friday or Saturday.[6]

As planning for the unity rally quickly gathered steam, it occurred to Brian Tobin that he should inform the prime minister and the cabinet of his activities. At the Tuesday morning cabinet meeting, he pitched his plan. "We can't just sit on our hands," he told his colleagues. "[Lucien] Bouchard has been successful at convincing Quebecers that the rest of us are indifferent, that we don't care. That's not true, as everyone in this room knows, but it is a very effective line. We must give Canadians a chance to show Quebecers that they *do* care."[7] Jean Chrétien opened the floor to discussion of Tobin's proposal. Reactions were mixed. Some Quebec ministers worried that a mass influx of Canadians orchestrated by the feds would play poorly among not only the sovereignists but also among their own provincial allies. (They were correct about this. "Operation English Canada Saves the Day" is how some provincial No organizers referred to the planned rally.)[8] But in the end, Chrétien and his ministers agreed that they had little to lose in backing Tobin's venture, so they thanked him for his efforts and wished him good luck.

~

Brian Tobin was not the first Canadian to imagine that Quebecers might respond warmly to expressions of affection from people living in the rest of Canada. Far from it.

As early as the spring, when it looked as though Jacques Parizeau's draft bill might proceed directly from the consultation phase to a referendum vote, Canadians had begun thinking of ways to appeal to

Quebecers' sentimental side. In March 1995, for example, Dalhousie University student Dominic Cardy organized a cross-country trek intended to bring hundreds of students, from Vancouver to Halifax, into Quebec City. (This initiative was postponed when Parizeau announced that the referendum would not be held in the spring.) A Cornwall, Ontario, group sponsored a cross-Canada bike ride in support of national unity in June 1995. Musicians of every stripe wrote and recorded "unity songs." Pilots towed banners shouting "Canada without Quebec is not an option" and other slogans.[9] A Woodbridge, Ontario, group calling itself Canadians for a Unified Canada was one of dozens of local organizations to sponsor letter-writing campaigns. Investment planner Tony Duscio launched one such initiative from his home in Kitchener, Ontario. "Somewhere along the line, people in Quebec have been sold the story that the rest of Canada doesn't care about them," said Duscio. "Most ordinary people I've talked to don't want Quebec to separate."[10]

In late September 1995, the Association canadienne-française de l'Alberta paid $24,000 to run an ad in *La Presse*, *Le Journal de Montréal*, and *Le Soleil*. Accompanied by a map showing communities where Alberta's 65,000 francophones were concentrated, the ad read "There are ties which should not be broken. There's a place for French in Canada, Quebec has its place in Canada."[11] The same organization would later run letter-writing and postcard campaigns. "It's not a question of meddling," insisted spokesperson Paul Denis. "It's a question of bringing to Quebecers a point of view from other Canadians who speak French."[12] Leo Boileau organized a group of franco-Calgarians to call up Quebecers at random and urge them to vote No. "If we had a magic formula to reach out and touch Quebecers, to tell them to stick with us, I'd use it," said Boileau. "But there is no magic word, no magic formula. The least we can do is pick up the phone."[13]

Canadians from all walks of life—but especially the students, teachers, and parents involved in French-immersion education—pitched in with phone calls, postcards, letters, faxes, and in-person trips to Quebec to persuade Quebecers not to leave. "Please stay in Canada," wrote the grade five and six students of St. Stephen's School in Rencontre East, Newfoundland. "What will Canada be without you? We are proud to have you as our brothers and sisters. Your ancestors and our ancestors built this country. We can all work together to make this country a better place to live in. We wouldn't want to lose a great part of our country."[14] Prayer vigils for national unity were held in churches across Canada. Unity rallies were organized virtually anywhere there was a town square, including several at Toronto's Nathan Phillips Square. Syndicated newspaper cartoonist Ben Wicks asked Canadian schoolchildren to send him their "love letters" for Canada and was overwhelmed when he got 50,000 submissions in response. Wicks quickly put out a book of their drawings and letters entitled *Cher Canada: Une lettre d'amour à mon pays* (*Dear Canada: A Love Letter to My Country*).[15]

On October 1, *Toronto Star* publisher John A. Honderich invited readers from English Canada to "tell Quebecers how you feel."[16] The *Star* received 1,100 letters in response, selecting sixty-five for publication in a special section of the newspaper. Three hundred and fifty thousand copies of a French translation of the section were bundled up and shipped to *La Presse* in Montreal, which had agreed to run it as a "From Us to You" supplement to its Saturday edition on October 21. Unfortunately for the *Star*, the entire shipment was returned to Toronto after *La Presse* publisher Roger D. Landry, in consultation with his lawyers, decided that the section, valued at $16,000, violated Quebec's referendum spending law. Honderich was "disappointed and surprised" at Landry's decision, but added, "I'm not going to break the law for the *Toronto Star* or anybody else."[17]

The *Star* was down but not out. Over the last week of the campaign, the newspaper urged its readers to bombard Quebecers with emails, faxes, and phone calls. "There will be endless expressions of good wishes in fractured French," observed a *Star* editorial. "In an era of corrosive political cynicism, when people are supposedly terminally tuned out, this is a remarkable tribute. Canadians aren't about to let the country be wrecked without being heard. That is why they are reaching out over the heads of separatist politicians, to deliver their messages in person. Sentimental? You bet. Excessive? Not a bit, considering the high stakes. Too late? Maybe."[18] Oddly, perhaps, it did not seem to occur to anyone at the *Star* that such sticky sentimentality might be at odds with the paper's editorial position on the referendum. For the better part of a year, the *Star* had led the attack on Quebec's sovereignist leaders as "cynical and manipulative," intent on tricking gullible voters with their "big lie." Having positioned Quebecers as naive, the paper now sought to win them over with its own emotional appeals.

Motions appealing to Quebecers to remain in Canada were tabled in the legislatures of Newfoundland, Nova Scotia, Prince Edward Island, and British Columbia. Quebec flags were flown over government buildings across Canada. The New Brunswick legislature passed a resolution expressing "deep affection for and kinship with the people of Quebec," and later followed with an all-party motion committing New Brunswickers to work with Quebecers to entrench distinct-society status in the Canadian Constitution.[19] PEI Premier Catherine Callbeck reminded Quebecers that her province had always supported distinct society status for Quebec, and it did still. "A country is not like an oil painting that stays the same once it's finished," she said. "It's a picture that changes and evolves." The government of Ontario passed a resolution urging Quebecers to vote against sovereignty. *"Nous aimons le Canada"* Mike Harris declared in the Ontario legislature. *"Nous aimons le Québec."*[20]

~

Having won the support of the prime minister and the federal cabinet, Brian Tobin mobilized his entire staff in the cause of the unity rally. "I had young junior staffers, who had never been involved in any kind of campaign, receiving commitments of money from one area of the country and directing it to other areas that needed it," he later recalled. "Local committees began springing up to handle things in their districts, and the entire process assumed a life of its own."[21]

The morning of Wednesday, October 25, Tobin appeared on the CBC-TV and CTV network morning shows to promote the rally. Even before Canadians had heard about the airlines' discounted fares, roughly 5,000 had booked flights to Montreal on their own dime. When Tobin announced the special unity fares on national television, the floodgates opened. "The reservation lines haven't stopped ringing," said Canadian Airlines spokesperson Laurie Schild. "People can't believe it."[22] Within hours, Canadian Airlines announced that it had sold all 25,000 of its unity-fare seats.[23] The company quietly asked Tobin to stop promoting the cheap flights.

To keep pace with the airlines, Via Rail announced a 60 per cent discount on all round-trip tickets to Montreal. Buses were hired by the dozens, in some cases by private companies like the *Toronto Star* and Connaught Laboratories, to carry people to Montreal from New Brunswick, Ottawa, and Toronto. Even with every available Ontario bus rerouted, managers at Greyhound and Voyageur reported that they could not keep up with demand.[24] How many people would simply hop in their cars and drive to Montreal was impossible to know. But with some of Ontario's biggest employers giving their workers the day off to attend, particularly in the Ottawa region, it was expected to be a good number.

By Thursday, October 26, estimates of the number of Canadians likely to descend on Montreal ran to the tens of thousands. "Interest in this rally is growing minute by minute, second by second," gushed Jean-François Viau, executive director of the Quebec Business Council for Canada. "People want to make a last emotional stand for Canada before the vote."[25] Brian Tobin was equally enthusiastic. "This is pure, national Canadian pride finding, at last, a way in this campaign to express itself," he said. "My feeling is that Lucien Bouchard and the separatists have almost cast a spell [over Quebecers] and part of that spell is the notion that the rest of Canada is some kind of a monolith that's uncaring and disinterested in what's happening in this referendum campaign and frankly unaware what the stakes are. I think it's time to break the trance."[26] Like other Canadians of like mind, Tobin did not seem to realize that from the perspective of many Quebecers, the idea of Canadians riding into Montreal to break the sovereignist "trance" was at least as condescending as the alleged trance itself. Asked what he thought of the deluge of Canadians planned for his city, mayor Pierre Bourque's cool response was typical of many Montrealers'. "I guess it will be good for tourism," he said with a shrug.[27]

Some Quebecers were not so nonchalant, not nearly. On October 25, Pierre-Ferdinand Côté, Quebec's chief electoral officer, sent Canadian Airlines a formal letter warning the company to terminate its cheap unity fares. Côté had been alerted to the issue by the Yes committee, which understood the fares (and their attendant advertising and administrative costs) as unauthorized campaign expenses under the *Referendum Act*. "Sending us testimonials, that's fine," said Pauline Marois, Quebec treasury board president. "But we aren't going to just watch this happen, with the consequences it could have."[28] Both of the national airlines responded to Côté's complaint with light-hearted indifference. They had been offering special fares to Quebec for weeks, they said, and in any case, there was no law against patriotism. "It's Canadian's way of making a meaningful contribution to national unity," said airline spokesperson Shannon Ohama.[29]

The debate over illicit campaign spending moved into the House of Commons on October 26, when Bloc MP Michel Bellehumeur accused Brian Tobin of meddling in the referendum. "How can the Minister of Fisheries and Oceans not only be in collusion but, moreover, entice a private company to contravene the *Referendum Act*, especially when he now knows the decision of the Chief Electoral Officer on the matter?"[30] Tobin played the innocent. "What various transportation companies are doing is entirely up to them," he replied. "The only thing I am doing is taking my wife [and] my children and I am going to Montreal. I suspect some other Canadians who love this country and love Quebec may join me."[31]

Lucien Bouchard called the unity rally a cynical federalist ploy. "We know what it means—this bogus demonstration that they're going to hold, to trick us and make us believe that they love us," he railed. "They are going to come here to tell us that they love us at 10 per cent of the ticket price that is being subsidized by Canadian [Airlines] contrary to our law. A law of Quebec isn't as important or respectable as a law of Alberta or Ontario or the federal government."[32] Daniel Johnson had his doubts about the rally, too, but in public at least spoke respectfully about the sentiments that had inspired it. "Obviously there is an out-pouring of affection and a very real feeling in the rest of Canada that Quebec is a very integral part of this country," he said. "No one should be surprised by it. It's not concocted or invented. It's a new Canadian reality."[33]

But the question remained. Could the one-day spectacle of Canadians descending en masse into downtown Montreal influence the referendum vote? The day before the rally, *Globe and Mail* Quebec correspondent André Picard penned a sardonic column entitled "A Nation United by a Seat Sale." Quebecers were not likely to forget their "emotion-laden history" just because a throng of out-of-towners showed up in Montreal waving flags, he wrote. They might see the rally as more of a "tawdry closing-time seduction" than an "outpouring of abiding love."[34]

Globe readers did not want to hear it. They assailed Picard for his cynicism and his terrible timing. Picard held his ground. "As much as many readers hate to hear it," he wrote the next day, "the outburst of love is not likely to make a big difference in Monday's vote."[35]

～

Yet seen from the perspective of many ordinary Canadians—those who could not fathom why anyone would want to destroy Canada from within—a mass rally in the heart of separatist Quebec struck exactly the right chord. A Southam News/Angus Reid poll conducted just days before the rally showed an unprecedented level of anxiety among Canadians about Quebec's future in Canada. Two-thirds of respondents said that national unity was now the pre-eminent issue facing the country. Fully 90 per cent expressed the hope that Quebecers would vote No. Ninety-seven per cent said that they felt "a profound attachment to Canada," while 80 per cent were "truly saddened" by the thought of Quebec's departure.[36]

These were the sentiments that inspired ordinary Canadians from every corner of the country to go to Montreal. Some spoke of feeling helpless and thus were relieved to be able to contribute to the message that Quebec should remain in Canada. "I love my country and I feel just absolutely sick about what is happening to it," said Sybil Rowe, a fifty-nine-year-old physiotherapist from Victoria. "I feel so small over what is going on. I just feel so tiny in trying to take [the Yes side] on. I'm hoping this message of love will reach some hearts and after that it's up to God."[37] Barry Fowler, a thirty-one-year-old salesman from Windsor, made a similar point. "I don't know if this is the best thing to do. But I just felt I had to do something. If [the referendum] ends up a Yes and I didn't do something to try to stop it, I'd regret it for the rest of my life."[38] Greg Thomason of Oyama, B.C., drove eight hours through a snow-storm to catch a flight from Calgary to Montreal. "I have eight cousins in Montreal," said Thomason. "Half are voting Yes. Half are voting No. If I can change one mind, then it will be worth it. I just got tired of sit-ting in front of my TV and not contributing. It's too important not to be there. This is the best country in the world and it just wouldn't be the same [without Quebec]."[39]

Claudette Roy, vice-principal at École Maurice Lavallée, joined fifty other Edmontonians on one of Air Canada's charter flights. "I've been itching to get into this for awhile now," said Roy, who was born in St. Paul, Alberta, where her father settled in 1912 after leaving Quebec. "I love Canada," she says. "I'm a francophone from Alberta, not a Québécois. I really want them to stay. I am going to be travelling all night to go down there and say that. I don't think that message is getting through, that there are people outside of Quebec who really care about this."[40] Denis Meilleur, general manager of the Association canadienne-française de l'Alberta, agreed with Roy. "United we stand," he said. "But we're doomed if the vote is Yes on Monday." Meilleur said he was heading to Montreal to demonstrate to Quebecers that Calgary was not "the redneck capital of Canada" but rather the Canadian city with the highest percentage of stu-dents in bilingual education outside Quebec. "I want to show them that Canada cares and Calgary cares deeply," he added.[41]

Some participants, particularly high school and university students, understood the unity rally as an opportunity to see history in the making. "It's a historical event that you don't want to miss," commented seventeen-year-old René Tourangeau of École secondaire l'Essor in St. Clair Beach (now Tecumseh), Ontario, who planned to attend the rally with her aunt. "The future of Canada is going to depend on what happens in Montreal. I'm against separation because it will decrease the value of the French language throughout the rest of the country. That's not fair to the French-speaking population outside Quebec."[42] Maggie Gilmour was one of several senior girls from Toronto's Jarvis Collegiate heading to Montreal after being swept up in the "excitement and energy" of the referendum campaign. "This is the Woodstock of our generation," she said. "I want to attend McGill University next year and I don't want to go to school in a foreign country."[43] Carleton University student Michael Coteau, now an Ontario Liberal MPP, planned to attend the rally because he knew that it would be a "wonderful day in Canadian history" and a once-in-a-lifetime opportunity for proud Canadians like him to stand up for his country.[44]

~

Cars and buses left Toronto for Montreal at 5 a.m. Friday, October 27. They travelled along Highway 401 in a convoy, meeting up with vehicles from eastern Ontario cities en route. *Fleurs-de-lis* and Canadian flags were displayed in car windows, and on antennas and bumpers. Motorists smiled and waved to each other as they passed on the highway. "They were hopeful," observed Kingston resident Lynn Messerschmidt, "and it was infectious."[45]

At 7 a.m., 13,000 people met at Ottawa's Lynx Stadium to board one of the 200 buses leaving for Montreal. Ten thousand got seats, the rest were left scrambling for an alternate means of transportation.[46]

A bus had left Windsor Thursday evening and arrived in Montreal at roughly 7 a.m. the next morning, well ahead of enthusiasts from other Ontario cities. Quebecers' reactions to the flag-draped bus were not what the Windsorites had expected. "For about half an hour just about everybody gave us the finger," said Patrick Gignac, a fifteen-year-old student from F.J. Brennan Catholic High School. "Some people said 'Go home, get out!' They didn't even want us here."[47] Marc Chayer, the Windsor Harbour manager who had organized the trip, later recalled being unprepared for this cool reception. "Until you get here, you don't realize how divided it is," he said. "It was a really sobering experience."[48] Chayer's group brought along a huge Canadian flag—six metres by nine metres—that had been donated by the Windsor Jaycees. That flag, carried aloft over the heads of rally participants and photographed from the air, would become the event's most enduring icon.

Starting at the break of dawn on Friday, October 27, a rising tide of pedestrian traffic filled Place du Canada. At 11 a.m., Montreal police closed Boulevard René-Lévesque, allowing the sea of Canadians to move freely between Place du Canada and Square Dorchester immediately to the north. Over the noon hour, Montreal office workers joined the crowd, along with the thousands of Quebecers who, like other Canadians, had travelled by bus, car, and train to participate in the rally.

At its largest, the crowd numbered between 100,000 and 150,000 people. Some participants wore Canadian flags tied around their necks like capes. Others had painted maple leaves and *fleurs-de-lis* on their faces, hair, and clothing. Many people carried Quebec and Canadian flags—hoisted aloft on hockey sticks, or on strollers, or even strapped onto their dogs. Some had brought along signs and banners. "*Non au Péquistan*," "*C'est notre pays*," and "Let's talk" were among the most popular slogans, along with the ubiquitous "*Non!*" Many of the Calgarians in the crowd wore white Stetsons. Some Maritimers and Westerners carried their own provincial flags. "Ca-na-da! Ca-na-da!" the crowd cheered. There was a party atmosphere. People danced, sang, and embraced.

For some Canadians, the unity rally was one of the most moving events in their lives as citizens. "We were proud," freelance writer Patsy Fleming later wrote of her own experience in Montreal. "Some people were in tears; a lot of people were cheering. It was a very great moment. On Friday, evidence that Canada had a heart was irrefutable."[49] For

Montrealer Keith Murray, who had been fretting for weeks about the possible loss of Canada, the congregation of Canadians in his city came as a great salve. "When you see people coming here from all over you feel there is still hope," he said.[50]

Some Quebec sovereignists attended the rally. Nineteen-year-old Jean-Yves Lamarre and his friend Robert Goudreau arrived early Friday morning and hoisted a large *Oui* banner between two trees across from the main stage. For hours, they stood under their sign, the targets of many Canadians' earnest pitches for a united Canada. "I find it really sickening," said Lamarre. "They're here just to piss us off." Asked whether he thought the rally would help the No vote, Lamarre scoffed. "Even if there were a million [people] it wouldn't change our minds," he said.[51] Goudreau, on the other hand, seemed to be receptive to the emotional intensity of the scene. "It impresses me, all these people saying they want us to stay," he said. "It warms my heart. But I wish they'd do it in their own province." Around noon, Lamarre and Goudreau's banner was ripped down by a group of young federalists. "There were five or six of them," said Goudreau. "They tore it down and this woman pulled my hair and called me a fascist."[52]

Politicians in attendance—many of them recruited by Brian Tobin—included Prime Minister Chrétien, Jean Charest, Daniel Johnson, Sheila Copps, Paul Martin, and nearly every other federal cabinet minister. Premiers McKenna of New Brunswick, Savage of Nova Scotia, and Callbeck of PEI were there. Also present in the crowd were Ontario premier Mike Harris and his ten-year-old son Mike Jr. The two had decided on the spur of the moment to drive to Montreal and attend the rally as ordinary citizens. When his Queen's Park aides discovered that the premier had left for Montreal, they tried to persuade him to participate officially. Harris declined. "I felt that if I went with my son, I could go and represent Ontario families that overwhelmingly wanted to send this signal to Quebecers that we wanted them to be part of Canada," Harris said. "It was very exciting."[53]

Just after noon, when the crowd was at its largest, the leaders of the No camp took the stage. Jean Chrétien gave a short speech. "When

I see you all, coming from the provinces in Canada and from all parts of Quebec, I have never felt as proud today to be a Quebecer and as proud to be Canadian," he said. "*Vive le Québec! Vive le Canada!*"[54] Daniel Johnson offered the crowd similar well-wishes. "Quebecers, Canadians, Quebecers and Canadians," he said. "Can they stop us from loving Quebec? Can they stop us from loving Canada and from being Canadian? Do we want to break our country, Quebec and Canada?"[55] It was one of the only times in the campaign when Johnson evinced a genuine passion for Canada, and the crowd responded all the more warmly for it.

One after another a steady stream of prominent federalists took the mic, happy to add their voices to the unity chorus. With each speech, the audience cheered enthusiastically and waved their Maple Leafs and *fleurs-de-lis*. Photographers and videographers captured the surging sea of red and blue as it rippled over the massive crowd. When the speeches concluded, Canadians broke into a rousing rendition of "O Canada." They all knew that they had experienced something without precedent in modern Canada—the kind of patriotic outpouring that other countries reserve for the return of their conquering heroes or their gold-medal athletes. Never in living memory had Canadians congregated in such numbers to express such a powerful love of country.

"What happened in Montreal on Friday, October 27, 1995, was a spontaneous reaction from Canadians who had been waiting for an opportunity to make themselves heard, to stand up and be counted," Brian Tobin later recalled. "All they needed was someone to tell them when and where to appear."[56]

~

Lucien Bouchard was disgusted by the unity rally. He could barely contain his vitriol. "It was an attempt by Mr. Johnson and Mr. Chrétien to manipulate the enthusiasm of English Canada," said the Bloc leader. "It's obvious they want to make us feel guilty by saying: 'Why do you want to do that [become sovereign]? We love you.' At the last minute, they say, 'We love you, we love you, you are distinct.' It's sickening. Two little polls showing that we are ahead and you see this outpouring of love for us. Imagine what will happen with a Yes vote. They'll absolutely adore us!"[57] Bouchard estimated the total cost of the rally at $4.3 million and accused the No camp of knowingly violating Quebec's rules on referendum spending. "It's clear it was a political operation staged in part with public funds and in an illegal way," he said. "I think that strongly taints the value of the operation."[58] Over the last weekend of the campaign, Bouchard mocked the Canadians who had come to Montreal. "Canada loves us, boom-boom," he said, his hand on his heart, his words dripping with sarcasm.[59]

Some Canadians returned the sentiment. "There was a palpable contempt in the way Lucien Bouchard dismissed the beating heart of Canadians gathering for this rally," wrote Ken MacQueen in the *Ottawa Citizen*. "It was a rare, unguarded glimpse at the raw anger fueling this man."[60] A *Globe and Mail* editorial blasted the Bloc leader. Canadians from all walks of life had flooded Bouchard's office with expressions of genuine sympathy when his life was threatened less than a year earlier, asserted the *Globe*. "Did Mr. Bouchard recall any of that when he so cavalierly heaped scorn on the thousands who travelled to Montreal yesterday to show their solidarity with Quebecers? We have come to know well the dark rages of Lucien Bouchard, and we despair of his mercurial manner. This is a man of chemical impulse and deep obsession, who thinks so little of loyalty that he changes parties the way he changes shirts. This is an eloquent man who spits the language of defiance and ethnic nationalism."[61]

Quebec's French-language press was for the most part unimpressed with the "*touristes de fédéralisme*" that had descended on Montreal—except to commend them for their discipline.[62] Some editorialists admitted that they had been impressed with Jean Chrétien's unscripted speech to the crowd. But most were unmoved by the sentiments that had ostensibly drawn Canadians to Quebec, suggesting that Canadians were months and years too late in their efforts to make Quebecers feel at home in Canada. Quebec voters were not likely to be fooled by Canadians' "*débordements d'amour*" ("excesses of love"), they agreed.[63]

"How many [Quebecers] asked themselves where all these Canadians of good will were during the repeated constitutional failures of the past few years?" wondered Chantal Hébert of *La Presse*.[64] "Where were you when we needed you?" asked *Le Soleil*'s Jean-Jacques Samson.[65]

Under the headline "*Apparences d'amour*" ("Appearances of Love"), Lise Bissonnette of *Le Devoir* penned a scathing critique of Canadians living outside Quebec. They told anyone who would listen that they love Quebecers, she fulminated, but 84 per cent of them refused to grant Quebec any special powers to protect their French culture. "*Nous ne sommes pas en situation d'amour, ici, mais de chantage mutuel*," she concluded. ("We are not in a position of love here, but mutual black-mail.")[66] Bissonnette's column was accompanied by a cartoon showing two tee-shirts hanging on a clothesline. "We Love You" said the Canadian shirt. "*Pas cette fois-ci, j'ai mal à la tête!*" ("Not now, I have a headache!") read the Quebec shirt.

Canada's English-language pundits knew very well that the rally had been fired by Canadians' love of country—but also by the desperation and panic that had accompanied bad-news polls late in the campaign. "The outpouring of emotion by many Canadians outside Quebec is heartening and understandable," observed an editorial in the *Edmonton Journal*. "Canadians love their country. But what are they prepared to do about it, besides spend an emotional day at Place du Canada in Montreal?"[67] *Journal* editorialist Linda Goyette was even even less forgiving. "Canadians cling to their own stubborn concept of a country they might be losing," she wrote. "Their last-minute pleading in Montreal is self-love, pragmatic politics, and Quebecers know it. Referendum voters should be left in peace to contemplate their decision. They don't need thousands of noisy Romeos on the balcony at this late hour."[68]

Resignation and fatigue dominated at the *Toronto Star*, an unexpect-edly pessimistic tone for the newspaper that had invested so heavily in the unity rally. "The Crusade for Canada that swept through Montreal yesterday was a beacon of light in a gloomy referendum campaign that has left Quebecers sadly divided, perplexed and anxious, and the rest of us frustrated to the point of fury," said the *Star*. "The hour of crisis is at hand, and no one can say which way it will go."[69] The Montreal *Gazette* was more optimistic. "Several months before the referendum was called, Premier Parizeau told an American newspaper that all he needed was for a couple of Ontarians to stomp on a Quebec flag and sovereignty was in the bag," said a *Gazette* editorial. "Yesterday, thousands from across Canada gathered in Montreal to show Quebecers that they want to praise the Quebec flag, not stomp on it. Yesterday's demonstration was more than just a love-in. It was a heartfelt demonstration of a desire among Canadians, confirmed by an Angus Reid poll published this week, to accommodate Quebec's special character and needs."[70]

The thousands of anxious Canadian patriots who had assembled in Montreal would not have wished to hear it, of course, but the net effect of the unity rally may have been to increase the sovereignist Yes vote. According to Grégoire Gollin of Créatec-Plus, the feds' private pollster, daily surveys conducted the day of the rally and the day after showed a drop in the No lead, from 3.7 per cent to 2.5. Gollin concluded reluctantly that the love-in and the massive media coverage it had garnered must have figured into the 1.2 per cent slide.[71]

~

The weekend of October 28–29 saw both camps pulling out all the stops to cap off their grassroots campaigning and get their vote out. In the streets of Montreal, groups of sovereignists and federalists passed out leaflets and orchestrated spontaneous mini-rallies. In other Canadian cities, unity rallies were held, including a celebration at Toronto's Nathan Phillips Square that drew 25,000 people.

On Sunday afternoon, thousands of No supporters marched across the Alexandra Bridge from Ottawa to Hull, where, outside the Museum of Civilization, Prime Minister Jean Chrétien gave his last speech of the campaign to a crowd of 10,000. "We have learned that never, never, should we take our country Canada for granted," he said. "We saw thousands upon thousands of Canadians from every province, from both territories, they came together with more than 100,000 Quebecers in the streets of Montreal. Everybody understood that Canada without Quebec, it's no more Canada, and Quebec without Canada, is no more Quebec. And that is why, my friends, that is why I know that Canada will emerge from this experience even stronger."[72] Daniel Johnson, too, now more confident of a No victory than he had been in weeks, spent the weekend on the hustings. "The next generation will never forgive us for abandoning Canada," he told a group of 400 Montrealers on Sunday. "Voting Yes means putting an X on Canada. Voting No guarantees the future that we have built and guarantees the future of our children. That's what we have to decide tomorrow."[73]

On Saturday, Lucien Bouchard urged Yes voters in Îles-de-la-Madeleine to do their own work of persuasion. "It's urgent," he said. "There remain two days for the future of Quebec. Everyone must use the hours that are left to convince one or two undecided voters. Talk to your friends, neighbors, parents and co-workers. The race is tight. The responsibility is in your hands."[74] The next day, the Bloc leader attended a Yes rally in the Quebec City suburb of Beauport, accompanied by his wife, Audrey Best, and their two sons, Alexandre and Simon. "I know that the Yes of Monday evening will be the Yes of all those who are proud of having said Yes to René Lévesque in 1980," he told the crowd. "I know also that it will be the Yes of so many people who, since 1980, have regretted not having said Yes to René Lévesque. We have no right to let it pass. God knows when it will [again] present itself. We have it before us. Seize it and vote Yes. Say Yes to ourselves. Say Yes to the people of Quebec."[75]

Jacques Parizeau gave a speech at Longueuil on Sunday, the last of the campaign for Quebec's foremost separatist. He, too, invoked the memory of Lévesque. "In the polling booth, if there is a moment of doubt, a moment of hesitation, we only have to ask ourselves: What would René Lévesque do in my place?" As he had so many times during the campaign, Parizeau spoke of the historic opportunity that now lay before Quebecers. "The entire world, today and tomorrow, has its eyes riveted on the Quebec people," he said. "Hundreds of journalists and tens of millions of people throughout the world are watching us.

In fact, the 185 peoples represented in the United Nations are asking themselves today if, tomorrow, another people will arise. If tomorrow another people will decide to take its place in the concert of nations, serenely, proudly and naturally."[76]

Pundits spent the weekend in watch-and-wait mode, speculating feverishly on what-ifs and what-went-wrongs. Op-ed writers and editorialists offered their most perspicacious nuggets of wisdom and their best prognostications. In the Quebec press, there was a last crush of appeals to influence the undecided. At *La Presse*, Alain Dubuc urged Quebecers to vote No. The idea that a Yes vote would bring an end to interminable federal-provincial quarrels was an "illusion," he wrote. "Sovereignty would require an unbelievable detour to get to the same point [as the current federalism], creative years devoted to negotiating Quebec's status, struggling against the inevitable degradation of the economy."[77] As she had throughout the campaign, Lise Bissonnette at *Le Devoir* exhorted Quebecers to vote Yes. "A No will be interpreted, in the rest of Canada, as an acceptance of the constitutional order of 1982," she declared. Daniel Johnson would have to bear the weight of history for having "submitted" to the feds' strategy—a strategy "based on the total, intentional absence of any formal commitment to modify Quebec's status within the federation." It was true that Quebecers had built Canada, Bissonnette concluded, but only "a Canada that could have been."[78]

～

Quebec voters had been polled, polled, and polled again. And yet, on the eve of the historic 1995 referendum vote, no one had the faintest idea of what the outcome would be. It was astounding.[79]

Daniel Johnson and Jean Chrétien had blown a twenty-point lead, but it remained far from certain whether Jacques Parizeau and Lucien Bouchard could deliver on their sovereignist dream. As decision day approached, as Quebecers readied themselves to vote not merely on their future but on their destiny, as Jacques Parizeau liked to say, both camps believed that they were poised for victory. On October 29, the feds' number-crunchers had the No vote in a 1.5 per cent lead with 70 per cent of the undecideds leaning the same way.[80] For their part, the sovereignists believed that their come-from-behind campaign had crested at precisely the right moment. "It was only in the last 48 hours," Jean-François Lisée later recalled, "that we felt that victory was probable, and in hand. It wasn't until the last 48 hours that we gave ourselves the right to believe."[81]

Across Canada and throughout Quebec, Canadians awaited the verdict of history. It was going to be a nail-biter.

CHAPTER THIRTEEN

The Night Canada Stood Still

Prime Minister Jean Chrétien awakened in his Shawinigan home the morning of October 30 in a "nervous but also fatalistic" state of mind. After casting his own referendum ballot, he flew immediately back to Ottawa to await the verdict of his fellow Quebecers. He remained confident of victory, but not as he had been just weeks earlier. "I assumed that most of the undecideds were No supporters who had been intimidated into silence," he later wrote.[1] It was an odd turn of phrase for a man who had done a good deal of intimidating himself, evidence that *le p'tit gars de Shawinigan* had not entirely lost his brawling instinct.

Quebec premier Jacques Parizeau, too, was nervous. "I said to myself, *What if it doesn't work out?*" he later recalled. "Can you imagine the responsibility that represents? Towards thousands, tens of thousands of people I had led on this adventure for years, people who in amounts of $20 and $50 had raised $32 million. Driven by what faith? Faith in a goal, in an ideal, in a man whom they thought made a certain amount of sense. Well, that morning, I said, 'My God, I hope it's going to work!'"[2]

Both men braced themselves for a long and tumultuous day.

The question that appeared on the referendum ballot was the one Premier Parizeau had tabled in the National Assembly on September 7, 1995:

Do you agree that Quebec should become sovereign, after having made a formal offer to Canada for a new Economic and Political Partnership, within the scope of the Bill respecting the future of Quebec and of the agreement signed on June 12, 1995?

The ballot was standard Canadian fare. It showed the question in both official languages in the top half. Below the two texts, set against a solid black background, were two white circles clearly marked *Oui*/Yes and *Non*/No. According to Quebec law, voters would have to mark their ballots with one of only four symbols—a check mark, an *X*, a cross, or a line. Any other marking, irrespective of how obviously it may have been inscribed into one or the other circle, could be rejected by electoral officers. Experts worried that in a close race, this stricture might turn out to be not only a colossal headache for Quebec's chief electoral officer, Pierre-Ferdinand Côté, but also a possible game-changer for the referendum vote itself.

The electoral apparatus for the referendum was identical to that of a provincial election. Each of Quebec's 125 National Assembly ridings would run neighbourhood polls under the supervision of a returning officer employed by the directeur général des élections du Québec (DGE). An army of 92,000 DGE workers would run the referendum machine, at a total cost of $15 million in salaries.[3] What distinguished this particular contest, of course, was that only two numbers counted— the province-wide tallies of Yes and No votes. It seemed improbable, indeed surreal, to philosophically minded Canadians and Quebecers that their common future could boil down to a binary choice, *Oui* or *Non*, on a single-sentence question. Most could not have chosen a dinner entrée or a baby name under such stipulations. Yet here they were, distilling their complex lives as citizens into a single *X*.

The cliché that every vote counts was never more apposite than on October 30, 1995, and both sides knew it.[4] Eligible voters numbered 5,086,979. Roughly 40,000 Quebecers had left the province within the two previous years, and they were also eligible to vote. Imagining that most members of this group would be federalists, the provincial

Liberals had paid to have the official *Non* booklet mailed out to them in mid-October, along with personalized letters from the party. (The DGE refused a request from the No organizers for a full listing of these Quebecers, so they cobbled together their own list.[5])

Former prime minister Joe Clark attached his name to the Calgary-based Committee to Register Voters Outside Quebec. Similar efforts were made in other cities across Canada. Lawyer Murray Rankin, for example, worked with the Victoria Public Library to make the requisite forms available to Quebecers living there. "There's a lot of people who don't know about the process," said Rankin. "We're not saying how to vote, we just want them to be able to exercise their right."[6] By October 4, 10,559 Quebecers living outside the province had registered to cast a referendum ballot. As of October 26, however, several hundred of them had not received their ballots in the mail. Canada Post had no explanation for the glitch, but Montreal lawyer Casper Bloom attributed it to political interference. "This is scandalous," said Bloom. "You can blame the mail sometimes, but when you're talking about hundreds and hundreds of ballots, something is cooking. People are calling me in panic. Some are crying, some are shouting at me."[7]

Fifteen thousand new immigrants to Quebec were also eligible to vote in the referendum, thanks to Ottawa's controversial decision to expedite citizenship applications in the province. The vast majority were expected to follow Quebec's established allophone communities and vote No. Roughly 30,000 aboriginals from across the province were also eligible to vote, but only Cree leaders expressly urged their people to do so.[8]

The polls opened at 10 a.m. and closed at 8 p.m. For both camps, voting day represented an opportunity to cap off months of campaigning with a monumental effort at the grassroots level. Even before dawn on October 30, party workers and volunteers from both camps began checking and rechecking electoral lists, phoning voters still thought to be undecided, and arranging means of getting their loyalists out to the polls.[9] Volunteer drivers tasked with taking elderly and infirm voters to local polling stations numbered in the hundreds.[10]

The weather in Quebec was clear and crisp throughout the day, and unseasonably chilly in the evening. Some observers thought the clement weather would contribute to a high voter turnout. Others suggested that the gloomy evening weather might sour the optimism of some undecided voters and compel them to vote No. Classes in all of Quebec's public schools were cancelled for the day. Public offices and many private institutions closed early to allow their employees ample time to vote. DGE officials reported heavy traffic at the polls, heightening expectations that voter turnout would exceed the 88 per cent recorded for the 1980 referendum on sovereignty—itself a provincial record.[11]

At some polling stations, there were long lineups and delays of several hours, prompting some non-francophone voters to accuse the Yes side of obstructionism.[12] Nothing about this day, it seemed, was going to come without a fight.

~

In keeping with the time-honoured Canadian tradition, media saturation on referendum night was total. Every major television network in both official languages built special sets and designed visually arresting on-screen graphics designed to heighten viewers' white-knuckle experience of watching the referendum returns roll in. Broadcasters competed ferociously with each other, both to attract viewers and, after the fact, to claim bragging rights about who had put on the best show. Front and centre on every network were the familiar anchors and senior correspondents, some of whom provided colour commentary, others real-time coverage from Yes and No headquarters, party venues, and even local pubs and homes. Alongside the media stars appeared an endless parade of experts, from cabinet ministers and provincial premiers to artists and academics.[13] Peter Mansbridge, who anchored the CBC's English-language broadcast, spoke for many of his colleagues about all the hoopla. "I've always said journalists aren't neutered at birth," he said. "We all have our own feelings about things. I have personal feelings about this issue, sure. But the personal feelings can't get in the way of telling the story."[14]

Virtually the only members of the Canadian and Québécois political elites to spend the evening off-camera were the politicians who had together brought the country to a standstill. Prime Minister Chrétien watched the televised broadcasts from 24 Sussex Drive, in the company of a small group of his top advisors, friends, and family. Quebec Liberal leader Daniel Johnson and his top aides awaited the verdict of the people of Quebec in a private suite at the Métropolis amphitheatre in Montreal, where the No camp was hoping to hold its victory celebration. Premier Jacques Parizeau and six of his closest advisors watched the returns from a suite on the second floor of the Palais des congrès de Montréal. Bloc Québécois leader Lucien Bouchard and fifteen of his aides were ensconced in a suite on the third floor of the same venue. ADQ leader Mario Dumont and a group of his advisors were staying at the Delta Hotel but would later move to the main ballroom at the Palais des congrès for what he and the other sovereignists hoped would be an historic victory celebration.

Most referendum broadcasts took to the air at 7 or 7:30 p.m. Eastern Standard Time, commencing with background reports, polling updates, and scene-setting introductions from roving correspondents. Tension and anticipation were the prevalent atmospherics at Yes and No headquarters in Montreal. Live from the floor of the Métropolis, veteran CTV reporter Craig Oliver captured the anxious mood among No supporters. "I have to tell you that after something like 40 years of hanging around campaign headquarters election nights, I've never seen a stress level so high," Oliver told CTV anchor Lloyd Robertson. "These people are putting on a show of confidence, talking about polls which show them slightly ahead as of last night but still not enough to win. They are plainly scared, fearful that a lost campaign may result yet in a lost country."[15]

Oliver's CTV colleague Alan Fryer then set the stage from the floor of the Palais des congrès. "Well, for many committed Quebec separatists, especially the four to five thousand who are already gathered here tonight, [there is] a sense that this could be the end of a very long road, a thirty-year struggle for Quebec independence. I was just speaking to a PQ official just moments ago who seemed to be fairly encouraged by the fact that the voter turnout is apparently extremely high, perhaps over ninety per cent and they figure that is going to help their cause."[16]

For Canadians and Quebecers tuning in to one of the many referendum broadcasts on television, the running totals shown in blue (Yes) and red (No) at the bottom of their screens heightened the intensity of the viewing experience. Pollsters had hammered home the message that the contest was too close to call. Yet the first images available to viewers showed the sovereignist blue bar outstripping the federalist red by 15 per cent. This dramatic opening occurred, as broadcasters dutifully reminded Canadians, because the first polling stations to report were in Îles de la Madeleine, a group of islands in the Gulf of St. Lawrence that happened to be in the Atlantic time zone. In the 1980 referendum, the islands had voted 54 per cent No. This time out, with only 0.1 per cent of the province's polls reporting, the Yes side in Îles de la Madeleine had taken a commanding lead straight out of the gate—a lead it would maintain well into the evening.

As polls from elsewhere in the Gaspé region started to trickle in, the Yes lead receded and stabilized at 53–47, a six-point spread guaranteed to unsettle even the most rock-ribbed federalists. Yet among the top strategists in the Yes camp, too, this early tabulation came as a worrisome portent. They knew that they would have to do better than 53 per cent outside Montreal to win. The rule of thumb among sovereignists was that the Yes vote would have to exceed 60 per cent in francophone ridings to take the referendum, since non-francophones were expected to vote No overwhelmingly.

At 8:15, with under 4 per cent of the ballots counted, the flow of data from the riding offices suddenly ceased. The blue and red bars froze, but now with the blue (Yes) vote out in front by almost 20 per cent. At the Colisée in Quebec City, where roughly 10,000 Yes supporters were assembled to watch the returns, the crowd exploded in exuberant cheers. The same was true for the Yes crowd at the Palais des congrès in Montreal. Chants of *"On veut notre pays!"* reverberated through both venues, as the dream of an independent Quebec came into view. "It's an amazing feeling when you first see those numbers come up," exclaimed Christine Lachance, one of the Montreal Yes enthusiasts. "You think, My God, it's possible."[17] Montreal businessman Robert Aubin agreed. "The atmosphere here tonight is different than the night in 1980," he observed. "This is a crowd which has dealt with the rejection of Meech Lake and Charlottetown. If we win, even narrowly, we will know the great majority of French-speaking Quebecers have spoken for sovereignty."[18]

As they waited for new numbers, anchors and their guests did their best to fill the dead air with informed banter. "It doesn't just matter who won," veteran reporter Mike Duffy reminded CTV viewers. "Every single ballot must be counted before we know the result tonight which means it's going to be [a] long, slow [night]. I can imagine there will be a lot of scrutineers fighting with each other in those counting booths as well, saying, that's a Yes, no it isn't, it's a No. And that's always part of the tension that slows things down."[19]

The data flow resumed. Early results from the heavily sovereignist Saguenay–Lac-Saint-Jean region showed the Yes vote leading 72–28, which surprised no one. From Montreal, the first polls showed the No leading 83.4 to 16.6, which was also widely expected. From the Outaouais region—the area north of Ottawa, which included Hull (now Gatineau)—the No also took an early lead, 77–23.

At 8:35, the trickle of numbers became a torrent. It showed the No side gaining, and fast. All of a sudden, the cheering at the Yes venues gave way to an eerie silence. The sea of *fleur-de-lis* flags disappeared. There was stillness, as all eyes fixed on the numbers on the overhead screens. By 9 p.m., the Yes lead had shrunk to 51–49, a mere 40,000 votes. The momentum was entirely on the No side. At the Palais des congrès, some demoralized sovereignists began looking for the exits. A rally organizer took to the stage, imploring the crowd that all was not lost and they should not go home. "*On veut notre pays!*" he shouted. The message buoyed people's spirits momentarily, but before long the mood again turned despondent.

The sobering reality that the vote would split along linguistic lines was by now evident to everyone. In predominantly francophone ridings, the Yes side was ahead 53.8 to 46.2 per cent. In mainly anglophone and allophone ridings, the No was running a decisive lead, 83.8 to 16.2 per cent.

At 9:30, with just under 40 per cent of polls reporting, the Yes lead continued to hold, 50.7 per cent to 49.3. Jacques Parizeau, still ensconced in his private suite in the Palais des congrès, discussed the numbers with his top strategist, Jean Royer. The two men agreed that they had hoped for better numbers outside Montreal and conceded that it did not look good for a Yes victory. When Montreal went No, just minutes later, Royer told the premier, "We don't stand a chance now."[20] Lisette Lapointe, who was by her husband's side at that moment, later recalled the agony conveyed in his silence. "It was a dreadful moment, sending shivers down your spine," she said. "It was not just a disappointment. It was a major blow. His entire dream went up in smoke. It had been the struggle of a lifetime."[21]

Jean-François Lisée sat at his computer in the same suite, preparing to draft the concession speech for Parizeau that he had hoped he would never have to write. Lisée was disheartened, naturally, but also philosophical. There would be other battles. "History will judge you on what you are going to say tonight," he told the premier. But he could see that Parizeau could not hear him through his seething emotions. "From what I observed," Lisée later recalled, "it was as if he had never prepared himself for the eventuality of a No victory. Even though there were times during the campaign that we thought we might lose, even though we had talked about it in the afternoon, it was as if, for him, this was a new situation."[22]

At 9:34, with 3 million ballots counted, the No side jumped into the lead by 6,000 votes. Then, just moments later, that number dropped. The screens flashed. People could not believe their eyes. *Twenty-eight ballots separated the two sides.*

Just at this moment, with the referendum race at its most precarious, broadcasters reported that the number of spoiled ballots was 37,000 and counting. Sovereignist Jean Lapierre, who spent referendum night as Lloyd Robertson's colour commentator on CTV, was nonplussed.

"That's most incredible," exclaimed Lapierre. "Why would those people go and bother to go to vote. They had to wait for hours in line, just to spoil it. I mean there must be something wrong. I can't believe it."[23]

Finally, at 9:40, there came the dramatic surge in the No vote that Yes strategists had been dreading for over an hour. They had been watching the returns painstakingly, riding by riding, and they knew that the counts from the predominantly English-speaking ridings of west end Montreal had been delayed (reportedly due to "long lineups and disputes over voting credentials").[24] Sure enough, as the Montreal numbers flowed in, the No side took a quick 13,000 vote lead and then, within minutes, added another 4,000. The crowd of No supporters gathered at the Métropolis in Montreal, who until then had had very little to celebrate, erupted into euphoric cheering. "*Le Québec au Canada! Le Québec au Canada!*" they roared. A moving sea of red and blue Canadian and Quebec signs suddenly illuminated the ballroom.[25]

From that point on, the No side never looked back. The lead was never great, but it was sufficient to carry the No side on to victory. At 10:20 p.m., with 97.8 per cent of polls reporting, Radio-Canada made it official. The No side had won—by an estimated margin of 43,000 votes, or 50.5 per cent to 49.5.

Canadian federalists exhaled. They had dodged a bullet, but with the referendum vote so close, so unbelievably close, they fully expected that it would not be the last. The math alone was momentous. If 22,000 Quebecers had cast their ballots differently, the sovereignists would have had their victory. "What this indicates," Mike Duffy told Lloyd Robertson, "is that the polls that the government has been getting in the last two days that show that they were far ahead—that had Liberal MPs talking about a 55 to 59% No vote—all of that was out the window. And just think what might have happened had the prime minister not gone on national TV last week and had there not been that massive outpouring of support in Montreal. We would be in really deep trouble tonight. As it is, I think the Canadian political system is already in paralysis."[26]

After almost two hours of roller-coaster suspense, the crowd at the Palais des congrès could see that the sovereignist cause in which they had invested so much of themselves was lost. When Radio-Canada announced the No victory, a shout of anguished protest could be heard from the floor. Then there was silence. The terrible reality took its toll. "As you look around, [there are] a lot of long faces, a lot of tears, people hugging each other, consoling each other," Alan Fryer reported. "[It is] reminiscent of that night in 1980 at the Paul Sauvé Arena the last time the Yes side lost in a referendum. There was a brief cheer that went up here a few minutes ago when a camera picked up a picture of Jacques Parizeau who is now in the building. He waved to the camera."[27] It fell to Pauline Marois to take the podium and break the news that everyone in the room dreaded hearing. The vote was close, she told the crowd, but their adversaries had prevailed. It was not an easy outcome to bear, but sovereignists must respect the verdict of Quebecers.[28]

At the Colisée in Quebec City, it was the same story. With the crushing announcement of the No victory, most of the crowd of 10,000 left the building in stunned silence and made their way home. Those who remained, many with tears in their eyes, watched the talking heads on the screens overhead, booing Jean Chrétien and various provincial Liberal MNAs whenever they appeared.[29]

In Ottawa, a small crowd gathered by the Centennial Flame on Parliament Hill to sing "O Canada." Abroad, where Canada's national-unity crisis had never been well understood, the country's near-miss was met with palpable relief.[30] The moment the referendum ticker began to edge in the direction of a No victory, Asian currency traders bid up the Canadian dollar by two cents.

∼

As the leaders of both camps prepared their post-referendum speeches and made their way towards their respective podiums, television crews sought out senior ministers and advisors for their views on the evening's extraordinary events.

Monique Simard was one of the first Yes organizers to be interviewed on live television after the announcement of a No victory. She was disappointed with the outcome of the vote, of course, but insisted that Quebecers' aspirations could no longer be ignored. "It's not a bluff, it's not frivolous," she told CTV Television. "It shows how the Quebec society has moved forward to being very serious about wanting fundamental change and I think that cannot be overlooked by anybody."[31] Bernard Landry was interviewed on Radio-Canada. "I've said for years that never will a people accept being a simple province of another people," he said. "So if the No won, especially under the circumstances we see tonight, with an immense francophone majority [for the Yes], all of this will unfortunately have to be redone."[32] Jean-François Lisée agreed. "The notion of sovereignty will never die," he told a reporter. "There will be people who will fight very hard to recreate the conditions that could make it possible."[33] "This result is very meaningful," added PQ minister Louise Beaudoin. "Canada can't go on like this. The result is so close that Canada still persists as a country on paper, but there's clearly something wrong with it."[34]

However relieved they may have been with the No victory, federalist organizers knew that this was no time to gloat. "Everybody wants change," said No committee chair Michel Bélanger. "That means a great deal of responsibility on the part of all governments."[35] Liberal MNA Yvon Charbonneau agreed. "I would have preferred a clearer majority," he said. "One thing that the two camps had in common was a desire for profound change. That is what is required now: profound change."[36] Yet change was not likely to come easily, constitutional expert Patrick J. Monahan told CTV's Lloyd Robertson. Far from it. "I think it's put us in a really difficult box," Monahan said of the close vote. "If you think about it, the difficulty really is that you still have a Parti Québécois government in Quebec City which really has no interest in reaching agreements on the Constitution, for example. So going back to the constitutional table to discuss with Jacques Parizeau is surely a recipe for disaster."[37]

Preston Manning was the first national leader to comment on the referendum results. He was far from exultant. "The day of the Quebec referendum and the weekend before it were the three most miserable days of my political life," he later recalled.[38] It was a great relief that

Quebecers had chosen to remain in Canada, he told a press scrum in the House of Commons, but the narrow No victory could be interpreted only as a rejection of the status quo in Canada and a sharp indictment of "all the politicians" who had fumbled the ball on national unity. "The closeness of the No vote tonight should serve as a wake-up call to all of us," he said, "in particular the prime minister and the traditional feder-alists that federalism simply must change in the days ahead." Manning concluded with an appeal to ordinary Canadians, who he believed had been sidelined in the referendum debate, much as he and his Reform colleagues had been. "Tonight, I hope that the close vote in Quebec has awakened a sleeping giant—the giant of Canadian nationalism—and will fill that giant with an unquenchable resolve to build a better coun-try for all who are proud to be called Canadian."[39]

ADQ leader Mario Dumont gave a short speech after Manning's. "The world in its entirety has seen that one of the founding peoples of Canada is not part of it," he asserted. "Quebec is not really part of Canada." Dumont thanked the people in Rivière-du-Loup for voting Yes and reassured Quebec sovereignists that, although they had lost this fight, time was on their side. "Mr. Chrétien likes to recall that in the fifties when he started in politics there were literally no supporters for sovereignty in Quebec," he said. "Today, thirteen years after the uni-lateral repatriation [of the Constitution] he engineered, nearly half of Quebecers are in favour of the major change the Yes side proposed."[40]

Lucien Bouchard took the stage at the Palais des congrès at 11 p.m., with his wife Audrey Best at his side. Over the previous months, he had come to personify the aspirations of Quebec sovereignists, inspiring them, mobilizing them, carrying them to the brink of victory. The loss of the referendum was all the more bitter for having been so close, and it fell to Bouchard, more than anyone else, to pick up the pieces and illuminate for disheartened sovereignists the path forward.

"I am disappointed by this evening's verdict," Bouchard told the crowd. "Many Quebecers who had never fully recovered from the defeat of 1980 had tried to protect themselves from new wounds by hoping against hope that things could change. Recently they had begun to believe that the sovereignist side could perhaps take over. Never had the victory of the Yes seemed closer than it had over the last couple of days. And to see it escape at the very point when we thought we had it firmly within our grasp, that hurts." But democracy, said Bouchard, had to be esteemed over and above even the most worthy partisan dreams. Like René Lévesque in 1980, sovereignists had to now "accept with calm and with dignity the decision taken this evening by Quebecers."

The crowd cheered as Bouchard reminded them that they had come too close to their dream of sovereignty to let it die. "There are people in Ottawa who may believe that now they have a free rein but they must be told that they are wrong," he said. "Let us tell them, let us tell them, my friends, that they do not have, as they had hoped, they have not achieved what they had hoped for which was to uproot the sovereignist ideal. It is an ideal and an idea that is still in the hearts of too many Quebecers, too many for it to simply die away. The Yes has never been as numerous as this evening and we are still all of us here. Let us keep hope. Let us keep hope because next time we'll make it. And that next time, that next time could come sooner than people think."[41]

With that terse shot across the federalists' bow, Bouchard waved to the crowd and escorted his wife backstage. There he passed Jacques Parizeau, who was waiting in the wings before making his own concession speech. The two men exchanged words of consolation and shook hands. "There was a sadness that passed between them," Jean-François Lisée said later of that moment. "There was a certain complicity in the failure."[42] Bouchard might have been expected to accompany Parizeau to the podium, as a final act of the sovereignist solidarity he had himself invoked. But neither he nor his closest advisors were confident that Parizeau would be gracious in defeat.[43]

At 11:15, Parizeau alone took the stage. Tucked into his coat pocket was the concession speech written for him by Jean-François Lisée, whose every instinct was to concede defeat honourably and ready sovereignists to fight another day.

"Friends, we failed, but not by much," Parizeau began. His bearing was sober and intense, his voice assertive. Lisée's notes remained in his pocket. It was immediately apparent that, on this most inauspicious of nights, the premier was going to shoot from the hip. "Let's stop talking about the French-speaking Quebecers, let's talk about us," he said. "Sixty per cent of us, we voted Yes. And we fought a hard battle. We succeeded in stating clearly what we wanted and we missed it by a little, little bit, just a few tens of thousands of votes. Well, in that kind of a case, what can we do? Well, we start right up again!" Parizeau congratulated the young Quebecers who had come out in ever-increasing numbers during the campaign to make their "*On veut notre pays!*" heard. "When young people want it," the premier insisted, "we will have our country!"

Parizeau would have done well to conclude his remarks then and there. But he did not have it in him. His disappointment was too great, his anger too close to the surface.

"It's true that we were beaten but we were beaten by what?" he asked. "By money and ethnic votes."

Some people in the crowd cheered Parizeau, possibly as a reflex, but many others stood in awkward silence. Like many francophone Quebecers watching the speech live on television, they could not be certain that they had heard the premier's words correctly. For Canadian anglos listening to one of the networks' real-time translation of the premier's speech, however, there was no ambiguity. He had actually said it. "*L'argent et des votes ethniques.*"

The premier carried on with his speech, exhorting his followers to prepare themselves for the hard fight ahead. "Never forget," he said sternly, "three-fifths of who we are voted Yes. That was not quite enough but soon it will be enough. We are going to have our country!"[44]

But that acid phrase "*l'argent et des votes ethniques*" hung in the air, clouding every word that followed. "Suddenly, I heard Mr. Parizeau say things I hadn't written, two horrible sentences," Jean-François Lisée later recalled. "For the last year and a half, our discourse had been one of unity, and there, he was setting us years back, just with a single sentence."

As Parizeau left the stage, he turned to his young aide and said, "Well, Mr. Lisée, too bold?"

"If you were afraid people might insult you," replied Lisée, "now you can be sure they will. You have ruined your exit."[45]

Lucien Bouchard had returned directly to his suite at the Palais des congrès after his own speech but, with all of the distractions around him, did not follow Parizeau's remarks closely. It fell to one of his aides to tell him what the premier had said. "Did he really say that?" replied an incredulous Bouchard.[46] Parizeau's angry slur had set the sovereignist movement back incalculably, and no one knew it better than the Bloc Québécois leader.

"Did we hear him correctly when he said, 'Money and the ethnic vote have defeated us'?" asked CTV anchor Lloyd Robertson.[47]

"You heard it exactly right, Lloyd," replied Alan Fryer from the floor of the Palais des congrès, "and I'll tell you, the premier has pressed some pretty hot buttons here tonight with that speech. Whereas Mr. Bouchard was actually extending an olive branch, asking for conciliation, Mr. Parizeau has I think pressed some very dangerous buttons. He said that we Quebecers, French-speaking Quebecers, have been denied our country by money and the ethnic vote and that is a very, very dangerous statement. Very dangerous indeed."[48]

Sovereignist Jean Lapierre agreed with Fryer. "Well I couldn't believe my ears that the premier of all Quebecers would say stupid things like that," he told Robertson. "And frankly, calling for revenge, I mean that's the worst thing this guy could do. It's a classless act that he performed tonight and I think he'll have to pay dearly for that. Every Quebecer must be ashamed of his premier tonight."[49]

Former Liberal cabinet minister Marc Lalonde, also serving as a network colour commentator, was asked his opinion. "The most charitable thing I can say is that he probably was not sober when he made that speech," Lalonde replied. "Otherwise this is a speech by a demagogue and a fascist and I think he should be thrown out by his own party as fast as possible. This is a disgrace to Quebec."[50] Former Ontario premier Bob Rae had the same visceral response. "I thought it was the most disgraceful speech I have ever heard from any premier of any province in my lifetime," he said. "It was disgusting. It was vicious.

It was an attack on anyone of any other race other than Mr. Parizeau. Perhaps alcohol was an explanation? I cannot think of any other reason why he would have made such a statement on such an important night in Quebec history."[51]

Some Quebecers were outraged by Parizeau's comments. "Defeat is a test of character which Parizeau has failed this evening," said Rabbi Reuben Poupko, president of the Rabbinical Council of Montreal. "His vocabulary reveals that he does not understand that he is premier of all Quebecers. [His] speech [was] replete with racism and crass demagoguery."[52] Alliance Quebec spokesperson David Birnbaum called Parizeau's statement "shocking and completely anti-democratic," adding that the premier had "lost the moral mantle of leadership."[53] Nick Pierni of the National Congress of Italo-Canadians called Parizeau's comment "a disgrace," but was quick to add that it should not undermine Canadians' obligation to Quebecers after such a close vote. Quebec must be recognized as a distinct society, said Pierni.[54] Interviewed just moments after Parizeau had finished speaking, Liberal MNA Christos Sirros called the speech divisive and hurtful to foreign-born Quebecers like him. "I don't believe Quebecers in their collective wisdom will follow somebody who is so bitter and so unable to accept a democratic verdict," he said.[55]

Some sovereignists defended Parizeau. "It's not racism, it's reality," said Emmanuel Marcotte of the Outaouais Yes committee. "Parizeau was just giving statistics."[56] But most Quebecers, already stunned by the polarized referendum vote, agreed with Alain Dubuc at *La Presse,* who called Parizeau's angry reaction "*un véritable dérapage*" ("a true gaffe").[57]

In an influential front-page editorial in *Le Devoir* the next day, sovereignist Lise Bissonnette would lay bare the question of Quebec's language divide, but without any mention of the premier or his speech. All votes have equal weight, Bissonnette affirmed, and their validity is beyond question if the people of Quebec are going to define themselves as modern, pluralist, and inclusive. But it would be morally negligent to treat this linguistic chasm as "a taboo," she insisted. The "internal reconciliation" of Quebec—to say nothing of any sort of reconciliation with Canada—must begin with the acknowledgement that a "clear majority" of francophones voted Yes, a "massive majority" of anglophones and allophones voted No, and the difference between them determined the outcome of the referendum vote. "The question of identity among French-speaking Quebecers is no longer the only source of inspiration for the sovereignist movement, but historically it has been the centre." For this reason, Bissonnette concluded, the national aspirations of "the majority within the majority" in Quebec cannot be ignored.[58]

Like many Québécois intellectuals, Université Laval political scientist Louis Balthazar agonized over Parizeau's outburst. The premier's reference to money and ethnic voters was "deplorable," Balthazar would later reflect. "Even worse, he clearly established a distinction between 'we,' the Francophone majority, and 'they,' the others." But even so, it was only fair to gauge Parizeau's unfiltered remarks against his political record. The premier "has never entertained any racist feeling whatsoever, nor has he given any evidence of harboring such feelings," said Balthazar. His first wife was born in Poland, and he had close friends in every corner of the globe. He had consistently extolled "a broad conception of a pluralist Quebec based on the equality of all citizens." Indeed, as a public servant and later as finance minister, Parizeau tried to epitomize "a civic conception of the Quebec state" that included constitutional protections for the rights of aboriginal and English-speaking people. "Were these just good intentions?" Balthazar asked. "Did the real Parizeau reveal himself on referendum night? Or was his bad speech the unwanted effect of deep disappointment and total exhaustion?"[59]

Parizeau himself never apologized for his referendum night speech, then or later. He did, however, qualify it, telling journalist Mario Cardinal in 2005 that he had been overcome by anger—with "the whole world and with myself." If he had it to do over again, Parizeau mused, he would likely make "the same statement" but certainly "not in the same words."[60]

~

Daniel Johnson took the stage at the Métropolis at 11:25 p.m., by which time the crowd of thousands of No supporters had shrunk to hundreds. If he had heard Jacques Parizeau's controversial speech, Johnson did not let on. He knew that the federalist referendum victory presented a singular opportunity for statesmanship and reconciliation, and he intended to deliver on both.

"I want to speak to all Quebecers," said Johnson. "I cannot help thinking of those hundreds of thousands of our fellow citizens who this evening feel definite sadness. We can understand how disappointed we would have been if our dream had been ended. What I say to them now is not to give up hope. What I tell them is that together we can continue working towards the kind of success and progress that is the feature of Quebec today and that paves the way for the Quebec of tomorrow." After thanking Jean Chrétien, Jean Charest, Michel Bélanger, and all of those who laboured on the No campaign, Johnson singled out "our fellow citizens in the rest of Canada." Quebecers rejected separation, he observed, but on the No side, too, there was "talk about change and our pride as Quebecers." The work of co-operating to build a better Canada must begin anew, he concluded, both for Quebecers who had been divided by the referendum campaign and for Canadians more generally.[61]

It was close to midnight when a "happy and relieved" Jean Chrétien arrived at his Parliament Hill office to address Canadians.[62] The prime minister and his aides had heard Jacques Parizeau's speech before leaving 24 Sussex. They knew that it offered the No side an opportunity to cap off a tumultuous campaign with a powerful *coup de grâce*. Eddie Goldenberg later regretted that they did not take a few extra minutes to "adjust" Chrétien's speech so he could respond to Parizeau's remarks "there and then." But it did not happen. "Instead, in the emotion, hurry, and plain exhaustion of the evening, we did nothing," Goldenberg lamented. "We allowed ourselves to be prisoners of our original planning."[63]

Whether Jean Chrétien had any inclination to eviscerate Jacques Parizeau for his referendum speech remains an open question, however. Over his long career, Chrétien had cultivated a remarkable capacity for compartmentalization. He knew—far better than his mentor Pierre Trudeau, in fact—that what was said in the heat of the moment, in front of the cameras, for partisan advantage, was part of the cut and thrust of Canadian politics. And although he sometimes felt the sting of others' slights against him, Chrétien had grown a thick skin. More than a decade after the 1995 referendum, Chrétien's abiding sense of Parizeau's referendum-night faux pas remained that of a political pro, clinical and detached. "Over the years, I have seen too many politicians ruin their careers because they could not accept defeat graciously," he wrote of Parizeau.[64] That was it.

Not surprisingly, when the prime minister sat down to address the nation, just after midnight, he stressed the need for reconciliation. Canadian federalism had survived the referendum, but just barely. The unofficial result, showing a 1 per cent margin of victory for the federalists, had left Canadians and Quebecers alike in a state of bewilderment. There was no getting around the fact that Chrétien himself bore a great deal of responsibility for the near-miss. This was no time for triumphalism.

"Quebecers have expressed themselves and now we must respect their verdict," Chrétien said solemnly. "This evening I call upon the Premier of Quebec to join the efforts of his government to those of the efforts of the Canadian government so that together we can meet the true and pressing needs of Quebec citizens." Chrétien lauded Canadians living outside Quebec for "the incredible outpouring of good feelings and good will [they] demonstrated over the last week." But he also put them on notice. "It is up to you now not to forget [Quebecers]. Let us work together to bring about the necessary change to make sure that our country remains united and in part this includes the recognition of the distinct nature of Quebec society." Canadians had together built "the country that has made us the envy of the world," concluded Chrétien. "Let us get on with the job. *Bonsoir et merci.* Good night."[65]

～

Canadians are famously boring and polite, or so goes the cliché.

Never was this national stereotype more resonant than in the fall of 1995, when societies the world over were being consumed by "ethnic," "sectarian," and other forms of civil violence. The Bosnian War—which had been triggered by a referendum on the independence of Bosnia and Herzegovina in 1992—was in its fourth year. The full horror of the 1994 genocide in Rwanda was still coming into view. The worst act of domestic terrorism in U.S. history had taken place in April 1995 when Timothy McVeigh bombed an office building in Oklahoma City as an act of protest against his own government. Canadians like Lieutenant-General Roméo Dallaire had borne witness to some of this carnage at extremely close range, providing a window on a world of civil strife that seldom intruded on Canada or Quebec. From Northern Ireland to South Africa, multicultural societies struggled to find new formulas for peace and reconciliation. The phrase "ethnic cleansing" entered the world's lexicon, as incendiary new incarnations of nationalism appeared—or as old ones reappeared. The Canadian historian and future Liberal leader Michael Ignatieff spent much of the 1990s obsessing about these developments in books like *Blood and Belonging* (1993), and he was not alone.

It was surely a credit to the leadership of both sides in the referendum contest, therefore—and to Canadians and Quebecers more generally—that words and ballots were their weapons of choice. Passions had run high throughout the campaign, but never did the leaders of either side lose sight of the liberal-democratic rules of engagement. They agreed from the outset that the sovereignty debate must be conducted with respect for the rights of all participants, democratically and without violence. As head of the sovereignist camp, Jacques Parizeau had sought a revolution of sorts. But he was no revolutionary. The Parti Québécois had no paramilitary wing, nor would it tolerate extra-legal activities of any kind. This was the enduring legacy of René Lévesque, the arch-democrat who had once called the radicals in the Front de libération du Québec (FLQ) "a couple of dozen young terrorists, whose ideology was a hopeless hodgepodge of anarcho-nationalism and kindergarten Marxism."[66] Jacques Parizeau's refrain that everyone "keep their shirts on" carried more than merely symbolic value. The premier was a student of Quebec and of world history. He well knew that nationalism had the power to excite the worst emotions as well as the best.

Over the course of the referendum campaign, partisans on both sides had engaged in illegal acts. In late September, Martin Clark, a PQ executive member living in Longueuil, had his computer stolen by vandals who also spray-painted No slogans on his walls. The Ahuntsic house of Bloc Québécois MP Michel Daviault was spray-painted with the word *No,* as was the house of one of his separatist constituents. Both Yes and No committee headquarters in Montreal had their windows broken and their walls defaced with graffiti. Two youths threw a Molotov cocktail through the window of the No committee office in Fabreville. The office of the Notre-Dame-de-Grâce Yes committee had its front window smashed and, in a separate incident, had swastikas spray-painted on it. An anonymous leaflet distributed in west Montreal threatened executions and a "war against the English invader." In mid-October, Montreal police assigned a special squad to investigate what they called "minor" referendum-related incidents—death threats, assaults, and vandalism—which by then numbered roughly one hundred.[67]

Police in Quebec's major cities were prepared for rioting on referendum night, particularly in Montreal, where the Yes and No venues were but five minutes' walking-distance apart.[68] "This is the same thing we do for any election or referendum," commented Corporal Richard Bourdon. "Normally, everything goes smoothly."[69]

Everything did go smoothly, with only a couple of notable exceptions. Just before Daniel Johnson took the stage, a group of roughly one hundred Yes supporters made its way down Rue Sainte-Catherine in the direction of the Métropolis, smashing store windows and setting off firecrackers along the way. When they arrived at No headquarters, they were met by hundreds of police officers in riot gear. Reporters on the scene described the crowd as drunk, angry, and "looking for trouble."[70] The police maintained a barrier in front of the Métropolis, preventing the No revellers inside from leaving and the Yes protesters outside from entering. A standoff ensued. The crowd chanted "*F-L-Q*" and "*On veut notre pays!*" Some bottles and rocks were thrown, and some billboards torched. After about an hour, the police moved to break up the mob, arresting eight people who refused to co-operate. Scuffles broke out between police and some of the youths.

Further down Rue Sainte-Catherine groups of Yes and No loyalists taunted each other in the street. "*Le Québec aux québécois*" and "*On veut notre pays!*" cheered the Yes group. "Ca-na-da" and "Losers, losers" jeered the No. Fist fights and "sporadic brawls" were reported. Again helmeted police intervened, this time with their helicopters hovering overhead. When the dust settled, forty people had been arrested and four police officers hurt, none of them seriously.

In Vaudreuil, Daniel Johnson's riding office was torched just before midnight, sending forty firefighters into action and gutting the three-storey building. "We think the fire was deliberately set," said dispatcher Clément Guérin with characteristic understatement. At about the same time, Montreal police dismantled a homemade bomb found at federal Liberal party headquarters.[71] In Quebec City, police responded to three bomb threats.[72]

For the most part, these were minor incidents, fuelled by youthful exuberance and alcohol. Quebecers could take heart. The famous "Richard Riot" of March 1955, in which thousands of Montrealers had taken to the streets to protest the suspension of Canadiens hockey star Maurice Richard, had been far worse. Beyond downtown Montreal, in fact, in cities and towns across the province, the streets remained eerily quiet.[73] Some eggs were thrown in residential areas, and pedestrians were occasionally regaled with slogans shouted from passing cars. But by and large, referendum night had come and gone without incident—in typical Canadian fashion.

It had been a long and emotionally charged twenty-four hours. Many Quebec sovereignists were disconsolate, even heartbroken. Yet the response of the vast majority of Quebecers to the dramatic dénouement of the campaign was to take it in stride, to ponder what the politicians might do next, and to get a few hours' sleep before heading back to work the next day.[74]

Canadians elsewhere in the country responded in exactly the same way—except perhaps in British Columbia, where it was still early enough to go down to the local pub for a final post-mortem on the day's extraordinary events.

Numb and Number[1]

The official referendum results confirmed not merely how divided Quebecers were on the sovereignty question but also how invested they were in it. The final tally showed 2,362,648 votes for the No side and 2,308,360 for the Yes—a difference of only 54,288 (for a spread of 50.58 per cent to 49.42). Almost 94 per cent of eligible voters had cast a ballot, a new provincial record.[2] If the litmus test of democratic engagement is the voter participation rate, Quebecers had left no doubt about how much their lives as citizens mattered to them.

~

Canadians awakened the morning of October 31 to an intact country, for which most were eminently grateful. But the dominant mood everywhere, even in Quebec, was one of gnawing uncertainty and morbid introspection. "If this is victory, why do I feel so sad?" asked *Ottawa Citizen* columnist Ken MacQueen. "I have to reach back 14 years to recall a weekend of such collective national grief and preoccupation. It was the death of Terry Fox."[3] Alain Dubuc at *La Presse*, who had days earlier urged Quebecers to plug their noses and vote No, called the federalist near-miss *"une victoire sans joie"* ("a victory without joy").[4]

Within Quebec, where the referendum debate had divided families, friends, and co-workers, there was much talk of reconciliation, which everyone agreed would take time.[5] There was also widespread acknowledgement that despite their agonizing loss, the sovereignists had carried René Lévesque's *projet de souveraineté* to lofty new heights.[6] Many Quebec nationalists, Daniel Johnson foremost among them, had voted to remain in Canada. But this did not change the obvious fact that the referendum vote was epochal when foregrounded against Quebecers' historic dream of nation.

Elsewhere in Canada, the sovereignists' loss was greeted with palpable relief. "I know some people will say this is such a narrow win, it isn't something you should be jubilant about," observed Thomas d'Aquino, head of the BCNI. "But it's like in hockey or football games, 5–5 is a tie, 6–5 is a win. We look at this as a win."[7] In the West, where approval ratings for all of the principals in the referendum debate were the lowest in the country, there were outbursts of pent-up resentment. "There'll be no noble Canadian tolerance here," fumed Trevor Lautens in the *Vancouver Sun*. "Now, as hotly as any separatist, I want to see [Lucien] Bouchard's and Jacques Parizeau's narrow little Quebec invited out."[8] Calgary-based columnist Catherine Ford assailed the Bloc leader. "I never understood, on a visceral level, why Americans hissed at the name Benedict Arnold," she wrote. "Try saying *Lucien Bouchard* anywhere but Quebec today. I suppose we've matured since we hanged Louis Riel, but is it too much to ask that he resign from the House of Commons?"[9] Reform Party leader Preston Manning added his voice to this bitter chorus. Jean Chrétien's performance during the campaign had been "pathetic," he railed, and as for Lucien Bouchard, he should quit the federal parliament.[10]

At a breakfast meeting the morning of October 31, mere hours after he had lost the fight of his life, Jacques Parizeau informed his cabinet colleagues that he was resigning. He made it official at a press conference in the Salon Rouge of the National Assembly later the same day. Almost no one was surprised. Two-thirds of Quebecers and virtually every senior member of the Parti Québécois believed that it was the right decision in light of his incendiary remarks the night before.[11] "My feeling was that he must announce his resignation today, because the wound had to be cauterized immediately," said Jean-François Lisée. "His speech threatened to destroy the collective achievement of Quebec the day before."[12] December 15, 1995, would be Jacques Parizeau's last day as Quebec premier and also as a member of the legislature. In an emotional farewell speech to the National Assembly on that day, he praised the "Yes Generation" of Quebec youth that had coalesced during the referendum campaign. Gesturing towards twenty-nine-year-old MNA André Boisclair, who would ten years later be elected leader of the Parti Québécois, Parizeau said, "On the question of Quebec sovereignty, it's his generation which will, I hope, have the final word."[13]

Even before Parizeau had announced his resignation, there was broad agreement among Canada's political elites that Prime Minister Chrétien should move quickly to honour his "Verdun promises" to Quebecers—and do so before Canadians in the rest of the country lapsed into complacency. "Mr. Chrétien and the premiers of the other provinces can no longer wait for 1997 (the next scheduled constitutional conference) to try to bring about modifications in the division of powers between Ottawa and the provinces and to press for formal recognition of Quebec as a distinct society," wrote editorialist Jean-Jacques Samson at Le Soleil.[14] "Let us take that emotion that has been so evident over the past few days," urged the Windsor Star, "and let it become a message to politicians in Ottawa and all the provinces to resolve our constitutional problems once and for all."[15] Daniel Johnson was the most assertive advocate of reform, but federal Tory leader Jean Charest and the provincial premiers were not far behind. "There has to be an open hand. There has to be a welcoming heart," said Saskatchewan premier Roy Romanow. "We have to make accommodation with respect to the province of Quebec."[16] Romanow and Alberta's Ralph Klein together called on Jean Chrétien to convene a first ministers meeting right away.

Despite the misgivings of some of Chrétien's own cabinet ministers, the prime minister's inclination was never in doubt. On November 1, Chrétien announced that he intended to honour his referendum pledge. He would move immediately to recognize Quebec as a distinct society and to give the Quebec government a veto over constitutional change. "I'm asking you to be bullish on Quebec," Chrétien implored Canadians. "You all have a responsibility to give real hope to those who voted Yes on

Monday because a lot of them thought that they had nothing to lose. Let's show them that Canada can work for them."[17]

~

Much had been said and written during the campaign about the 15 to 20 per cent of Quebec voters who were undecided. Sovereignists had been accused of trying to trick these elusive butterflies into voting Yes with an intentionally cloudy referendum question and promises of a new partnership with Canada. Pollsters had routinely described undecideds as confused—and so had the prime minister.[18] Exit polls taken on referendum night showed that a significant number of Quebecers had indeed voted Yes in the belief that they would continue to use Canadian currency and Canadian passports, and even to send elected representatives to Ottawa. For many Canadians living outside Quebec, this revelation merely confirmed the obvious. As the influential *Canadian Annual Review* concluded, "Many Yes supporters believed they were endorsing a new federal-provincial arrangement, not the outright political independence of Quebec."[19]

Within Quebec, however, such talk had always been condescending, and it remained so. Like Canadians everywhere, Quebecers are citizens of an advanced democracy, where the rights and responsibilities of membership are well understood. Jean-François Lisée, principal author of the PQ's referendum question, based the text on the question that had been put to Canadians during the 1992 referendum on the Charlottetown Accord: "Do you agree that the Constitution of Canada should be renewed on the basis of the agreement reached on August 28, 1992?" The *péquistes'* question referenced the June 1995 tripartite agreement and Bill 1, it is true, but it also contained the declarative phrase "Quebec should become sovereign." At critical points in the campaign, most notably when polls started showing the Yes side leading, both Parizeau and Lucien Bouchard had reiterated the fundamentals of their *projet de souveraineté*. "We're going to make Quebec sovereign," Parizeau had said. "If there is a new partnership, bravo, perfect, and I believe there will be one. If there isn't, we declare sovereignty."[20]

Over the course of the campaign, the premier's toughest franco-phone critics, in the National Assembly but also in the press, took Parizeau to task for a steadily lengthening number of transgressions. He had rigged the commission hearings, they said; he had abandoned his own principles, making common cause with people whose views he loathed; he had hoped to provoke hotheads in English Canada and thus to benefit from a backlash in Quebec; he had understated the economic and the social costs of sovereignty; most egregiously, he had cynically endorsed a partnership scheme that he knew in his heart Canadians outside Quebec would never accept. But with very few exceptions—and in stark contrast with what was said about Parizeau in the rest of Canada—his francophone critics did not accuse him of trying to hoodwink Quebec voters. The premier may well have imagined that Quebecers were like lobsters in boiling water. But as they had demon-strated since the day he took power, they were notoriously hard to trap.

As political scientist Louis Balthazar later wrote, there was more to the referendum result than "ignorance, confusion, deception, or just plain fraud." Many Quebecers understood a Yes vote as their only option if they wished to maintain both their unique francophone soci-ety in North America and their strong attachment to Canada. "In spite of all denials of any possibility of partnership," wrote Balthazar, "many Quebecers stubbornly continued to believe that one form or another of Canadian union would impose itself after a Yes victory. Quebecers seem to be quite persistent in their belief that sovereignty can be accompan-ied by a Canadian union. This belief may be idealistic and naive, but it certainly is not completely devoid of common sense."[21]

Exit polls conducted on referendum night supported Balthazar's view. One-quarter of Quebecers who voted Yes had considered voting No, and vice versa. More than one-third of Yes voters said that their primary motivation for voting as they did was to "send a message" to Ottawa. "Rather than trying to break up the Canadian political sys-tem," concluded the authors of the definitive academic study of these polling data, "they were trying to use the opportunity provided by the referendum to change it."[22] Anecdotal evidence points in the same direction. During the referendum campaign, the Canadian Press tracked the evolving ideas of three undecided voters who ended up supporting the sovereignty option. "I voted Yes to make sure the No side would have the smallest possible majority," said forty-nine-year-old Roger-Daniel Laberge of Beauport. "I voted *Oui* with my head, not my heart, because I thought it would make things move," said twenty-seven-year-old Montreal teacher Diane Boucher. Eighteen-year-old Outremont student Myriam Fredette said she voted Yes believing that it would not necessarily "bring about any great change immediately" but might "be the first step towards something else."[23]

Lucien Bouchard's elevation to *négociateur en chef* on October 7 had been widely credited with drawing a good number of undecided voters to the Yes side. His talk of a new partnership with Canada, it was said, had emboldened many Quebecers who were otherwise reluctant to plunge into the deep end of the sovereignty pool alongside Jacques Parizeau.

Jean Chrétien bore his fair share of responsibility for the butter-flies' migration into sovereignist territory. For over a year, he had blithely insisted that he did not have to talk Quebecers into anything. All the chatter about sovereignty was "hypothetical," he declared. "You all know that Canada will win." It did not seem to occur to the prime minister or his advisors that such brash confidence in a feder-alist victory—bolstered by the best polling money could buy—gave undecided Quebec voters little incentive to vote No. By mid-October, when the once-incontestable premises of the feds' campaign were in shreds and the Yes forces were ascendant, it was too late. Worse yet for Chrétien, Lucien Bouchard's withering attacks on him had had the effect of broadening the sovereignty debate into a contest over his political record and even his character. By the time the prime minister appeared at the massive No rally in Verdun, the evening of October 24, he felt compelled to remind Quebecers that the referendum was not "a popularity contest" but "a fundamental and irreversible choice of a country." Little wonder that some critics had concluded even before Quebecers cast their ballots that Chrétien had lost the sovereignty debate, and lost badly.[24]

Yet post-referendum polls revealed that 65 per cent of non-Quebecers thought Chrétien had acquitted himself well during the campaign (compared with only 35 per cent of Quebecers).[25] Such numbers underscored one of the most enduring aspects of the referendum debate within Quebec, namely how little it invoked Canadians living elsewhere.

Jacques Parizeau, Lucien Bouchard, and even Daniel Johnson had always said that Quebecers had to be free to chart their own course, and all three had demonstrated during the campaign that they meant it. With the exception of Bouchard's repeated assertion that English Canada would have no choice but to negotiate a new partnership with a sovereign Quebec, the debate was focused almost entirely on the aspirations of Quebecers alone. More than this, it was conducted almost entirely by politicians representing no outside constituencies and beholden to no outside voters. (Jean Chrétien, Jean Charest, and Paul Martin were the most notable exceptions, but it remains significant that even former prime ministers Pierre Trudeau, Brian Mulroney, and Joe Clark were not invited to participate.) This insularity helps to explain why many Canadians watching the campaign from the periphery thought it had a surreal, Alice-in-Wonderland air. It also helps to account for the feelings of frustration and helplessness that carried so many of them to the unity rally in Montreal.

~

Inside Quebec, the referendum outcome was tainted by charges from the No camp of voting irregularities, and from the Yes camp of funding irregularities. For weeks, such "shenanigans" were the talk of the province.[26]

Spoiled ballots numbered 86,388 (or 1.8 per cent), which was greater than the margin of victory but in line with earlier electoral contests in the province. (In the 1992 Charlottetown referendum, 2.2 per cent of ballots were rejected; in the 1994 provincial election, 1.96 per cent; and in the 1980 sovereignty referendum, 1.74 per cent.) The No camp accused the sovereignists of any number of dirty tricks at the polling stations, including vote tampering. Liberal MNA Thomas Mulcair was particularly incensed, claiming that in a single polling station in his riding of Chomedey, eighty-two of a total of 149 No votes were rejected by sovereignist scrutineers. "I've got shell-shocked workers," he exclaimed. "I've got workers who knew the Duplessis era and they say they've never known anything like this. This is systematic electoral fraud."[27] For their part, Parti Québécois officials remained irate about the undeclared corporate subsidies that had underwritten the feds' unity rally, in blatant contravention of Quebec law.[28]

As Quebecers had anticipated, some even before the official campaign had begun, chief electoral officer Pierre-Ferdinand Côté found himself at the centre of a storm of accusations and counter-accusations. Swamped with 225 formal complaints in the aftermath of the vote, Côté announced in late November 1995 that he was enlisting the services of a team of legal and academic experts to undertake what would be the largest investigation in Quebec's electoral history.[29] "I'm taking these exceptional measures because of the large number of complaints and the gravity of the allegations," said Côté.[30]

Yet, tellingly, the deadline by which either committee could petition to have the referendum vote overturned, November 15, came and went. The victorious No side had no interest in a recount. As for the Yes side, Quebecers speculated that since the unity rally appeared to have benefited the sovereignist and not the federalist vote, there was not much of a case to be made that spending irregularities had bought the referendum.[31]

On December 20, 1995, Pierre-Ferdinand Côté published a discussion paper recommending the loosening of restrictions on how Quebecers could mark their ballots and the tightening of rules about who had the authority to reject them.[32] Not until May 13, 1996, did he issue a full report on his investigations. Citing Judge Alan B. Gold's analysis of the ballots from thirty-four electoral divisions, Côté concluded that "there was no plot or conspiracy in the upper echelons of the Yes National Committee."[33] He noted as well, however, that an unusually high number of votes had been rejected in certain Montreal ridings and thus instigated proceedings against twenty-nine scrutineers and two PQ delegates. Thirty-one charges of electoral fraud followed. In all cases, the defendants were acquitted by the Court of Quebec. In 1997, the DGE, now headed by chief electoral officer François Casgrain, appealed the decision of the lower court, only to have the acquittals upheld by Judge Ginette Piché of the Quebec Superior Court in April 1998.[34] The following year, a panel of three judges of the Quebec Court of Appeal dismissed the chief electoral officer's appeal of Justice Piché's decision. The panel ruled that the young scrutineers' zealous rejections of No ballots at two Montreal polling stations were more compatible with "*une erreur de jugement*" than with "*un acte malhonnête*" ("a dishonest act").[35]

In September 2006, Quebec's chief electoral officer, Marcel Blanchet, launched an inquiry into allegations of federal spending irregularities made in Robin Philpot's book *Le Référendum volé* (*The Stolen Referendum*).[36] After fifty-two days of hearings and the investigation of more than 18,000 documents, directeur général des élections du Québec chief investigator Bernard Grenier concluded that Option Canada and the Canadian Unity Council had indeed spent roughly $11 million on the No campaign—and that the money had come from the federal department of Canadian heritage.[37] Only $539,000 had been spent illegally, according to Grenier, but only because the rest of the money had never been channelled through the official No committee, where it would have been subject to provincial law. Not surprisingly, sovereignists were outraged by these revelations—and are still. In 2012, Jean-François Lisée wrote extensively about "*le cover-up d'Option Canada*," noting that the $11 million spent by the feds on the No vote amounted to a tripling of the spending limit proscribed by Quebec law.[38] Jacques Parizeau urged Quebecers to read *Le Référendum volé* for themselves to judge whether they had been "deprived of an extraordinary opportunity to have their own country."[39]

～

There was never much doubt about who would step into Parizeau's ample shoes as Quebec premier. Well before Quebecers had cast their referendum ballots, Lucien Bouchard had been spoken of as the heir apparent, and not always in whispers.[40] Post-referendum polls confirmed that roughly 55 per cent of Quebec voters thought he should succeed Parizeau.[41] Indeed, Prime Minister Chrétien and his cabinet colleagues had reacted to Parizeau's resignation with a feeling of foreboding, knowing that Bouchard remained a threat. "The question on everyone's mind," Eddie Goldenberg later recalled, "was whether Bouchard might use his immense popularity to call and win a snap referendum."[42]

On November 22, Bouchard affirmed that he was willing to take over as premier of Quebec. But to the great relief of Canadian federalists everywhere, he announced at the same time that he would not hold another referendum before the next provincial election. His priority as premier, he said, would be the Quebec economy. "Setting public finances in order once more is no longer simply a matter of good management, but rather, it is an imperative duty," he said. There would be a third referendum on sovereignty, he added, but "I don't know when."[43]

Bouchard's decision turned out to be a fork in the road for national unity. For sovereignists, it may also have been a missed opportunity. A Léger and Léger poll published on November 25 found not only that a Bouchard-led PQ would soundly defeat Daniel Johnson's Liberals if an election were held that day, but that 54.8 per cent of decided voters would have said Yes to sovereignty.[44]

Lucien Bouchard filed his nomination papers for the leadership of the Parti Québécois on December 22, his fifty-seventh birthday. He was acclaimed as leader on January 12, 1996, and sworn in as premier of Quebec seventeen days later. True to his word, Bouchard plunged into the thankless task of getting the government's finances in order. On May 9, 1996, the National Assembly passed Quebec's first-ever zero-deficit law, mandating the elimination of the provincial deficit by the year 2000. This was tough medicine, and many Quebecers, particularly in the left-leaning ranks of the sovereignist movement, felt betrayed by it. By the autumn of 1996, with the first anniversary of the referendum looming, Premier Bouchard found himself being burned in effigy by

Quebec protesters, who saw him as a convert to the same heartless neo-liberalism that he had claimed to revile in Mike Harris's Ontario.

Jean Chrétien, in the meanwhile, demonstrated that he was serious about moving quickly on his Verdun promises. Less than a month after the referendum, on November 28, 1995, he tabled a motion in parliament recognizing Quebec as a distinct society, paired with a resolution granting the government of Quebec (and other provinces) a veto on constitutional change. "These initiatives are substantial," said Chrétien. "They are not constitutional in nature, because the government of Quebec has stated categorically that it does not want to participate in constitutional discussions."[45]

What followed the tabling of the prime minister's reform package was two and a half weeks of blistering acrimony in Ottawa—and, indeed, across Canada. Against the objections of the Reform Party, the Bloc Québécois, the federal NDP, some provincial and aboriginal leaders, and a majority of Canadians living outside Quebec, the Liberals used their parliamentary majority to limit debate on the distinct-society motion and ram it through the House of Commons.[46] Daniel Johnson commended Chrétien for taking this important "first step."[47] Lucien Bouchard called the initiative meaningless, since it was not written into the Constitution and could be rescinded unilaterally by the federal government at any time.[48] Preston Manning and his Reform colleagues claimed to be so disgusted by the prime minister's "lame-brained" handling of both the referendum campaign and its aftermath that they sought out a means of "impeaching" him.[49] Among Quebecers, there was widespread acknowledgement that if Chrétien had suggested before the referendum vote that he was prepared to offer only these reforms, the Yes side would have won.[50]

No one, least of all the prime minister himself, was sorry to see the raucous session of parliament break for Christmas on December 15.

~

The referendum debate had demonstrated, to Canadians outside Quebec at least, that the legal and constitutional uncertainties of a

Yes vote played to the advantage of the sovereignists. On November 1, therefore, just two days after the vote, the prime minister announced that he could not allow the federal government to be held hostage any longer by threats of secession. "We cannot play that game where there will be a referendum every six months or year or two years until [the sovereignists] win and after that there will be no more referendum," said Chrétien. "It's not the way that I will play the game. This country has the right to political stability and as prime minister of Canada I will make sure that we have political stability in this land."[51] A two-track strategy thus emerged. The government's efforts to mollify Quebec voters (by fast-tracking the distinct-society resolution but also by ceding power to Quebec in manpower training and elsewhere) became known as "Plan A." "Plan B" referred to the feds' evolving legal strategy for protecting Canada's interests should Quebecers vote Yes to sovereignty in the future.[52] If Jean Chrétien had envisaged Plan A as a velvet glove, Plan B was the iron fist.

In January 1996, the prime minister brought constitutional law professor Stéphane Dion into the cabinet as his point man on Quebec. Dion had no great love for the sovereignists, and vice versa. "I believe very strongly that a secessionist process is very difficult to reconcile with democracy," he said flatly. "I believe it is unrealistic for a government to think that it can unilaterally break up a modern democratic state."[53] One month into Dion's tenure, by which time Lucien Bouchard was serving as premier of Quebec, the federal government codified its legal obligations to Canadians in its Speech from the Throne. "As long as the prospect of another Quebec referendum exists," it stated, "the Government will exercise its responsibility to ensure that debate is conducted with all the facts on the table, that the rules of the process are fair, that the consequences are clear, and that Canadians, no matter where they live, will have their say in the future of their country."[54]

In September 1996, the feds announced their intention to refer the question of Quebec's right to secede to the Supreme Court of Canada. Premier Bouchard dismissed the move as yet another cynical power play, declaring that the government of Quebec had no choice but to boycott the court's hearings and ignore its ruling. Almost two years later, on August 20, 1998, the Supreme Court handed down its opinion. The unilateral secession of Quebec was contrary to both Canadian constitutional law and international law, it ruled, but even so, Ottawa and the provinces had a "constitutional duty" to negotiate with Quebec if a "clear majority" of Quebecers voted in favour of secession "on a clear question."[55]

Since most Quebecers, not all of them sovereignists, believe that the terms and conditions by which Quebecers will achieve sovereignty are theirs alone to decide, the Supreme Court reference was widely acknowledged as having done little to break Canada's constitutional "deadlock."[56] This did not prevent the federal Liberals from adopting Bill C-20, the *Clarity Act*, in June 2000, a statute that forbids Ottawa from negotiating with Quebec on the terms of secession if the question "is not clear" or if it does not result "in a clear expression of the will of the population."[57] The National Assembly of Quebec responded quickly and forcefully to the *Clarity Act* by passing Bill 99. "No other parliament or government may reduce the powers, authority, sovereignty or legitimacy of the National Assembly," it asserted, "or impose constraint on the democratic will of the Québec people to determine its own future."[58]

Both the federal *Clarity Act* and Quebec's Bill 99 remain on the books, and both remain highly contentious. In October 2013, Quebec's Superior Court agreed to hear a constitutional challenge to Bill 99 that had been working its way through the legal system for years. What vaulted news of the court's decision onto the nation's front pages was the discovery that the federal government, now headed by Prime Minister Stephen Harper, had "quietly" joined the legal challenge to Bill 99 on the grounds that some of its sections violate federal law.[59] Spokespersons for all four parties in the National Assembly leapt to the defence of Bill 99, demonstrating that Quebec's prerogative to determine its own future retains broad public support. In criticizing the Harper Conservatives, Quebecers did not fail to notice that this was the same government that had in 2006 passed its own motion, stating "That this House recognize that the Québécois form a nation within a united Canada."

Questioned in 2013 about his government's role in the legal challenge to Bill 99, Prime Minister Stephen Harper sounded very much like Jean Chrétien circa October 1995. "Everybody on this side [of the House of Commons], including the minister of intergovernmental affairs, is an unconditional supporter of the unity of this country," said Harper. "I believe that Quebecers, as much as anyone else, do not want another referendum. They do not want to be arguing about this. They want to be taking this country, united together, forward into the future."[60]

Plus ça change . . .

~

It is, of course, impossible to know anything with certainty about the road not taken—about what might have happened if the referendum vote on October 30, 1995, had gone the other way. But what is known is suggestive.

The day of the referendum vote, Premier Jacques Parizeau pretaped a speech to Quebecers to be broadcast in the event of a Yes win. "A simple and strong decision has been taken tonight," said the premier solemnly. "Quebec will become sovereign. It has taken great courage for the men and women of Quebec to overcome the formidable obstacles placed in their path, from the very beginning right up to this day. Today, you have outdone yourselves. You have inscribed your name on the face of the earth. Each of you should know, tonight, that the Government of Quebec will proceed in the coming days with the same clarity, the same serene determination, the same courage and the same openness that you, the citizens of Quebec, have shown today."[61]

Whether Parizeau considered pressing forward with a unilateral declaration of independence after a Yes vote remains an open question. All that can be said with certainty is that he laid the groundwork for any eventuality, a UDI included. The week before the referendum, for example, Parizeau had Bernard Landry write directly to foreign ambassadors posted to Ottawa requesting that their governments act quickly in the event of a Yes vote to recognize Quebec as a sovereign nation.[62] International recognition of Quebec sovereignty would have buttressed a UDI, without question, but it might also have served the less ambitious goal of leveraging the federal government in a negotiated partnership deal *à la* Bouchard. But the symbolism of Landry's letters to the embassies—postdated to October 30 and dispatched in flagrant violation of diplomatic protocol—was unmistakable. The PQ government was prepared to act, as early as October 31, as though it were sovereign.

In 1996, Benoît Aubin, information director of Quebec's TVA network, recounted his impression of Parizeau's demeanour as he recited his victory speech before the network's rolling cameras. "They were ready," wrote Aubin of the sovereignists. "Not, as we thought from what they had been saying during the campaign, to negotiate patiently with Ottawa for at least a year, but ready to move ahead. Immediately, forcefully, on all fronts. More quickly, more actively, and more irremediably than anything they had implied during the campaign, and even in the wording of the question they had gone to the people with that day."[63] In 2005, journalist Mario Cardinal offered a more measured reading of the premier's intentions. "Jacques Parizeau's first move, should the Yes vote prevail, would be to appoint a transition committee, which would gather around him the ministers responsible for Public Safety, Intergovernmental Affairs, the Treasury Board and Justice. Provisions would immediately be made to convene the National Assembly as soon as possible. As regulations require 48 hours' notice, members of the National Assembly would be called to sit on Thursday, November 2, to adopt a motion to bring a proclamation of sovereignty within the year."[64]

Back in Ottawa, it had fallen to Eddie Goldenberg to write Jean Chrétien's concession speech in the event of a sovereignist victory. "The draft speech certainly put a brave face on the outcome," Goldenberg later recalled. "It recognized that Quebecers wanted change in Canada, but it firmly rejected the interpretation of a close Yes vote—or even any Yes vote—on an ambiguous question as a genuine vote to separate Quebec from Canada." Even if the sovereignists had won by a significant margin, Goldenberg affirmed, the prime minister would have refused to enter into negotiations to break up Canada "based on the question on that referendum ballot."[65]

Jean Chrétien had hinted as much in the immediate aftermath of the referendum, telling journalists in year-end interviews for 1995 that he had never understood the referendum vote as legally binding. "It was a plebiscite," said the prime minister, "it wasn't a legal act. It didn't mean the end of Canada."[66] In his 2007 memoir, Chrétien made the same case: "I did not debate—and never will debate—what I would have done if the Yes side had won. No matter what tricks Jacques Parizeau might have held up his sleeve, the reality was that the crooked question had not asked for a mandate to separate. Events would have been chaotic, emotions would have run high, but a very slight majority for the Yes side could not have been interpreted as irrefutable proof that the majority of Quebecers wanted to sever their historic links with Canada. Resolving the problems would have taken a long, long time, without any certainty that the separatists would triumph in the end. If Parizeau had been able to grab power back from Lucien Bouchard and had proclaimed independence unilaterally without the support of the people, he would have had to act on it. He would have had to establish borders and take control of federal institutions in Quebec. And he would have had to face a hell of a fight from Jean Chrétien."[67]

Within Quebec sovereignist circles, the blunt revelations of Goldenberg's and Chrétien's memoirs were nothing short of incendiary. In light of his admission that he had no intention of allowing a Yes vote to break up Canada, Jean Chrétien's appeal to Quebecers at Verdun and again during his emergency broadcast—his insistence that their decision would be "serious and irreversible"—is today remembered as one of the "*grands mensonges de notre histoire*" ("great lies of our history").[68] Jean-François Lisée spoke for many *péquistes* when he observed in 2010 that Jean Chrétien's dishonesty during the 1995 campaign had exceeded even Pierre Trudeau's in 1980.

~

Jacques Parizeau and Lucien Bouchard entered the 1995 referendum campaign believing that it would be the last battle for sovereignty for both of them. "It would be unrealistic of a man of 55 to think that there will be another shot at it," said Bouchard early in the campaign. "The last one was in 1980. There is no way we can anticipate such a sequence for 20 or 10 years. People of our generation have to consider this as a last fight."[69]

But, to judge from their recent pronouncements at least, for both Parizeau and Bouchard the referendum contest has by no means been consigned to ancient history. Their dream of nation is alive and well, bolstered by every new poll that sheds a favourable light on the sovereignist option for Quebec, and especially by the successes of the generation of separatists that is presently making its mark in Quebec politics. "Quebec will make a third bid for independence," Jacques Parizeau prophesied in 2010. "The strategy and the tactics remain to be defined."[70]

Lucien Bouchard is perhaps not quite so bullish. "There's no referendum in sight and I don't want to suffer another defeat," he remarked in 2010. "In the meantime, we have a lot to do."

Reflecting on his own experience of the 1995 referendum, Bouchard has said that he dove head-first into the campaign "not even checking if there was water in the pool." If only he had been able to win his sovereignist comrades to a two-referendum option, he mused. "We would have won. I'm convinced. That's the ultimate goal, it's to win."[71]

ABBREVIATIONS USED IN NOTES

BG — *Boston Globe*
CBCDA — CBC Digital Archives
CH — *Calgary Herald*
CP — Canadian Press
EJ — *Edmonton Journal*
FP — *Financial Post*
GM — *Globe and Mail*
HCH — *Halifax Chronicle Herald*
KWS — *Kingston Whig-Standard*
LD — *Le Devoir*
LDR — *Le Droit*
LAT — *Los Angeles Times*
LP — *La Presse*
LS — *Le Soleil*
MG — Montreal *Gazette*
NP — *National Post*
NYT — *New York Times*
OC — *Ottawa Citizen*
TS — *Toronto Star*
VP — *Vancouver Province*
VS — *Vancouver Sun*
VTC — *Victoria Times-Colonist*
WS — *Windsor Star*

NOTES

PROLOGUE: FREE FALLING

1. Eddie Goldenberg, *The Way It Works: Inside Ottawa* (Toronto: McClelland & Stewart, 2006), 212.
2. Ibid.
3. Jean Chrétien, *My Years as Prime Minister* (Toronto: Knopf, 2007), 144–5.
4. Sandro Contenta, "Quebec: It's Neck and Neck Poll Finds," *TS* (October 18, 1995); and Chantal Hébert, "La marée haute du OUI," *LP* (October 18, 1995).
5. Chrétien, *My Years as Prime Minister*, 137.
6. Ibid., 144–5.
7. Guy Laforest, *Trudeau and the End of a Canadian Dream* (Montreal: McGill-Queen's University Press, 1995), 15.
8. Pierre Trudeau, "Speech at the Paul Sauvé Arena" (May 14, 1980), http://www.cbc.ca/archives/categories/politics/federal-politics/a-la-prochaine-fois-the-1980-quebec-referendum/trudeau-promises-a-renewed-confederation.html.
9. Pierre Trudeau, cited in Kenneth McRoberts, "English Canada and Quebec: Avoiding the Issue," Sixth Annual Robarts Lecture, York University (March 5, 1991), http://robarts.info.yorku.ca/files/lectures-pdf/rl_mcroberts.pdf, 8.
10. Laforest, *Trudeau and the End*, 33.
11. Jacques Parizeau, cited in Katherine Wilton, "Parizeau Hits Back at Chrétien," *MG* (May 5, 1995); Mario Fontaine, "Chrétien fait le sale travail," *LP* (May 5, 1995); André Picard and Rhéal Séguin, "Parizeau Calls Chrétien a Traitor," *GM* (May 5, 1995); and Donald Charette, "Parizeau rappelle une page d'histoire au pays de Chrétien," *LS* (July 10, 1995).
12. Jean Chrétien, cited in Goldenberg, *The Way It Works*, 206.
13. Chrétien, *My Years as Prime Minister*, 143–4.
14. See Mollie Dunsmuir and Brian O'Neal, "Quebec's Constitutional Veto: The Legal and Historical Context," BP-295E (Ottawa: Government of Canada, Law and Government Division, 1992), http://www.parl.gc.ca/Content/LOP/researchpublications/bp295-e.pdf.

15. Chrétien, *My Years as Prime Minister*, 143–4.

16. "Meech Marathon" CBCDA, http://www.cbc.ca/archives/categories/politics/the-constitution/constitutional-discord-meech-lake/meech-marathon.html.

17. See, for example, Charles Taylor, *Reconciling the Solitudes: Essays on Canadian Federalism and Nationalism* (Montreal: McGill-Queen's University Press, 1993); Charles Taylor, "The Politics of Recognition," *Multiculturalism: Examining the Politics of Recognition,* Amy Gutmann, ed. (Princeton, NJ: Princeton University Press, 1994); Will Kymlicka, *Multicultural Citizenship* (Toronto: Oxford University Press, 1995); Peter H. Russell, *Constitutional Odyssey: Can Canadians Become a Sovereign People?* (Toronto: University of Toronto Press, 1992); Alan C. Cairns, *Charter Versus Federalism: The Dilemmas of Constitutional Reform* (Montreal: McGill-Queen's University Press, 1992); and Alan C. Cairns, *Reconfigurations: Canadian Citizenship and Constitutional Change* (Toronto: McClelland & Stewart, 1995); and Michael Ignatieff, *The Rights Revolution* (Toronto: Anansi, 2000).

18. Joe Clark, *A Nation Too Good to Lose: Renewing the Purpose of Canada* (Toronto: Key Porter Books, 1994), 105.

19. Jean Chrétien, cited in Mario Cardinal, *Breaking Point Quebec–Canada: The 1995 Referendum*, trans. Ferdinanda Van Gennip and Mark Stout (Montreal: Bayard Canada Books, 2005), 288–9.

20. John Ibbitson, "The Charter Proves To Be Canada's Gift to World," *GM* (April 15, 2012).

21. Jean Chrétien, cited in Joan Bryden, "Chrétien Says Referendum Question 'One-Way Ticket Out of Canada,'" *OC* (September 12, 1995).

22. See Brian O'Neal, "Distinct Society: Origins, Interpretations, Implications," BP-408E (Ottawa: Government of Canada, Political and Social Affairs Division, December 1995), http://publications.gc.ca/Collection-R/LoPBdP/BP/bp408-e.htm#A.

23. Pierre Trudeau and Jean Chrétien, cited in Chrétien, *My Years as Prime Minister*, 122–3.

24. Ibid., 143–4.

25. Ibid., 144–5.

26. Avrum Stark, cited in Sarah Scott, "'No' Rally Tinged with Pride, Fear," *MG* (October 25, 1995).

27. Victor Debbas, cited in Edison Stewart, "We're Open to Change Passionate PM Vows," *TS* (October 25, 1995).

28. Michelle Paiement, cited in Stewart, "We're Open."

29. France Héroux, cited in Scott, "'No' Rally Tinged."

30. Sylvie M. Beaudreau, cited in David Leyton-Brown, *Canadian Annual Review of Politics and Public Affairs 1995* (Toronto: University of Toronto Press, 2002), 134.

31. Jean Chrétien, cited in "Demanding Changes in Quebec's Referendum," CTV National News, transcript (December 7, 1994).

32. See William Johnson, "Bouchard Is a Leader Who Could Never Lead," *KWS* (October 10, 1995).

33. Jane Stewart, cited in Cardinal, *Breaking Point,* 307.

34. Chrétien, *My Years as Prime Minister,* 145–6.

35. Lysiane Gagnon, "Trop peu, trop tard," *LP* (October 25, 1995). See also Vincent Marissal, "Chrétien parle de changement," *LS* (October 25, 1995); and Michel Vastel, "Les dés sont jetés," *LDR* (October 25, 1995); Chantal Hébert, "Un test crucial pour Chrétien," *LS* (October 25, 1995); "Le NON contre-attaque," *LP* (October 25, 1995); and Joël-Denis Bellavance, "Chrétien change son plan de match," *LS* (October 25, 1995).

36. Jean H. Leroux, *Hansard* (October 25, 1995), 15802.

37. Jean Chrétien, cited in Lawrence Martin, *Iron Man: The Defiant Reign of Jean Chrétien* (Toronto: Viking Canada, 2003), 129.

38. Chrétien, *My Years as Prime Minister,* 145–6.

39. Jean Chrétien, cited in Edward Greenspon and Anthony Wilson-Smith, *Double Vision: The Inside Story of the Liberals in Power* (Toronto: Doubleday, 1996), 324–5.

CHAPTER ONE: OTTAWA, 1993

1. Jeffrey Simpson, *The Friendly Dictatorship* (Toronto: McClelland & Stewart, 2001).

2. Eddie Goldenberg, cited in Mario Cardinal, *Breaking Point Quebec–Canada: The 1995 Referendum,* trans. Ferdinanda Van Gennip and Mark Stout (Montreal: Bayard Canada Books, 2005), 34.

3. Jean Chrétien, *My Years as Prime Minister* (Toronto: Knopf, 2007), 124.

4. Ibid., 115.

5. Ibid., 118.

6. Tom Axworthy and Pierre Elliott Trudeau, *Towards a Just Society: The Trudeau Years* (Toronto: Penguin, 1992), 7.

7. Eighty-one per cent of voters in Quebec and Canada cited an economic issue as the "most important" of the campaign. See Harold D. Clarke, Allan Kornberg, and Peter Wearing, *A Polity on the Edge: Canada and the Politics of Fragmentation* (Toronto: University of Toronto Press, 2000), 147.

8. See Manon Cornellier, *The Bloc* (Toronto: James Lorimer & Company, 1995), 80.

9. Lucien Bouchard, *On the Record,* trans. Dominique Clift (Toronto: Stoddart, 1994), 233.

10. Lucien Bouchard, cited in Cornellier, *The Bloc,* 74–5.

11. Bouchard, *On the Record,* x–xi.

12. Harold D. Clarke, Allan Kornberg, and Peter Wearing, *A Polity on the Edge: Canada and the Politics of Fragmentation* (Toronto: University of Toronto Press, 2000) 147.

13. Bouchard, *On the Record,* xi. See also Gilbert Lacasse, "Chrétien face à la tourmente," *LS* (October 26, 1993); Denis Lessard, "Bouchard sera notre honneur, dit Parizeau," *LP* (October 26, 1993); and Lia Lévesque, "Le Bloc entend faire honneur au Québec," *LS* (October 26, 1993).

14. Philip Authier, "Yes: What Went Right," *OC* (October 28, 1995), A4.

15. See Bouchard, *On the Record*, 228–9. Italics in the original.
16. Ibid., 228.
17. Jean Charest, *My Road to Quebec* (Montreal: Éditions P. Tisseyre, 1998), 101.
18. Brian Mulroney, *Memoirs 1939–1993* (Toronto: McClelland & Stewart, 2007), 754.
19. Jean Lapierre, cited in Cornellier, *The Bloc*, 12. See also Paul Roy, "Jeux de bloc," *LP* (May 18, 1991); "Le Bloc va empêcher Mulroney de remporter une élection référendaire," *LP* (February 25, 1991); and Denis Lessard, "Québec-Ottawa, copain-copain comme jamais," *LP* (May 18, 1991).
20. Bouchard, *On the Record*, 256.
21. Ibid., 251–2.
22. Lucien Bouchard, cited in Paul Wells, "Preparing for Final Combat," *MG* (November 27, 1994).
23. Bouchard, *On the Record*, 276–7.
24. Lucien Bouchard, *Un Nouveau parti pour l'étape décisive* (Montreal: Fides, 1993), 89.
25. Bouchard, *On the Record*, xi.
26. Bouchard, *Un Nouveau parti*, 87, 122.
27. Lucien Bouchard, cited in Hubert Bauch and Philip Authier, "Quebec Would Force Canada to Negotiate Pact, Bouchard Says," *MG* (October 10, 1995). See also Donald Charette, "Au lendemain d'un OUI," *LS* (October 10, 1995).
28. Bouchard, *On the Record*, 251–2.
29. Richard Gwyn, "'Bolter' Bouchard Is Headed Straight for Quicksand," *TS* (April 24, 1995).
30. Bouchard, *On the Record*, 251.
31. Ibid., 258.
32. On polling data, see David Johnston, "In PQ Circles the Word is 'Sovereignty,'" *MG* (November 26, 1994).
33. Lucien Bouchard, cited in Eric Siblin, "PM Blind to English Canada," *KWS* (October 20, 1995).
34. Alan C. Cairns, "Why Is It So Difficult to Talk to Each Other?" *McGill Law Journal/ Revue de droit de McGill 42* (1997), 71.
35. Preston Manning, *Think Big: Adventures in Life and Democracy* (Toronto: McClelland & Stewart, 2002), 122.
36. Ibid., 137.
37. Preston Manning, cited in Steve Patten, "The Reform Party's Re-imagining of the Canadian Nation," *Journal of Canadian Studies / Revue d'études canadiennes* 34:1 (Spring 1999), 27–52.
38. Chrétien, *My Years as Prime Minister*, 132.
39. Deborah Grey, cited in Norm Ovenden, "Reform Plans to Displace Bloc as Effective House Opposition," *EJ* (September 14, 1995).
40. Alan C. Cairns, "An Election To Be Remembered: Canada 1993," *Canadian Public Policy—Analyse de Politiques* 20:3 (1994), 224. See also Gilles Paquin, "Le Reform Party tente de se donner une image moins extrémiste," *LP* (April 6, 1991).

41. Preston Manning, cited in Tu Thanh Ha and Edward Greenspon, "Referendum Just a Step, Manning Tells Quebec," *GM* (December 15, 1994).

42. Stephen Harper, cited in Susan Delacourt, "Reform Joins Referendum Fray with Own Spin on Separation," *GM* (October 16, 1995).

43. William Thorsell, "Initials as Destiny," *GM* (December 31, 1994).

44. Pascale Gemme, cited in Peter Menzies, "Quebec Media Turns Deaf Ear on Manning Message," *CH* (October 18, 1995).

45. Manning, *Think Big*, 125.

46. Sheila Copps, *Hansard* (December 6, 1994), 8697.

47. Manning, *Think Big*, 124.

48. Chrétien, *My Years as Prime Minister*, 134.

49. Ibid., 3.

50. Goldenberg, *The Way It Works*, 197.

51. Richard S. Conley, "Sovereignty or the Status Quo? The 1995 Pre-referendum Debate in Quebec," *Journal of Commonwealth & Comparative Politics* 35:1 (March 1997), 89.

52. Editorial "Broadening the Federalist Tent" *GM* (January 4, 1995).

53. Patrick J. Monahan, "Why Are the Sovereignist Forces in Such Disarray?" *GM* (May 15, 1995).

54. The largest public opinion poll in Canadian history, held in January 1995, showed that that "60 per cent of Quebecers would vote against independence if Premier Jacques Parizeau asked the question: 'Do you want Quebec to separate from Canada and become an independent country?'" See Rod MacDonell, "Question Murky, Huge Poll Finds," *MG* (January 26, 1995); and Philip Authier, "No 60%, Yes 40%: Poll," *MG* (February 17, 1995).

55. John Samuel, cited in Terrance Wills, "Quebec's Population Is Growing Too Old for Sovereignty: Study," *MG* (November 16, 1994). The numbers: In 1980, 54 per cent of Quebec voters were under 40; in 1995, the proportion dropped to 45 per cent. Voters between 40 and 49 in 1980 represented 15 per cent in 1980, but were up to 20 per cent in 1995. Quebecers over 50 rose from 31 to 35 per cent.

56. See Hubert Bauch, "The Age Gap," *MG* (December 17, 1994).

57. See Rod MacDonell, "Sovereignty Slipping Among Educated Young," *MG* (March 31, 1995).

58. Richard Gwyn, "If Quebec Is Crying for Help, How Will You Reply?" *TS* (January 4, 1995). See also Ken MacQueen, "Quebec's Race with Its Biological Clock," *VS* (April 22, 1995); and Carolyn Abraham, "In the Demography of Quebec Lies a Time Bomb," *EJ* (November 2, 1995).

59. PQ pollster Michel Lepage predicted right up to election day, September 12, 1994, that the party would win eighty-five seats and 48 or 39 per cent of the popular vote. See Don Macpherson, "Parizeau Assuages the Pequistes' Lingering Doubts," *MG* (November 8, 1994).

CHAPTER TWO: QUEBEC CITY, 1994

1. John Gray, "Moxy No Proxy for Separatism," *GM* (December 13, 1994).
2. Craig Turner, "Jacques Parizeau: Creating a New Nation from French Quebec," *LAT* (December 11, 1994). Jean Chrétien: "Jacques Parizeau had none of the warmth, charm, or oratorical skills of René Lévesque. Though Parizeau could be pleasant enough in person, he came across on TV or on the platform as proud, puffed up, and extremely pompous." See Jean Chrétien, *My Years as Prime Minister* (Toronto: Knopf, 2007), 136.
3. "Parizeau may have been perceived as the logical heir to the legacy of René Lévesque but many observers found that he came across as coldly rational, overconfident, distant, and moreover, incapable of enflaming nationalist passions." David Leyton-Brown, *Canadian Annual Review of Politics and Public Affairs 1995* (Toronto: University of Toronto Press, 2002), 126.
4. Lucien Bouchard, *On the Record*, trans. Dominique Clift (Toronto: Stoddart, 1994), 77.
5. Ibid., 84.
6. See "Jacques Parizeau: How I Became a Separatist," CBCDA, http://www.cbc.ca/archives/categories/politics/federal-politics/separation-anxiety-the-1995-quebec-referendum/remembering-jacques-parizeau.html.
7. Jacques Parizeau, *An Independent Quebec: The Past, the Present and the Future*, trans. Robin Philpot (Montreal: Baraka, 2010), 23.
8. Jacques Parizeau: "The words *sovereignty*, *independence* and *separation* all mean the same thing. In early years, *separatism* was associated with violence and the army, while *independence* was linked to conflict that had so often marked the period of decolonization. *Sovereignty*, and even more so *sovereignty-association*, referred implicitly to negotiation and recognition. Polls clearly confirmed these different perceptions. To my mind all three terms mean the same thing and I tend to use them as synonyms." See Parizeau, *An Independent Quebec*, 24.
9. Jacques Parizeau, cited in Chantal Hébert, "Sois belle et tais-toi!" *LP* (August 16, 1994). See also Robert McKenzie, "PQ Readying for the Big One," *TS* (May 21, 1995).
10. In early May 1995, the *Globe and Mail* ran a front-page story under the headline "Parizeau Calls Chrétien a Traitor." Parizeau was mortified, saying, "My God, my God, I never used that word. I never said anything of that sort. The political debate is very heated. Could everyone please keep his shirt on?" Cited in Richard Mackie, "Calm Urged by Parizeau" *GM* (May 6, 1995). See also André Picard and Rhéal Séguin, "Parizeau Calls Chrétien a Traitor," *GM* (May 5, 1995).
11. John Moore, "PQ Victory Is Nothing to Fear," *NP* (September 4, 2012).
12. National Executive Council of the Parti Québécois, *Quebec in a New World: The PQ's Plan for Sovereignty*, trans. Robert Chodos (Toronto: James Lorimer & Company, 1994), 42–3.
13. Ibid., 44. See also Donald Charette, "Les Québécois doivent choisir entre deux thèses opposées," *LS* (July 27, 1994).

14. National Executive Council of the Parti Québécois, *Quebec in a New World*, 65.

15. Desmond Morton, "Defeating Parizeau's Referendum Will Be No Cakewalk," *TS* (September 14, 1994).

16. Daniel Johnson, cited in John Gray, "Johnson Urges Flexible Federalism," *GM* (January 19, 1995).

17. Robert Sheppard, "Daniel Johnson's Studied Ambiguity," *GM* (January 19, 1995).

18. Jacques Parizeau, cited in Rhéal Séguin, "Quebeckers to Vote Sept. 12," *GM* (July 25, 1994). See also Gilbert Leduc, "Parizeau: Johnson est un tricheur," *LS* (July 24, 1994); and Donald Charette, "Johnson accuse Parizeau d'inventer des problèmes et de désinformer," *LS* (July 27, 1994).

19. See Elizabeth Thompson, "Johnson to Focus on His Love for Canada," *MG* (October 20, 1995).

20. Daniel Johnson, cited in Rhéal Séguin, "Johnson Embraces Federalism," *GM* (January 12, 1994).

21. Daniel Johnson, cited in Ann Gibbon, "Johnson Wants Separation Costs Aired," *GM* (August 27, 1994).

22. André Picard, "PQ Wins Quebec Election," *GM* (September 13, 1994).

23. Jean Charest, *My Road to Quebec* (Montreal: Éditions P. Tisseyre, 1998), 182.

24. Jacques Parizeau, cited in Richard Mackie, "Parizeau Starts Taking Win for Granted," *GM* (August 22, 1994).

25. Daniel Johnson, cited in Richard Mackie, "Johnson Steps Up Attack on Separatists," *GM* (July 30, 1994).

26. Wendy Mesley, "Voting for change: Quebec Election 1994" CBCDA http://www.cbc.ca/archives/categories/politics/provincial-territorial-politics/quebec-elections-1960-2007/voting-for-change.html.

27. See Hugh Winsor, "Many May Point at Wrong Villain," *GM* (September 13, 1994).

28. See Don Macpherson, "Parizeau Assuages the Péquistes' Lingering Doubts," *MG* (November 8, 1994).

29. Rhéal Séguin, "PQ to Cast Wide Net in Referendum," *GM* (November 7, 1994). See also Phillippe Dubuisson, "Toronto pousse un soupir de soulagement... pour le moment," *LP* (September 14, 1994).

30. Donald Charette, "Parizeau en route vers le pays," *LS* (September 13, 1994).

31. Jacques Parizeau, cited in Anne McIlroy, "Parizeau Pledges Referendum in 1995," *CH* (September 15, 1994).

32. Jacques Parizeau, cited in Brian Kieran, "PQ Bravado 'Presumptuous,'" *VP* (September 13, 1994); Colin Nickerson, "Separatists Gain Victory in Quebec," *BG* (September 13, 1994); Gilles Normand, "Parizeau parle de l'immense défi à relever," *LP* (September 13, 1994); and Pierre-Paul Noreau, "Pour Parizeau, il ne reste ... qu'à livrer la marchandise!" *LS* (September 13, 1994).

33. Jacques Parizeau, cited in McIlroy, "Parizeau Pledges Referendum."

34. Lucien Bouchard, cited in Edison Stewart, "Federalist 'Dominoes' Falling, Bouchard Says," *TS* (September 13, 1994).

35. Lucien Bouchard, cited in "Parizeau Has Team at Work," *GM* (September 13, 1994).

36. Lucien Bouchard, cited in Susan Delacourt, "Stay Calm, Chrétien to Tell Canadians," *GM* (September 13, 1994).

37. Daniel Johnson, cited in Richard Mackie, "Johnson Picks Up Vote of Confidence," *GM* (September 13, 1994); and Sandro Contenta, "Johnson Vows Federalist Win in Referendum," *TS* (September 13, 1994).

38. Daniel Johnson, cited in "Johnson Calls for Referendum," *GM* (September 14, 1994).

39. Ibid.

40. Don Macpherson, "Action Mario Puts New Spin on the Sovereignty Ball Game," *OC* (June 15, 1995).

41. See Gilbert Leduc, "Dumont qualifie le chef du Bloc de valet de Parizeau," *LS* (September 16, 1994); and "Dumont refuse le 'carcan' référendaire du PQ," *LS* (December 2, 1994).

42. Jean Chrétien, cited in André Picard, "PQ Wins Quebec Election," *GM* (September 13, 1994). See also Michel Vastel, "De 'p'tit gars' à grand monsieur," *LDR* (September 19, 1994).

43. Chrétien, *My Years as Prime Minister*, 127.

44. Cited in Edward Greenspon, "What Hand Will PM Play?" *GM* (September 13, 1994).

45. Sheila Copps, cited in Edison Stewart, "Bouchard's Views Sway PQ Strategies," *TS* (September 15, 1994); and Joan Bryden, "Keep Cool on Quebec, Copps Urges," *MG* (September 15, 1994). See also Susan Delacourt, "Stay Calm, Chrétien to Tell Canadians," *GM* (September 13, 1994).

46. Preston Manning, cited in Derek Ferguson and Shawn McCarthy, "Don't be Hostage, Ottawa Warned," *TS* (September 13, 1994).

47. Stephen Harper, cited in Delacourt, "Stay Calm."

48. Roy Romanow, cited in Susan Delacourt, "Premiers Urge Parizeau to Be Careful," *GM* (September 14, 1994).

49. Frank McKenna, cited in Monte Stewart and Patrick Nagle, "Premiers on Same Page," *WS* (September 14, 1994). Nova Scotia premier John Savage: "We have to make it abundantly clear to the people of Quebec that we accept this as a democratic election, but we do not accept it as a vote in favor of separation." Prince Edward Island premier Catherine Callbeck: "I feel that if Quebecers are asked a simple question, then they'll choose Canada as they have in the past." Manitoba premier Gary Filmon: "I think it would be very difficult for the PQ to argue they have anything like a solid mandate to pursue separation." Alberta premier Ralph Klein: "Mr. Parizeau, Canada is a pretty good country. Stick with us." See Susan Delacourt, "Premiers Urge Parizeau to Be Careful," *GM* (September 14, 1994); and Derek Ferguson and Shawn McCarthy, "Don't be Hostage, Ottawa Warned," *TS* (September 13, 1994).

50. Editorial "On Guard for Thee," *VP* (September 13, 1994). *Edmonton Journal:* "A separatist government is about to settle into office in Quebec City with no mandate to separate. The endless process of defining relations between Quebec and

the rest of Canada begins anew. It requires a certain faith and a certain openness, and some ability too. If Canadians still retain those aspects, the Parti Québécois will never get its mandate to separate." See Editorial "Quebec Gives Parizeau a Limited Mandate," *EJ* (September 13, 1994). The *Calgary Herald*: "All Canadians, within and outside Quebec, should take this opportunity to quietly reaffirm the successes—the cultural richness, the economic well-being, the social harmony and the political security—which have come with Confederation." See Miro Cernetig, "Westerners Urged to Ease Off Quebec," *GM* (September 14, 1994).

51. David J. Bercuson, "Building the Will to Rebuild," *GM* (September 13, 1994).

52. Desmond Morton, "Defeating Parizeau's Referendum."

53. Jonathan Ferguson, "Loan Rates Fall as Dollar Soars," *TS* (September 14, 1993).

54. John Gray, "Johnson Wants Fast Referendum," *GM* (September 14, 1994).

55. Jean Chrétien, cited in Rosemary Speirs, "PM Dares Parizeau to Hold Unity Vote," *TS* (September 14, 1994).

56. Jean Chrétien, cited in Speirs, "PM Dares Parizeau."

57. Jacques Parizeau, cited in Denis Lessard, "Régions et souveraineté: L'Autre façon de gouverner," *LP* (September 27, 1994). See also Jean-Jacques Samson, "L'Heureux cocktail de Parizeau," *LS* (September 27, 1994).

58. Jacques Parizeau, cited in Rhéal Séguin, "Parizeau Tailors Cabinet to Build Support for Sovereignty," *GM* (September 27, 1994). See also Gilles Normand, "Le temps des luttes partisanes est terminé," *LP* (September 27, 1994).

59. Jacques Parizeau, cited in Rhéal Séguin and John Gray, "Parizeau Pleads for Civil Debate," *GM* (September 15, 1994).

60. Jacques Parizeau, cited in "Separation Vote in '95, Parizeau Says," *GM* (September 29, 1994). See also Gilles Boivin, "Date du Référendum: Parizeau se garde du jeu," *LS* (September 27, 1994); and Denis Lessard, "Parizeau: Le référendum aura lieu d'ici la fin de '95," *LP* (September 29, 1994).

61. Lucien Bouchard, cited in Edison Stewart, "Federalist 'Dominoes' Falling, Bouchard Says," *TS* (September 13, 1994); and "Le vote au Québec a déçu Bouchard," *LP* (September 23, 1994).

62. Lucien Bouchard, cited in Susan Delacourt, "Bouchard Refuses to be Goaded," *GM* (September 20, 1994). See also Manon Cornellier, "Bouchard est pour un référendum rapide 's'il peut être gagné,'" *LS* (September 20, 1994); and Lysiane Gagnon, "Le 'side show' de Chrétien," *LP* (September 22, 1994).

63. Jean Chrétien, cited in "Parizeau Denies Promising PM Early Vote," *GM* (September 21, 1994); and Chantal Hébert, "Parizeau tiendra parole, soutient Chrétien," *LP* (September 21, 1994).

64. Paul Martin, cited in "Parizeau Denies Promising."

65. See Donald Charette, "Parizeau en route vers le pays," *LS* (September 13, 1994); and Alain Dubuc, "Que doit faire le Canada? Rien!" *LP* (September 24, 1995).

CHAPTER THREE: SOVEREIGNTY FOR WHAT?

1. Gurbax Singh Malhi, *Hansard* (October 18, 1995), 15520.
2. Jean Chrétien, cited in "Francophones Powerful, PM Says," *VTC* (October 7, 1995). English-Canadian pundits regularly noted that Quebecers were also disproportionately influential in shaping national policies. Free trade, for example, would never have come to pass without the massive support Quebecers gave Mulroney in the 1988 federal election.
3. Jacques Parizeau, *An Independent Quebec: The Past, the Present and the Future,* trans. Robin Philpot (Montreal: Baraka, 2010), 218.
4. Sarah Scott, "Language Issue Comes off the Back Burner," *MG* (September 23, 1995). See also John Richards, *Language Matters: Ensuring That the Sugar Not Dissolve in the Coffee,* C.D. Howe Institute Commentary 84 (1996).
5. See Marie C. Agen, "The Politics of the Societé Saint-Jean-Baptiste de Montreal," *American Review of Canadian Studies* 29:3 (Fall 1999), 495.
6. Lucienne Robillard, cited in Scott, "Language Issue Comes."
7. Richard Martineau, cited in Anne McIlroy, "Montreal—in 1980," *VS* (September 30, 1995). See editorial "Why Separatism Is Falling Flat," *GM* (August 30, 1995): "In the past generation, the Quebec provincial government has passed laws—some of them restrictive, arbitrary laws—that favour French over English in Quebec society. Because Quebec used its power to override the Constitution—an extraordinary power for a supposedly downtrodden people to possess—those laws have survived all challenges. As a result, polls show that francophone Quebecers no longer fear the future of French."
8. See Ingrid Peritz, "Massive Anglo Opposition Puzzles Francophones," *MG* (April 1, 1995).
9. William Johnson, *A Canadian Myth: Quebec, Between Canada and the Illusion of Utopia* (Montreal: Robert Davies, 1994), 14; and Andrew Phillips, "Changing Advocacy During the History of *The Gazette,*" *Canadian Issues* (Summer 2007), 51–2.
10. See Ed Bantey, "Greek Community Meeting Tuesday Might Set Good Example," *MG* (January 29, 1995); and Don Macpherson, "Bourgault Overlooks Sovereignty's Major Flaw," *MG* (March 1, 1995). In early April, the results of a "mega-poll" were published. Roughly 10,000 Quebecers were polled. The poll found that 93 per cent of anglophones in Quebec would vote No in a referendum—including many bilingual anglophones who in other ways evinced great sympathy for Quebec nationalism. Asked to comment on the poll, Université de Montréal political scientist Stéphane Dion said: "[I] can understand why some francophones might be tempted by sovereignty—they would go from a minority status to a majority status. They might be willing to take the risks. But why would non-francophones accept it? What will they gain?" See Ingrid Peritz, "Massive Anglo Opposition."
11. See Jill Wherrett, *Aboriginal Peoples and the 1995 Quebec Referendum: A Survey of the Issues* (Ottawa: Political and Social Affairs Division, Library of Parliament,

1996), 7. Apart from the Inuit, there were ten aboriginal nations in Quebec: the Crees, Mi'kmaq, Malecite, Algonquin, Huron, Montagnais, Abenaki, Atikamekw, Naskapi, and Mohawk.

12. On February 7, 1995, Cliche stated that the PQ government would not honour the outcome of any referendum purporting to assert the right of aboriginal people to secede from Quebec. "The Inuit can hold their own referendum if they want to and so can the Cree. But where we disagree is on the impact of such a referendum.... We cannot accept that the territory of Quebec be taken apart. This position is not new. We've been saying that for years. But we do respect the right to (aboriginal) self-determination." See "PQ Would Ignore Referendum by Aboriginals," *OC* (February 7, 1995).

13. See Jack Aubry, "Cree Might Join Ontario, Chief Suggests," *OC* (March 14, 1995). See also Reg Whitaker, "Sovereignties Old and New: Canada, Quebec, and Aboriginal Peoples," *Studies in Political Economy* 58 (Spring 1999), 84.

14. Matthew Coon Come, "Consenting Partners: The James Bay Crees, Quebec Secession and Canada," in *If You Love This Country: Fifteen Voices for a Unified Canada*, ed. Cynthia Good (Penguin Books Canada Ltd., 1995), 94–6.

15. Matthew Coon Come, cited in Rhéal Séguin, "Stop Separatists, PM Urged," *GM* (December 14, 1994). See also Matthew Coon Come, "Separatism and the Crees," *GM* (November 24, 1994).

16. Ghislain Picard: "We don't have to follow Quebec's calendar either for the dates or the content. We must be less passive. Quebec says it wants to maintain the integrity of its territory after independence. We say we have our own territorial integrity. And our territories and Quebec's overlap." See "Natives Plan Active Role in Referendum," *MG* (February 1, 1995).

17. Joe Norton, cited in Robert McKenzie, "Indian Chiefs Demand Ottawa Act on Quebec," *TS* (December 14, 1994). See also Wherrett, *Aboriginal Peoples*, 6–8; and Denis Arcand, "Des chefs veulent négocier avec Parizeau, pas Cliche," *LP* (February 10, 1995).

18. Paul De Villers, cited in Terrance Wills, "We're Still Alive and Even Thriving, Ontario Francophones Inform Bloc," *MG* (October 20, 1995).

19. Robert Thibault, cited in Alan Jeffers, "The Morning After," *MG* (October 12, 1995).

20. Cited in William Johnson, "Secessionists Caught in a Dilemma," *EJ* (March 25, 1995). Montreal *Gazette* columnist Jean-Claude Leclerc: "Separation would not extract dead or sick organs, it would sever very real heritages and lives. This surgery of separation—as difficult to do as separating Siamese twins—would be more painful than any future constitutional reform." See "Pulling Teeth," *MG* (November 28, 1994). See also Eva Ferguson, "Local French Canadians Fear Loss of Rights," *CH* (December 7, 1994).

21. Suzanne Tremblay, cited in Johnson, "Secessionists Caught."

22. Pierre Pelletier, cited in Terrance Wills, "We're Still Alive and Even Thriving." Pelletier spoke for the Coalition pour le developpement et l'épanouissement de la communauté franco-ontarienne et des minorités raciales de l'Ontario. See also Don

Retson, "Franco-Albertans Fear Pitch by Que. Minister," *EJ* (November 20, 1994); and Luc Bouvier, "La disparition des francophones hors Québec," *LDR* (February 21, 1995).

23. "Quebec Is Proud of Nation, Grits Find," *GM* (May 9, 1995).

24. Cited in Edison Stewart, "65% Object to Granting Quebec Special Powers," *TS* (September 16, 1995).

25. See Paul Gessell, "MPs Should Refuse Petitions that Fight French as an Official Language," *OC* (May 8, 1995).

26. Peter C. Newman, "Standing By Is Not Enough," in *If You Love This Country*, 50.

27. Tom Connors, "The Liberation of Quebec?" in *If You Love This Country*, 37.

28. Conrad Black, "Canada's Continuing Identity Crisis," *Foreign Affairs* 74:2 (March 1995), 99–115. See also Conrad Black, *A Matter of Principle* (Toronto: McClelland & Stewart, 2011), ch. 1.

29. Alan C. Cairns, "The Charlottetown Accord: Multinational Canada v. Federalism," in *Constitutional Predicament: Canada After the Referendum of 1992*, ed. Curtis Cook (Montreal: McGill-Queen's University Press, 1994), 52. University of British Columbia political theorist Philip Resnick: "Quebec nationalists of our day who aspire to 'sovereignty' are seeking to do what other [independent] peoples— the Slovaks and Slovenians, the Israelis and Algerians—have accomplished. For English-speaking Canadians, there is nothing ambiguous about the term 'sovereignty.' It suggests a total break between Quebec and Canada, two quite independent states. There is little enthusiasm for future negotiations with a partner that has just walked out of the common household." See "From Sea to Shining Sea, Some Words—Nation, State—Get Lost in the Translation," *VS* (October 23, 1995).

30. See Charles Taylor, "A Qualified No," *MG* (September 28, 1995); Reg Whitaker, "Sovereignties Old and New: Canada, Quebec, and Aboriginal Peoples," *Studies in Political Economy* 58 (Spring 1999); Kenneth McRoberts, "English Canada and Quebec: Avoiding the Issue," Sixth Annual Robarts Lecture, York University (5 March 1991), http://robarts.info.yorku.ca/files/lectures-pdf/rl_mcroberts.pdf; Robert M. Gill, "The 1995 Referendum: A Quebec Perspective," *American Review of Canadian Studies* 25:4 (Winter 1995), 409; John F. Conway, *Debts to Pay: English Canada and Quebec from the Conquest to the Referendum* (Toronto: James Lorimer & Company, 1992); Joseph H. Carens, ed., *Is Quebec Nationalism Just? Perspectives from Anglophone Canada* (Montreal: McGill-Queen's University Press, 1995); Robert Bothwell, *Canada and Quebec: One Country, Two Histories*, trans. Robin Philpot (Vancouver: UBC Press, 1998); and Luther A. Allen, "Thinking as a Quebec Canadian: Charles Taylor and the 1995 Referendum," *Quebec Studies* 24 (Fall 1997), 55–73.

31. Anne Michele Meggs, "Bloc Québécois Member's View," *OC* (May 7, 1995).

32. Editorial "Separatist Racism," *TS* (February 28, 1995). See also William Johnson, *A Canadian Myth: Quebec Between Canada and the Illusion of Utopia* (Montreal: Robert Davies, 1994); and especially Jeremy Webber, "Just How Civic Is Civic

Nationalism in Quebec?" in *Citizenship, Diversity, and Pluralism: Canadian and Comparative Perspectives*, Alan C. Cairns et al., ed. (Montreal: McGill-Queen's University Press, 1999).

33. John Gray, "Ethnic Base of Yes Drive Inescapable Despite Denials," *GM* (October 27, 1995).

34. Johnson, *A Canadian Myth*, 402.

35. Lucien Bouchard, *On the Record*, trans. Dominique Clift (Toronto: Stoddart, 1994), 251.

36. Cited in Daniel Latouche, "There's Desperation in the Air," *GM* (February 23, 1995).

37. John F. Conway, "Québec and English Canada: The Politics of Territory" *Constitutional FORUM constitutionnel* 6:1–4 (1994), 23.

38. Jacques Parizeau, cited in Rhéal Séguin, "Separation Express Unstoppable, Premier Says," *GM* (November 21, 1994).

39. Bob Rae, *From Protest to Power: Personal Reflections on a Life in Politics* (Toronto: Penguin, 1996), 314.

40. Jacques Parizeau, cited in Séguin, "Separation Express Unstoppable."

41. Jacques Parizeau, cited in Anne McIlroy, "Parizeau Out to Fix 'Skewed View' of Quebec," *VS* (November 23, 1994).

42. Jacques Parizeau, cited in Séguin, "Separation Express Unstoppable."

43. Bob Rae, cited in John Gray, "Parizeau Treats Toronto to Flattery, Reassurance,"*GM* (November 23, 1994); editorial "Rae Roils Waters on Parizeau's First Visit," *WS* (November 23, 1994); Philippe Cantin, "Un non ramènera le pays sur la chaise du dentiste," *LP* (November 23, 1994); and Raymond Giroux, "Le bon voisinage," *LS* (November 23, 1994).

44. Jacques Parizeau, "Notes for a Speech Delivered to the Canadian Club," *GM* (November 24, 1994).

45. Jacques Parizeau, cited in Gray, "Parizeau Treats Toronto." See also Clinton Archibald, "Parizeau à Toronto," *LDR* (November 24, 1994).

46. Editorial "Parizeau Invents Quebec's Enemies" *TS* (November 23, 1994).

47. Robert Sheppard, "Too Many Decibels in the Quebec Debate," *GM* (November 24, 1994).

48. Richard Gwyn, "The First Borderless State," *TS* (November 26, 1994). See also editorial "Reach Out to Quebec," *TS* (November 28, 1994).

CHAPTER FOUR: NOUI

1. Jacques Parizeau, *An Independent Quebec: The Past, the Present and the Future*, trans. Robin Philpot (Montreal: Baraka Books, 2010), 53–4. Italics added.

2. Jacques Parizeau, cited in "Premier Tells PQ to Shed Referendum Pessimism," *TS* (November 6, 1994); Gilles Boivin, "Parizeau fouette ses troupes," *LS* (November 6, 1994); and Michel David, "Le blues du PQ," *LS* (November 8, 1994).

3. Jean-François Lisée: "Political life in Quebec has been flooded with surveys for 40 years, and we know there is no majority for independence in Quebec and no majority for the current federalism. Only two majorities are possible: renewed federalism of the sovereignty of Quebec with an association, in one form or another, with the rest of Canada. To try to reduce Quebecers to either the current federalism or secession without any desire for an agreement [with the rest of Canada] is to reject their political reality and their political will." Cited in Mario Cardinal, *Breaking Point, Quebec–Canada: The 1995 Referendum,* trans. Ferdinanda Van Gennip and Mark Stout (Montreal: Bayard Canada Books, 2005), 67.

4. Jacques Parizeau, cited in Rhéal Séguin, "PQ to Cast Wide Net in Referendum," *GM* (November 7, 1994).

5. Ibid.

6. Anne McIlroy, "PQ Pins Hopes on the Undecided," *EJ* (December 22, 1994).

7. Michel Lemieux, cited in "No Vote No Longer a Sure Thing as PQ Opens Door to 'Association,'" *TS* (April 22, 1995). See also Louis-Guy Lemieux, "L'Insoutenable légèreté du 'oui,'" *LS* (September 27, 1995); and Michel Vastel, "Le Noui de Robert et Lucien," *LDR* (October 31, 1995).

8. Jean Kerwin, cited in "The Undecideds in Quebec Will Likely Determine the Referendum's Outcome," CTV National News, transcript (October 26, 1995).

9. Jean-Marc Léger, cited in "Quebeckers Called 'Legendary Ambivalents,'" *GM* (September 30, 1995).

10. Grégoire Gollin, cited in "Quebeckers Called 'Legendary Ambivalents.'" Deputy premier Bernard Landry: "We are launching the quote-unquote invasion of the undecideds. And in that sense it could be an interesting psychological turning point." See Hubert Bauch, "Landry Sidesteps Voting-Date Questions," *MG* (April 8, 1995).

11. John Fox, Robert Andersen, and Joseph DuBonnet, "The Polls and the 1995 Quebec Referendum," *Canadian Journal of Sociology/Cahiers canadiens de sociologie* 24:3 (Summer, 1999), 411–24.

12. Jacques Parizeau, cited in Philip Authier, "Premier to Unveil Referendum Plan as Session Opens," *MG* (November 29, 1994).

13. Don Macpherson, "Parizeau's Plan Is to Administer Some Group Therapy to Try and Get the Right Answer in Referendum," *MG* (November 30, 1994). See also "Big Winds of Sovereignty," *MG* (November 30, 1994); and Hubert Bauch, "Speech a Triumph of Form over Content," *MG* (November 30, 1994).

14. Jean-François Lisée, cited in Cardinal, *Breaking Point,* 67.

15. Ed Bantey, "Assembly Speech Challenge of a Lifetime for Parizeau," *MG* (November 27, 1994).

16. See Robert McKenzie, "Parizeau Sets the Stage," *TS* (November 29, 1994).

17. Jacques Parizeau, cited in "Chrétien 'Happy' at PQ's Promise of a Vote in '95," *TS* (November 30, 1994); Denis Lessard, "D'Abord combattre la peur," *LP* (November 30, 1994); Rhéal Séguin, "Parizeau Promises Debate Will Clarify Quebec's Future,"

GM (November 30, 1994); "Don't Fear Independence: Parizeau," *OC* (November 30, 1994).

18. Stéphane Dion, cited in "Parizeau's Delay Has Pundits Wondering," *KWS* (December 2, 1994).

19. Editorial "Parizeau's Problem," *OC* (November 30, 1994).

20. Daniel Johnson, cited in "Chrétien 'Happy.'" See also Gilles Boivin, "Daniel Johnson plutôt froid envers la main qui se tend," *LS* (November 30, 1994); and Anne McIlroy, "Parizeau Pitch Targets Non-Separatists," *OC* (November 30, 1994).

21. Daniel Johnson, cited in Rhéal Séguin, "Johnson Calls for Federal Change," *CM* (December 1, 1994). See also Philippe Cantin, "Johnson accuse le PQ de détournement d'état," *LP* (December 1, 1994).

22. Daniel Johnson, cited in Séguin, "Johnson Calls."

23. Daniel Johnson: "We are not going to defend the constitutional status quo. I am not a fan of the status quo and I am not resigned to it, either. If the government holds a referendum quickly, for the good of Quebec, I can assure Quebecers one thing, that a rejection of independence, even massive, will not signify that Quebecers are satisfied with the status quo. Quebecers can say No to separation, knowing that other Canadians will not found their opposition to any reform on that vote." See Séguin, "Johnson Calls." See also Robert McKenzie, "Johnson Lashes Out at Separatism," *TS* (December 1, 1994).

24. Cited in Edison Stewart, "Chrétien, Johnson Talk Referendum Strategy," *TS* (November 3, 1994).

25. Jean Chrétien, cited in "Chrétien 'Happy.'"

26. Ibid.

27. Ibid. See also Jim Brown, "Chrétien Rallies Federalist Troops," *KWS* (November 30, 1994).

28. Lucien Bouchard, cited in "Referendum Battle Is On, Bloc Declares," CP, *TS* (November 28, 1994); and Pierre-Paul Noreau, "Bloc québécois: Le plan de mobilisation est en place," *LS* (November 28, 1994).

29. Lucien Bouchard, cited in Rhéal Séguin, "BQ Plans to Bait Chrétien to Tip Hand on Referendum," *GM* (November 28, 1994).

30. Ibid.

31. Lucien Bouchard, cited in Philip Authier, "Premier to Unveil Referendum Plan as Session Opens," *MG* (November 29, 1994).

32. Editorial "Bouchard's Strategy for Politics of Fear," *TS* (November 1, 1994).

33. Lucien Bouchard, cited in "Bouchard's Strategy."

34. Michel Poisson, cited in "Hold On, Old Friend," CP (December 2, 1994).

35. Jacques Parizeau, cited in "Bouchard's Crisis Stuns Allies, Foes," *GM* (December 2, 1994); and Donald Charette, "La nouvelle a sidéré Parizeau," *LS* (December 2, 1994).

36. Daniel Johnson, cited in "Bouchard's Crisis."

37. Jean Chrétien, cited in "Bouchard's Crisis."

38. Carol Goar, "Brush with Death Shakes All Parties," *TS* (December 3, 1994). See also "C'est aussi la consternation à Ottawa," *LS* (December 2, 1994); Michel Vastel, "Un drame qui ébranle tout le Québec," *LDR* (December 2, 1994); and Chantal Hébert, "Bouchard amputé," *LP* (December 2, 1994).

39. Patrick D'Amico, cited in Goar, "Brush with Death"; and Carole Thibaudeau, "Le chef du Bloc québécois l'aura échappé belle!" *LP* (December 3, 1994); and Éric Trottier, "Bouchard est hors de danger," *LP* (December 3, 1994).

40. Jacques Parizeau, cited in "Bouchard's Illness Affects Strategy," *GM* (December 3, 1994); and Denis Lessard, "'Un ami revenu de l'abysse,' dit Parizeau," *LP* (December 3, 1994).

41. Lise Bissonnette, "Solidarity Truly Appears in Moments of Crisis," *GM* (December 3, 1994).

42. Don Macpherson, "Legend of Lucien Bouchard," *MG* (December 3, 1994).

43. William Johnson, "Bouchard Will Loom Larger in Hearts, Minds of Quebecers," *MG* (December 3, 1994).

44. Robert Sheppard, "The Life of Lucien Bouchard," *GM* (December 5, 1994).

45. Chantal Hébert, "Ripping at Bloc's Very Soul," *OC* (December 3, 1994).

46. Robert McKenzie, "A Defining Moment," *TS* (December 3, 1994).

47. Gilbert Charland, cited in Joan Bryden, "Bouchard Issues Bedside Instructions," *KWS* (December 6, 1994).

48. Jean-François Lisée, cited in Cardinal, *Breaking Point*, 74.

49. Michel Vastel, "Le chef bloquiste mène ses troupes de son lit d'hôpital," *LS* (December 6, 1994).

50. Jacques Parizeau, cited in Philip Authier, "'Referendum Plan Holds': Parizeau," *MG* (December 4, 1994); and Denis Lessard, "Pour l'instant, la stratégie référendaire suit son cours," *LP* (December 4, 1994).

CHAPTER FIVE: CLEVER, QUITE CLEVER

1. Daniel Johnson, *Assemblée nationale du Québec* (December 1, 1994).

2. Jacques Parizeau, *Assemblée nationale du Québec* (December 6, 1994).

3. Ibid.

4. Daniel Johnson.

5. Ibid.

6. Jacques Parizeau, Assemblée nationale du Québec (December 6, 1994). See also Philippe Cantin, "Des échanges musclés ponctuent le débat à l'Assemblée nationale," *LP* (December 8, 1994).

7. Jean-François Lisée, cited in Pierre Duchesne, *Jacques Parizeau: Le Régent 1985–1995* (Montreal: Les Éditions Québec Amérique, 2004), 319.

8. Jacques Parizeau, cited in "PQ Bill Declares Quebec a Sovereign Country," *GM* (December 7, 1994).

9. Jacques Parizeau, cited in Philip Authier, "Parizeau's Map for Sovereignty Outlined in Bill," *MG* (December 7, 1994).

10. Jacques Parizeau, cited in "Parizeau Unveils Separation Plan," *TS* (December 7, 1994).

11. Daniel Johnson, cited in Rhéal Séguin, "PQ Unveils Sovereignty Declaration," *GM* (December 7, 1994). See also Gilles Normand, "Johnson crie à l'abus de pouvoir," *LP* (December 7, 1994); and Denis Lessard, "Les fédéralistes disent non à la démarche de Parizeau," *LP* (December 7, 1994).

12. Jacques Parizeau, *Assemblée nationale du Québec* (December 7, 1994).

13. Daniel Johnson, cited in Philip Authier and Andy Riga, "Referendum Process Is Democratic: Premier" *MG* (December 8, 1994); and Gilles Boivin, "Boycott des libéraux," *LS* (December 7, 1994). Liberal MNA Yvon Charbonneau: "[T]he PQ has decided not to submit its option to the population, but to subject the population to its option." See *Assemblée nationale du Québec* (December 8, 1994).

14. Raymond Brouillet, *Assemblée nationale du Québec* (December 9, 1994).

15. Mario Dumont, cited in Philip Authier, "Parizeau's Map for Sovereignty Outlined in Bill," MG (December 7, 1994).

16. Daniel Johnson, cited in Philip Authier and Lynn Moore, "Dumont Might Take Referendum Bait," *MG* (December 18, 1994).

17. See Murray Maltais, "La souveraineté, prise deux," *LDR* (December 7, 1994).

18. Léon Dion, cited in Rod MacDonell, "Constitutional Expert Attacks Bill," *MG* (December 7, 1994). See also Desmond Morton, "Referendum Will Affect Us All But We Still Shouldn't Butt In," *TS* (December 13, 1994).

19. Guy Laforest, cited in Hubert Bauch, "On the Defensive," *MG* (December 10, 1994).

20. Camille Laurin, cited in "Premier Parizeau's New Draft Bill Declaring Quebec a Sovereign State Before a Referendum," *Question Period*, CTV Television, transcript (December 11, 1994).

21. Cited in Hubert Bauch, "The PQ's Breathtakingly Blatant Attempt to Stack the Procedural Deck in Favour of Sovereignty Might Yet Turn Out to Be Too Clever by Half," *MG* (December 10, 1994). See also Jean-Jacques Samson, "L'anesthésie d'un peuple," *LS* (December 7, 1994); and editorial "Parizeau Baits a Trap," *TS* (December 11, 1994.)

22. Jean-Jacques Samson, cited in Tombs, "Parizeau's Independence Plan." Gilles Lesage: "Everything is on the table? ... [B]eware if you do not agree with Article I. The *beau risque* [sic], after all, is only a one-way street." Cited in André Picard, "The Deck Is Stacked at the Hearings on Sovereignty," *GM* (February 9, 1995).

23. Alain Dubuc, cited in Tombs, "Parizeau's Independence Plan." See also Alain Dubuc, "L'Arme à double tranchant de Jacques Parizeau," *LP* (December 7, 1994).

24. Daniel Latouche, cited in George Tombs, "French Media Say Federalist Strategy is Way Off-Base," *MG* (December 29, 1994). Michel C. Auger: "[T]his is the way referendums are done in most democracies, by asking the people to vote on a bill adopted by their legislative body." Cited in "Parizeau Picks Wrong Strategy to Lead Quebec to Independence," *EJ* (December 9, 1994).

25. Lysiane Gagnon, "Sovereignty Bill as Designed Is a Siren Call to Undecided Voters," *GM* (January 28, 1995). See also Michel David, "Une astuce préparée de longue date," *LS* (December 7, 1994); Michel Vastel, "Le piège des mots de la souveraineté," *LDR* (December 9, 1994); and Pierre Bergeron, "La fiction pulpeuse de Jacques Parizeau," *LDR* (December 10, 1994).

26. Editorial "Premier Parizeau's Bag of Tricks," *MG* (December 7, 1994). See also editorial "Legalities of Separation Important," *MG* (January 9, 1995).

27. Joan Fraser, "Deceit in the Guise of Democracy," *OC* (December 7, 1994).

28. Don Macpherson: "[I]f federalists boycott the process, they'll be taking the chance that Quebec will become sovereign with a constitution drafted by sovereignists alone. But if they participate, they'll be helping to create an impression of gathering momentum in favor of sovereignty in time for a spring referendum." See "Parizeau Plan a Masterpiece of Political Manipulation," *EJ* (December 7, 1994).

29. Hubert Bauch, "Bare-Knuckle Tactics" *MG* (December 7, 1994). See also Jean-Claude Leclerc, "PQ's Strategy: Act as If a Yes Vote Would Bring Economic Paradise," *MG* (December 7, 1994); and George Tombs, "Parizeau's Independence Plan Elicits Widespread Scorn," *MG* (December 8, 1994).

30. Bob Rae, cited in Susan Delacourt, "Parizeau Assuming Too Much, Federalists Argue," *TS* (December 7, 1994). See also editorial "Harris and McLeod Attack Wrong Foe," *TS* (December 9, 1994).

31. See Leslie Papp, "Rae Urges 'Firm' Warnings about Sovereignty Risks," *TS* (December 7, 1994). See also "All Provinces Must Okay Quebec Exit, Klein Warns," *TS* (December 19, 1994).

32. Editorial "The Presumption of Mr. Parizeau," *GM* (December 8, 1994).

33. Andrew Coyne, "Beware the Third Option, Between Separation and the Status Quo," *GM* (December 12, 1994). Italics in original. See also Editorial "Splitting Canada Won't Be Cost-Free," *TS* (December 8, 1994). *Star* columnist Richard Gwyn compared Jacques Parizeau to "a brattish kid insisting he must end a game by taking away his bat and ball even though unable to describe any changes in the rules he feels must be made." See "PQ's Only Hope Is to Provoke Anti-Quebec Backlash," *TS* (December 9, 1994). See also Don MacDonald, "Recreating Separatist Fervour," *KWS* (December 7, 1994). *Vancouver Province*: "[D]emocracy just got flushed into the St. Lawrence." See editorial "Parizeau's Push" *VP* (December 7, 1994). See also Duart Farquharson, "Clever Parizeau Trying to Fool Quebecers," *EJ* (December 11, 1994).

34. See Andy Riga, "Poll Finds Support for Process But Not Independence," *MG* (December 10, 1994).

35. See Hubert Bauch, "In the Referendum, One Word Is All Important," *MG* (December 17, 1994). See also Richard Gwyn, "Quebecers Must be Sure about What They Are Voting For," *TS* (December 21, 1994).

36. See Doug Fischer, "We Have a Say in Canada's Future: Non-Quebecers," *MG*

(December 23, 1994). Jacques Parizeau: "It's rather an interesting example of how, when you are using a certain kind of question, you can swing public opinion in one way or another. The way some of the questions are asked, I'm surprised that the negative percentages are not higher." See Conway Daly, "Parizeau Dismisses Poll on Quebec Separation," *KWS* (December 23, 1994).

37. Colleen O'Connor, cited in Aaron Derfel, "Montrealers Critical of Strategy," *MG* (December 7, 1994).

38. Christine Smith, cited in Derfel, "Montrealers Critical."

39. Eduardo Pereira, cited in Derfel, "Montrealers Critical."

40. René Rénaud, cited in Derfel, "Montrealers Critical."

41. Other English-rights organizations included the Townshippers Association (in the Eastern Townships), the Outaouais Alliance (in the Hull region), the Chateauguay Valley English-Speaking Peoples Association, and the Committee for Anglophone Social Action in the Gaspé. See Harvey Shepherd, "Anglo Group Gets Hostile Ride at Hearing," *MG* (March 2, 1995).

42. Jacques Parizeau, cited in Philip Authier, "Come Aboard, Premier Tells Anglos," *MG* (February 6, 1995).

43. Zebedee Nungak, cited in "Quebec Inuit Put Faith in Canada," *OC* (December 9, 1994).

44. Cited in Rhéal Séguin, "Stop Separatists, PM Urged," *GM* (December 14, 1994).

45. Michel Audet, president of the Quebec Chamber of Commerce: "If it was a Bélanger-Campeau operation, we certainly would have participated, but the bill on sovereignty does not now propose this framework. To get involved in a process we have to be able to be sure we can have a balanced point of view." See Philip Authier and Andy Riga, "4 Big Groups Refusing to Participate in Process," *MG* (December 8, 1994).

46. See Richard S. Conley, "Sovereignty or the Status Quo? The 1995 Pre-referendum Debate in Quebec," *Journal of Commonwealth & Comparative Politics* 35:1 (March 1997), 77–8.

47. Eddie Goldenberg, *The Way It Works: Inside Ottawa* (Toronto: McClelland & Stewart, 2006), 190–1.

48. Jean Chrétien, cited in Goldenberg, *The Way It Works*, 190–1.

49. Gilles Duceppe, *Hansard* (December 6, 1994), 8693–4.

50. Preston Manning, ibid., 8696.

51. Sheila Copps, ibid.

52. Ibid.

53. Jean Chrétien, cited in Joan Fraser, "Federal Vote on Quebec 'An Option,' PM Says," *OC* (December 8, 1994); and "Demanding Changes in Quebec's Referendum," CTV National News, transcript (December 7, 1994).

54. Jean Chrétien, cited in Joan Fraser, "Federal Vote."

55. Paul DeVillers, *Hansard* (December 7, 1994), 8475–8.

56. Monique Guay, ibid.

57. Marcel Massé, *Hansard* (December 8, 1994), 8790–8820.

58. Sheila Copps, *Hansard* (December 7, 1994), 8475–8.

59. Gilles Duceppe, cited in "Copps's Attack Surprises Reformers," *WS* (December 8, 1994). See also Susan Delacourt, "Parizeau Assuming Too Much, Federalists Argue," *TS* (December 7, 1994).

60. Claude Charron, cited in André Picard, "Chickens on Ice, and Other Referendum Views," *GM* (December 29, 1994).

61. Don Macpherson, "Wrong Message," *MG* (December 22, 1994).

62. William Johnson, "Copps's Response to Parizeau Move Was Pathetic," *MG* (December 7, 1994).

63. Michel Gauthier, *Hansard* (December 8, 1994), 8824–5.

64. Jean Chrétien, ibid.

65. Preston Manning, cited in "The Parti Québécois Referendum Strategy Held Centre Stage in the Commons Today," CTV National News, transcript (December 8, 1994).

66. See "Parizeau Puts Federalists at Head of 2 Key Panels," *GM* (December 22, 1994).

67. Daniel Johnson, cited in "Parizeau Taunts 'Disorganized' Federalist Forces," *OC* (December 22, 1994).

68. Jean Chrétien, *Hansard* (December 9, 1994), 8877–8.

69. Ibid.

70. Jean Chrétien, cited in Edison Stewart, "Chrétien Slams PQ Plan as 'Scam,'" *TS* (December 8, 1994).

71. Jean Chrétien, cited in Jim Brown, "Not Our Job to Negotiate Split: PM," *MG* (December 20, 1994).

72. Jean Chrétien, cited in Edison Stewart, "PQ Strategy Is Gutless, Chrétien Says," *TS* (December 20, 1994). See also editorial "Wrong Way to Woo Quebec," *TS* (January 5, 1995).

73. Jacques Parizeau, cited in Robert MacKenzie, "Parizeau Defends Right to Pass Law," *TS* (December 8, 1994).

74. Jacques Parizeau, cited in Craig Turner, "Jacques Parizeau: Creating a New Nation from French Quebec," *LAT* (December 11, 1994).

75. Lawrence Bergman, cited in "Parizeau Hoping for New Flag-Stomping Incident," *OC* (December 11, 1994).

76. Jacques Parizeau, cited in "Premier Parizeau's New Draft Bill Declaring Quebec a Sovereign State before a Referendum," *Question Period*, CTV Television, transcript (December 11, 1994).

CHAPTER SIX: SOVEREIGNIST SETBACKS

1. Lucien Bouchard, cited in "Bouchard: Thanks But Nothing Has Changed," *GM* (February 23, 1995).

2. Lucien Bouchard, cited in Mario Cardinal, *Breaking Point, Quebec–Canada: The 1995 Referendum*, trans. Ferdinanda Van Gennip and Mark Stout (Montreal: Bayard Canada Books, 2005), 80.

3. Editorial "Bouchard Wants a Yes, Any Yes," *MG* (February 21, 1995).

4. Lucien Bouchard, cited in "Bouchard: Thanks But Nothing."

5. Lucien Bouchard, cited in Susan Delacourt, "Bouchard Would Alter the Question," *GM* (February 22, 1995).

6. Lucien Bouchard, cited in "Bouchard: Thanks But Nothing."

7. Jean Chrétien, *Hansard* (February 22, 1995), 9939.

8. Preston Manning: "On behalf of all Reform members, including myself, I wish to welcome back the honourable member for Lac-Saint-Jean. We parliamentarians are all professional politicians. Although, in the course of our public lives, we often express heartfelt and varied opinions on matters of public policy, we remain human beings united by our shared love of life and health and by our vulnerability to disease and tragedy." Audrey McLaughlin: "Beyond all our differences, compassion is the bond that unites us. I would like to offer my best wishes to the leader of the Bloc Quebecois and to his courageous family." See *Hansard* (February 22, 1995), 9939.

9. Lucien Bouchard, *Hansard* (February 22, 1995), 9939–41.

10. Lucien Bouchard, cited in Edison Stewart, "'Don't Rush Vote': Bouchard," *TS* (February 20, 1995).

11. Lucien Bouchard, cited in André Picard, "Bouchard Ready for Battle," *GM* (February 20, 1995). See also George Tombs, "Parizeau's Independence Plan Elicits Widespread Scorn," *MG* (December 8, 1994).

12. Jean Chrétien, *My Years as Prime Minister* (Toronto: Knopf, 2007), 129.

13. Jean Chrétien, cited in Linda Drouin, "Grits Take All for Hat Trick," *VTC* (February 14, 1995).

14. Lucien Bouchard, cited in Edison Stewart, "Ottawa Calls for a Quick Referendum," *TS* (February 15, 1995).

15. Jacques Parizeau, paraphrased by Jean-François Lisée, cited in Cardinal, *Breaking Point*, 65.

16. Jean-François Lisée: "There was a 'dance' between Mr. Bouchard and Mr. Parizeau for several months, which put us somewhat at odds with the people from the Bloc." Cited in Cardinal, *Breaking Point*, 65. Jacques Parizeau: "We need a winning question and a clear one. The only thing we must avoid is getting nailed down too soon." See Philip Authier, "We'll Vote This Year: Parizeau," *MG* (February 21, 1995).

17. Alain Dubuc, cited in George Tombs, "Michel Bélanger Seen as Solid Catch for No Side in Referendum," *MG* (January 12, 1995).

18. Michel Bélanger, cited in "A Look at the Shape of the Referendum Campaign," *Question Period*, CTV Television, transcript (January 15, 1995).

19. Cited in Philip Authier, "Referendum Question Could Change," *MG* (December 21, 1994). See also Katia Gagnon, "Comment intéresser les 18–35 ans à la question

nationale?" *LP* (December 12, 1994); and Michel David, "La bonne question," *LS* (December 15, 1994).

20. Jacques Parizeau, *Assemblée nationale du Québec* (December 20, 1994). See also editorial "Question Should Be Clear," *MG* (December 23, 1994).

21. Guy Bertrand, cited in "Referendum: PQ Plan Labelled 'Suicide' by Separatist," *KWS* (January 17, 1995). See also "La conversion de Guy Bertrand enchante les libéraux fédéraux," *LS* (December 19, 1995); and Lysiane Gagnon, "La cape et la toge," *LP* (January 19, 1995).

22. Jean Chrétien, cited in Edison Stewart, "Chrétien Eases Stand on Legality of PQ Plan," *TS* (January 17, 1995).

23. Marcel Massé, cited in "Separatist's Conversion Celebrated," *EJ* (January 19, 1995).

24. Pierre Bourgault, cited in Don MacDonald, "It Would Be 'Dangerous' for Anglos to Thwart Separation: Bourgault," *MG* (January 16, 1993).

25. Stephen Scheinberg, cited in Andy Riga, "Bourgault's Views Spark Criticism," *MG* (January 17, 1995).

26. Jean-V. Dufresne, cited in George Tombs, "Bourgault Was Roundly Denounced by French-Language Media," *MG* (January 19, 1995). See also Joan Fraser, "Talk of Terrorism Has No Place in Independence Debate," *MG* (January 18, 1995).

27. Jacques Parizeau, cited in Andy Riga, "I Won't Fire Bourgault: Premier," *MG* (January 18, 1995).

28. Jean Chrétien, cited in Riga, "Bourgault's Views," *MG* (January 17, 1995).

29. Jacques Parizeau, cited in "Parizeau Pal Resigns Over Warning," *EJ* (January 19, 1995).

30. Jacques Parizeau, cited in Rhéal Séguin, "Parizeau Accepts Adviser's Resignation," *GM* (January 19, 1995).

31. Cited in "PQ Adviser Says Interviewer Trapped Him," *KWS* (January 20, 1995).

32. Pierre Bourgault, cited in "Parizeau Pal Resigns."

33. Don MacDonald, cited in Robert McKenzie, "PQ Adviser Quits Over Flub on Anglos," *TS* (January 19, 1995).

34. Pierre Bourgault, cited in Philip Authier, "Bourgault Accuses Premier of Bowing to Anglo Pressure in Dumping Him," *MG* (January 20, 1995).

35. Pierre Bourgault, cited in André Bellemare, "Bourgault accuse les anglophones d'exercer un 'vote carrément raciste,'" *LP* (February 27, 1995).

36. Pierre Bourgault, cited in Anne McIlroy, "Censured Separatist Says He'll Shut Up," *VS* (March 2, 1995).

37. Philippe Paré, cited in Daniel Sanger, "'Old-Stock' Voters Proponent Demoted," *VS* (February 28, 1995).

38. Lucien Bouchard, cited in Sanger, "'Old-Stock' Voters." See also Donald Charette, "Lucien Bouchard blâme et destitue Paré," *LS* (February 28, 1995).

39. Jean-Marc Léger, cited in Rollande Parent, "'Unilingual Anglos, Newcomers Shouldn't Vote': Sovereignist," *MG* (March 2, 1995).

40. Editorial "Separatist Racism," *TS* (February 28, 1995). See also editorial "Separatism's Dark Side," *GM* (March 1, 1995).

41. Editorial "Hate-Mongering Won't Help Yes Side," *MG* (March 1, 1995).

42. Marc-André Coallier: "We want to open the doors to all the young people who don't feel included, not necessarily just in the referendum debate, but in politics in general." See Richard Mackie, "Sovereignists Target Young, Elderly," *GM* (February 6, 1995).

43. See David Johnston, "Commissions to Offer Mixture of Formal Hearings and Town-Hall Meetings," *MG* (February 4, 1995).

44. Jean-Paul L'Allier: "We have to make tremendous efforts to keep it above party lines if possible. We want it to be a very deep debate that will not necessarily solve everything for the future but maybe help us go forward together.... What will be the form [of the country] at the end of that negotiation? What will be the form of the political organization? I don't know. But I know one thing for sure: we are not, and I say we as Canadians all together, quite at ease with this country the way it is at the moment." See "Big Names Bagged for PQ Panels," *TS* (December 22, 1994).

45. Editorial "Masse Confusion," *TS* (December 23, 1994). See also editorials "Quebec Hearings Rigged," *MG* (February 7, 1995) and "A False Start for Quebec Road Show," *TS* (February 7, 1995). *Globe and Mail* editorial "Mr. Parizeau's Twenty Questions" (February 7, 1995): "Mr. Parizeau urges Quebeckers to build a new country—even if he ignores the risks of political instability, economic calamity, social upheaval and international isolation—rather than remain in Confederation. It is our country (Quebec) or their country (Canada), he says, and Canada is bankrupt, paralyzed and indifferent to Quebec. Of course this claim is so demonstrably false that Mr. Parizeau risks his credibility whenever he utters it." Jean-Jacques Samson: "The mandate given to the commissions by Mr. Parizeau is indecipherable. One day 'everything is on the table'; the next day, he denounces the boycott by federalists, by natives and groups like Alliance Quebec, before adding that it is out of the question to renounce sovereignty. How can opponents seriously participate in an exercise that is so fundamentally biased?" See André Picard, "The Deck Is Stacked at the Hearings on Sovereignty," *GM* (February 9, 1995).

46. See Anne McIlroy, "Referendum Budget Set at $70M," *OC* (March 24, 1995).

47. Cited in David Leyton-Brown, *Canadian Annual Review of Politics and Public Affairs 1995* (Toronto: University of Toronto Press, 2002), 125–6.

48. Yves Ducharme, cited in Mike Shahin, "West Quebec Speaks," *OC* (February 14, 1995).

49. Richard S. Conley, "Sovereignty or the Status Quo? The 1995 Pre-Referendum Debate in Quebec," *Journal of Commonwealth & Comparative Politics* 35:1 (March 1997), 72. See also Rhéal Séguin, "Quebeckers Question Sovereignty as a Solution," *GM* (March 18, 1995); Robert McKenzie, "Parizeau Advised Not to Rush Vote," *TS* (March 21, 1995); Robert Sheppard, "Tactics Before the Referendum," *GM* (March 23, 1995); Rhéal Séguin, "Rift Developing among Separatist Forces," *GM* (March 16, 1995); and editorial "Waiting for Parizeau," *TS* (March 21, 1994).

50. Cited in Rod MacDonell, "Question Murky, Huge Poll Finds," *MG* (January 26, 1995).

51. See Andy Riga, "'Panels Will Clarify Referendum Query': Minister," *MG* (January 27, 1995).

52. See Philip Authier, "No 60%, Yes 40%: Poll," *MG* (February 17, 1995).

53. See Richard Mackie, "Most Voters Not Heeding PQ Panels," *GM* (February 25, 1995). Hubert Bauch: "[T]he province-wide commission hearings faded into background babble last week, amid the sounds of rising panic in the senior ranks of the separatist movement as the anticipated momentum failed to materialize." See "Unless It's Over for Sovereignty, the PQ Can't Have a Worse Week," *MG* (February 26, 1995).

54. André Pépin, cited in Hubert Bauch, "Backtracking on Separation," *MG* (February 18, 1995).

55. Jean-Jacques Samson, cited in André Picard, "Inertia Has Given Way to Inertia," *GM* (March 16, 1995).

56. See Marcel Côté, *Rêve de la terre promise cout* (Montreal: Stanké, 1995). See also "Bouchard Links Budget to Vote," *KWS* (March 1, 1995).

57. Jean Chrétien, cited in Susan Delacourt, "Flag-Waving to Greet Winners," *GM* (February 15, 1995). See also Don Macpherson, "Parizeau's Lost Cause," *MG* (February 18, 1995); editorial "Separatist Woes," *VTC* (March 2, 1995); and Lysiane Gagnon, "The Search Is on for a Face-Saving Device," *GM* (February 18, 1995).

58. Marcel Masse, cited in Rod MacDonell and Alexander Norris, "Sovereignty Bill Needs Changes," *MG* (March 5, 1995).

59. Jacques Parizeau, cited in Sandro Contenta, "Quebecers Not Ready for Sovereignty," *TS* (March 27, 1995).

60. Jacques Parizeau, cited in Philip Authier and Monique Beaudin, "We'll Vote in the Fall: Parizeau," *MG* (April 6, 1995). See also Gilles Normand, "Oui ou Non: Pas avant l'automne, précise Parizeau," *LP* (April 6, 1995); and Claude Beauregard, "La première défaite de Jacques Parizeau," *LD* (April 7, 1995).

61. Bernard Landry, cited in Pierre Duchesne, *Jacques Parizeau: Le Régent 1985–1995* (Montreal: Éditions Québec Amérique, 2004), 381. See also Donald Charette, "Oubliez le référendum en juin," *LS* (March 28, 1995). Landry's remark hurt Parizeau, and still does. "I had better not comment," Parizeau said in 2005, "because I could say something rude. And I don't like to be rude. But episodes like this are a part of life." See Cardinal, *Breaking Point*, 105.

62. Daniel Johnson, cited in Authier and Beaudin, "We'll Vote in the Fall"; and Denis Lessard, "'On fait durer le supplice,' dit Johnson," *LP* (April 7, 1995). On March 15, Johnson's Liberals tabled a motion in the National Assembly demanding that the PQ government honour its election promise to hold a referendum in 1995. See *Assemblée nationale du Québec* (March 15, 1995).

63. Jean Chrétien, cited in Terrance Wills, "Hold Referendum Now, PM Urges Parizeau," *MG* (April 5, 1995).

64. Jean Chrétien, cited in Edison Stewart, "PM Urges Quick Referendum," *TS* (April 5, 1995). See also Julian Beltrame, "PM Rakes Parizeau for Vote Delay," *CH* (April 7, 1995). Montreal *Gazette* journalist Josh Freed: "Only in Quebec. The people

most enthusiastic about holding a referendum these days are federalists, who are increasingly cocky about winning. Many separatists seem so demoralized they don't even want a referendum any more." See "Federalist Cry in Quebec: *NON* Delay on Referendum Vote," *MG* (February 18, 1995).

65. Daniel Johnson, cited in Alexander Norris, "'PQ Is Sacrificing Separatist Principles to Trick Voters': Johnson," *MG* (March 5, 1995).

66. Michael Bliss, "You Can Ignore the Doomsayers: Separatism Is Dead," *TS* (April 7, 1995).

67. Richard Gwyn, "Separatism Goes the Way of Monty Python's Parrot," *TS* (April 9, 1994). See also Edison Stewart, "Ottawa Calls for a Quick Referendum," *TS* (February 15, 1995); and "Why Bother?" *CH* (March 2, 1995).

68. Jean-François Lisée, *Des Histoires du Québec* (Montreal: Rogers Publishing Limited, 2012), 148–9.

CHAPTER SEVEN: LES VIRAGES

1. Guy Laforest, cited in "PQ Prepares to Make Difficult Decisions," *GM* (March 3, 1995).

2. In an interview with CTV Television, Laforest summarized his sense of Quebecers' state of mind: "The message is: okay guys you had a plan, that plan is going nowhere, please do something." See "Is There a New Question Coming in the Quebec Referendum?" CTV National News, transcript (March 1, 1995).

3. On "persistent pens," see Robert McKenzie, "No Vote No Longer a Sure Thing as PQ Opens Door to 'Association,'" *TS* (April 22, 1995). On Laforest's position in the academic debate, see, for example, Alan C. Cairns, "Why Is It So Difficult to Talk to Each Other?" *McGill Law Journal/ Revue de droit de McGill 42* (1997), 76.

4. Lucien Bouchard, cited in Huguette Young, "Bouchard Wants Vote on Canada Connection," *KWS* (March 1, 1995).

5. Lucien Bouchard, cited in "Bouchard Wants 'Economic' Question," CP (March 1, 1995).

6. Don Macpherson, "Dust Off the Hyphen," *MG* (March 2, 1995).

7. Bernard Landry, cited in "Referendum Question May Change," *KWS* (March 2, 1995). Lysiane Gagnon: "If [Landry] so vehemently dissociated himself from his leader's position—a very risky move—it's because he knew the cabinet and the party were on his side." See "An Erosion in the Credibility of Parizeau," *GM* (April 8, 1995).

8. Lucienne Robillard, cited in Paul Wells, "Robillard Enters Cabinet," *MG* (February 23, 1995).

9. Eddie Goldenberg, *The Way It Works: Inside Ottawa* (Toronto: McClelland & Stewart, 2006), 193.

10. Lucienne Robillard, cited in Sandro Contenta, "Winner Warns Foes of 'Big Fight,'" *TS* (February 14, 1994).

11. Gilles Duceppe, cited in "Decision to Call 3 By-elections Attacked," *GM* (December 24, 1994). See also Bob Cox, "New Minister Takes Point for PM in Quebec Vote," *VS* (April 7, 1995).

12. Jean Chrétien, *Hansard* (February 16, 1995), 9724–5.

13. Marcel Massé, cited in "Liberals to Sell 'Flexible Federalism,'" *EJ* (December 11, 1994).

14. Allan Rock, cited in Mario Cardinal, *Breaking Point Quebec–Canada: The 1995 Referendum*, trans. Ferdinanda Van Gennip and Mark Stout (Montreal: Bayard Canada Books, 2005), 92.

15. Jean Chrétien, cited in "Is There a New Question Coming in the Quebec Referendum?" CTV National News, transcript (March 1, 1995). During a Radio-Québec interview, Chrétien responded equally dismissively to the suggestion that the referendum might have multiple questions. "If they want a three-part question they can ask, 'Do you prefer apple pie, sugar pie or blueberry pie.' They would still not get a consensus." See Sue Montgomery, "PQ Forcing Their Option on Quebeckers says Chrétien," *OC* (March 4, 1995). Lucienne Robillard: "I think that [Landry]'s so afraid to lose that he wants to change the question. First of all, they use the word sovereignty. This is a very confusing word, as you know, for Quebecers. Many Quebecers believe that if they vote for sovereignty, they will still be part of Canada. Now they want to add economic association. That's just unbelievable. They must be very worried and they are afraid to lose." Cited in Philip Authier, "Question on Economic Association Is Likely on Ballot, Landry Says," *MG* (March 2, 1995).

16. Jean-François Lisée: "Il y a même, à Ottawa, sorti de convalescence avec une rapidité qui force l'admiration, un leader souverainiste au faîte de sa popularité qui critique publiquement la stratégie, dit que tout va mal, ce qui devient donc automatiquement vrai : Lucien Bouchard." See Jean-François Lisée, *Des Histoires du Québec* (Montreal: Rogers Publishing Limited, 2012), 148–9.

17. Jacques Parizeau, cited in "Parizeau Rules Out Association Option," *OC* (March 9, 1995).

18. Jacques Parizeau, cited in Rhéal Séguin, "Parizeau Amenable to Linking Canada, Sovereign Quebec," *GM* (March 9, 1995).

19. Daniel Turp, "The June 12 Agreement: A Common Project for Quebec's Future," http://www.rocler.qc.ca/turp/eng/Future/Works5.htm.

20. Lucien Bouchard, cited in Paul Wells, "Bouchard Wants Economic Union," *MG* (April 8, 1995).

21. Lucien Bouchard, cited in Cardinal, *Breaking Point*, 108–9.

22. Wells, "Bouchard Wants Economic Union"; Chantal Hébert, "Bouchard prône une union économique avec le Canada," *LP* (April 8, 1995); Michel Vastel, "Bouchard réclame un 'virage,'" *LDR* (April 8, 1995); Gilles Gauthier, "Le 'virage' Bouchard adopté, on craint les chausse-trappes," *LP* (April 10, 1995); and Anne McIlroy, "Bouchard Says Vote Could Wait 4 Years," *OC* (April 9, 1995).

23. Jean-François Lisée: "It was Lucien Bouchard who had put the word *virage* in his text. It was a code word, but *we* knew what he meant by it: he meant a second referendum. And he was emphasizing the need for a radical change of direction in the sovereignty proposal. He wanted the referendum question changed so that it would allow for a second referendum. That is, there would be a first referendum on sovereignty, accompanied by the statement that any agreement with Canada would be ratified in a second referendum. He wanted to reintroduce the notion of association, as in the 1980 referendum." Cited in Cardinal, *Breaking Point*, 110.

24. See Edison Stewart, "Bloc Tells PQ to Back Off," *TS* (April 9, 1995); Michel Vastel, "Bouchard réclame un 'virage,'" *LDR* (April 8, 1995); "Le projet d'institutions communes de Bouchard ne fait pas l'unanimité," *LP* (April 9, 1995); Claude Masson, "Le 'virage' de l'option souverainiste," *LP* (April 10, 1995); and Jean-Jacques Samson, "Lucien Bouchard a pris le volant," *LS* (April 10, 1995).

25. Lucien Bouchard, cited in Stewart, "Back Off."

26. See "Rift Widens in Sovereignty Ranks," *GM* (April 10, 1995); and Chantal Hébert, "Bouchard attend un signal," *LP* (April 10, 1995).

27. Jacques Parizeau, cited in Robert McKenzie, "Parizeau to Bloc: I'm Still in Charge," *TS* (April 10, 1995); and Denis Lessard, "Parizeau réaffirme son autorité," *LP* (April 10, 1995).

28. Jacques Parizeau, cited in McKenzie, "Parizeau to Bloc."

29. Lucien Bouchard, cited in Rod MacDonell, "Bouchard Might Not Campaign," *MG* (April 11, 1995); and Rhéal Séguin, "Sovereignists Try to Heal Rift," *GM* (April 11, 1995).

30. See "Rift Widens."

31. Jacques Parizeau, cited in "Parizeau Unmoved by BQ Views on Links," *GM* (April 10, 1995).

32. English Canada was in no mood for Bouchard's partnership proposal. "The big lie coming out of Quebec is that somehow sovereignty will happen without any input from the rest of the country," observed pollster Angus Reid. "Well, guess what? The rest of Canada has opinions, too, and they simply aren't interested in any kind of special deal for Quebec—either inside or outside Canada. It's time for a reality check." Cited in MacDonell, "Bouchard Might Not Campaign."

33. Jacques Parizeau, cited in Ed Bantey, "Bouchard Might Have Strengthened Parizeau's Image as Man of Principles," *MG* (April 16, 1995).

34. Tu Thanh Ha, "Why Bouchard Triggered Fight with Parizeau," *GM* (April 18, 1995); Lysiane Gagnon, "Virage ou lutte de pouvoir?" *LP* (April 11, 1995); and Claire Hoy, "Parizeau Losing the Separatist Debate," *VP* (April 11, 1995).

35. Jacques Parizeau, cited in Sandro Contenta, "Parizeau Tries to End Split with Bloc," *TS* (April 11, 1995).

36. Daniel Johnson, *Assemblée nationale du Québec* (April 13, 1995). See also Denis Lessard, "Dure semaine pour les souverainistes," *LP* (April 15, 1995).

37. According to sources cited by Jeffrey Simpson, Bouchard had been swamped with

appeals from PQ caucus members—some of them in cabinet—to prevent Parizeau from "leading them to referendum slaughter." Change the question, delay the vote, they urged Bouchard. Deputy premier Bernard Landry was part of this *putsch*. Simpson: "The Bouchardistes force the premier to swallow his intellectually silly, but perhaps electorally alluring, Economic Association with Canada." See "What Will Happen in Quebec Should the Secessionists Lose," *GM* (September 21, 1995). See also Anne McIlroy, "Two Solitudes Within Separatist Camp," *KWS* (April 13, 1995); and Lysiane Gagnon, "Once Muted, the Power Struggle Is Out in the Open," *GM* (April 15, 1995).

38. Mario Dumont, cited in Robert McKenzie, "'Rainbow Coalition' Wins Dumont Favor," *TS* (April 11, 1995).

39. See Robert McKenzie, "No Vote No Longer a Sure Thing as PQ Opens Door to 'Association,'" *TS* (April 22, 1995).

40. Jacques Parizeau, cited in "Parizeau: Rift or Not, We'll Vote in Fall," CP (April 11, 1995).

41. Jacques Parizeau, *Assemblée nationale du Québec* (April 11, 1995). See also "Parizeau: Sovereignty Report May End Ruckus," CP (April 13, 1995).

42. Université Laval political scientist and member of the Quebec City commission Louis Balthazar: "Parizeau will find a way to rally towards Bouchard's position by saying 'I'm a democrat, the people have told us it is important to have economic association with Canada.'" Cited in Jack Branswell, "Sovereignty Commissions' Report Expected to Ease Parizeau-Bouchard Rift," *MG* (April 19, 1995).

43. *Rapport de la Commission nationale sur l'avenir du Québec*, cited in Robert McKenzie, "Now Parizeau Talks of Major Changes to Sovereignty," *TS* (April 20, 1995). See also "Commission Opens Escape Hatches," *MG* (April 20, 1995); and John Gray, "Highlights of Report," *GM* (April 20, 1995). The super-commission put forward forty recommendations, which were left-liberal as well as sovereignist. A Quebec "declaration of sovereignty," said the report, "must reflect respect for democracy, family life, the importance of education, social solidarity, equality of men and women, the fight against poverty and social exclusion, respect for the environment and international solidarity." The commission also recommended the election of a Founding Assembly, which would draft a new constitution that would include a charter of rights and freedoms as well as entrenched rights for anglophones and native people. Measures in the commission report clearly designed to assuage Quebecers' economic worries included a call for the government of Quebec to assume its share of the federal debt, to employ civil servants currently working within the federal bureaucracy, and to honour all pensions, including federal ones.

44. Jacques Parizeau, cited in Daniel Sanger, "Bouchard Vision Prevails over Parizeau Plan," *OC* (April 20, 1995).

45. Jacques Parizeau, cited in Rhéal Séguin, "Parizeau Agrees to Include Political Union in Bill," *GM* (April 20, 1995); Vincent Marissal, "Un rapport qui 'arrange' Parizeau,"

LS (April 20, 1995); Gilles Normand, "Un vrai coup de main pour la souveraineté," *LP* (April 20, 1995).

46. Jacques Parizeau, cited in Sandro Contenta, "Parizeau Ends Feud with Bloc's Bouchard," *TS* (April 23, 1995).

47. Lucien Bouchard, cited in Anne McIlroy, "Economic Union on Agenda," *EJ* (April 25, 1995).

48. Jacques Parizeau, cited in "PQ Wants Canada's Answer First," *GM* (April 25, 1995).

49. Jacques Parizeau, *Assemblée nationale du Québec* (April 26, 1995).

50. Jacques Parizeau, cited in "Parizeau 'Game' to Try Offer of Political Union," *GM* (April 29, 1995).

51. See Jules Richer, "Rapport de la Commission nationale sur l'avenir du Québec," *LDR* (April 22, 1995); Lia Lévesque, "'Un rapport rassembleur,' selon les syndicats et les étudiants," *LP* (April 20, 1995); Marissal, "Un rapport qui 'arrange' Parizeau"; Normand, "Un vrai coup de main"; and Mario Fontaine, "Le rapport va simplement plus loin que la position officielle," *LP* (April 20, 1995).

52. Sanger, "Bouchard Vision." See also editorial "Parizeau Lost," *OC* (April 20, 1995); and Don Macpherson, "Another Showdown Looming for No-Show Bouchard, Parizeau," *MG* (April 20, 1995).

53. Daniel Latouche, "The Partnership Speech," *GM* (April 21, 1995). See also Latouche, "Where Have All the Political Clichés Gone?" *GM* (April 28, 1995).

54. William Johnson, "Bouchard has Shown Breathtaking Arrogance," *MG* (April 12, 1995).

55. Rosemary Speirs, "Bouchard Can't Stand Anyone Else Being in Charge," *TS* (April 11, 1995).

56. Jeffrey Simpson, "The Knife Wounds in Jacques Parizeau's Back Look Familiar," *GM* (April 11, 1995). See also "Conservative Leader Takes Swipe at Bouchard," *GM* (April 11, 1995); Duart Farquharson, "Bouchard Trying to Hoodwink Quebecers," *EJ* (April 16, 1995); Christopher Young, "Bouchard's History of Defection Shows He Strives to be the Boss," *KWS* (April 17, 1995); and Suzanne Dansereau, "Le projet d'union politique agace le Canada anglais," *LP* (April 21, 1995).

57. Andrew Coyne, "Separatism Dies a Slow Death, Caught in Its Own Contradictions," *GM* (April 24, 1995).

58. See Tu Thanh Ha, "Sovereignists Can't Ensure Political Union," *GM* (April 20, 1995).

59. Editorial "Separatists Dish Up Dishonest Report," *TS* (April 22, 1995). The *Calgary Herald*: "Don't be fooled by imitations. Parizeau wants unequivocal, irreversible independence. Sovereignists are not in retreat, they are simply regrouping." See "Independence Lite," *CH* (April 22, 1995).

60. Editorial "Quebec Separatists Kick Off Silly Season," *TS* (May 2, 1995).

61. Robert McKenzie, "No Vote No Longer a Sure Thing as PQ Opens Door to 'Association,'" *TS* (April 22, 1995).

62. See Hugh Winsor, "Bouchard Bests Parizeau in Survey," *GM* (April 22, 1995). The same Léger and Léger poll showed the gulf that had grown between Parizeau's and

Bouchard's popularity in Quebec. Only 35.7 per cent of Quebec voters would follow Parizeau into sovereignty. Under Bouchard, the number rose to 46.2 per cent.

63. Lucien Bouchard, cited in Sandro Contenta, "Referendum Win Sure Thing Now, Bouchard Says," *TS* (May 20, 1995).

64. Jean-Marc Léger, cited in "Pollster Gives Even Odds to Separatists for Fall Win," *KWS* (June 13, 1995).

65. Michel Bélanger, cited in Paul Mooney, "Federalists Will Stick to Game Plan as Referendum Looms, Bélanger Says," *MG* (June 7, 1995).

66. Jean Chrétien, cited in "If You Leave, Don't Come Back, PM Tells Quebec," *EJ* (April 22, 1995). Lucienne Robillard professed astonishment at Parizeau's endorsement of political union. "This is not mentioned in his party's platform or any section of his draft bill and the issue was almost never raised at the hearings of the various commissions on the future of Quebec," she said. See Bob Cox, "Parizeau's Flip-Flop on Political Association Is Astonishing: Robillard," *MG* (April 21, 1995).

67. Jean Chrétien, cited in "Chrétien Turns Up the Heat," *GM* (May 4, 1995); and Mario Fontaine, "Jean Chrétien accuse le camp souverainiste de mépriser la démocratie," *LP* (May 4, 1995).

68. Rafe Mair, "No Divorce with Bedroom Privileges," *MG* (May 6, 1995). See also editorial "Chrétien Is Right to Mock PQ Tactics," *TS* (May 5, 1995). Chrétien himself liked the metaphor: "I don't know a lot of divorces where people walk out of the court house and back into the family home." Cited in Terrance Wills, "Federalists Slam Quebec Plan," *OC* (June 13, 1995).

69. Preston Manning, *Hansard* (April 25, 1995), 11755–6.

70. Jean Chrétien, cited in "Parizeau's Offer Finds No Takers," CP (April 26, 1995).

71. Jacques Parizeau, cited in Don MacDonald, "Separatist Leaders Sign Strategy Pact," *KWS* (June 13, 1995).

72. Jacques Parizeau, cited in Philip Authier and Paul Wells, "Sovereignists Unite on Strategy," *MG* (June 12, 1995).

73. Jacques Parizeau, *An Independent Quebec: The Past, the Present and the Future,* trans. Robin Philpot (Montreal: Baraka, 2010), 51–2.

74. Lucien Bouchard, cited in "PM Slams Separatists as Gutless," *TS* (June 13, 1995).

75. Parizeau, *An Independent Quebec*, 51–2.

76. Mario Dumont, cited in Elizabeth Thompson, "Dumont Wants to Keep His Distance from Parizeau and Bouchard," *MG* (July 6, 1995). Dumont in 2005: "We [had] to save our own skin, too. The day after the referendum, we would be going right back into the political game and the PQ would become our opponent. We would have another election to prepare for. [During the referendum], of the 2,000 people who might turn out to cheer me on, perhaps 1800 were PQ. In the next election, these same people would be going around saying the ADQ was a ridiculous party and they would be working against us." See Cardinal, *Breaking Point*, 211.

77. Gilles Lesage, cited in André Picard, "Three Parties in Search of a Yes Vote," *GM* (June 15, 1995). See also Gilles Lesage, cited in Alexander Norris, "Dumont's Jump Will Make Federalists' Job More Difficult, Editorials Say," *MG* (June 15, 1995).

78. Jean-Jacques Samson, cited in Picard, "Three Parties."

79. Lysiane Gagnon, "Autre parcours, même objectif," *LP* (June 6, 1995).

80. Pierre Gravel, cited in Norris, "Dumont's Jump."

81. Jean-Marc Léger, cited in Douglas Gold, "Bleak Forecast for Quebec," *GM* (June 13, 1995). See also Don Macpherson, "Canadians Don't Expect a Yes Victory, Pollster Says," *MG* (June 21, 1995).

82. Jean Chrétien, cited in Terrance Wills, "Federalists Slam Quebec Plan," *OC* (June 13, 1995). Lucienne Robillard: "Can you imagine all the other Canadian provinces accepting to give a veto to an independent Quebec over monetary policy and citizenship? It's pretty unbelievable. But that's what is in the proposal." See "PM Slams Separatists as Gutless." Jean Chrétien in 2007: "Their agreement promised to negotiate a totally fanciful treaty between Quebec and the rest of Canada in which the two partners would manage the government and the economy jointly, like some two-headed animal." See Jean Chrétien, *My Years as Prime Minister* (Toronto: Knopf, 2007), 130.

83. Stephen Harper, cited in Wills, "Federalists Slam" and "Pollster Gives Even Odds."

84. Jean Charest, cited in Wills, "Federalists Slam."

85. Joe Clark, cited in "Wake Up to Strong PQ Threat, Clark Says," CP (June 22, 1995). See also "Clark: No Side Didn't Want Me," *VTC* (November 6, 1995).

86. Editorial "Why Let Separatists Set the Agenda?" *TS* (June 23, 1995).

87. Jonathan Ferguson, "Shrill Clark Should Stay Out of Quebec Debate," *TS* (June 23, 1995).

88. Editorial "Separatist-Trio Proposal a Joke," *MG* (June 13, 1995).

89. Joan Fraser, "It's Sad to See Purist Jacques Parizeau Twist into a Moral Pretzel," *MG* (June 14, 1995).

90. Editorial "Unnatural Alliance," *OC* (June 13, 1995).

91. Editorial "A Question of Independence," *GM* (June 13, 1995).

92. Don Macpherson, "Despite Flip-Flops, Parizeau Will Probably Live Up to Deal," *MG* (June 22, 1995).

93. Lucien Bouchard, cited in Chantal Hébert, "Finie l'opposition officielle pour le Bloc," *LP* (June 22, 1995); Manon Cornellier, "Le Bloc en campagne référendaire," *LS* (June 22, 1995); and Bob Cox, "Separatist Campaign Intensifies," *OC* (June 22, 1995).

94. Jean Chrétien, cited in "Chrétien Challenges Bloc Québécois to Give up Salaries," *VTC* (June 23, 1995).

95. Jacques Parizeau, cited in Robert McKenzie, "End-of-July Launch for Sovereignist Push," *TS* (June 24, 1995).

CHAPTER EIGHT: DECLARING SOVEREIGNTY

1. See Joan Bryden, "Separation Vote Low on Canadians' Worry List, Poll Finds," *EJ* (August 1, 1995).

2. Claude Masson, cited in Sandro Contenta, "Even Quebecers Jaded by Referendum," *TS* (September 26, 1995).

3. Guylaine Chabot, cited in Anne McIlroy, "Few Show Any Passion for Fight Over Power," *OC* (September 29, 1995). See also André Picard, "Politicians Ignore Important Issues in Puerile Debate," *GM* (September 29, 1995); and Mike Gasher, "The Word on the Street? There Is None," *GM* (October 2, 1995).

4. Hélène Jutras, cited in "I Don't Believe in Independence Anymore," *VS* (September 30, 1995).

5. Jean-Herman Guay, Pierre Drouilly, Pierre-Alain Cotnoir, and Pierre Noreau, "Les souverainistes risquent de 'rencontrer une dure défaite,'" *LP* (August 26, 1995); "For Mr. Parizeau: The Courage to Say 'Another Time,'" *GM* (August 29, 1995); and Donald Charette, "Pas d'excès de confiance," *LS* (August 29, 1995).

6. Ken MacQueen, "Parizeau Feels Budget Pressure," *EJ* (August 31, 1995).

7. See Jack Branswell, "Chrétien May Yet Prove an Asset to No Campaign," *OC* (July 23, 1995).

8. Jean Chrétien, cited in Bob Cox, "PM on Referendum," *MG* (September 2, 1995).

9. Claude-Éric Gagné, cited in Elizabeth Thompson, "Johnson Should Take Constitutional Stand, Young Liberals Say," *MG* (August 2, 1995); and Vincent Marissal, "Propositions du camp du NON," *LS* (August 2, 1995).

10. Daniel Johnson, cited in Lysiane Gagnon, "Daniel Johnson May Be Shrewder than He Seems," *GM* (August 12, 1995).

11. Daniel Johnson, cited in editorial "Johnson Should Learn Virtue of Silence," *VTC* (August 15, 1995); Marcel Adam, "Johnson est trop nationaliste pour renouveler le discours fédéraliste," *LP* (August 19, 1995); and Murray Maltais, "Daniel Johnson en terrain miné," *LDR* (August 15, 1995).

12. Pierre O'Neill, "Johnson s'engage à réclamer le droit de veto et la société distincte," *LD* (August 14, 1995); Alain Dubuc, "Retour à la case départ," *LP* (August 16, 1995); and Michel Vastel, "Un vocabulaire à réinventer," *LDR* (August 18, 1995).

13. Bernard Landry: "Johnson, like ourselves, has the duty to tell Quebecers what he intends for their future." See "The Quebec Referendum," CTV National News , transcript (August 14, 1995).

14. See Don Macpherson, "Caving in to Young Liberals, Johnson Shows Lack of Leadership," *MG* (August 15, 1995).

15. Stephen Harper, cited in Norm Ovenden, "Special Status 'Off the Table,'" *EJ* (August 17, 1995). Harper on August 23: "If this gets more serious, if the federal government is actually talking about having a real effort to get comprehensive constitutional change ... they will lose the referendum if they pursue that kind of a strategy. There's no reason to offer Quebecers special deals, because they already benefit

from Confederation. We know that separation is a losing question. The federalists are crazy to fight on anything else. If we say that Quebecers' loyalty is conditional upon getting a wish list, that is surrendering the high ground." See Sheldon Alberts, "Strategy Warning Sounded," *CH* (August 24, 1995). See also Catherine Ford, "We Westerners Want a Say in Canadian Unity, Too," *VS* (August 18, 1995).

16. Jean Chrétien, cited in Linda Drouin, "Federalists Try to Repair Cracks in the Ranks," *OC* (August 16, 1995). Marcel Massé (also cited in Drouin): "I am not surprised that Mr. Johnson has a different constitutional position from ours because that's what it was in the past. But he's not in power."

17. Jean Chrétien, cited in Allan Thompson, "Constitution Offers Out, PM Insists," *TS* (August 27, 1995).

18. Joël-Denis Bellavance, "Chrétien ferme la porte à Johnson," *LS* (August 16, 1995); and Chantal Hébert, "Accueil glacial d'Ottawa aux propos de Johnson," *LP* (August 16, 1995).

19. Lucien Bouchard, cited in Philip Authier, "Be Proud, Vote Yes, Quebecers Told," *MG* (August 16, 1995); Vincent Marissal, "Coup d'envoi de la campagne préréférendaire," *LS* (August 16, 1995); and Lucien Bouchard, cited in Don MacDonald, "'No' Decision Will Humble Quebec, Bouchard Warns," *OC* (August 16, 1995).

20. Daniel Johnson, cited in Philip Authier, "Bouchard Arrogant, Johnson Says," *MG* (August 17, 1995).

21. Michel C. Auger, "Federal Liberals Embarrass Johnson," *EJ* (August 18, 1995); Gilbert Lavoie, "Le 'camp du changement,'" *LS* (August 17, 1995); and Lysiane Gagnon, "Les deux pieds dans l'ornière," *LP* (August 19, 1995).

22. Cited in Hugh Winsor, "Quebeckers Want Proposals from Ottawa," *GM* (August 26, 1995).

23. Chantal Hébert, "Après un OUI, les québécois seront comme des homards," *LP* (July 11, 1995).

24. Cited in "Comments Attributed to Parizeau Cause Flap," *GM* (July 12, 1995). See also Philippe Cantin, "Le homard, était-il dans le casier ou dans la marmite?" *LP* (July 13, 1995).

25. Jan Fietelaars, cited in Wells, "'Lobster' Caldron Boils Over," and Joël Bellavance, "Ambassades dans l'eau bouillante," *LS* (July 12, 1995).

26. Bernard Landry, cited in Wells, "'Lobster' Caldron."

27. Chantal Hébert, cited in Wells, "'Lobster' Caldron."

28. Jean-François Lisée, cited in Mario Cardinal, *Breaking Point Quebec–Canada: The 1995 Referendum*, trans. Ferdinanda Van Gennip and Mark Stout (Montreal: Bayard Canada Books, 2005), 143.

29. Leslie Swartman, cited in "Comments Attributed to Parizeau Cause Flap," *GM* (July 12, 1995).

30. Daniel Johnson, cited in "Comments Attributed to Parizeau"; and Daniel Johnson, cited in Wells, "'Lobster' Caldron."

31. Cited in Wells, "'Lobster' Caldron."

32. Lysiane Gagnon, cited in Alexander Norris, "Parizeau Lands in Hot Water with Some Writers for Lobster Remark," *MG* (July 20, 1995).

33. Joan Fraser, "'Lobster' Quote Has Potential to be PQ's Big Mistake of Referendum," *MG* (July 12, 1995).

34. Editorial "Mr. Parizeau's Lobster Dinner," *GM* (July 12, 1995). See also editorial "Lobsters in the Pot?" *TS* (July 13, 1995).

35. Barry Nelson, "Executives Silent on Quebec," *CH* (September 21, 1995).

36. Sophie Beaudoin, "Chrétien nie toute implication," *LP* (July 16, 1995).

37. Jacques Hébert, cited in Hubert Bauch, "*Cité Libre* Jokers Keep Parizeau's Lobster Gaffe Alive," *MG* (September 8, 1995).

38. See "The Lobster Clause,"*GM* (September 30, 1995).

39. See John Gray, "Bouchard by Far Most Popular Political Leader in Quebec," *GM* (August 18, 1995).

40. Lucien Bouchard, cited in Edison Stewart, "'No' Vote Would Be a Disaster: Bouchard," *TS* (August 24, 1995).

41. Lucien Bouchard, cited in Tu Thanh Ha, "Bouchard to Raise Separatism in Commons," *GM* (August 23, 1995).

42. "Partnership Issue Largely Avoided," *GM* (September 7, 1995).

43. Jean Claude Lemoine and Claude Peron, cited in Sandro Contenta, "The Big Question," *TS* (September 9, 1995). See also Donald Charette, "Souverainistes injuriés," *LS* (September 7, 1995).

44. Jacques Parizeau, cited in "Partnership Issue Largely Avoided", *GM* (September 7, 1995).

45. Denis Lessard, "Une question et une démarche radicalement différentes de 80," *LP* (September 9, 1995). See also Pierre Bergeron, "La question," *LDR* (September 8, 1995).

46. Patrick Gagnon, cited in Edison Stewart, "Ottawa Low-Key in Reaction to Proposal," *TS* (September 7, 1995).

47. Daniel Johnson, cited in "Partnership Issue Largely Avoided"; and Philippe Cantin, "La fierté ne se donne pas en spectacle," *LP* (September 7, 1995).

48. Daniel Johnson, cited in Sandro Contenta, "Johnson Slams 'Biased' Declaration," *TS* (September 7, 1995).

49. "Une Déclaration de souveraineté toute en lyrisme," *LD* (September 7, 1995). See also Donald Charette, "Le projet est sur la table," *LS* (September 8, 1995); and Denis Lessard, "Le train référendaire est lancé," *LP* (September 9, 1995).

50. Jean-V. Dufresne, cited in Sarah Scott, "French Media Give Initiatives a Mixed Greeting," *MG* (September 8, 1995).

51. Alain Dubuc, "La complainte des dinosaures," *LP* (September 7, 1995). See also Michel David, "L'interminable strip-tease," *LS* (September 7, 1995).

52. Lysianne Gagnon, cited in Scott, "French Media." See also Lysiane Gagnon, "Parizeau: promesse tenue," *LP* (September 9, 1995); Vincent Marissal, "Une baffe au reste du pays," *LS* (September 7, 1995); and Denis Lessard, "Le préambule promet la société parfaite," *LP* (September 7, 1995).

53. Jeffrey Simpson, "Quebec's Politicians Catch a Disease Shared by Poets and Intellectuals," *GM* (September 7, 1995).

54. Editorial "Separatist Theatrics Sell Quebec Short," *TS* (September 7, 1995).

55. Editorial "Before Voting, Quebecers Need a Reality Check," *VS* (September 8, 1995).

56. Michael Bliss, "Words Can't Hide Separatists' Nakedness," *TS* (September 8, 1995).

57. Joël-Denis Bellavance, "Les médias anglophones s'en prennent à Parizeau," *LS* (September 9, 1995).

58. Jacques Parizeau, cited in Cardinal, *Breaking Point*, 154.

59. Daniel Johnson, cited in "Trick Question?" *VTC* (September 8, 1995).

60. Jacques Parizeau, *Assemblée nationale du Québec* (September 7, 1995).

61. "Since 1980, the referendum period has begun on the day that the government issues the writ. The writ instituting the holding of a referendum cannot be issued before the 20th day following the adoption of the question or the bill by the National Assembly. But following the amendments made by Bill 36 in 1992, the writ instituting the holding of a referendum may not be issued before the 18th day following that on which the question or the bill is tabled in the National Assembly. The duration of the campaign can vary according to the day on which the writ is issued. Voting must be on a Monday. A writ instituting a general election automatically cancels a referendum writ." See Julien Côté, *Instruments of Direct Democracy in Canada and Québec,* 3rd ed. Edition (Sainte-Foy, Quebec: Le Directeur général des élections du Québec, 2001), 31.

62. Jacques Parizeau, *Assemblée nationale du Québec* (September 11, 1995).

63. Ibid.

64. Ibid.

65. Ibid.

66. Ibid.

67. Daniel Johnson, *Assemblée nationale du Québec* (September 12, 1995).

68. Ibid.

69. See André Picard, "Johnson Wants Treaty on Table," *GM* (September 13, 1995).

70. Daniel Johnson, *Assemblée nationale du Québec* (September 12, 1995).

71. Ibid.

72. Ibid.

73. Jean Chrétien, cited in Joan Bryden, "Chrétien Says Referendum Question 'One-Way Ticket out of Canada,'" *OC* (September 12, 1995). Chrétien's later recollection of the phrasing of Parizeau's referendum question evinced still-raw emotion. "Instead of asking Quebecers whether they wanted to separate from Canada, yes or no, he decided to go with a question that was even trickier than the one Lévesque had presented in 1980 ... as though every voter in the province knew what bill it was referring to or what the hell was in the fine print of the deal Parizeau had signed with Bouchard and Dumont.... [T]he separatists had replaced the scary words 'independence' and 'separatism' with the fuzzy notion of 'sovereignty.'" See Chrétien, *My Years as Prime Minister*, 132.

74. Jean-V. Dufresne, cited in Alexander Norris, "Three Commentators Urge Parizeau to Plan a Second Referendum," *MG* (September 14, 1995). Alain Dubuc: "It is patently ridiculous to think that commercial interests would force Canada to sign a partnership agreement of a political nature." See André Picard, "Referendum Refrains," *GM* (September 21, 1995). Jean-Jacques Samson: "Can one for one moment imagine that Canada will [agree] to be handcuffed in its monetary and trade policies by a neighboring country that is three times less populous?" Cited in Norris, "Three Commentators."

75. See Susan Delacourt and Tu Thanh Ha, "Liberal, Reform Leaders Cool Rhetoric," *GM* (September 21, 1995).

76. Stéphane Dion, cited in Sarah Scott, "Wording Will Have Little Impact: Experts," *MG* (September 8, 1995). See also Vincent Marissal, "Une question confuse," *LS* (September 8, 1995); and Philippe Cantin, "Oui ou non," *LP* (September 8, 1995).

77. Anne McIlroy, "In Pursuit of a Coy Electorate," *VS* (September 9, 1995).

78. Sara Perry, cited in Mike King, "Referendum Hard for Illiterates, Expert Says," *MG* (September 8, 1995).

79. Louis Balthazar, "Within the Black Box: Reflections from a French Quebec Vantage Point," *American Review of Canadian Studies* 25:4 (Winter 1995), 519.

80. See editorial "PQ's Best Weapon Is Mass Confusion," *MG* (September 26, 1995).

81. Keder Hyppolite, cited in Ingrid Peritz, "We Feel Left Out, Ethnic-Community Leaders Say," *MG* (September 8, 1995).

82. Nick Pierni, cited in Peritz, "We Feel Left Out."

83. Mordecai Richler, "Have We Got a Deal for You," *FP* (September 23, 1995).

84. Stephen Harper, cited in Susan Delacourt, "Rest of Canada Cool to Partnership Stratagem," *GM* (September 8, 1995).

85. Clyde Wells, cited in Linda Drouin, "Yes Vote Means Goodbye," *KWS* (September 8, 1995); and Delacourt, "Rest of Canada Cool."

86. Mike Harcourt, cited in Drouin, "Yes Vote Means Goodbye."

87. Frank McKenna, cited in Drouin, "Yes Vote Means Goodbye."

88. Roy Romanow, cited in Drouin, "Yes Vote Means Goodbye."

89. Editorial "Stacking the Deck for a Yes Vote," *MG* (September 8, 1995).

90. Editorial "The Question Is Clumsy, the Choice Is Clear," *GM* (September 8, 1995).

91. Jeffrey Simpson, "There Are Two Kinds of Economic Association, and They're Very Different," *GM* (September 8, 1995).

92. Editorial "Quebec Question Aims to Dupe Voters," *TS* (September 8, 1995).

93. Richard Gwyn, "PQ's Soft Question Dodges Hard Answers," *TS* (September 8, 1995).

94. See "Forget Using Dollar, Majority Says," *TS* (September 16, 1995).

95. See Doug Fischer, "Canada Uneasy about Economic Deal with Quebec," *CH* (October 11, 1995).

96. Lucien Bouchard, cited in Peter O'Neil, "B.C. City Angers Bouchard by Selling Quebec Bonds," *OC* (October 3, 1995).

97. "No Ties with Solo Quebec: Petition," *MG* (October 7, 1995).

98. Paul Gessell, "Anti-Parizeau Views Enjoy Renaissance," *OC* (June 6, 1995).

99. Guy Bertrand, *Enough Is Enough: An Attorney's Struggle for Democracy in Quebec* (Toronto: ECW Press, 1996), 61, 87, 92.

100. See François Crépeau, "The Law of Quebec's Secession," *American Review of Canadian Studies* 27:1 (Spring 1997), 27–50.

101. Robert Lesage, cited in Elizabeth Thompson, "Plan Illegal but Vote OK," *MG* (September 9, 1995).

102. See Don Macpherson, "Winning at Judicial Roulette," *MG* (September 9, 1995); and Gilbert Leduc, "La démarche référendaire: Illégale, mais non interdite," *LS* (September 9, 1995).

103. Bertrand, *Enough Is Enough,* 100. See also Rod MacDonell, "Province Lacks Power to Split, Lawyer Claims," *MG* (October 28, 1995).

104. Gilles Lesage, cited in Norris, "Three Commentators." See also Gilles Normand, "Un jugement à la Salomon," *LP* (September 9, 1995).

105. Alain Dubuc, "Des coups de toge dans l'eau," *LP* (September 12, 1995).

106. Michel C. Auger, cited in Norris, "Three Commentators."

107. William Johnson, "To the Courts," *MG* (August 15, 1995). See also William Johnson, "The Justice Minister Had a Duty to Defend the Constitution," *MG* (September 12, 1995).

108. Andrew Coyne, "Some People Actually Think the Constitution Is Worth Defending," *GM* (August 14, 1995). See also Andrew Coyne, "Yes Vote Not the End," *GM* (October 26, 1995).

109. Patrick J. Monahan, *Cooler Heads Shall Prevail: Assessing the Costs and Consequences of Quebec Separation* (Toronto: C.D. Howe Institute, January 1995), 26. See also Denis Lessard, "Parizeau court-circuite la cour," *LP* (September 6, 1995).

110. Jean Chrétien, cited in John Colebourn, "Debate's Taking a Toll on Me: PM," *VP* (October 11, 1995).

111. New Brunswick premier Frank McKenna: "In the absence of specific requests from the people who are leading our side in Quebec, we think it would be not only not useful but possibly harmful for us to be intervening with information or messages which we may not be as sensitive about as we should." See Alan Jeffers, "Atlantic Premiers Stay Mum on Referendum," *MG* (October 5, 1995).

112. Thomas d'Aquino, cited in Bertrand Marotte, "Business Loath to Spark Separatist Cause," *CH* (September 21, 1995). See also Richard Gwyn, "PM Wants Us to Level with Quebec, but Respectfully," *TS* (September 13, 1995).

113. Bill Beacon, "Habs Avoid Giving Any Offence in Referendum Debate," *MG* (October 5, 1995).

114. William Gold, "Shhhhh... Just be Very, Very, Very Quiet!" *CH* (September 8, 1995). See also William Gold, "Passion Missing from Referendum," *CH* (September 25, 1995).

CHAPTER NINE: DOWN TO BUSINESS

1. Louise Beaudoin, cited in Rhéal Séguin, "PQ Vows to Have Deal Ready Quickly," *GM* (September 13, 1995).
2. Daniel Johnson, *Assemblée nationale du Québec* (September 13, 1995).
3. Jacques Parizeau, ibid.
4. Ibid.
5. Daniel Johnson, ibid.
6. Jacques Parizeau, ibid.
7. Daniel Johnson, ibid.
8. Jacques Parizeau, *Assemblée nationale du Québec* (September 14, 1995).
9. Daniel Johnson, ibid.
10. Hubert Bauch, "Assembly Session Fails to Spark Separatist Momentum," *MG* (September 23, 1995).
11. Mario Dumont, *Assemblée nationale du Québec* (September 14, 1995).
12. Richard Le Hir, ibid.
13. Richard Le Hir, *Assemblée nationale du Québec* (September 18, 1995).
14. Daniel Johnson, *Assemblée nationale du Québec* (September 19, 1995).
15. Daniel Johnson, *Assemblée nationale du Québec* (September 20, 1995).
16. Daniel Johnson, ibid.
17. Jacques Parizeau, ibid. See also Philippe Cantin, "Johnson demande la tête de Le Hir," *LP* (September 21, 1995).
18. See Rhéal Séguin, "PQ Strategy in Tatters as Parties Take to Road," *GM* (September 21, 1995).
19. John Ciaccia, cited in Bauch, "Assembly Session Fails."
20. Jacques Parizeau, cited in Mario Fontaine, "Parizeau admet que la grogne s'est manifestée dans son caucus," *LP* (September 22, 1995).
21. Cited in Philip Authier, "PQ Troops Trying to Make Up for 'Lost Week,'" *MG* (September 22, 1995).
22. See Michel C. Auger, "Liberals Make Political Hay over Referendum Question," *EJ* (September 25, 1995).
23. Cited in Bauch, "Assembly Session Fails."
24. Julien Côté, *Instruments of Direct Democracy in Canada and Québec,* 3rd ed. (Sainte-Foy, QC: Directeur général des élections du Québec, 2001), 30.
25. See Côté, *Instruments of Direct Democracy,* 49–52. See also "Separatist Spending," *TS* (November 16, 1995).
26. Cited in "Parizeau Gears Up for Summer Referendum Blitz," *TS* (July 3, 1995). See also Norman Delisle, "Le Conseil pour l'unité canadienne prépare activement le référendum," *LP* (November 15, 1994).
27. Cited in "Parizeau Gears Up."
28. Yves Duhaime, cited in "Parizeau Gears Up."

29. Eddie Goldenberg, *The Way It Works: Inside Ottawa* (Toronto: McClelland & Stewart, 2006), 190–1.

30. Chrétien, *My Years as Prime Minister* (Toronto: Knopf Canada, 2007), 134.

31. Jean Pelletier, cited in Gilbert Lavoie, *Jean Pelletier: Entretiens et témoignages: Combattez en face* (Montreal: Éditions du Septentrion, 2009), 126.

32. Ibid.

33. Gilles Duceppe, cited in Terrance Wills, "'Unity Group' of 40 Bureaucrats to Monitor Quebec Referendum Campaign" *MG* (February 11, 1995).

34. Marcel Massé, cited in Wills, "'Unity Group.'"

35. Cited in John Gray, "Ottawa Briefs Business on Quebec," *GM* (February 21, 1995).

36. There had been at least one false start. On September 21, Quebec Superior Court justice Nicole Benard ordered the No campaign to remove hundreds, possibly thousands, of No-side billboards from Quebec highways that had been erected on September 16 and 17, ruling that they contravened the *Referendum Act*. The No committee agreed immediately to take down the signs, saying it had been an innocent mistake.

37. André Picard, "Battle of Posters Goes to Yes Side," *GM* (October 3, 1995).

38. Joan Fraser, "Yes Side Uses Retro Ads to Push Its Retro Referendum Message," *MG* (October 4, 1995).

39. See Anne McIlroy, "Women of Quebec Hold Power to Cast Deciding Votes," *EJ* (October 30, 1995).

40. Wayne Lowrie, "CBC's 'No' Stirs Tempest in a TV Ad," *EJ* (October 12, 1995).

41. Lucien Bouchard, cited in Lowrie, "CBC's 'No' Stirs Tempest."

42. Daniel Johnson, cited in Elizabeth Thompson, "Sovereignist TV Spot 'a Fraud,'" *MG* (October 13, 1995).

43. Lucien Bouchard, cited in Joan Bryden, "Battle for Quebec Shifts to Commons," *VS* (September 16, 1995).

44. Jean Chrétien, cited in Bryden, "Battle for Quebec Shifts."

45. Stephen Harper, cited in Terrance Wills, "Separation Battlefield Shifts to Commons," *MG* (September 18, 1995).

46. Lucienne Robillard, cited in "We'll Respect Vote, Says Minister," *KWS* (September 13, 1995).

47. Jean Chrétien, cited in "The Chrétien Government's Referendum Minister Learned an Important Lesson in Referendum Politics Today," CTV National News, transcript (September 12, 1995). See also "Chrétien refuse d'endosser Robillard et Johnson," *LS* (September 13, 1995); and Gilles Normand, "Parizeau critique l'hésitation de Chrétien," *LP* (September 14, 1995).

48. Patrick J. Monahan, *Cooler Heads Shall Prevail: Assessing the Costs and Consequences of Quebec Separation*," C.D. Howe Institute, Commentary 65 (January 1995), 27.

49. Jean Dion, "Reconnaîtra, reconnaîtra pas?" *LD* (September 13, 1995).

50. Lucien Bouchard, *Hansard* (September 18, 1995), 14528.

51. Jean Chrétien, ibid.

52. Jean Chrétien, ibid.

53. Lucien Bouchard, ibid., 14528–9.

54. Michel Gauthier, ibid., 14529.

55. Jean Chrétien, ibid.

56. Preston Manning, ibid., 14530.

57. Jean Chrétien, ibid.

58. Lucien Bouchard, *Hansard* (September 19, 1995), 14608.

59. Jean Chrétien, ibid.

60. Johnson: "How can you break up a country on a judicial recount? That's the real question. Isn't it a little bizarre to have a judicial recount to find out if you break up a country or not?" Mario Dumont: "Never in the National Assembly has a party caved in so much before the federal government as Daniel Johnson did today, to cave in before Jean Chrétien, who surely told him to not repeat his commitment now to recognize the referendum in Quebec." See Philip Authier and Terrance Wills, "Slim Win Won't Do," *MG* (September 20, 1995).

61. Preston Manning, *Hansard* (September 19, 1995), 14609.

62. Jean Chrétien, ibid., 14610.

63. Edison Stewart, "PM Won't Pledge to Honour Yes Vote," *TS* (September 19, 1995); "Chrétien met en doute la reconnaisance d'un OUI serré," *LD* (September 19, 1995); and Chantal Hébert, "Ottawa n'acceptera pas un résultat serré en faveur du OUI," *LP* (September 19, 1995).

64. Michel C. Auger, cited in André Picard, "Referendum Refrains," *GM* (September 21, 1995). See also Jules Richer, "La Planète du Référendum," *LDR* (September 19, 1995); Joël-Denis Bellavance, "Chrétien ne laissera pas un OUI majoritaire 'détruire le Canada,'" *LS* (September 19, 1995); Joël-Denis Bellavance, "Une curieuse alliance," *LS* (September 20, 1995); and Chantal Hébert, "Manning et Chrétien font une brèche dans le front fédéraliste," *LP* (September 20, 1995).

65. See Stewart MacLeod, "Tag Team," *VTC* (November 24, 1994). A March 1995 poll put the number at 67 per cent. See "Poll: Most Quebecers agree with Chrétien," CP (September 20, 1995). A December 1994 CROP poll showed that only 23 per cent of Quebecers believed a simple majority should be sufficient. See "50% + 1 Not Good Enough," *WS* (December 12, 1994).

66. Cited in "Citizens Feeling MP Debate Ripples," CP (September 20, 1995).

67. Editorial "No Waffling," *OC* (September 21, 1995).

68. Lysianne Gagnon, "It's Too Late for Chrétien to Change the Rules," *GM* (September 23, 1995).

69. Jean Charest, cited in Joan Bryden, "PM Says Yes Vote Not Enough," *WS* (September 19, 1995).

70. William Johnson, "Chrétien's Gambit Carried the Day, But He's Wrong," *MG* (September 19, 1995).

71. Paul Minvielle, "Jean Mustn't Follow Lucien's Game Plan," *VTC* (September 20, 1995).

72. Norm Ovenden, "Manning Won't Play Unity Game," *EJ* (September 22, 1995). Lysianne Gagnon: "Reform, a party alien to Quebec, cannot dream of forming the government as long as Quebec is in. If Quebec is out, though, it's another story. Then Reform *could* win a federal election." See Gagnon, "It's Too Late for Chrétien."

73. Lucien Bouchard, cited in Authier and Wills, "Slim Win Won't Do."

74. Jean Chrétien, *Hansard* (September 20, 1995), 14642.

75. Preston Manning, *Hansard* (September 21, 1995), 14719.

76. Lucien Bouchard, cited in Susan Delacourt and Tu Thanh Ha, "Liberal, Reform Leaders Cool Rhetoric," *GM* (September 21, 1995).

77. Preston Manning, cited in "Interview with Preston Manning," *Question Period*, CTV Television, transcript (September 24, 1995).

78. Preston Manning, *Think Big: Adventures in Life and Democracy* (Toronto: McClelland & Stewart, 2002), 139. See also "Manning, Harper to Enter Que. Fray," *EJ* (October 6, 1995).

79. Lucien Bouchard, *Hansard* (September 20, 1995), 14641.

80. Michel Gauthier, ibid., 14642.

81. Jean Chrétien, ibid.

82. Lucien Bouchard, cited in Edison Stewart, "Bloc MPs' Number Dwindle in Commons as Tactics Shift," *TS* (October 3, 1995).

83. Jean Chrétien, cited in Alexander Norris, "Polls Won't Make Me Change Strategy: Chrétien," *MG* (October 15, 1995).

84. Lucienne Robillard, cited in Paul Mooney, "No Forces Confident They Will Win," *KWS* (September 25, 1995).

85. Jean Charest, cited in Elizabeth Thompson and Hubert Bauch, "Federalists Court Soured Followers of Dumont," *MG* (September 25, 1995).

86. Daniel Johnson, cited in Denis Lessard, "Johnson prie les adéquistes de quitter le 'camp du refus,'" *LP* (September 25, 1995).

87. Claude Garcia, cited in "Insurance Boss Sorry for Remark," *VS* (September 29, 1995).

88. Jean Royer, cited in Mario Cardinal, *Breaking Point Quebec–Canada: The 1995 Referendum*, trans. Ferdinanda Van Gennip and Mark Stout (Montreal: Bayard Canada Books, 2005), 171.

89. Jean-François Lisée, *Des Histoires du Québec* (Montreal: Rogers Publishing Limited, 2012), 137.

90. Daniel Johnson, cited in Sarah Scott, "Johnson Doesn't Want Vote to 'Crush' Any Quebecers," *MG* (September 26, 1995).

91. Jacques Parizeau, cited in "Debate Degenerating, Parizeau Says," *VS* (September 27, 1995). See also Alain Dubuc, "Nous sommes tous des Québécois," *LP* (September 27, 1995).

92. Cited in "Insurance Boss Sorry."

93. Claude Garcia, cited in "Insurance Boss Sorry." See also Jean-Claude Leclerc, "Francophones Have Deep Fear of Being 'Crushed,'" *MG* (October 2, 1995); and Andy Riga, "Garcia Resigns as Chairman of UQAM," *MG* (November 7, 1995).

94. Jacques Parizeau, cited in "'Crushing' Comment Could Cost Insurance Firm $11.5-Million Contract," *MG* (September 30, 1995).

95. Editorial "It's Not Over Till 'Fat Lady' Votes," *MG* (October 3, 1995).

96. Ibid.

97. Lucien Bouchard, cited in Tu Thanh Ha, "Bouchard: No Way to Halt Vote," *GM* (September 26, 1995).

98. Cited in Colin Leslie, "Copps Predicts No Vote in Quebec," *TS* (September 26, 1995).

CHAPTER TEN: L'EFFET LUCIEN

1. Jacques Parizeau, cited in Wayne Lowrie, "Parizeau Starts on Emotional Note, Johnson Tackles Economic Issues," *OC* (October 3, 1995).

2. Murray Campbell, "Blueprint for Separate Quebec Offers Tempered Idealism," *GM* (October 31, 1995).

3. Jacques Parizeau, cited in Richard Mackie, "Yes Campaign Plays to Fears," *GM* (October 2, 1995); and "Parizeau évoque son départ," *LS* (October 3, 1995). Daniel Johnson followed Parizeau with his own televised address, calling the sovereignists' proposal "a jump into the unknown." The day after the referendum vote, said Johnson, "we won't be more Québécois than the day before, nor less Québécois, no matter what the decision." See Denis Lessard, "Le compte à rebours est commencé," *LP* (October 2, 1995); and Philippe Cantin, "'Parizeau dit n'importe quoi,' soutient Daniel Johnson," *LP* (October 3, 1995).

4. Cited in Anne McIlroy, "Referendum Campaign Officially Underway," *KWS* (October 2, 1995).

5. Henri Massé, cited in Robert McKenzie, "Sovereignists Criticize 'Defensive' Yes Camp," *TS* (October 5, 1995).

6. Mario Dumont, cited in McKenzie, "Sovereignists Criticize."

7. The son of Power Corp. chief Paul Desmarais married Jean Chrétien's daughter. Top Liberal aides Michael Pitfield and John Rae worked for Power Corp. Seagram's board of directors was interwoven with Power Corp.'s, and Edgar Bronfman's charitable foundation was directed by Liberal Tom Axworthy.

8. Pierre Côté, cited in Peter Hadekel, "Business to PQ: Prove Sovereignty Is Profitable," *MG* (February 15, 1995).

9. Jacques Parizeau, cited in Rhéal Séguin, "Parizeau Broadens Scope of Referendum Struggle," *GM* (September 27, 1995).

10. Lucien Bouchard, *Hansard* (October 3, 1995), 15178.

11. Lucien Bouchard, cited in Hugh Winsor, "Document Coercive, Bouchard Charges," *GM* (October 4, 1995).

12. Jean Chrétien, *Hansard* (October 3, 1995), 15178.

13. Lucien Bouchard, cited in Terrance Wills, "Business Blackmailed, Bloc Charges," *EJ* (October 4, 1995).

14. Jacques Parizeau, cited in Wayne Lowrie, "Federal Minister Denies Blackmail of Quebec Firms," *OC* (October 4, 1995); Paul Cauchon, "Le chef du OUI dénonce le 'colonialisme de l'esprit,'" *LD* (October 4, 1995); and Gilles Normand, "Parizeau accuse Laurent Beaudoin de pratiquer un 'colonialisme de l'esprit,'" *LP* (October 4, 1995).

15. Laurent Beaudoin, cited in Kathryn Leger, "Bombardier, Power Chiefs Lash Out at Separatist Tactics," *FP* (October 4, 1994); Michel Vastel, "Le roi Beaudoin," *LDR* (October 4, 1995).

16. See Michel Vastel, "Beaudoin menace de quitter le Québec," *LS* (October 4, 1995); and Mario Fontaine, "Beaudoin: Bombardier pourrait quitter le Québec advenant un OUI," *LP* (October 4, 1995).

17. "La campagne du OUI manque d'agressivité, déplore la FTQ," *LP* (October 5, 1995).

18. Jacques Parizeau, cited in Robert McKenzie, "Parizeau Attacks Business Leaders," *TS* (October 4, 1995).

19. Jacques Parizeau, cited in Rhéal Séguin, "Parizeau Blasts Corporate Elite for Siding with Federalists," *GM* (October 4, 1995); Robert McKenzie, "Parizeau Attacks Business Leaders," *TS* (October 4, 1995); and Donald Charette, "Jacques Parizeau: 'Nous on ne crache pas dans la soupe,'" *LS* (October 6, 1995).

20. Jacques Parizeau, cited in "Mulroney Set to Wade into Debate" *VTC* (October 6, 1995).

21. Jacques Parizeau, cited in "Parizeau Derides 'No Clan' at Rally," *TS* (October 8, 1995). See also Denis Lessard, "Parizeau poursuit sa charge contre les 'milliardaires,'" *LP* (October 8, 1995); and Donald Charette, "Parizeau dénonce 'l'État-Desmarais,'" *LS* (October 8, 1995).

22. See, for example, Gilbert Lavoie, "De Laurent Beaudoin à Marcel Masse," *LS* (October 7, 1995); Elizabeth Thompson, "Can PQ Survive a No Vote?" *MG* (October 6, 1995); and Sandro Contenta, "PQ Should 'Govern' After Vote: Johnson," *TS* (October 6, 1995).

23. Daniel Johnson, cited in Philip Authier and Elizabeth Thompson, "Big Business 'Spitting on Us,'" *MG* (October 6, 1995); and Vincent Marissal, "Langage de ruelle," *LS* (October 6, 1995).

24. Guy Laforest, cited in Peter Hadekel, "Yes–No Split Seen as Class Division," *MG* (October 7, 1995).

25. Lucien Bouchard, cited in Hubert Bauch, "Businesspeople Who Back Yes Side Should Speak Up, Bouchard Says," *MG* (October 7, 1995).

26. Editorial "Cynical Separatists Resorting to the Big Lie," *TS* (October 8, 1995).

27. See Ed Bantey, "Parizeau Might Let Bouchard Handle Crucial Yes-Panel Post," *MG* (September 24, 1995); and "Bouchard Role Seems to Spark Sovereignists," *GM* (October 9, 1995).

28. Denis Lessard, "Les péquistes veulent que Bouchard prenne plus de place," *LP* (October 7, 1995).

29. Goldenberg, *The Way It Works: Inside Ottawa* (Toronto: McClelland & Stewart 2006), 203.

30. See "Bouchard Role."

31. Jacques Parizeau, cited in Rhéal Séguin, "Parizeau Announces Watchdog Committee," *GM* (October 7, 1995); and Gilles Normand, "Parizeau veut négocier vite et fait déjà cinq nominations," *LP* (October 7, 1995).

32. Denise Verrault, cited in Séguin, "Parizeau Announces Watchdog Committee."

33. Jacques Parizeau, cited in Mario Cardinal, *Breaking Point Quebec–Canada: The 1995 Referendum,* trans. Ferdinanda Van Gennip and Mark Stout (Montreal: Bayard Canada Books, 2005), 227.

34. Jean-François Lisée, cited in Cardinal, *Breaking Point*, 227; Gérald Leblanc, "Personne ne comprend ce qui se passe au Québec," *LP* (October 7, 1995); and Michel David, "Tout commence," *LS* (October 8, 1995).

35. Lucien Bouchard, cited in "Parizeau Derides 'No Clan' at Rally," *TS* (October 8, 1995); Denis Lessard, "Bouchard sera chef négociateur," *LP* (October 8, 1995); and Donald Charette, "Bouchard, négociateur en chef," *LS* (October 8, 1995).

36. Gérald Larose, cited in "Bouchard Role."

37. Cited in Philip Authier, "I'm Still in Charge: Parizeau," *MG* (October 10, 1995).

38. Jacques Parizeau, cited in Authier, "I'm Still in Charge."

39. Lucien Bouchard, cited in Rhéal Séguin, "Bouchard Key to Rallying Yes, Premier Allows," *GM* (October 10, 1995).

40. Jean Chrétien, cited in Joan Bryden, "Canada Easier to Sell than Separation, PM Says," *OC* (October 13, 1995).

41. Daniel Johnson, cited in Richard Mackie, "Johnson Laughs Off 'Separator-in-Chief,'" *GM* (October 9, 1995); and Johnson, cited in Jack Branswell, "Don't Expect to Keep Jobs after Yes Vote, Johnson Warns," *OC* (October 10, 1995).

42. Daniel Johnson, cited in Cardinal, *Breaking Point*, 229.

43. Claude Masson, "Le tout pour le tout avec Lucien Bouchard," *LP* (October 10, 1995).

44. Don Macpherson, "All for the Cause," *MG* (October 10, 1995). *Globe and Mail* correspondent Rhéal Séguin: "Not only has Mr. Parizeau all but relinquished leadership of the Yes forces to Quebec's most popular politician, but he has given up control to the more moderate wing of the pro-sovereignty movement." See Séguin, "Parizeau Saw that He Was the Enemy," *GM* (October 9, 1995).

45. Editorial "Mr. Bouchard Takes Centre Stage," *MG* (October 11, 1995).

46. Editorial "From Turncoat to Negotiator," *TS* (October 11, 1995).

47. Ken MacQueen, "Quebec Politics: Will Quebecers Finally Come to the Aid of a New Parti?" *WS* (October 13, 1995).

48. Donald Charette, "À deux doigts de la 'bouchardmanie,'" *LS* (October 19, 1995).

49. Raymond Lefebvre, cited in Authier, "I'm Still in Charge."

50. Roger Langlois, cited in Authier, "I'm Still in Charge."

51. Vincent Marissal, "L'effet Lucien Bouchard," *LS* (October 13, 1995); Denis Lessard, "Bouchard à l'avant-plan: sage décision," *LP* (October 11, 1995); and Alain Dubuc, "Le facteur Bouchard," *LP* (October 14, 1995).

52. Jeffrey Simpson, "Bouchard Electrifies Yes Voters, Fulfilling an Old and Powerful Dream," *GM* (October 12, 1995).

53. Lucien Bouchard, cited in Hubert Bauch and Philip Authier, "Quebec Would Force Canada to Negotiate Pact, Bouchard Says," *MG* (October 10, 1995); and Donald Charette, "Absolument ridicule," *LS* (October 14, 1995).

54. Lucien Bouchard, cited in Peter O'Neil, "Bouchard Forecasts Union with West," *EJ* (October 12, 1995); Donald Charette, "Frontières avec l'Ontario," *LS* (October 15, 1995).

55. Lucien Bouchard, cited in Philip Authier, "With Religious Fervor, Bouchard says Quebecers Have 'Sacred Duty' to Stop the NOs," *MG* (October 28, 1995).

56. Lucien Bouchard, cited in Bauch and Authier, "Quebec Would Force Canada to Negotiate Pact."

57. Lucien Bouchard, cited in "Bouchard Buoys Yes Activists," *TS* (October 9, 1995).

58. Lucien Bouchard, cited in Philip Authier, "Bouchard Drops Studies," *MG* (October 11, 1995).

59. Lucien Bouchard, cited in Philip Authier, "Business Needs Plan B: Bouchard," *MG* (October 13, 1995).

60. Lucien Bouchard, cited in Andy Riga, "Federalist Side Is Running Scared from Our New Energy," *MG* (October 12, 1995); Chantal Hébert, "La contre-attaque du NON à l'effet Bouchard," *LP* (October 12, 1995); and Chantal Hébert, "La maison de verre du OUI," *LP* (October 13, 1995).

61. Lucien Bouchard, cited in editorial "Talk of Trudeau 'A Sign of Panic,'" *VS* (October 12, 1995).

62. Mike Harris, cited in "Harris 'Sets the Record Straight,'" *TS* (October 13, 1995).

63. Lucien Bouchard, cited in "Border Crossings a 'Ludicrous' Idea, Bloc Leader Says," *OC* (October 15, 1995).

64. Lucien Bouchard, cited in "Ontario's Menu for Poor Gets a No-Star Rating," *VS* (October 24, 1995). Another popular staple of Bouchard's routine was his impersonation of a phone call between Jean Chrétien and Daniel Johnson. "Listen, Daniel," Bouchard had Chrétien saying, "don't forget you're in the No camp." See Authier, "With Religious Fervor." Mike Harris's common-sense revolution was a gift to Bouchard. "A vote for sovereignty would mean endorsing a kinder, gentler, made-in-Quebec solution to the problem of balancing the government's books. There would be no workfare programs, no homeless people, no soup kitchens, no hospital closings and school board amalgamations of the kind seen in Mike Harris's Ontario.... Saying 'oui,' then, would not only be about creating a new country, it would also be about saying 'yes' to a more caring society." See David Leyton-Brown, *Canadian Annual Review of Politics and Public Affairs 1995* (Toronto: University of Toronto Press, 2002), 132.

65. "'No' Side Leads, 18% Waver," *VS* (October 14, 1994).

66. Richard Mackie, "Yes Side Narrows Gap in Latest Poll," *GM* (October 14, 1995).

67. See, for example, Sarah Scott, "Race Too Close to Call," *CH* (October 15, 1995).

68. Lucien Bouchard, cited in "Apôtres du vide infini," *LS* (August 27, 1995).

69. Jean Chrétien, cited in Alexander Norris, "Polls Won't Make Me Change Strategy: Chrétien," *MG* (October 15, 1995); and Philippe Cantin, "Le camp du NON nie une remontée de l'option souverainiste," *LP* (October 13, 1995).

70. See Chris Cobb, "Both Sides Run in Fear of Disastrous Slip," *OC* (October 16, 1995); Doug Fischer, "Unity Biggest Worry for Canadians," *EJ* (October 7, 1995); and "The Referendum Campaign in Quebec Is Having a Huge Impact on the Rest of Canada," CTV National News, transcript (October 7, 1995).

71. Lucien Bouchard, cited in Gilles Gauthier and André Pépin, "Bouchard dit n'avoir eu aucune intention négative en parlant de..." *LP* (October 17, 1995). See also "Bouchard choque les femmes," *LP* (October 16, 1995); "Des 'tactiques de désespoir,'" *LS* (October 17, 1995); Paul Wells and Philip Authier, "Johnson Challenges Bouchard on Jobs," *OC* (October 16, 1995); and Mario Fontaine, "Bouchard sur la défensive," *LP* (October 17, 1995).

72. Kathleen Lévesque and Michel Venne, "Tempête autour des femmes," *LD* (October 18, 1995).

73. Paul Gessell, "Was Bouchard Being Racist and Sexist, or Was He Just Stupid?" *OC* (October 17, 1995).

74. Jean Chrétien, *Hansard* (October 16, 1995), 15400–1.

75. Lucien Bouchard, ibid., 15401.

76. Jean Chrétien, ibid. See also Manon Cornellier, "Bouchard violemment pris à partie à Ottawa," *LS* (October 17, 1995).

77. Lucien Bouchard, cited in Joan Bryden, "'Slip-up' Slows Yes Momentum," *WS* (October 17, 1995); and Lucien Bouchard, cited in Tu Thanh Ha, "Bouchard Defends 'White Race' Remark," *GM* (October 17, 1995).

78. Jacques Parizeau, cited in Peter O'Neil, "No Forces Play Racism, Sexism Cards on Bouchard," *VS* (October 17, 1995); and Ha, "Bouchard Defends 'White Race' Remark." On Université de Montreal demographer Evelyne Lapierre-Adamcyk, see Andy Riga, "Quebec's Fertility Rate Not Even Lowest Among Canadian Provinces," *MG* (October 18, 1995); and Yves Boisvert, "Dénatalité: le Québec loin du record," *LP* (October 17, 1995).

79. Daniel Johnson, cited in Sandro Contenta, "Federalists' Economic Theme Getting Lost, Johnson Admits," *TS* (October 19, 1995).

80. Suzanne Marcil, cited in O'Neil, "No Forces Play Racism, Sexism Cards." Lucienne Robillard: "Linking a woman's personal choice whether or not to have children with the sovereignty of Quebec is an absurd idea. It proves that Mr. Bouchard is completely out of touch with reality. The woman of 1995 in Quebec is not the woman described by Lucien Bouchard." See Allan Thompson, "Bouchard Comments on Women Attacked," *TS* (October 17, 1995).

81. Ivyline Fleming, cited in Gessell, "Was Bouchard Being Racist?"

82. Cited in "SOS Racisme veut des excuses mais pas la LAM," *LS* (October 17, 1995). *Montreal Gazette* columnist Don Macpherson: "At the very least, it may be a Freudian slip showing that deep down inside, Bouchard really doesn't believe his own 'territorial' nationalist talk about all us Quebecers forming one big, happy, multiethnic and multiracial family." See "Bad Timing," *MG* (October 17, 1995).

83. Bouchard: "Whether I like it or not, history made me Québécois of old stock. Nowadays, one almost has to apologize for this. My roots have struck deep into a small part of this earth. I don't think it is better or richer than others, but it is mine. Some may think that it nourishes outmoded values and isolates me from other Québécois who joined us more recently to build here, with us, a new future for themselves. I do not think so. The particular is reductionist only if it prevents access to the universal. But I want my village to be part of a real country that broadens the range of my thoughts and opens to the outside world, starting with the one that has already settled among us, the ethnic communities." See Lucien Bouchard, *On the Record*, trans. Dominique Clift (Toronto: Stoddart, 1994), 275.

84. See Peter O'Neil, "No Forces Play Racism, Sexism Cards."

85. Françoise David, cited in André Picard, "Attack on Bouchard Wrong-Headed, Group Says," *GM* (October 18, 1995).

86. Pierrette Venne, *Hansard* (October 17, 1995), 15478.

87. Lucien Bouchard, cited in "J'ai employé une expression malheureuse," *LS* (October 18, 1995). See also Mario Fontaine, "Bouchard sur la défensive," *LP* (October 17, 1995); and Denis Lessard, "Bouchard regrette ses allusions à la 'race blanche,'" *LP* (October 18, 1995).

88. "Vache séparatiste," *LS* (October 14, 1995).

89. Jean Chrétien, *Hansard* (October 16, 1995), 15399.

90. Jean Chrétien, *My Years as Prime Minister* (Toronto: Knopf, 2007), 137.

91. Lucien Bouchard, cited in Philip Authier, "Bloc Leader Compares Yes Vote to 'a Wave of a Wand,'" *MG* (October 16, 1995); and Philippe Cantin, "Un OUI, ça a quelque chose de magique," *LP* (October 16, 1995).

92. Lucien Bouchard, cited in Authier, "Bloc Leader Compares." See also Alain Dubuc, "Abracadabra," *LP* (October 17, 1995).

93. Jean Chrétien, *Hansard* (October 16, 1995), 15399. Chrétien: "The magic wand that was to solve all the problems. Imagine if I had said things like that. Here I see *The Globe and Mail, The National Post* and all the gang dumping by the truckload on me. And, in Quebec, nobody picked up the pen and said that makes no sense." Cited in Cardinal, *Breaking Point*, 262.

94. Jeffrey Simpson, "Visions of Sugar Plums Are Dancing in Mr. Bouchard's Head," *GM* (October 18, 1995).

95. Editorial "Bouchard Rhetoric Invites Disbelief," *TS* (October 17, 1995).

96. See Michel David, "Sondage SOM/Le Soleil/The Gazette: À égalité," *LS* (October 17, 1995).

97. Alain Giguère, cited in Janet Bagnall, "Survey Examines Voters' Motivations," *MG* (October 30, 1995).
98. Jacques Parizeau, cited in Robert McKenzie, "Sovereignty Declaration Possible in 'Months,'" *TS* (October 17, 1995). See also Don MacDonald, "Quebec Might Move Fast," *KWS* (October 21, 1995).
99. Lucien Bouchard, cited in Denis Lessard, "Lucien Bouchard à *La Presse:* Un OUI, cest la souveraineté," *LP* (October 19, 1995); and Philippe Cantin, "Souveraineté d'abord, négociations ensuite?" *LP* (October 20, 1995).
100. Lucien Bouchard, cited in "Separatists Seek Double Mandate," *MG* (October 20, 1995).
101. Lloyd Robertson, cited in "Lucien Bouchard says Yes Means Independence," CTV Television, transcript (October 19, 1995).
102. Chrétien, *My Years as Prime Minister,* 137.
103. Goldenberg, *The Way It Works,* 203.
104. Norman Webster, "The Smell of Fear," *MG* (October 28, 1995).
105. Chantal Hébert, "There's No Dark Mystery to Lucien Bouchard's Appeal in Quebec," *OC* (October 24, 1995).

CHAPTER ELEVEN: FEDERALIST SETBACKS

1. See *Non* (Quebec: Directeur général des élections du Québec, 1995).
2. *Oui* (Quebec: Directeur général des élections du Québec, 1995), 3.
3. *Quebec, Canada, The Future* – Text of an interview with Thomas d'Aquino, President and Chief Executive, Business Council on National Issues (October 3, 1995), 3.
4. "Yes Vote Would Cost Quebec Billions: Group," *MG* (October 7, 1995).
5. Edward Neufeld, cited in Paul Wells, "Parizeau's Promise of No New Taxes Doesn't Add Up," *MG* (October 12, 1995). See also Peter Hadekel, "Financial Analysts See Rocky Times If Quebec Votes Yes," *MG* (October 18, 1995).
6. Dave Gower, "Canada's Unemployment Mosaic in the 1990s," *Statistics Canada Perspectives* 16 (Spring 1996), 4; and Statistics Canada, "Annual Average Unemployment Rate, Canada and Provinces, 1976–2012" (January 2–13), 1.
7. Cited in "Job Concerns Top Sovereignty: Poll," *MG* (August 17, 1995).
8. Vincent Marissal, "92 300 emplois menacés," *LS* (October 11, 1995).
9. Paul Martin, cited in Paul Wells, Terrance Wills, and Philip Authier, "No Economic Union," *MG* (September 27, 1995).
10. Lucien Bouchard, cited in Joan Bryden, "Quebec Threatens to Walk Away from Its Share of National Debt," *EJ* (September 28, 1995).
11. See Terrance Wills, "Business Survey Is Fear-Mongering: Bouchard," *MG* (September 21, 1995).
12. Paul Martin, cited in Laurier Cloutier, "Un OUI menacerait un million d'emplois, selon Martin," *LP* (October 18, 1995); and François Pouliot, "1 million d'emplois menacés," *LS* (October 18, 1995).

13. Paul Martin, cited in David Vienneau, "Million Quebec Jobs at Risk with Yes Vote, Martin Says," *TS* (October 18, 1995).

14. Jacques Parizeau, cited in Donald Charette, "On va devoir 'importer des chômeurs,'" *LS* (October 18, 1995).

15. Pollster Jean-Marc Léger: "When it's a battle between statistics and emotion, emotion wins, and Daniel Johnson doesn't understand this. There's an old saying in French—you can't write on a shaky page." Cited in Sarah Scott, "Emotion Defeating Reason in Referendum Debate," *MG* (October 20, 1995). For a defence of Martin, see Alain Dubuc, "Un million de trop," *LP* (October 19, 1995).

16. Bernard St-Laurent, cited in Edward Greenspon and Anthony Wilson-Smith, *Double Vision: The Inside Story of the Liberals in Power* (Toronto: Doubleday, 1996), 315. See also Jules Richer, "Hull," *LDR* (October 21, 1995). In late October, when political uncertainty caused the Canadian dollar and the TSX to drop, Jacques Parizeau blamed Paul Martin and his outrageous comment about a million jobs. "Could that man, for God's sake, act as a finance minister? I know what a finance minister should be. I've been at it for eight years. The man wanted to be alarmist for home reasons. He's now taken up by a world currency commotion. If he can make nice noises, or at least, at the very least, shut up, it's going to help." Jacques Parizeau, cited in Tu Thanh Ha et al., "2 Sides Swap Blame for Dollar's Drop," *GM* (October 24, 1995).

17. "Yes, No Sides in a Virtual Deadlock, New Poll Says," *VS* (October 17, 1995); and "A New Quebec Referendum Poll Was Released Today," CTV National News, transcript (October 17, 1995).

18. Sandro Contenta, "Quebec: It's Neck and Neck Poll Finds," *TS* (October 18, 1995).

19. Lucien Bouchard, cited in Philip Authier, "Bouchard Buoyed by Latest Poll," *MG* (October 18, 1995).

20. See Chantal Hébert, "Le Canada sans le Québec n'est pas un pays," *LP* (October 19, 1995).

21. Jean Chrétien, cited in "PM Challenges 'Magician' of Yes," *TS* (October 19, 1995).

22. Jean Chrétien, cited in Paul Wells, "Chrétien Lashes Bouchard 'Hocus-Pocus,'" *OC* (October 19, 1995).

23. *Toronto Star*: "Jean Chrétien's forceful intervention yesterday in the referendum campaign should help boost the federalist cause and reverse the lift Lucien Bouchard gave the Yes campaign over the last week. The Prime Minister did well to expose the separatist dream merchants for the reckless ideologues they are." See editorial "Chrétien's Warning," *TS* (October 19, 1995).

24. Jean-Jacques Samson, "Ottawa doit bouger," *LS* (October 14, 1995).

25. Michel Gauthier, *Hansard* (October 19, 1995), 15598–9.

26. Jean Chrétien, ibid., 15599.

27. Lucien Bouchard, cited in "Bouchard Urges PM to Speak Up," *OC* (October 19, 1995).

28. Chrétien, *My Years as Prime Minister* (Toronto: Knopf, 2007), 137.

29. Michel Bélanger, cited in "Interview with the President of the 'NO' Campaign, Michel Bélanger," *Question Period*, CTV Television, transcript (October 22, 1995).

30. Goldenberg, *The Way It Works: Inside Ottawa* (Toronto: McClelland & Stewart), 2006), 204.

31. John Parisella, cited in Lawrence Martin, *Iron Man: The Defiant Reign of Jean Chrétien* (Toronto: Viking, 2003), 124.

32. Daniel Johnson, cited in Philip Authier and Elizabeth Thompson, "PM Rebuffs No's Plea for Help," *EJ* (October 22, 1995); Vincent Marissal, "Un NON garde les portes ouvertes," *LS* (October 21, 1995); and Lysiane Gagnon, "Deux NON égalent un OUI," *LP* (October 23, 1995).

33. Mario Fontaine, "Chrétien dit non à Johnson," *LP* (October 22, 1995).

34. Edward Greenspon and Alan Freeman, "No Side Splinters over Strategy," *GM* (October 23, 1995).

35. Daniel Johnson, cited in Goldenberg, *The Way It Works*, 207–8.

36. Daniel Johnson, cited in Philip Authier and Elizabeth Thompson, "We're Almost There: Parizeau," *MG* (October 23, 1995); and "Le camp du NON tente de colmater la fissure," *LP* (October 23, 1995).

37. See, for example, Joël-Denis Bellavance, "Chrétien n'a pas toujours appuyé la société distincte," *LS* (October 24, 1995).

38. Cited in Joan Bryden, "PM Backs Distinct Society," *OC* (October 23, 1995).

39. Daniel Johnson, cited in Sandro Contenta, "No Side Denies 'Snub' by Chrétien," *TS* (October 23, 1995).

40. Lucien Bouchard, cited in Authier and Thompson, "PM Rebuffs No's Plea"; Donald Charette, "Bouchard 'invite' Johnson à joindre le camp du OUI," *LS* (October 22, 1995); and Robert McKenzie, "Bouchard Says PM Won't Help Johnson," *TS* (October 22, 1995).

41. Lucien Bouchard, cited in "Optimistic Yes Side Says Nothing Can Halt Separatist Tide," *OC* (October 25, 1995).

42. Lucien Bouchard, cited in Rhéal Séguin, "Separatists Pounce on PM for Remarks on Recognition," *GM* (October 23, 1995); and in Authier and Thompson, "We're Almost There."

43. Jacques Parizeau, cited in Authier and Thompson, "We're Almost There."

44. Clyde Wells, cited in "Wells dit NON à un statut spécial," *LS* (October 24, 1995).

45. Clyde Wells, cited in "Clyde Wells Wishes He'd Kept Quiet," *KWS* (October 26, 1995).

46. Jean Chrétien, "Quebec Referendum," transcript (October 25, 1995). See also Joël-Denis Bellavance, "Messages à la nation," *LS* (October 26, 1995); and Chantal Hébert, "Ultime appel," *LP* (October 26).

47. Norman Webster, "The Smell of Fear," *MG* (October 28, 1995).

48. Lucien Bouchard, cited in "Quebecers Know Well the Risks of Their Decision," *CH* (October 26, 1995).

49. Lucien Bouchard, cited in "Chrétien Called 'Not Credible' in French Speech," *EJ* (October 26, 1995).

50. Jacques Parizeau, cited in "Yes Rally Jeers Chrétien," *MG* (October 26, 1995); Philippe Cantin, "Chrétien pris pour cible," *LP* (October 26, 1995); and Donald Charette, "Tir groupé sur Chrétien," *LS* (October 26, 1995).

51. Lucien Bouchard, cited in "Yes Rally Jeers Chrétien."

52. Angus Reid pegged the Yes vote at 44 per cent, the No at 40 percent, and the undecided at 16 per cent. A SOM poll had the Yes vote at 45.6, the No at 40.4, and the undecided at 14. CROP's numbers showed the narrowest spread, with the Yes vote at 44.5, the No at 42.4, and the undecided at 13.2. See Hugh Winsor, "Surge for Separatism Stalled," *GM* (October 27, 1995).

53. Hugh Winsor, "Poll Disputes No Rally's Success may have Helped Yes Forces More," *GM* (November 11, 1995).

54. Goldenberg, *The Way It Works*, 216.

55. Jean Charest, *My Road to Quebec* (Montreal: Les Éditions Pierre Tisseyre, 1998), 194–5.

56. Chrétien, *My Years as Prime Minister,* 147–8.

57. Daniel Johnson, cited in Hubert Bauch, "Johnson Stresses Message of Change Across Canada," *MG* (October 26, 1995); and "Johnson satisfait de l'ouverture de Chrétien," *LS* (October 26, 1995). See also Gilles Normand, "Johnson invite Parizeau à dire NON," *LP* (October 24, 1995).

58. Editorial "No Fireworks, Just the Facts," *VTC* (October 27, 1995).

59. Dalton Camp, "PM's Change of Heart Cuts Ties with Trudeau," *TS* (October 29, 1995).

60. Don Braid, "Passionate Embrace May Be Too Late," *CH* (October 28, 1995).

61. Catherine Ford, "Will Separatists Wake Up Before It's Too Late?" *CH* (October 24, 1995).

62. Mark Lisac, "Constitutional Battle Like a Horror Movie with Infinite Sequels," *EJ* (October 21, 1995).

63. Jay Bryan, "Separate Quebec Would Have Serious Deficit Shock," *MG* (October 26, 1995).

64. Heather MacIvor, cited in Ted Shaw, "Bouchard Dangerous, Kiwanis Club Told," *WS* (October 25, 1995).

65. Conrad Black, "Hope for a No, But See the Opportunities in a Yes," *GM* (October 27, 1995).

66. Black, "Hope for a No." An Angus Reid survey of 501 Ontario voters, published on October 27, contradicted Black's prognostications. "If Ontarians could name a single political leader to represent their position in future negotiations with Quebec, 38 per cent would choose Jean Chrétien. Only nine per cent would choose Ontario Premier Mike Harris and just two per cent would choose Reform Party leader Preston Manning." Cited in Paul McKeague, "Attitudes Harden in Ontario, Poll Shows," *WS* (October 27, 1995). See also Nick Lomonossoff, "Black's Shock Therapy and Redneck Protein," *GM* (November 4, 1995).

67. See Norman Webster, "We've Heard Too Much from 'Anti-Kweebec' Noisemakers," *MG* (September 30, 1995).

68. Cited in Mark Kennedy, "Keep Ottawa as Canada's Capital, Poll Says," *OC* (October 28, 1995).

69. The Crees' announcement was accompanied by the reissue of the 1991 book *Sovereign Injustice*, which claimed that the government of Quebec was undermining their aboriginal and treaty rights. See Grand Council of the Crees of Québec, *Sovereign Injustice: Forcible Inclusion of the James Bay Crees and Cree Territory into a Sovereign Québec* (Ann Arbor: University of Michigan Press, 1995); and Aaron Derfel, "Crees Plan Their Own Sovereignty Referendum," *MG* (October 13, 1995).

70. In 1995, there were more than 11,000 Cree living in northern Quebec but more than half were under age 18. Voter turnout was 77 per cent, for a total of 4,849 ballots. See Jill Wherrett, *Aboriginal Peoples and the 1995 Quebec Referendum: A Survey of the Issues* (Ottawa: Political and Social Affairs Division, Library of Parliament, 1996), 5–6.

71. Matthew Coon Come, cited in Felicity Munn, "Cree Refuse to Leave," *KWS* (October 26, 1995).

72. See Michael Ignatieff, *Blood and Belonging: Journeys into the New Nationalism*

73. "A Message to Canadians and their Governments," *GM* (October 26, 1995).

74. David Cliche, cited in Jack Aubry, "Cree Vote Overwhelmingly to Stay in Canada," *OC* (October 26, 1995); and Yves Boisvert, "'Nèmoué,' disent les Cris à 96 p. cent," *LP* (October 26, 1995).

75. Guy Bellefleur, cited in Aaron Derfel, "Quebec Inuit Strongly Reject Sovereignty in Own Vote," *MG* (October 27, 1995). Of 3,896 eligible Inuit voters, 2,944 cast a ballot. See "Inuit Will Hold Separate Vote on Simple Question," *CP* (October 6, 1995).

76. Zebedee Nungak, cited in Jack Aubry, "More Inuit Reject Separation," *CH* (October 27, 1995).

77. Of 1,500 eligible Montagnais voters, 1,010 cast a ballot. See Aaron Derfel, "Montagnais Reject Quebec Independence," *MG* (October 28, 1995).

78. See Derfel, "Montagnais Reject."

79. Jack Aubry, "96% of Inuit Vote Against Sovereignty," *OC* (October 27, 1995).

80. Matthew Coon Come, cited in Aubry, "96% of Inuit."

81. Darrell Bricker, cited in Jack Aubry, "If Canada Is Divisible, So Is Quebec," *CH* (October 28, 1995).

82. Ron Irwin, cited in Jack Aubry, "Natives Protected: Minister," *KWS* (October 28, 1995).

83. Cited in "Eyes of World Watch with Surprise," *CP* (October 28, 1995). See also Michel Corbeil, "Les yeux du monde entier tournés vers le Québec," *LS* (October 30, 1995); Julian Beltrame, "Americans Shocked Their Neighbor Might Unravel," *EJ* (November 12, 1995); and Alexander Norris, "Foreign Reporters Flock in to Cover Referendum Finale," *MG* (October 29, 1995).

84. George Bush, cited in Miro Cernetig, "Stay United, Bush Tells Canada," *GM* (October 10, 1995).

85. Mikhail Gorbachev, cited in Cernetig, "Stay United."

86. Chrétien, *My Years as Prime Minister*, 138.

87. Patrick J. Monahan: "If the old constitutional order disappears and officials, judges and the general public acquiesce in the laws, rules, and orders issued by the new holders of power, then sooner or later a new legal order will have come into being. This reality explains how the rebellion of the 13 American colonies led to the creation of a new legal order, the United States of America, even though their 1776 declaration of independence was wholly illegal under British law." See Patrick J. Monahan, *Cooler Heads Shall Prevail: Assessing the Costs and Consequences of Quebec Separation*, C.D. Howe Institute Commentary 65 (January 1995), 10.

88. Warren Christopher, cited in James Blanchard, *Behind the Embassy Door: Canada, Clinton, and Quebec* (Ann Arbor: Sleeping Bear Press, 1998), 236–8.

89. Bernard Landry, letter to Warren Christopher, cited in "Landry Tells U.S. to Keep Its Nose out of Quebec Vote," *MG* (October 27, 1995); "Lettre de Landry," *LS* (October 27, 1995); and "Landry avait prévenu Clinton de rester coi," *LP* (October 27, 1995).

90. Daniel Johnson, cited in Ingrid Peritz, "My Letter of Warning to U.S. Wasn't a Threat, Landry Says," *MG* (October 27, 1995).

91. Bill Clinton, cited in Chrétien, *My Years as Prime Minister*, 139.

92. Bill Clinton, cited in Blanchard, *Behind the Embassy Door*, 248.

93. David Leyton-Brown, *Canadian Annual Review of Politics and Public Affairs 1995* (Toronto: University of Toronto Press, 2002), 15.

94. "Queen Duped into Chat with Chrétien Imposter," CP (October 28, 1995).

95. Editorial "Call to Action," *CH* (October 27, 1995). William Gold: "That's my country, our country, that Lucien Bouchard and Jacques Parizeau are attacking by way of Yes. Daniel Johnson and Jean Charest are fighting back for No, yet I'm not sure I recognize the Canada for which they fight. A fifth man from Quebec attempts to project his voice above the voices of all those others. Yet I am not sure just where Jean Chrétien is coming from, either." See "I Shout for Canada, But No One Hears," *CH* (October 23, 1995).

CHAPTER TWELVE: AMOUR À MONTRÉAL

1. Brian Tobin (with John Lawrence Reynolds), *All in Good Time* (Toronto: Penguin, 2002), 142–3.

2. Frank McKenna, cited in Tobin, *All in Good Time*, 144.

3. Lloyd Axworthy, cited in Tobin, *All in Good Time*, 144.

4. Tobin, *All in Good Time*, 144.

5. Hollis Harris, cited in Tobin, *All in Good Time*, 146. Tobin later acknowledged that corporate funding had fuelled the Unity rally. "One part of the story that has not been told in detail until now was the solid backing of corporate Canada; all the major business leaders that my office approached opened their cheque books and asked how much we needed."

6. "Cheap Fares to No Rally Are Illegal, Official Rules," CP (October 26, 1995).

7. Tobin, *All in Good Time*, 146.

8. Edward Greenspon and Anthony Wilsom-Smith, *Double Vision: The Inside Story of the Liberals in Power* (Toronto: Doubleday, 1996), 328.

9. Gerard Young, "Banners Fly to Court Quebec," *VTC* (October 22, 1995).

10. Tony Duscio, cited in "Postcards to Push for No Supporters," *MG* (October 1, 1995).

11. Cited in Jack Danylchuk, "Franco-Albertans Place Unity Advertisements," *CH* (September 27, 1995).

12. Paul Denis, cited in Erin Ellis, "Pro-Canada Postcards from the Edge," *EJ* (September 19, 1995).

13. Leo Boileau, cited in Sheldon Alberts, "Reach Out and Convince Someone," *CH* (October 21, 1995).

14. Cited in Irwin Block, "Canadians Rally Today for Their Nation," *MG* (October 27, 1995). See also Katherine Wilton, "Keep Canada Together, Fax Messages Plead," *MG* (October 29, 1995); Kerry Powell, "Edmonton Woman's Tiny Light for Unity," *EJ* (October 29, 1995); Denise Helm, "Fervent Few Call for Unity," *VTC* (October 30, 1995); and Daniel Drolet, "Thousands Make Last-Ditch Unity Plea," *OC* (October 30, 1995).

15. Ben Wicks, *Cher Canada: Une lettre d'amour à mon pays* (Toronto: Ben Wicks & Associates, 1995). When Wicks's book was launched in Ottawa, eighteen Canadian children who had contributed to it were feted in the House of Commons. The fanfare that accompanied the launch in Ottawa left Wicks open to accusations that he was exploiting children to promote federalism. "I did not use seven-year-olds for this purpose," he said. "All I did was ask them to write a love letter to their country." See Tim Harper, "Kids Hailed for Unity Love Letters," *TS* (October 3, 1995).

16. John A. Honderich, "Here's a Way to Tell Quebecers How You Feel," *TS* (October 1, 1995).

17. John A. Honderich, cited in Ingrid Peritz, "Passionate Appeal from English Canada Runs into Referendum Rules," *MG* (October 19, 1995).

18. Editorial "Messages of Hope in a Dark Hour," *TS* (October 26, 1995).

19. "The Rest of Canada Shows How Much It Really Cares," *GM* (October 26, 1995).

20. Mike Harris, cited in John Ibbitson, "Ontario MPPs Make Emotional Plea for Unity," *OC* (October 27, 1995).

21. Tobin, *All in Good Time*, 147.

22. Laurie Schild, cited in David Johnston, "Tens of Thousands to Rally for No," *MG* (October 26, 1995).

23. Tobin, *All in Good Time*, 144–8.

24. Desmond Bill, "All Aboard for Giant Montreal Rally," *TS* (October 27, 1995).

25. Jean-François Viau, cited in Johnston, "Tens of Thousands to Rally."

26. Brian Tobin, cited in Joan Bryden, "Montreal Rally Aims to Shore Up Unity," *WS* (October 25, 1995).

27. Pierre Bourque, cited in André Picard, "Patriotic Display May Not Alter Votes," *GM* (October 27, 1995).

28. Pauline Marois, cited in Johnston, "Tens of Thousands to Rally"; Michel Corbeil, "Une incitation à la désobéissance civile," *LS* (October 27, 1995); and Denis Lessard and Gilles Gauthier, "Manif de la Place du Canada," *LP* (October 26, 1995).

29. Shannon Ohama, cited in "Cheap Fares to No Rally."

30. Michel Bellehumeur, *Hansard* (October 26, 1995), 15876.

31. Brian Tobin, ibid.

32. Lucien Bouchard, cited in "Bouchard Denounces Bogus Rally," *VTC* (October 27, 1995).

33. Daniel Johnson, cited in "Bouchard Denounces Bogus Rally."

34. André Picard, "A Nation United by a Seat Sale," *GM* (October 26, 1995).

35. André Picard, "Patriotic Display May Not Alter Vote," *GM* (October 27, 1995).

36. Cited in Doug Fischer, "Majority Favor Post-No Talks," *KWS* (October 27, 1995).

37. Sybil Rowe, cited in "Love Is in the Air from B.C. to Quebec," *VTC* (October 27, 1995).

38. Barry Fowler, cited in David Morelli and Chris Vander Doelen, "Unity Crusaders Embark on Mission," *WS* (October 27, 1995).

39. Greg Thomason, cited in Dave Pommer, "Crusaders for Unity Stream into Montreal," *CH* (October 27, 1995).

40. Claudette Roy, cited in Andy Ogle, "Albertans Ready to Ask Quebec to Stay in Canada," *EJ* (October 26, 1995).

41. Denis Meilleur, cited in Dave Pommer, "Albertans Talk from the Heart," *CH* (October 28, 1995).

42. René Tourangeau, cited in Morelli and Vander Doelen, "Unity Crusaders Embark."

43. Maggie Gilmour, cited in Edison Stewart, Dale Brazao, and Theresa Boyle, "Vive le Canada! Nearly 150,000 Ask Quebecers to Stay United," *TS* (October 28, 1995).

44. Michael Coteau, personal interview (June 2011).

45. Lynn Messerschmidt, cited in "Swept Along by a Patriotic Tide," *KWS* (October 28, 1995).

46. See Brad Evenson, "Crusade for Canada," *OC* (October 28, 1995).

47. Patrick Gignac, cited in Paul McKeague, "A Cry for Canada," *WS* (October 28, 1995).

48. Mark Chayer, cited in McKeague, "A Cry for Canada."

49. Patsy Fleming, "A Journey to the 'Heart of Canada,'" *KWS* (October 31, 1995).

50. Keith Murray, cited in Jack Knox, "O Canada! What a Rally Cry," *VTC* (October 28, 1995).

51. Jean-Yves Lamarre, cited in "Separatists Brave Flak."

52. Robert Goudreau, cited in "Separatists Brave Flak at Unity Rally," *CP* (October 28, 1995).

53. Mike Harris, cited in Mario Cardinal, *Breaking Point Quebec–Canada: The 1995 Referendum*, trans. Ferninanda Van Gennip and Mark Stout (Montreal, Bayard Canada Books, 2005), 336.

54. Jean Chrétien, cited in Anne McIlroy, "Canada, Canada: Thousands Show Love for Quebec," *CH* (October 28, 1995).

55. Daniel Johnson, cited in McIlroy, "Canada, Canada."

56. Tobin, *All in Good Time*, 150.

57. Lucien Bouchard, cited in "Pressure Builds on Undecideds," *EJ* (October 29, 1995).

58. Lucien Bouchard, cited in Philip Authier, "'Illegal' Rally Cost $4.3 Million: Bouchard," *MG* (October 28, 1995).

59. Lucien Bouchard, cited in Peter O'Neil, "PM's Final Tone Confident," *VS* (October 30, 1995).

60. Ken MacQueen, "Montreal Rally Was an Earthquake in the Emotional Life of the Nation," *OC* (October 28, 1995).

61. Editorial "Mr. Bouchard's Lament," *GM* (October 28, 1995).

62. Sylvain Blanchard, "Les touristes du fédéralisme," *LD* (October 28, 1995); Julie Lemieux, "Québec, on t'aime!" *LDR* (October 28, 1995); Éric Clément, "Une manif particulièrement pacifique," *LP* (October 28, 1995); and Marie-Claude Lortie, "Un bruyant message d'amour pour les Québécois," *LP* (October 28, 1995).

63. Philippe Cantin, "Les Québécois ne seront pas dupes de 'ces ébordements d'amour,'" *LP* (October 28, 1995); Julie Lemieux, "À bord de la croisade," *LDR* (October 28, 1995); and Donald Charette, "Qu'on nous fiche la paix," *LS* (October 29, 1995).

64. Chantal Hébert, "Thérapie de groupe," *LP* (October 28, 1995).

65. Jean-Jacques Samson, "Bons baisers aux Québécois," *LS* (October 28, 1995). Ray Conlogue: "The massive descent of Canadians in Montreal last October is a metaphor for cultural deafness. The English speakers who went there thought they were demonstrating 'love'; French-speaking Montrealers felt invaded by a callous throng with which they have nothing in common." See Ray Conlogue, *Impossible Nation: The Longing for Homeland in Canada and Québec* (Toronto: Mercury Press, 1996), 8.

66. Lise Bissonnette, "Apparences d'amour," *LD* (October 28, 1995). The Quebec press was also interested in prosaic questions surrounding the rally—why so many federal employees appeared to have the day off with pay and free passage to Montreal, whether the airlines had violated the *Referendum Act,* and whether the day's events had been inspired by the tone of panic that had gripped the English-Canadian press in the final days of the campaign. See Pasquale Turbide, "Vent de panique dans la presse ontarienne," *LP* (October 29, 1995); Mario Gilbert, "Le Canada anglais a tenté de convaincre les indécis," *LDR* (October 28, 1995).

67. Editorial "Getting Emotional about Canada," *EJ* (October 27, 1995).

68. Linda Goyette, "We'll Need More than Valentines to Save Our Country," *EJ* (October 27, 1995). Lorne Gunter: "Most of these paratroopers of love were not, as portrayed, ordinary Canadians eager to show affection for Quebec. Most were die-hard Liberals and federal Tories, economic and cultural nationalists, and holdovers from the 1992 Charlottetown referendum Yes committee who were flying to Montreal to salvage Canada's 70-year-old experiment in manufacturing a centralized national identity." See "Unity Gang in Love with Mirage," *EJ* (October 30, 1995).

69. Editorial "Canada's Too Good to Throw Away," *TS* (October 28, 1995).

70. Editorial "Why Quebecers Should Vote No," *MG* (October 28, 1995).

71. See Hugh Winsor, "Poll Disputes No Rally's Success may have Helped Yes Forces More," *GM* (November 11, 1995). See also Barbara Yaffe, "We're Going to Have to Start Listening to Each Other," *VS* (October 31, 1995); and Jean-Philippe Warren and Eric Ronis, "The Politics of Love: The 1995 Montreal Unity Rally and Canadian Affection," *Journal of Canadian Studies/Revue d'études canadiennes* 45:1 (Winter 2011), 21.

72. Jean Chrétien, cited in O'Neil, "PM's Final Tone Confident."

73. Daniel Johnson, cited in Sandro Contenta, "Johnson Makes Final Plea for 'Existence of Canada,'" *TS* (October 30, 1995). See also Elizabeth Thompson, "Yes and No Forces Wrap Up Campaigns," *MG* (October 30, 1995).

74. Lucien Bouchard, cited in "Pressure Builds on Undecideds," *EJ* (October 29, 1995).

75. Lucien Bouchard, cited in Authier, "Yes and No Forces Wrap Up"; and Robert McKenzie, "World Watching, Quebecers Told," *TS* (October 30, 1995). After the speech, Bouchard spoke at a news conference: "Do we found the future of Quebec on pride or resignation? Do we found the future of Quebec on change or immobility? Do we found the future of Quebec on confidence or fear? Do we found the future of Quebec on solidarity or division? Do we found the future of Quebec on enthusiasm or torpor? Is Quebec big enough for me? Am I big enough for Quebec? If in our minds, the answer is Yes to this question, the hand will answer the question. Tomorrow, at different hours and in diverse places, with different opinions in mind, we will all enter the voting booth. That night a people will emerge."

76. Jacques Parizeau, cited in McKenzie, "World Watching."

77. Alain Dubuc, cited in Graham Fraser, "Newspapers Mirror Divided Quebec," *GM* (October 27, 1995).

78. Lise Bissonnette, cited in Fraser, "Newspapers Mirror."

79. "Dead Heat: Experts Say the Quebec Referendum Is Too Close to Call," *VP* (October 29, 1995).

80. Blanchard, *Behind the Embassy Door*, 256. See also Rick Pedersen, "Polls Exaggerate Yes Vote," *CH* (October 30, 1995).

81. Jean-François Lisée, *Des Histoires du Québec* (Montreal: Rogers Publishing Limited, 2012), 166–7. See also Norman Webster, "Smell of Fear Pervades Desperate No Side," *CH* (October 30, 1995).

CHAPTER THIRTEEN: THE NIGHT CANADA STOOD STILL

1. Jean Chrétien, *My Years as Prime Minister* (Toronto: Knopf, 2007), 149. See also Huguette Young, "Chrétien face au plus grand défi de sa carrière," *LS* (October 30, 1995).

2. Jacques Parizeau, cited in Cardinal, *Breaking Point Quebec–Canada: The 1995 Referendum,* trans. by Ferdinanda Van Gennip and Mark Stout (Montreal: Bayard Canada Books, 2005), 381. See also "Parizeau visiblement nerveux," *LP* (October 31, 1995).

3. Alison Ramsey, "How Things Work at Polling Stations," *MG* (October 30, 1995).

4. "In a Referendum, Every Vote Counts," *MG* (October 30, 1995).
5. See "Former Quebecers Informed," *TS* (September 7, 1995).
6. Murray Rankin, cited in "Lawyer Hopes to Flush Out Quebec Referendum Voters," *VTC* (September 28, 1995).
7. Casper Bloom, cited in "Hundreds of Voters Furious at Being Left Off Electoral Lists," *EJ* (October 26, 1995).
8. Jack Aubry, "Federalists Lobby Aboriginals to Break Tradition and Vote," *OC* (October 30, 1995).
9. See Andy Riga, "Now Their Work Begins," *MG* (October 30, 1995).
10. Andy Riga, "Grass-Roots Workers Fight to the Finish," *MG* (October 29, 1995).
11. See Hubert Bauch, "Canada Survives," *MG* (October 31, 1995).
12. Ann McLaughlin, "Anglo Voters Accuse Yes Side of Stalling at Polling Stations," *OC* (October 23, 1995).
13. See Greg Quill, "Six Days in October," *TS* (October 24, 1995).
14. Peter Mansbridge, cited in "Canadians at the Crossroads," *WS* (October 30, 1995).
15. Craig Oliver, cited in "The Quebec Referendum: A Nation in Question," CTV National News, transcript (October 30, 1995).
16. Alan Fryer, cited in "The Quebec Referendum."
17. Christine Lachance, cited in Tim Harper and Dale Brazao, "Yes, No Sides Fight in Streets," *TS* (October 31, 1995).
18. Robert Aubin, cited in Harper and Brazao, "Yes, No Sides Fight."
19. Mike Duffy, cited in "The Quebec Referendum," CTV National News.
20. Jean Royer, cited in Cardinal, *Breaking Point*, 389.
21. Lisette Lapointe, cited in Cardinal, *Breaking Point*, 390.
22. Jean-François Lisée, cited in Cardinal, *Breaking Point*, 390.
23. Jean Lapierre, cited in "The Quebec Referendum," CTV National News.
24. Bauch, "Canada Survives." See also Brad Evenson, "Narrow No Win Little Comfort to Outaouais Region," *OC* (October 31, 1995).
25. Vincent Marissal, "Au Métropolis: De l'angoisse au soulagement," *LS* (October 31, 1995).
26. Mike Duffy, cited in "The Quebec Referendum," CTV National News. See also Michel David, "Une insignifiance statistique," *LS* (October 31, 1995).
27. Alan Fryer, cited in "The Quebec Referendum"; and Donald Charette, "Au Palais des congrès," *LS* (October 31, 1995).
28. John Gray, "Yes Side's Joy Seeps Out Quickly as Divisions Sink In," *GM* (October 31, 1995).
29. François Pouliot, "Des larmes coulaient," *LS* (October 31, 1995); and Ann Gibbon, "Quebec City's *Oui* Supporters Dejected by Results," *GM* (October 31, 1995).
30. "Washington soupire de soulagement," *LS* (October 31, 1995); and Michel Dolbec, "Paris prend acte du NON," *LP* (October 31, 1995).
31. Monique Simard, cited in "The Quebec Referendum," CTV National News.
32. Bernard Landry, cited in Sandro Contenta, "What Now? No Wins but Francophones Vote for Sovereignty," *TS* (October 31, 1995).

33. Jean-François Lisée, cited in Bauch, "Canada Survives."

34. Louise Beaudoin, cited in Bauch, "Canada Survives."

35. Michel Bélanger, cited in Graham Fraser, "'Le Québec au Canada' Rings Out at No Headquarters," *GM* (October 31, 1995).

36. Yvon Charbonneau, cited in Fraser, "'Le Québec au Canada.'" Eric Maldoff: "With a result like this, Canada ends up united with a clear message of change, and Quebec ends up divided with a profound need for reconciliation." See "The Quebec Referendum," CTV National News.

37. Patrick J. Monahan, cited in "The Quebec Referendum."

38. Preston Manning, *Think Big: Adventures in Life and Democracy* (Toronto: McClelland & Stewart, 2002), 142.

39. Preston Manning, cited in "The Quebec Referendum."

40. Mario Dumont, cited in "The Quebec Referendum"; and "Mario Dumont," *LS* (October 31, 1995).

41. Lucien Bouchard, cited in "The Quebec Referendum."

42. Jean-François Lisée, cited in Cardinal, *Breaking Point*, 397.

43. Bouchard's advisor Bob Dufour: "We saw Mr. Parizeau arrive. We knew what kind of politician he was. He used to say it himself: he was 'politically incorrect,' and he would say what he thought all the time. We had no idea what he was going to say." See Cardinal, *Breaking Point*, 397.

44. Jacques Parizeau, cited in "The Quebec Referendum."

45. Jean-François Lisée, cited in Cardinal, *Breaking Point*, 399.

46. Lucien Bouchard, cited in Cardinal, *Breaking Point*, 399.

47. Lloyd Robertson, cited in "The Quebec Referendum."

48. Alan Fryer, cited in "The Quebec Referendum."

49. Jean Lapierre, cited in "The Quebec Referendum."

50. Marc Lalonde, cited in "The Quebec Referendum."

51. Bob Rae, cited in "Parizeau Blames Loss on 'Money, Ethnic Vote,'" *TS* (October 31, 1995). Bob Rae later reflected on his own remarks in his memoir. "I was getting more and more agitated when Parizeau came on and unloaded at the end of the evening. I had never liked or trusted him personally, and when I heard him vent his spleen in language worthy of a Munich beer hall in the twenties, I went ballistic. I was even more upset by the namby-pamby response of the commentators, who seemed incapable of voicing honest anger. When my turn finally came, I said what I thought, that Parizeau's was a vicious outburst unworthy of anyone who aspired to be in a position of political responsibility in any part of Canada. He sounded drunk to me, and I said as much, which enraged the sovereignists on the other panels. At that point I was past caring. I simply had to say what I thought. I'm glad I did. If I contributed in only a minor way to Mr. Parizeau's demise, I am a happy man." See Bob Rae, *From Protest to Power: Personal Reflections on a Life in Politics* (Toronto: Penguin, 1996), 314.

52. Reuben Poupko, cited in Alexander Norris and Irwin Block, "Premier's Remarks Shock Minorities," *MG* (October 31, 1995).

53. David Birnbaum, cited in Norris and Block, "Premier's Remarks."

54. Nick Pierni, cited in Norris and Block, "Premier's Remarks."

55. Christos Sirros, cited in Norris and Block, "Premier's Remarks."

56. Emmanuel Marcotte, cited in Anne McIlroy, "Only 52,000 Votes Separate Two Sides," *OC* (October 31, 1995).

57. Alain Dubuc, "Une victoire sans joie," *LP* (October 31, 1995). See also Philippe Cantin, "Parizeau blâme l'argent et le vote ethnique," *LP* (October 31, 1995); and Pierre Gingras, "Les communautés culturelles unanimes contre Parizeau," *LP* (November 1, 1995).

58. Lise Bissonnette, "Le NON de 1995," *LD* (October 31, 1995).

59. Louis Balthazar, "Within the Black Box: Reflections from a French Quebec Vantage Point," *American Review of Canadian Studies* 25:4 (Winter 1995), 519.

60. Jacques Parizeau, cited in Cardinal, *Breaking Point,* 400.

61. Daniel Johnson, cited in "The Quebec Referendum," CTV National News; and Gilles Normand, "Johnson s'engage à élargir la coalition en faveur du changement," *LP* (October 31, 1995).

62. Chrétien, *My Years as Prime Minister,* 149–50.

63. Eddie Goldenberg, *The Way It Works: Inside Ottawa* (Toronto: McClelland & Stewart, 2006), 218.

64. Chrétien, *My Years as Prime Minister,* 149–50.

65. Jean Chrétien, cited in "The Quebec Referendum," CTV National News; and Joël-Denis Bellavance, "Chrétien tend la main à Parizeau," *LS* (October 31, 1995).

66. René Lévesque, "For an Independent Quebec," in *Quebec since 1945,* ed. Michael D. Behiels. (Toronto: Copp Clark Pitman, 1987), 272.

67. See "Debate Degenerating, Parizeau Says," *VS* (September 27, 1995); "West-End Residents Report Getting Hate Sheet Threatening Executions," *MG* (October 20, 1995); and Rhéal Séguin, "Vandalism, No Blunders Give Yes Campaign a Boost," *GM* (September 28, 1995).

68. "Quebec Police Prepared for Referendum Violence," *VTC* (October 30, 1995); and Lia Lévesque, "Actes de vandalisme contre un militant péquiste," *LS* (September 27, 1995).

69. "Police Create Referendum Squad," *EJ* (October 22, 1995).

70. Gerard Young, "Bottles, Rocks Fly in Clash," *VTC* (October 31, 1995).

71. "Montreal Police Dismantle Bomb," *KWS* (November 1, 1995).

72. Claude Vaillancourt, "Trois alertes à la bombe," *LS* (October 31, 1995).

73. See André Cédilot and Bruno Bisson, "Le scrutin s'est déroulé dans le calme," *LP* (October 31, 1995); François Foisy, "Le calme régnait dans les rues d'Ottawa," *LDR* (October 31, 1995); "Grabuge à Montréal, calme plat ici," *LDR* (October 31, 1995); and Claude Vaillancourt, "Calme plat dans un Vieux-Québec désert," *LS* (October 31, 1995).

74. Éric Clément, "On va tous rentrer au travail ce matin," *LP* (October 31, 1995).

CONCLUSION: NUMB AND NUMBER

1. "Numb and Number" cited in David Staples, "Muddy Referendum Result Doesn't Solve Quebec Question," *EJ* (October 31, 1995).

2. *La consultation populaire au Canada et au Québec* (Quebec City: Directeur général des élections du Québec, 2000), 51–7.

3. Ken MacQueen, "Canada Survived This October Crisis, but It Will Never Be the Same," *OC* (October 31, 1995); and "Le reste du Canada pousse un grand soupir de soulagement," *LP* (October 31, 1995).

4. Alain Dubuc, "Une victoire sans joie," *LP* (October 31, 1995).

5. See Marie-Claude Lortie, "Maintenant commence la grande guérison," *LP* (October 31, 1995).

6. Claude Masson, "Le pas de géant du camp du OUI," *LP* (October 31, 1995).

7. Thomas d'Aquino, cited in Gillian Shaw, "Entire Political System Needs Overhaul, Labor Business Says," *VS* (October 31, 1995).

8. Trevor Lautens, "No Tolerance Here for Any More of This," *VS* (October 31, 1995).

9. Catherine Ford, "Blame-Takers: Today Is the Time to Reflect on What It Means to Be a Canadian," *WS* (October 31, 1995).

10. Preston Manning, cited in Norm Ovenden, "Manning Calls Chretien's Handling of Referendum 'Sickening, Pathetic,'" *VS* (November 1, 1995); and Terrance Wills, "Bouchard Expects to Encounter Bitterness," *VS* (October 31, 1995).

11. Paul Gaboury, "Jacques Parizeau passe le flambeau," *LDR* (November 1, 1995); and Philippe Cantin, "Parizeau s'en va," *LP* (November 1, 1995).

12. Jean-François Lisée, cited in Pierre Duchesne, *Jacques Parizeau: Le Régent 1985–1995* (Montreal: Québec Amérique, 2004), 560.

13. Jacques Parizeau, cited in Philip Authier, "Parizeau Bids Adieu to Quebec Assembly," *MG* (December 16, 1995).

14. Jean-Jacques Samson, "Dans les deux capitales," *LDR* (October 31, 1995).

15. Editorial "No's Message: The Problems Are Unresolved," *WS* (October 31, 1995); editorial "Message Is Confusing but Full of Hope," *OC* (October 31, 1995); editorial "Recognize Quebec While There's Still Time," *TS* (November 1, 1995); Derek Ferguson, "Act Fast on Unity Claims, Charest Tells PM," *TS* (November 1, 1995); and Edie Austin, "Editorial Writers See Result as an Opportunity for Change," *MG* (November 1, 1995).

16. Roy Romanow, cited in "Premiers Offer Olive Branch," *VS* (October 31, 1995). See also Anne McIlroy, "Pressure on Chrétien to Make a Deal," *WS* (October 31, 1995); and Susan Delacourt, "All of Canada Faced with Continuing Unity Debate," *GM* (October 31, 1995).

17. Jean Chrétien, cited in Edward Greenspon and Jeff Salott, "Chrétien Promises Rapid Steps on Distinct Society, Quebec Veto," *GM* (November 1, 1995). See also Bob Cox, "As Prime Minister of Canada I Will Make Sure that We Have Political Stability in this Land," *KWS* (November 2, 1995).

18. See "Chretien Says No to Neverendums," *VTC* (November 2, 1995).

19. David Leyton-Brown, *Canadian Annual Review of Politics and Public Affairs 1995* (Toronto: University of Toronto Press, 2002), 133.

20. Jacques Parizeau, cited in Robert McKenzie, "Sovereignty Declaration Possible in 'Months,'" *TS* (October 17, 1995). See also Don MacDonald, "Quebec Might Move Fast," *KWS* (October 21, 1995).

21. Louis Balthazar, "Within the Black Box: Reflections from a French Quebec Vantage Point," *American Review of Canadian Studies* 25:4 (Winter 1995), 519. Richard Simeon: "Indeed, the term *sovereignty-partnership* encapsulates the fundamental belief (shared by sovereigntists and federalists alike) that from its inception Canada was seen as a partnership between the two great language groups. Quebecers have *always* thought of Canada as a partnership. The term is familiar and comfortable. And it is the growing rejection of this conception of Canada, as reflected in the *Constitution Act of 1982* and the defeat of the Meech Lake and Charlottetown Accords that has tipped the balance for many people from trust in federalism to belief in the need for sovereignty." See Richard Simeon, *Limits to Partnership: Canada-Quebec Relations in a Postsecession Era* (Toronto: C.D. Howe Institute, 1998), 397.

22. Harold D. Clarke, Allan Kornberg, and Peter Wearing, *A Polity on the Edge: Canada and the Politics of Fragmentation* (Toronto: University of Toronto Press, 2000), 183.

23. See Rob Bull, "Three Tell Why They Voted Yes," CP (November 1, 1995).

24. See, for example, Lysiane Gagnon, "Whatever Occurs, the Sovereignists Have Already Won," *GM* (October 28, 1995).

25. See Joan Bryden, "Majority Back PM's Role in Unity Debate, Poll Finds," *OC* (November 5, 1995).

26. Andy Riga, "Referendum Investigator Named Law Firm, Academics to Aid Probe of Vote-Fraud Allegations," *MG* (November 24, 1995). See also Andy Riga, "Post-Referendum Scandal Fest," *MG* (November 18, 1995); and "Rejected Votes Outnumber Margin of Victory," CP (October 31, 1995).

27. Thomas Mulcair, cited in "Liberal Irate as 12% of Ballots Rejected," *MG* (October 31, 1995).

28. "Unity-Rally Charges Are 'Quite a Spectacle,'" *MG* (November 20, 1995).

29. Directeur général des élections du Québec, press release (October 30, 1995), http://www.electionsquebec.qc.ca/english/news-detail.php?id=1606.

30. Pierre-Ferdinand Côté, cited in Riga, "Referendum Investigator."

31. See Don Macpherson, "It Was a Close Vote, but There's No Referendum Recount," *MG* (November 18, 1995).

32. See Don Macpherson, "Quebec's Chief Electoral Officer to Canadians: Stay Away," *VS* (December 20, 1995).

33. Directeur général des élections du Québec, press release "Referendum of October 30, 1995" (May 16, 1996), http://www.electionsquebec.qc.ca/english/news-detail.php?id=1537.

34. Directeur général des élections du Québec, press release "October 30, 1995 Referendum" (May 19, 1998), http://www.electionsquebec.qc.ca/english/news-detail.php?id=1092.

35. Québec (Directeur général des élections) c. Janie Fortin, No. 500-10-001318-987 (540-36-000108-984), Cour d'Appel, Province de Québec (December 17, 1999), 12, http://canlii.ca/fr/qc/qcca/doc/1999/1999canlii13532/1999canlii13532.html.

36. Robin Philpot, *Le référendum volé* (Montreal: Les Éditions des Intouchables, 2005).

37. Bernard Grenier, *Rapport d'enquête au sujet des activités d'Option Canada à l'occasion du référendum tenu au Québec en octobre 1995* (Québec: Directeur général des élections du Québec, 2007), 1.

38. Jean-François Lisée, *Des histoires du Québec* (Montreal: Rogers Publishing Limited, 2012), 217–19.

39. Jacques Parizeau, *An Independent Quebec: The Past, the Present and the Future,* trans. Robin Philpot (Montreal: Baraka, 2010), 61–2.

40. Denis Lessard, "Lucien Bouchard s'en vient," *LP* (November 1, 1995).

41. "Majority Happy Parizeau Left Office after Losing Referendum, Poll Shows," *EJ* (November 13, 1995).

42. Eddie Goldenberg, *The Way It Works: Inside Ottawa* (Toronto: McClelland & Stewart, 2006), 222. See also Chantal Hébert, "Shallowness of No Victory Becoming Increasingly Evident in Quebec," *OC* (November 21, 1995).

43. Kathryn Leger, "Bouchard Rules Out New Vote Before '97," *FP* (November 22, 1995); and "Bouchard Text: Pride, Family and Sovereignty," *VS* (November 22, 1995).

44. See Richard Mackie, "Quebec Referendum Poll," *GM* (November 25, 1995).

45. Jean Chrétien, cited in Alan Toulin, "PM Extends Hand to Quebec," *FP* (November 28, 1995). See also Gregory S. Mahler, "Canadian Federalism and the 1995 Referendum: A Perspective from Outside of Quebec," *American Review of Canadian Studies* 25:4 (Winter 1995), 449; and Mollie Dunsmuir and Brian O'Neal, "Background to the Introduction of Bill C-20" (Ottawa: Library of Parliament, 2000), http://publications.gc.ca/collections/Collection-R/LoPBdP/PRB-e/PRB9942-e.pdf.

46. See Brian O'Neal, "Distinct Society: Origins, Interpretations, Implications" (Ottawa: Library of Parliament, 1995), 21–2.

47. Daniel Johnson, cited in Elizabeth Thompson, "Johnson Welcomes PM's Move" *MG* (November 28, 1995); and "PM Acted Too Late on Vote: Johnson," *TS* (December 16, 1995).

48. Lucien Bouchard, cited in "Provinces Dislike Unity Deal," *MG* (December 5, 1995).

49. See Norm Ovenden, "Manning Releases Petition to Impeach 'Irrational' PM," *EJ* (December 14, 1995).

50. See Alain Dubuc, "Les québécois veulent beaucoup plus que cela," *LP* (November 29, 1995).

51. Jean Chrétien, cited in "Chretien Says No to Neverendums."

52. See Alan C. Cairns, "Looking into the Abyss: The Need for a Plan C" (C.D. Howe Institute, 1997), 32.

53. Stéphane Dion, *Straight Talk: On Canadian Unity* (Montreal: McGill-Queen's University Press, 1999), xvii.

54. Cited in Dunsmuir and O'Neal, "Background to the Introduction of Bill C-20."

55. Supreme Court of Canada, "Reference re Secession of Quebec" (August 20, 1998), 273, 291. http://scc-csc.lexum.com/decisia-scc-csc/scc-csc/scc-csc/en/item/1643/index.do.

56. See David Schneiderman, "Introduction," in *The Quebec Decision: Perspectives on the Supreme Court Ruling on Secession,* ed. David Schneiderman (Toronto: James Lorimer & Company, 1999), 11; Dunsmuir and O'Neal, "Background to the Introduction of Bill C-20"; and Peter Russell and Bruce Ryder, "Ratifying a Post-referendum Agreement on Quebec Sovereignty," *The Referendum Papers: Essays on Secession and National Unity,* ed. David Cameron (Toronto: University of Toronto Press, 1999), 324.

57. *Clarity Act* (2000), 3–4, http://laws.justice.gc.ca/PDF/C-31.8.pdf.

58. *An Act Respecting the Exercise of the Fundamental Rights and Prerogatives of the Québec People and the Québec State* (2000), http://www2.publicationsduquebec.gouv.qc.ca/dynamicSearch/telecharge.php?type=5&file=2000C46A.pdf.

59. L. Ian MacDonald, "Bill 99 Challenge Is the 1995 Referendum's Latest Echo," *MG* (October 30, 2013).

60. Stephen Harper, *Hansard* (October 22, 2013), http://www.parl.gc.ca/HousePublications/Publication.aspx?Language=E&Mode=1&Parl=41&Ses=2&-DocId=6263293.

61. Jacques Parizeau, cited in Mario Cardinal, *Breaking Point Quebec–Canada: The 1995 Referendum,* trans. Ferdinanda Van Gennip and Mark Stout. (Montreal: Bayard Canada Books, 2005), 384.

62. "Deputy Premier Asked Diplomats to Recognize Sovereign Quebec," *OC* (November 8, 1995).

63. Benoît Aubin, cited in Dunsmuir and O'Neal, "Background to the Introduction of Bill C-20."

64. Cardinal, *Breaking Point,* 358.

65. Goldenberg, *The Way It Works,* 220.

66. Jean Chrétien, cited in Tu Thanh Ha, "Chrétien Says Vote Was Not Binding," *GM* (December 21, 1995).

67. Chrétien, *My Years as Prime Minister,* 149–50.

68. Jean-François Lisée, "1995 versant Non: Les 15 ans du grand mensonge" (October 28, 2010), http://jflisee.org/1995-versant-non-les-15-ans-du-grand-mensonge.

69. Lucien Bouchard, cited in "Bouchard Calls Referendum His Last Battle for Separatism," *VTC* (November 27, 1994).

70. Parizeau, *An Independent Quebec,* 64.

71. Lucien Bouchard, cited in Rhéal Séguin, "Bouchard Says PQ on Cusp of 'Radicalism,'" *GM* (February 17, 2010).

INDEX

Aboriginal Peoples, 53–54, 87, 211–213, 240, 254

Action démocratique du Québec (ADQ), 44–45, 63, 70, 83, 118, 124–125, 157, 159, 174, 180, 242, 249. *See also* Dumont, Mario

Air Canada, 219–220, 227

Alberta, 29–30, 34, 209, 221, 226–227, 262

Allaire, Jean, 45, 180

Alliance for the Preservation of English Canada (APEC), 55

Alliance Québec, 52, 87, 253

Anctil, Pierre, 159, 200

Auger, Michel C., 84, 134, 150, 166

Axworthy, Lloyd, 219

Balloch, Howard, 160

Balthazar, Louis, 146, 254, 264

Beaudoin, Laurent, 175–177

Beaudoin, Louise, 48, 59, 154, 248

Bédard, Éric, 100

Bélanger, Michel, 100, 122, 159, 200, 248, 255

Bertrand, Guy, 101, 149–150, 164

Best, Audrey, 114, 235, 249

Bill 1 (*Act Respecting the Future of Quebec*), 139–140, 142–143, 145–147, 149, 151, 156–157, 171, 174, 179, 263

Bill 101 (*La Charte de la langue française*), 52–53

Bissonnette, Lise, 74, 141, 145, 233, 236, 253–254

Black, Conrad, 56, 209–210

Blanchard, James, 214

Bliss, Michael, 109, 142

Bloc Québécois (BQ)
  1993 election, 18–19, 22, 26, 30, 50
  Chrétien Liberals and, 48
  francophones outside Quebec, 54
  and Gilles Duceppe, 73, 75, 88, 118, 160
  and Lucien Bouchard, 18, 27, 43, 49, 70, 99, 169, 182, 242, 261
  and Michel Gauthier, 199
  national convention, 114
  as Official Opposition, 17, 22, 30 34, 75, 88
  and Parti Québécois, 34, 43, 50, 58, 63, 75, 88, 152, 160, 173

Boisclair, André, 262

Bouchard, Lucien
  Anglo-Canadians' view of, 19, 25–26, 76–77, 104, 167
  and Bloc Québécois, 18–19, 22, 27, 43, 70, 73, 99, 104, 114, 128, 182

Bouchard, Lucien (*cont.*)
  and Brian Mulroney, 18, 21–22, 24,
    27–28, 121, 193
  Canadian Constitution, 18–19, 22,
    33, 58, 70, 97, 164, 199, 205, 270
  charisma, 192–193
  concession speech, 249–250
  illness, 71–76, 96–99
  and Jacques Parizeau, 19, 22, 35–37,
    100, 111, 113–121, 124, 128, 137,
    178, 179, 184–185, 196, 236, 250,
    252, 263, 266, 275–276
  and Jean Chrétien, 19–20, 27, 49, 71,
    97–99, 128, 133, 137, 163–166,
    168–169, 176, 181, 186–188, 199,
    202–203, 206–208, 270
  Mario Dumont, 117, 123, 125, 133,
    136
  as *négociateur en chef*, 180, 182, 187,
    197, 265
  as opposition leader, 22, 75, 97–98,
    164–165, 182, 187
  as premier of Quebec, 268–270
  and Quebec economy, 23–24, 124,
    190, 196, 269
  races blanches remark, 186–188, 190
  tripartite accord, 123
  unity rally, 231–232
  view of Parti Québécois, 43
  views on English Canada, 19–20,
    24–27, 55, 57, 97–98, 182, 184,
    196, 198, 202, 206, 266
  virage speech, 114–115, 120–121
Bourassa, Robert, 23, 37, 39–40, 45,
  143, 160
Bourgault, Pierre, 101–104
British Columbia, 223, 259
Bryden, Joan, 202
Bush, George Sr., 213
Business Council on National Issues
  (BCNI), 152, 261

Cairns, Alan C., 26, 56
Callbeck, Catherine, 223, 230
Camp, Dalton, 208
Campeau, Jean, 48, 100
Canadian Airlines, 224–225
Canadian Broadcasting Corporation
  (CBC), 42, 64, 75, 162, 172, 197,
  223, 241
Canadian Charter of Rights and
  Freedoms, 3, 6–8, 25, 56
Canadian Unity Council (Conseil pour
  l'unité canadienne, CUC), 161
Charest, Jean, 10–11
  and Jacques Parizeau, 41
  Jean Chrétien's Verdun promises, 262
  and Lucien Bouchard, 21–22, 187,
    207
  and No campaign, 127, 159, 170,
    255, 266
  and Preston Manning, 167, 170
  sovereignty hearings, 90
  unity rally, 230
Charland, Gilbert, 75–76
Charlottetown Accord, 7–9, 16, 18–19,
  28, 37, 45, 58, 127, 137, 139, 244,
  263, 266
Chirac, Jacques, 214
Chrétien, Jean
  1993 election, 17–18, 143
  1995 referendum, 238, 242, 247
  1995 Yes vote, 151, 166–167, 169
  aboriginal people of Quebec, 212
  appointment of Lucienne Robillard,
    112–113
  Bill 1, 140, 145
  Bill Clinton, 215
  and Bloc Québécois, 128
  concession speech, 274
  and Daniel Johnson, 132–134,
    201–203
  dishonesty during 1995 campaign,
    275

distinct society status for Quebec, 6–8
draft bill, 88–90, 164
emergency address, 204–208
federal strategy, 32–34, 70, 122–123,
    127, 152, 171, 186, 193, 236,
    261, 265
flexible federalism, 39–40
French recognition of Quebec, 214
House of Commons debate,
    163–166
and Jacques Parizeau, 62, 66,
    135–136, 269
Liberal caucus meeting, 13–16
and Lucien Bouchard, 27, 72, 75,
    97–99, 187–188, 192
Lucien Bouchard's appointment as
    négociateur en chef, 181
as minister of justice, 2
Night of the Long Knives, The (*La
    Nuit des Longs Couteaux*), 4–5
Parti Québécois victory, 45–48
Pierre Brossard's impersonation, 216
Plan A and B, 271
popularity among Quebecers, 131,
    137, 266
popularity outside of Quebec, 172
and Preston Manning, 28, 31, 168
provincial No team, 159–160
Quebec Chamber of Commerce
    speech, 197–199
Quebec secession, 52, 91–92, 176, 210
Radio-Canada ad, 162
referendum timetable, 49–50, 91,
    108
refusal to campaign on
    Constitution, 32
sovereignty hearings, 107
tripartite accord, 126
United Nations delegates and, 213
unity rally, 220, 230–232, 234
Verdun promises, 262, 270
Verdun speech, 5, 9–13, 206

victory speech, 255–256
Yes strategy, 101–102, 190–191
Christie, Doug, 149
Christopher, Warren, 214–215
Ciaccia, John, 156
Clark, Joe, 7, 127, 240, 266
Clark, Martin, 257, 266
Cliche, David, 53, 211
Clinton, Bill, 214–216
Connors, Stompin' Tom, 56
Constitution of Canada
    1982 repatriation of, 6–7, 193
    Charlottetown Accord, 263
    Cree position on, 211
    Daniel Johnson's position on, 40,
        132, 134
    Jean Chrétien's position on, 17–19,
        32–33, 47–48, 70, 199–201
    Lucien Bouchard's position on, 97
    Pierre Trudeau's promise to renew,
        3–4
    Post-referendum reforms, 270
    Preston Manning's position on, 29
Conway, John F., 59
Coon Come, Matthew, 54, 87, 208,
    210–212
Copps, Sheila, 31, 46, 89–90, 172, 230
Côté, Marcel, 107, 195
Côté, Pierre, 175
Côté, Pierre-Ferdinand, 158, 225, 239,
    267
Coteau, Michael, 228
Cotnoir, Pierre-Alain, 131
Coyne, Andrew, 86, 91, 121, 150–151
Cree, 54, 87, 210–212, 240
CTV, 168, 192, 223, 242, 244–245, 248,
    252

d'Aquino, Thomas, 152, 195, 261
David, Françoise, 189
Desmarais, Paul, 39, 177

Dion, Léon, 84
Dion, Stéphane, 68, 84, 146, 271
Directeur général des élections du
    Québec (DGE), 239–241
Distinct society clause, 8, 201
Drouilly, Pierre, 131, 146
Dubuc, Alain, 84, 141, 145, 150, 236,
    253, 260
Duceppe, Gilles, 73, 75, 88–90, 112,
    118, 160
Duffy, Mike, 244, 246
Dufresne, Jean-V., 102, 141, 145
Duhaime, Yves, 158–159, 161
Dumont, Mario, 133, 138, 142, 155
    1995 referendum, 242, 249
    and ADQ, 44–45
    European Union–style partnership
        with Canada, 117
    Montreal rally, 202
    referendum hearings, 83–84
    tripartite accord, 123–125
    Yes campaign, 157, 170, 174, 183

Federal Government. *See* Chrétien,
    Jean
Fietelaars, Jan, 134–135
First Nations. *See* Aboriginal Peoples
Ford, Catherine, 208, 261
Fraser, Joan, 85, 127, 136, 162
Front de libération du Québec (FLQ),
    21, 257–258
Frulla, Lisa, 159
Fryer, Alan, 242, 252

Gagné, Claude-Éric, 132
Gagnon, Lysiane, 14, 85, 126, 136, 141,
    167
Garcia, Claude, 170–171, 174–175, 187
Gauthier, Michel, 73, 75, 90–91, 118,
    165, 169, 199

General Agreement on Tariffs and
    Trade (GATT), 78, 120, 124
Gold, William, 152
Goldenberg, Eddie
    Canadian constitution, 17, 32
    draft bill, 88
    impressions of Lucien Bouchard,
        192, 269
    Jean Chrétien's concession speech,
        274–275
    Jean Chrétien's emergency address,
        207
    as Jean Chrétien's senior policy
        advisor, 1, 5, 32
    and Lucienne Robillard, 112
    meetings with Daniel Johnson
        camp, 159, 200–201
    No victory speech, 225
    and U.S. Ambassador James
        Blanchard, 214
    Yes campaign, 179
Gollin, Grégoire, 65, 234
Gorbachev, Mikhail, 213
Gray, John, 35, 57
Grey, Deborah, 28
Gwyn, Richard, 24, 61, 109, 148

Harcourt, Mike, 85, 147
Harper, Stephen, 31
    anti-bilingualism petition, 55
    Chrétien-Bouchard Commons
        debate, 163
    distinct society status for Quebec, 133
    legal battle against Bill 99, 272
    legality of referendum process, 9
    Parti Québécois victory, 46
    Quebec secession, 30–31, 147, 273
    Reform Party, 29, 168
    tripartite accord, 126
Harris, Hollis, 219
Harris, Mike, 185, 223, 230, 270

Hébert, Chantal, 75, 134–135, 193, 233
Hébert, Jacques, 137, 185, 190
Honderich, John A., 222
Hydro-Québec, 36, 211

Ignatieff, Michael, 257
Inuit, 87, 210–211
Irwin, Ron, 212–213

Johnson, Daniel Jr.
  1995 referendum, 259
  access to federal resources, 159–160
  Bill 1, 141–143
  boycott of commission hearings,
    82–83, 86–87, 90–92, 105
  chef of No side, 2, 66, 100, 158, 170,
    242
  draft bill, 80, 83–84
  federalist strategy, 41–42, 66, 70,
    122, 171, 194, 236
  and Jacques Parizeau, 68, 77, 108,
    117, 120, 136, 142, 178
  Jean Chrétien's Verdun promises,
    262, 270
  and Lucien Bouchard, 181, 188, 193,
    269
  and Mario Dumont, 170
  NAFTA, 215
  position on Quebec secession,
    143–145, 150, 164, 235, 261, 266
  as premier of Quebec, 39
  Quebec unemployment, 195–197
  Radio-Canada ad, 162
  reaction to *projet de souveraineté*, 69,
    80, 84
  Richard Le Hir's studies, 154–156, 163
  schism with Chrétien, 200–203,
    207, 208
  speech in National Assembly, 144,
    153, 173

  stance on constitutional reform,
    131–134
  unity rally, 226, 230–231
  victory speech, 254, 258
  See also Parti libéral du Québec
Johnson, Daniel Sr., 23, 39, 194
Johnson, William, 53, 57–58, 74, 90–91,
  121, 150–151, 167

Klein, Ralph, 85, 209, 262

Laforest, Guy, 3–4, 84, 110–111, 117,
  178
Landry, Bernard, 48, 108, 111, 113, 117,
  135, 215, 248, 273–274
Landry, Roger D., 222
Langlois, Roger, 183
Lapierre, Jean, 22, 245, 252
Lapointe, Lisette, 59, 79, 118, 245
Latouche, Daniel, 84, 120–121
Laurin, Camille, 84, 105
Léger, Jean-Marc, 104
Léger, Jean-Marc (pollster), 65, 122,
  126
Léger and Léger, 64, 67, 106, 121, 134,
  186, 200, 269
Le Hir, Richard, 48, 153, 155, 163
Lesage, Gilles, 125, 150
Lesage, Jean, 13, 23
Lesage, Justice Robert, 149–151
Lévesque, René
  1980 referendum, 65, 144, 235, 250
  beau risque (beautiful risk), 37, 58
  dream of independent Quebec, 16, 23
  FLQ, 257
  and Jacques Parizeau, 63, 82, 85, 124
  Night of the Long Knives, The (*La
    Nuit des Longs Couteaux*), 4, 6,
    49, 58, 206–207
  Parti Québécois, 20, 36, 39, 115

Lévesque, René (*cont.*)
　projet de souveraineté, 261
　sovereignty-association option, 3,
　　42, 81, 69, 111
Liberal Party of Canada, 8, 17, 89, 113,
　　167, 199, 259, 270
　and Bill C-20, *Clarity Act*, 272
　See also Chrétien, Jean
Liberal Party of Quebec. *See* Parti
　　libéral du Québec
Lisée, Jean-François, ii
　1995 referendum, 237, 248
　author of referendum question, 263
　fledgling Yes campaign, 109
　Garcia remark, 170
　Jacques Parizeau's concession
　　speech, 245, 250–252, 261
　Jacques Parizeau's lobster remarks,
　　134–135
　on Jean Chrétien, 275
　"*le cover-up d'Option Canada,*" 268
　letter to heads of state, 215
　on Lucien Bouchard, 76, 179–180
　Quebec unemployment, 197
　rainbow coalition, 67
　sovereignty commissions, 81, 138

Macpherson, Don, 45, 67, 74, 85, 90,
　　111, 182
MacQueen, Ken, 182, 232, 260
Maldoff, Eric, 159
Malhi, Gurbax Singh, 51
Manitoba, 7, 17
Manning, Preston
　1995 referendum, 248–249
　as *agent provocateur*, 31
　decentralization, 29, 31
　distinct society status for Quebec, 28
　and Jean Chrétien, 31, 41, 89, 91,
　　122, 165–168, 261, 270
　Lucien Bouchard's illness, 72, 98

Parti Québécois's *projet de souver-
　ianeté*, 90–91
Parti Québécois victory in 1994, 46
Quebec secession, 27, 89
Quebecers' view of, 30, 55
Mansbridge, Peter, 241
Marois, Pauline, 67, 105, 171, 225, 247
Martin, Paul
　1990 Liberal Leadership race, 8
　1995 referendum, 11, 266
　budget cuts, 107, 176
　Meech Lake Accord, 143
　Quebec economy after Yes vote,
　　195–197
　unity rally, 230
　view of Jacques Parizeau and Lucien
　　Bouchard, 50
　voice of No camp, 169
Massé, Henri, 174, 177
Massé, Marcel, 90, 101, 104, 113,
　　159–160
Masse, Marcel, 104, 107, 143
Masson, Claude, 130, 181–182
Mathews, George, 154–155
McIlroy, Anne, 146
McKenna, Frank, 47, 85, 147, 219, 230
McLaughlin, Audrey, 17, 98
Meech Lake Accord, 7–8, 16, 18–19,
　　21–22, 24–28, 31, 33, 37, 55,
　　58–59, 65, 132, 139, 143, 193,
　　201, 203, 244
Meggs, Anne Michele, 57
Mercer, Rick, 149
Mercredi, Ovide, 212
Mohawk, 54, 211
Monahan, Patrick J., 33, 151, 212, 248
Montreal Canadiens, 152, 259
Morton, Desmond, 47
Mulcair, Thomas, 266
Mulroney, Brian
　1995 referendum campaign, 213,
　　266

changes to Canadian Constitution,
7, 18, 32, 37, 143
and Lucien Bouchard, 21–22, 121

National Assembly of First Nations,
87, 212
New Brunswick, 223–224
See also McKenna, Frank
New Democratic Party (NDP), 17, 98,
270
Newfoundland, 7, 89, 222–223
See also Wells, Clyde
Newman, Peter C., 55–56
Nolin, Pierre-Claude, 159, 218
North American Free Trade Agreement
(NAFTA), 29, 78, 120, 124, 177, 215
North Atlantic Treaty Organization
(NATO), 78
Norton, Joe, 54
Nova Scotia, 54, 223, 230
Nungak, Zebedee, 87, 211

O'Brien, Phil, 218–219
Oliver, Craig, 168, 242
Ontario
and Mike Harris, 186, 223, 230, 270
partnership deal with Quebec,
184–185
trade linkages with Quebec, 60
unity rally, 221, 224, 228
See also Rae, Bob

Paré, Phillipe, 103–104, 189
Parisella, John, 159, 200
Parisot, Patrick, 1, 159
Parizeau, Jacques, 4–5, 19, 22–23, 25
1994 provincial election, 38, 41–50
1995 referendum, 238, 242–245,
247–248

Anglo critics, 35, 69, 127–128, 142,
150, 261
Bill 1, 139–152, 157, 171
Bouchard's illness, 72, 74–75
comments made by Bourgault,
101–104
concession speech, 250–256
draft bill, 77–95, 99, 150, 164, 220
early career in politics, 35–37
France, 214–215
Le Hir studies, 153–157, 163
Le Référendum volé (The Stolen
Referendum), 268
lobster story, 134–139
Longueuil speech, 235
Montreal rally, 202–203
noui vote, 66, 70
perspective on ROC, 51–62, 234
postponement of referendum,
107–109, 112, 131
pretaped victory speech, 273–274
provincial unemployment, 195–198
and Quebec business elite, 175–178,
185
Quebec independence, 63, 67,
81–82, 84, 190–191, 263, 275–276
rainbow coalition, 63, 67
and René Lévesque, 36–37
resignation, 262
sovereignty commissions, 104–106,
163
as technocrat, 37, 183
tension between Lucien Bouchard
and, 76, 100, 110–111, 113–119
tripartite accord, 123–125
volte face, 120–121
Yes campaign kickoff, 173–174
Yes-side strategy, 178–183, 257
Parti libéral du Québec (PLQ), 4, 21, 82,
83, 125, 132, 157, 174, 202, 240
Parti Québécois (PQ)
1994 victory, 41–50

Parti Québécois (PQ) (*cont.*)
  after a 1995 Yes victory, 274
  Bill 1, 137–143
  and Bloc Québécois, 43, 130, 173,
    181
  draft bill, 83–95, 99
  Lucien Bouchard as leader of, 269
  Plan B, 178–180
  referendum strategy, 62–68, 76, 89,
    90, 115
  René Lévesque, 36, 115
  sovereignty commissions, 79–87,
    104–106, 115, 118, 121, 138, 143
  sovereignty studies, 156, 185, 191
  See also Parizeau, Jacques
Pelletier, Jean, 1, 32, 159–160
Picard, André, 162, 226
Pierni, Nick, 147, 253
Pinard, Maurice, 33
Plamondon, Louis, 22, 64
Prince Edward Island, 223. *See also*
  Callbeck, Catherine

Queen Elizabeth II, 6, 216
Quebec
  *Charte des driots et libertés de la
    personne* (Charter of Rights and
    Freedoms), 57
  as distinct society, 5–9, 13, 28, 117,
    132–133, 144, 198, 200–202, 208,
    223, 253, 256, 262, 270–271
Quebec Business Council for Canada,
  175, 218, 224
Quebec Manufacturers Association
  (QMA), 48, 87
Quebec Superior Court ruling on PQ's
  referendum process, 149–151
Quiet Revolution, 4, 25, 36, 84, 105,
  120, 139

Radio-Canada, 77, 86, 99, 162, 184,
  200, 246–247
Rae, Bob, 59–60, 85, 185, 252
Rae, John, 1, 32, 159
Referendum Act, 80, 91, 153, 157–159,
  161, 225
Reform Party
  and 1993 election, 17, 27, 29, 30
  decentralization, 209
  and Lucien Bouchard, 166, 168
  views on Quebec sovereignty, 126,
    133, 270
  See also Manning, Preston; and
    Harper, Stephen
Richler, Mordecai, 53, 147
Robertson, Lloyd, 192, 246
Robillard, Lucienne, 11, 99, 112, 113,
  160, 162–164, 170
Rocheleau, Gilles, 8, 22
Rock, Allan, 113
Romanow, Roy, 47, 85, 148, 262
Royer, Jean, 67, 170, 179, 245
Ryan, Claude, 39

Samson, Jean-Jacques, 84, 107, 125,
  145, 199, 233, 262
Saskatchewan. *See* Romanow, Roy
Sheppard, Robert, 40, 61, 74–75
Simpson, Jeffrey, 121, 141–42, 148, 183,
  191
Sirros, Christos, 253
Smith, Christine, 86
Societé Saint-Jean-Baptiste, 88
Stewart, Jane, 13–14
St-Laurent, Bernard, 197
Supreme Court of Canada, 5, 52, 91,
  271–272

Taylor, Charles, 57, 105
Thorsell, William, 30

Tobin, Brian, 14
    unity rally, 218–220, 223–225,
       230–231
Tory party, 17, 19, 21–22, 24, 28–29, 63,
       70, 159. *See also* Charest, Jean;
       and Mulroney, Brian
Trudeau, Pierre
    1980 referendum, 2–5, 33, 112–113,
       275
    1995 referendum, 185, 266
    Charlottetown Accord, 137
    and Jean Chrétien, 7–9, 17, 206–208
    Just Watch Me, documentary, i
    and Lucien Bouchard, 20
    obsession with Quebec, 32
    and Radio-Canada, 162
    repatriation of Canadian
       Constitution, 6, 21, 58, 143

Turner, Craig, 93–94
Turp, Daniel, 114
Two Rivers, Billy, 211

United Nations (UN), 39, 46, 236
United States, 120, 214–216

Vézina, Monique, 119, 143
Vigneault, Gilles, 138, 139

Webster, Norman, 192, 210
Wells, Clyde, 68, 143, 147, 203
Wells, Paul, 23
Whitaker, Reg, 57
Wicks, Ben, 222